The Taciturn Text

The Taciturn Text

The Fiction of Robert Penn Warren

Randolph Paul Runyon

Ohio State
University Press
Columbus

Copyright © 1990 by the Ohio State University Press.
All rights reserved.

Library of Congress Cataloging-in-Publication Data

Runyon, Randolph, 1947–
    The taciturn text : the fiction of Robert Penn Warren / Randolph
Paul Runyon.
      p. cm.
    Includes bibliographical references (p.   ) and index.
    ISBN 978-0-8142-5350-2 (alk. paper)
    1. Warren, Robert Penn, 1905–1989—Fictional works. I. Title.
PS3545.A748Z8644 1990
813'.52—dc20   90–7534
                                                                                                                       CIP

The paper in this book meets the guidelines for permanence and durability of the Committee on Production Guidelines for Book Longevity of the Council on Library Resources.∞

9 8 7 6 5 4 3 2 1

*For Elizabeth,
Ezekiel, and Augusta*

Contents

	Acknowledgments	ix
	Introduction. Ianthe and the Logic of the Dream	1
1	Night Writer: Or, the New Morpheus (*Night Rider*, 1939)	9
2	Unlocking the Gate (*At Heaven's Gate*, 1943)	37
3	Willie's Wink (*All the King's Men*, 1946)	60
4	The View from the Attic (*The Circus in the Attic and Other Stories*, 1947)	82
5	Beaumont's Dream (*World Enough and Time*, 1950)	107
6	Decomposing Angels (*Band of Angels*, 1955)	127
7	The Fictive Fetus in the Cave (*The Cave*, 1959)	146
8	Moses in the Wilderness (*Wilderness*, 1961)	163
9	Continent in Flood (*Flood*, 1964)	183
10	Christmas Gift (*Meet Me in the Green Glen*, 1971)	203
11	Old Buck's Golden Shower: Or, the New Perseus (*A Place to Come To*, 1977)	222
	Conclusion. "at the end of . . . life's long sorites"	250
	Notes	261
	Works Cited	279
	Index	285

Acknowledgments

I would like to express my appreciation to Miami University for the semi-sabbatical during which this book was begun. I am grateful, too, to Alex Holzman of the Ohio State University Press for his strong support and the skillful manner in which he guided this manuscript to publication. I especially want to thank James A. Grimshaw, Jr., James Justus, and Victor Strandberg for their gracious encouragement to a newcomer in the field.

Thanks most of all to Elizabeth, who miraculously made it possible to work at home.

Parts of chapters 3 and 9 previously appeared in *Southern Literature and Literary Theory,* ed. Jefferson Humphries (Athens: University of Georgia Press, 1990); part of chapter 5, as "The View from the Attic: Robert Penn Warren's *Circus* Stories," in *The Mississippi Quarterly* 38 (Spring 1985); an earlier version of chapter 6, as "The Beech, the Hearth, and the Hidden Name in *World Enough and Time,*" in *The Southern Literary Journal* 17 (Fall 1984); and chapter 8, in *Time's Glory: Original Essays on Robert Penn Warren,* ed. James A. Grimshaw, Jr. (Conway: University of Central Arkansas Press, 1986).

Introduction
Ianthe and the Logic of the Dream

In the dream Robert Penn Warren recounts in his poem "I Am Dreaming of a White Christmas," he returns to a childhood Christmas scene, frozen in time as in memory, although time has exacted its price. Dust obscures the newspapers whose dates the poet cannot bring himself to read, and his parents, still in their chairs, are skeletal mummies now—his father's skin brown as old leather and his eyes "Not there, . . . stare at what / Is not there." Under the denuded tree there's a present for Warren, and he reaches out to take it. But a parental voice forbids him, "*No presents, son, till the little ones come.*" Later in the poem, after the scene has shifted to Times Square and points west, the poet wonders, "Will I never know / What present there was in that package for me, / Under the Christmas tree?" And comments:

> All items listed above belong in the world
> In which all things are continuous,
> And are parts of the original dream which
> I am now trying to discover the logic of.

This book is an attempt to join him in the search for the logic of the dream—a search that, in part, is the logic of dream. This dream logic is explained in a book the son had once left behind and imagines his father reading, in another poem ("Reading Late at Night, Thermometer Falling") contained in the same book (*Or Else: Poem / Poems 1968–1974*) where "I Am Dreaming . . ." appears. The book is "Freud on dreams"—Freud's *Interpretation of Dreams*—which discovers the "dreamwork" through which the unconscious constructs its nightly fictions. Warren recently commented to Floyd Watkins that the gift the parental voice forbade him to open, which seems to symbolize the dream he cannot yet interpret, contains his "whole life, of course" (Watkins, 164). It contains to a remarkable degree his literary oeuvre as well, which itself is a "world / In which all things are continuous." Just how continuous is suggested by the recurring dream about a package to be unwrapped (analogous to "unwrapping" the dream itself) that first appears in *Night Rider* and reappears in one form or another throughout most of Warren's subsequent novels, as if it too were somehow an "original dream"—one that lies at the heart of his fiction.

This continuity is also suggested by the persistence with which texts in all of Warren's ten novels circulate between father and son: a text the father wrote for the son to read, a text the father should have written but did not, a text the son mistakenly thought the father had written, a text someone else wrote but the father came to possess and passes on to the son, a text whose existence the father refuses to acknowledge in the very moment he transmits it to the son, a text that denies its own existence, a text the father wants the son to write for him, or a text the son inherits from the father and rewrites to his own advantage.

Pervading each one of these relationships of fathers and sons is the old, old story of what happened to Oedipus at the crossroads and at Thebes. Just under the surface is an unremitting and murderous hostility—as Warren was to write in his autobiographical memoir disguised as a book on Jefferson Davis: "How often we learn in later life . . . that the love we long ago thought we had was a mask for hatred, or hatred a mask for love" (24–25). An undercurrent of violence is not entirely absent, either, from the relationship of author to critic thus already inscribed in these stories about sons trying to make sense of the text their fathers left them: ". . . I suppose that I am the last person, quite literally, whose comment on the book is relevant. It might be somewhat like a patient etherized upon the table jumping up to grab the scalpel from the surgeon and stabbing the surgeon to the heart" (letter from RPW to RPR, 10 June 1985).

Given the importance of this recurring pattern in the novels, the way in which Warren performs the symmetrically opposite gesture in "Reading Late at Night" appears all the more significant. It seems to present itself—at least to me—as some kind of response to the question posed by the insistent recurrence of that paternal textual legacy. What the son gives back to the father is Freud, and what Warren at the same time gives the reader who has puzzled over the recurring dreams, unopenable packages, and paternal texts in the novels is some valuable information about how to read. For "Freud on dreams" tells us how to read not only dreams but texts, as Warren himself has elsewhere said. In "A Poem of Pure Imagination," Warren's essay on Coleridge's "The Rime of the Ancient Mariner," he made use of Freud's concept of "condensation" from *The Interpretation of Dreams* to explain how literary symbols are infused with meaning:

> The symbol . . . has what psychoanalysts call condensation. It does not "stand for" a single idea, and a system of symbols is not to be taken as a mere translation of a discursive sequence. Rather, a symbol implies a body of ideas which may be said to

be fused in it. This means that the symbol itself may be developed into a discursive sequence as we intellectually explore its potential. To state the matter in another way, ... a symbol may be the condensation of several themes and not a sign for one. (352)

For Freud, condensation was one of the four principal phenomena of the dreamwork of the unconscious, along with "displacement," "the means of representation," and "considerations of representability." "The first thing," he wrote, "that becomes clear to anyone who compares the dream-content with the dream-thoughts is that a work of *condensation* on a large scale has been carried out. Dreams are brief, meagre and laconic in comparison with the range and wealth of the dream-thoughts. If a dream is written out it may perhaps fill half a page. The analysis setting out the dream-thoughts underlying it may occupy ... a dozen times as much space" (312–13).

What Warren calls the development of a discursive sequence out of a literary symbol is clearly analogous to Freud's drawing out the latent content of a dream: both are ways of describing what it is I shall try to do here, as I draw out of such a condensation—for example, the beech tree for which Warren, in a letter to me, could recall no "'reason' for putting ... there [in *World Enough and Time*] except that I have always liked going to woods, and the beech is a splendid thing"—an entire network of associations essential to the mystery at the heart of the ongoing story that underlies his fiction and poetry and reaches its conclusion only in his last novel.[1] The beech tree, despite Warren's denial, is a symbol that "may be developed into a discursive sequence as we intellectually explore its potential."

One may object that the analysis presented here is too ingenious; but both Warren and Freud can be called as witnesses for its defense. In his Coleridge essay, Warren declares that to say "Assuming that certain interpretations can be 'drawn out of' or 'put into' the poem by an 'exercise of ingenuity,' how do we know that the poet 'intended' them?" is to ask a "false" because "loaded" question (395). This is because, he goes on to assert, no specific intention precedes the creation of the poem other than the poem itself: "the only thing [the poet], in the ordinary sense, may 'intend' is to make a poem" (396).[2] Such a question also misrepresents the creative process, Warren argues, because it ignores the role played by the unconscious: "As Coleridge said, and as many other poets and even scientists have said, the unconscious may be the genius in the man of genius" (396).

Freud answered the accusation of overcleverness leveled at *The Interpretation of Dreams* by pointing out that the unconscious is more clever than we give it credit for:

> The first reader and critic of this book—and his successors are likely to follow his example—protested that "the dreamer

seems to be too ingenious and amusing." This is quite true so long as it refers only to the dreamer; it would only be an objection if it were to be extended to the dream-interpreter.... If my dreams seem amusing, that is not on my account, but on account of the peculiar psychological conditions under which dreams are constructed.... Dreams become ingenious and amusing because the direct and easiest pathway to the expression of their thoughts is barred. (332–33n)

It is precisely at this point, however, that I may have to disagree with Warren. In his estimation, poetic creation is not governed by the unconscious, nor does it work by the same rules the unconscious employs to create, for example, dreams. The role of the unconscious is limited, in his view, to providing raw material for the rational mind of the poet to select or reject. Poetic creation, he hastens to add immediately after quoting Coleridge on how the unconscious may be the genius in the man of genius, is not "an irrational process." Despite the fact that Warren is sufficiently comfortable with Freud to adopt a psychoanalytic critical vocabulary, it seems that he nevertheless displays a certain fear of the unconscious in that essay. The unconscious may have its uses, but it is something from which the poet, in his view, needs finally to escape: "creative reverie is, in the end, a liberation from the compulsiveness of the unconscious" (410).

But to give in to Warren's claim that it is the unconscious which is exploited by the poet and not vice versa, and then to read his literary production as if such a claim were true, would be uncomfortably close to disagreeing with him when he says that poems are not made with preexisting blueprints. It would be to treat such a critical theory[3] as something like the blueprint Warren had in mind when he wrote (as well as a blueprint for the reader to follow). Surely the way out of this dilemma is to read his critical writings with the same eye with which one reads his fictional and poetic texts—that is, open to the possibility that even here he may be saying more, and something other, than he means to say. In the end it is the text that we are obliged to read, not the man who wrote it:

> If the poet does not have a blueprint of intention (and if he does happen to have it, we ordinarily have no access to it), on what basis may a poem be interpreted? What kind of evidence is to be admitted? The first piece of evidence is the poem itself. And here ... the criterion is that of internal consistency. If the elements of a poem operate together toward one end, we are entitled to interpret the poem according to that end. Even if the poet himself should rise to contradict us, we could reply that the words of the poem speak louder than his actions. (397)

In any case, the chief reason why Freud on dreams is relevant to Warren—the fact that his narratives are not only sometimes *about* dreams but are possibly constructed *like* dreams—is that they contain dreams that belong not only to the dreamer. There are good reasons to conclude that they belong, on some level, to the novel as well, for there are connections between the dreams the story tells and the fabric of the narrative which go beyond the demands of the story. In one instance (*Night Rider*), the novel gives us clues to the interpretation of the dream before we are even told the dream. Although these clues are events in the hero's life that occur *after* the dream, in the reader's experience they precede it, in much the same way that Freud maintained that the events of the preceding day come before, and are recombined in, a night's dreaming—and in the way Warren himself describes the process in an early *Fugitive* poem:

> ... sleep, the dark wherein you all are piled,
> Poor fragments of the day, until there come
> Dreams to release from the troubled heart and deep
> The pageantry of thoughts unreconciled.
>   ("Images on the Tomb")

In another novel (*World Enough and Time*), the protagonist has a dream that he finds puzzling and that poses a riddle only the reader can answer, for it depends upon knowledge that the author and reader share but the hero knows nothing about. The answer to the riddle is a name the novel never speaks but which permeates its imagery and returns in later novels to haunt the reader who has noticed it here.

    A word should be said about what I mean by "the reader." To my knowledge, this is no reader who has gone before, for I believe this study brings to light aspects of Warren's fiction that have not been made explicit elsewhere, at least in print.[4] But it does seem to me that these narratives at times appeal to a certain kind of reader, one capable of profiting from the various clues they offer to their own interpretation, and that they often do so at the moment the characters in the story are engaged in deciphering a difficult text. For example, in a reading scene in *Night Rider* occurs a sentence in a letter that does not fit but that when analyzed emerges as the key to the real meaning of the letter; a similarly puzzling sentence appears in the novel itself, whose inappropriateness can jar us into a better understanding of what is going on in the text. In *All the King's Men,* Jack Burden's paradox about how reality arises from the combination of events that are in themselves not real both echoes something Warren says elsewhere about poetic creation and tells us something quite specific about that novel. *The Cave* is a parable that, in telling how a fiction can become real, illustrates the power of Burden's insight. The short story collection *The Circus in the Attic* speaks about how Time and the delay between writing something and reading it permit meaning to emerge that was not at first apparent; and the delay parallels the one between these stories' first, separate publication and their present appearance together in the book, during which they seem to have taken on new meaning. *Flood* shows us how the slight deformation of a text (putting a scratch on a record with the stylus, in this instance) can make it repeat its actual content, which turns out to be the very idea of content itself, an insight not without relevance to the interpretation not just of that novel but of all Warren's fiction.

It seems to me that a reader capable of being alert to such clues is implied by Warren's text; it is my hope that this reading of his fiction will encourage such readers to renew their acquaintance with this aspect of his work. Since so much of my analysis depends upon exactly what events take place in Warren's narratives, I have included detailed plot summaries of each of the novels and short stories.

Perhaps it will be argued that there is something a little eccentric, even perverse, about such an approach. After all, we already know what Warren's novels are about, don't we? The search for personal identity, self-knowledge, and redemption; the restoration of community; the inescapable reality of evil. To read his fiction without paying proper respect to what his work is manifestly about may well be to behave like Perse Munn's distant cousin, Ianthe Sprague, in Warren's first novel, who was bored by novels:

> The novel had a direction, it described lives that were moving toward fulfillments, it pretended to a meaning. Therefore she could not listen to it.... But the fragmentary, the irrelevant, the meaningless, such things she could receive and draw her special nourishment from.... [S]he was like some species of marine life that ... sustains itself on what the random currents bring, absorbing the appropriate matter and ejecting all else, with a delicate and punctilious, but unconscious, discrimination. (*Night Rider,* 212)

Ianthe herself may seem to be just such an irrelevant fragment in the novel. Her name fascinated Perse because he had read Walter Savage Landor's poem of that name in a book that had belonged to his father (the only mention of his father in the entire novel: so much of what happens in *Night Rider* and all the novels to follow will depend on a son's reading of texts of paternal provenance that even this detail of the origin of her name is no accident). But her very irrelevance is relevant, for Ianthe, with her "unconscious" power of discrimination, resembles nothing so much as the unconscious itself, as Freud saw it; particularly in its role as dreammaker, culling the events of the preceding day—those "Poor fragments of the day"—for the raw material with which it will compose the text—the dream—in which its repressed desire can find disguised fulfillment. If one wants to discover the logic of the dream[5] that repeats itself in Warren's fiction one has to pay attention to the figures it proposes for the unconscious and its power to dream. And one will have to take the risk of appearing to ignore the larger issues—the fulfillment and the meaning toward which non-Ianthian readers of Warren believe his fiction strives. What fascinated Freud about dreams was not their manifest content but their latent one, and not even the primal wish therein concealed, so much as the dreamwork itself, the way in which the unconscious both disguises and presents its hidden agenda—how, like that underwater creature to which Ianthe is compared, it finds its nourishment, the raw material for its fictions, in seemingly insignificant details.

Chapter 1

Night Writer: Or, the New Morpheus *Night Rider*, 1939

Chapter 1 The story begins on a hot August day in 1904 in Bardsville, Kentucky, where thirty-year-old Percy Munn has been practicing law for seven years. The Association of Growers of Dark Fired Tobacco has organized a huge rally to encourage farmers to pool their tobacco crops in order to force the buyers to offer a better price. Munn, who commutes to town from his tobacco farm, gets off the crowded train and meets Association firebrand Bill Christian and his daughter, Lucille, as well as Civil War veteran Captain Todd, the unctuous Senator Tolliver, and other members of the Association's board of directors. Tolliver gives a rousing oration before the crowd, and Munn is manipulated into making an impromptu speech, which turns out to be surprisingly successful. He chooses as his text the word *nothing* ("There is nothing here [in the Association] . . . except what you have brought with you . . .").

Chapter 2 A few days later Munn is talked into joining the board of the Association, to complete the unexpired term of "a Mr. Morphee." A Mrs. Bunk Trevelyan persuades him to defend her husband in court against a charge of having murdered a neighbor.

Chapter 3 At Trevelyan's trial, the prosecuting attorney introduces into evidence a newspaper-wrapped package from which he draws a knife. He establishes that Trevelyan had bought one identical to it and that the fatal wound could have been made by such a knife. Trevelyan had not told Munn about this and now claims that someone had stolen it from his house before the murder. Munn is able to locate the knife in the house of a black man, who is then convicted and hanged for the murder.

Chapter 4 The board meets at Senator Tolliver's country estate in late December. An anti-Association grower has received an anonymous threat; Captain Todd's motion to publicly condemn such threats is unanimously passed. Munn finds that he is losing his desire for his wife May, and that he is developing a liking for Lucille Christian—as is likewise Captain Todd's young son, Benton.

Chapter 5 In the spring, Edmund Tolliver, in a hand-delivered letter, tenders his resignation on the grounds that the board had voted not to accept what he considered a reasonable offer from the tobacco companies. The letter appears in the newspapers the next day—evidently Tolliver's own doing with the intention of discrediting the Association in the eyes of the public. It is revealed that Tolliver had considerable debts and that the tobacco companies must have "got to him."

Chapter 6 Munn meets Professor Ball, whose hands are permanently wrapped in bandages, and Ball's son-in-law, Dr. Mac-Donald. Munn is persuaded to join the night riders, who terrorize farmers into signing with the Association.

Chapter 7 Munn and his wife are drifting apart. The night riders, including Munn, are scraping the tobacco beds of those who refuse to sign up. Captain Todd resigns from the Association because "the night riders are running it." Munn is struck by the resemblance between the way Todd held up his hand for silence and the way his son Benton would raise his hand six weeks later to be sworn into the night riders.

Chapter 8 In August 1905, the night riders discover that Bunk Trevelyan, whom Munn had persuaded to join their number, has been trying to extort money from a farmer. They take him out and shoot him. Munn fires the first shot, having drawn that duty by lot but sufficiently motivated by his recent realization that an innocent man—because of Munn's overly zealous detective work in finding the knife—had been hanged for the murder Trevelyan in fact committed. When Munn returns home that night, he forces his affections on an unwilling May.

Chapter 9 Munn reminisces about Ianthe Sprague, an elderly woman he had befriended in Philadelphia and to whom he used to read aloud from the newspaper. May has left him and gone to live with her Aunt Lucy Burnham, who refuses access to Munn.

Chapter 10 Munn begins to stay at Bill Christian's house and—without her father's knowledge—to sleep with Lucille.

Chapter 11 Munn arrives at Professor Ball's with "a small packet, tied up in newspaper"—evidently a change of clothes, although this is not spelled out. Dr. MacDonald proposes that the night riders destroy the tobacco companies' warehouses. On the night of 30 December 1905, they successfully raid Bardsville, but during their escape Munn's company sustains one fatality—Benton Todd, who bleeds to death from a leg wound when they are attacked at the crossroads near the New Bethany church. As some of the raiders point out, Todd's death was Munn's fault: had he not been so determined to make it to the New Bethany church crossroads but had ambushed their pursuers from behind a stone fence along the road, as they had pleaded with him to do, no one would have died.

Chapter 12 When Senator Tolliver, no longer an imposing figure, makes a feeble speech at Bardsville in support of law and order, Munn realizes his hatred for the man. Tolliver's house is destroyed by fire, and so, ultimately, is Munn's, who gets the news while in bed with Lucille. Bill Christian discovers his daughter in Munn's room and suffers a paralyzing stroke.

Chapter 13 Lucille, troubled by her father's condition, tells Munn she doesn't feel anything for him anymore. Lucy Burnham informs Munn in a letter that her niece will not give him a divorce and that May is pregnant, but that he will never see her or the baby. MacDonald, pursued by the law for the Bardsville raid, eludes arrest on one occasion by disguising himself in his father-in-law's bandages. On another, he hides in the attic when the soldiers come to Ball's house and his sister-in-law, Isabella, distracts them with a shotgun; he gives himself up, though, when he hears the shotgun blast.

Chapter 14 At MacDonald's trial, when Al Turpin, the only witness who will positively identify MacDonald among the Bardsville raiders, takes the stand the defense lawyer successfully stalls for time, and court is adjourned until the next day. The following morning, Munn goes to his office before the trial and leaves it unlocked for his secretary. On his way back to his hotel room, Isabella Ball warns him that the soldiers are looking for him.

Chapter 15 Someone has assassinated Al Turpin with Munn's rifle through Munn's office window. Munn sneaked out of town and is now spending his days in a cave on Willie Proudfit's farm. Proudfit informs him that there are handbills all over Thebes with his picture on them and offering a reward. Since his first night there, Munn has had a mysterious recurring dream in which May holds out to him a bundle wrapped in old newspaper that flakes away to reveal the body of a fetus with the face of Bunk Trevelyan. Immediately upon waking one morning, he realizes that it must have been Professor Ball, despite his clumsy bandage-wrapped hands, who shot Al Turpin. Munn learns from Proudfit's niece Sissie that May has given birth to a boy. Proudfit tells the story of his years out west shooting buffalo, concluding with an account of his own mysterious dream of a place that, when he returned to Kentucky, turned out to be "the road come-en down to Thebes" by the New Bethany church.

Chapter 16 Lucille Christian visits Munn at the Proudfits' and says that her father has died and that she is willing to marry him if he will go away with her. Munn prefers to stay. She also tells him that Senator Tolliver used to put his hands on her every chance he got. After she leaves, Munn announces his own departure, asking Proudfit for the handkerchiefs he had got for him at Thebes. He makes his way on foot to Tolliver's place, tries to kill him but can't bring himself to, and is hunted down and killed by soldiers. His last gesture is suicidal: he shoots blindly upward to draw his pursuers' fire.

Percy Munn, who for most of *Night Rider* seems powerless and inarticulate, caught up in events beyond his control and for which he cannot give a clear account, did display a surprisingly effective eloquence when he addressed the crowd at the Bardsville rally in the first chapter of Warren's first published novel. Even then, however, he was the victim of someone else's design, manipulated into giving a speech he had neither the desire nor the preparation to give. Senator Tolliver, "a real orator" whose "flowing, full, compelling voice" (22) commanded the attention of his audience, was indeed a hard act to follow. Tolliver's performance, which Munn could not hope to match, is described in terms of a fullness that overcomes a void: "The Senator was speaking, his full, rich voice . . . dominating the hot emptiness of the afternoon air" (21). When Munn, after the shock of having been introduced as the next speaker, stood to face the crowd and tried to speak, at first no sound would come. He looked up to the sky and felt that emptiness even more intensely when he noticed that even the single buzzard that had "[a]t a great height . . . hung motionless" when the Senator was speaking was gone now, "leaving nothing but the empty and intense blue of the sky." That *nothing but* becomes the theme of his impromptu oration, as he makes the emptiness of his own speechlessness, and that of the sky and the crowd, the very substance of his speech. It is, almost, a discourse about nothing:

> "My friends. . . . You came here through the dust and heat"— and he felt his own voice growing stronger within him and the words coming—"because you thought you could get something here to help you." He came from behind the table and went to the edge of the platform, what seemed the tremendous emptiness of the crowd, like the emptiness of the sky when one fixes his steady gaze upon its depth, drawing him as though against his will. "But there is nothing here to help you. . . . There is nothing here in Bardsville for you."

At this point the Senator and his Association colleagues must have begun to realize how much of a gamble it had been to lure him into speaking to the crowd. "He heard the shuffling of feet on the boards behind him, and a short, nervous cough. 'There is nothing here,' he went on, 'except what you have brought with you. . . . There is no hope except the hope you bring here . . .'" (24–25). And so in the end it was a successful, rousing speech, one that urged the crowd to stand up and fight for their interests (and to join the Tobacco Association to further those interests)—one that cleverly made use of the rhetorical trick of getting the listener's attention by appearing to say the unspeakable and then twisting it into invigorating eloquence. This rhetorical solution finally became for Munn what had seemed so inimitable in the senator's oratory, a kind of fullness: "He could not tell whether they were listening to him, and found that he did not care, for his own voice filled him and he was completely himself."

The predicament in which Munn found himself, first enraptured by the Senator's style, by the way "he poured forth his full and powerful discourse" (22) and then enveloped by a "wave of nausea" as he heard his own name spoken and began to realize what it was he was being called upon to do—that predicament is one that will return with remarkable regularity in Warren's fiction. It is, essentially, the situation of a son who finds that he has been preceded by his father, and specifically by his father's *text*, and that now he must in his turn speak, act, or interpret that paternal text. My reading of Warren—which seeks, among other things, to show the profound unity underlying his fiction—will be centered, in part, around this recurring scene.

That Senator Tolliver played a fatherly role toward Munn, and that Munn responded—until the shock of betrayal—as a dutiful son, there is no question. To Tolliver, Percy Munn was "my boy" on more than one occasion (29, 30, 92), the protégé to whom he promised a bright future in return for his work in the Association. The Senator communicated a fatherly feeling (or the semblance of one) through his hand: "He reached out and laid his hand *paternally* on Mr. Munn's shoulder. Then, as though embarrassed at betraying his own feelings, he removed it" (92; emphasis added). Later, when Tolliver loses the vote (in which he had persuaded Munn to join him) to accept the companies' offer (the defeat that will precipitate his departure from the Association), he repeats the gesture: The Senator "reached out to touch him on the shoulder. 'Well, boy,' he said in a low voice, 'we did the best we could'" (98). And still later, after Tolliver's quitting the Association will make Munn turn against him, it will be that paternally laid hand that Munn most remembers: "If the Senator had never laid a hand on his shoulder, had never leaned confidentially toward him, had not used him and betrayed him, he might never have taken this step" (121).

This father will fall in the son's estimation, chiefly because of the letter by which Tolliver will announce his resignation from the Association in chapter 5, but confirmed on the occasion of yet a third paternal text (by that adjective I do not mean to suggest "fatherliness" but simply to express the fact that the text comes from the father), the pitiful speech the Senator will give after the Bardsville raid in chapter 12. Hearing it, Munn is made aware of the depth of his hatred for the man. That hatred was like "a token or a keepsake, which is nothing in itself, but which means the reality of one's past ... the fact of one's identity. The hatred was there now, perfect and safe within, something to hold to" (243). At the end of the novel, that hatred and that identity will be clearly figured as oedipal—Warren winks confirmation of this by inventing a Kentucky *Thebes*—when Munn tries to kill this father he hates.

This recurring scene, as I read the novels, will assume different forms but does not evolve; it was all there from the beginning (a beginning one can date, roughly, from *Night Rider*). My reading of Warren will not attempt to show change but rather the remarkable extent to which so many stories are variations on the same narrative, the surprising degree to which so much of Warren is all of a piece. I am in entire agreement with one of the characters whose conversation William Harmon stages in "Three Italians Visit Monticello": "In a sense, Warren has created but one character: R.P.W. And in each of his writings ... we can see R.P.W. ... heroically, engaged on one single quest" (though we may not have the same quest in mind). All of his works "are cognate and concentric ... so that any one work—early or late, prose or verse—is a variation of any other" (277).

Anyone who has read very much of Warren's poetry has probably been struck by the insistently recurrent image of a high-flying bird at which the poet gazes with fascination: the "sunset hawk" in "Kentucky Mountain Farm," the eagle that likewise stares at the sun in "Eagle Descending," the wild geese whose knowledge he envies in "Heart of Autumn," the hawk "climbing the last light" in "Evening Hawk," or the one the poet murdered in "Red-Tail Hawk and Pyre of Youth." Although all these are of apparently nobler lineage than the buzzard that had hung motionless in the sky during Senator Tolliver's eloquence but disappeared when Munn arose to speak,[1] it is not unlikely that this earlier bird should in some way anticipate them. For one of the most fascinating aspects of Warren's oeuvre is the fact that so much of what ultimately unfolds in the course of his long writing career was always already there. He consistently organized his self-selected poetic anthologies, of which there have been four, from the most recent poems to the earliest, and in each instance arrived in the end at the same beginning; the poem "To a Face in the Crowd" bears witness to this. The buzzard certainly appears to be a kind of totem for the Senator—ultimately ludicrous, like him, and a predator; but the language of *Night Rider* provides a surer clue, for just as the buzzard "At a great height ... *hung* motionless as though sustained *in* the incandescent blue of *the sky,*" so also the last word of the Senator's speech—"justice"—seemed to *hang in the* hot *air* for a long instant ..." (23; emphasis added). What hangs together in this reading—the identity of bird and word—is what is finally made explicit some forty-three years later in *Chief Joseph of the Nez Perce* when "The hawk hung high. / Gleamed white. A sign. It gleamed like a word in the sky."[2]

There is yet a third text from this father figure in Munn's life, within which lies a hidden meaning that Percy endeavors, and is finally able, to grasp. It is the letter in which Tolliver announced his resignation from the board of the Tobacco Association (brought on, as I have mentioned, by his having failed to persuade the board to accept the tobacco companies' offer). When it is read aloud to the board, the text of the letter becomes the subject of intense discussion. The members parse each sentence, looking for clues to what it really means. Bill Christian calls their attention to one passage in particular: "... even though it is my firm belief that the policy I have supported is the one of reason and peace and would be endorsed by an overwhelming majority of the actual members of the Association itself" (100). Is that true? they ask, or does the Senator think it is? Why would he say it if he didn't think it was?

That is as far as their analysis takes them. But Munn continues to think about the sentence, about how "it was the key to the letter. It was not like the rest of the letter. It really didn't belong in the letter...." He slept on the problem and suddenly realized its true significance the next morning when he discovered the same sentence in the newspaper. It was in all the papers; evidently Tolliver hoped that by stating it publicly he would make it true.

There is a sense in which Munn's insistence that the key to the letter was a sentence out of keeping with the rest can provide a clue to how to read the larger text of the novel itself. For in *Night Rider,* too, there is a sentence that does not fit. I do not imagine the parallel is intentional, but it is well worth discussing, if only to provide a transition to that other problematic sentence and to the extremely important—but as far as I can tell unread—submerged network of connections in which it figures. It appears in the last chapter, when Munn tells Willie Proudfit that he is leaving, and takes place on the day after Lucille Christian had told him that the Senator used to "put his hands on me every chance he got" (354). Although her visit, especially her unchaperoned visit to Munn's room after dark, had caused tension in the Proudfit household that might have made Munn uncomfortable enough to want to leave, the real reason for his departure is that he wants to kill Tolliver. Although he already hates the man who had once placed that paternal hand on his shoulder, the sexual jealousy Lucille's revelation causes him to feel evidently pushes him over the edge.

He goes back into the house to get what he will need for the journey: "'I just wanted to get a few things,' Mr. Munn explained, almost apologetically; 'those handkerchiefs you got for me over at Thebes, and a few things'" (360). It is already a little strange, in a novel as carefully constructed and as relatively free from unmotivated detail as this, that something as mundane as handkerchiefs would be the only thing Munn names among the equipment he deems necessary for his oedipal quest. That they should come from a place called Thebes—Oedipus's hometown—makes them, of course, a little less strange in that context. But what seems altogether fitting to a reader not unhappy to find some confirmation of the oedipal undercurrent he already suspected was there comes nevertheless at the expense of some verisimilitude: handkerchiefs seem too trivial for Munn to go back into the house for. The sentence, like Tolliver's, doesn't quite fit.

And it doesn't quite fit for an entirely other reason too. Proudfit may remember "*those* handkerchiefs," but the reader will not, for the prior mention that demonstrative pronoun assumes just does not exist. Search as you may, you will not find it. But you will find something, and what you find will make it clear that we are not dealing with an authorial lapse, or at least not with an unmotivated one. For there was an earlier Theban handsomething: "Willie Proudfit brought him one of the handbills offering the reward. . . . His picture was on the handbill. . . . 'They got them handbills every whar. You better keep lay-en low. Over at Thebes they got 'em all over the settlement, on walls and telephone poles, and lay-en in stores'" (313–14). What we appear to have are two interlocking pieces of a puzzle. But of what picture? There is considerably more to put together, and we could start by examining the other common element (other than oedipal Thebes) that links these two pieces: hands.

The hand Tolliver placed on Munn's shoulder was the most expressive sign of his seemingly paternal interest; it was what Munn most blamed for his falling into trap of behaving like a son ("If the Senator had never laid a hand on his shoulder . . ."). The word *justice,* the last word of the Senator's speech that hung motionless in the air as the buzzard hung in the sky, was accompanied by an extraordinarily expressive and powerful hand: "the Senator slowly raised his right hand in a gesture that suggested the solemnity of benediction and the incitement of salute. As the hand began, slowly, to descend, the first spatter of applause broke . . . like the first . . . tumescent drops exploding upon the dry roof before the storm breaks in full volume" (23). Munn's command of this sort of sign language seems to suffer by comparison: When he extended his hand to Bunk Trevelyan at the successful conclusion of his trial, his client "looked for an instant at Mr. Munn's outstretched hand as though he did not comprehend the gesture" (64). He suffered similar embarrassment later when he tried to shake hands with Professor Ball. Munn "was about to grasp the offered hand when he saw that it was completely swathed in bandages. Involuntarily he stopped, his glance resting on the carefully wound cloths. Each finger was wrapped separately to make a great, clumsy, club-like glove" (112). Ball's outlandish costume is a weird detail, but that weirdness makes it all the more useful for getting to the bottom of what the handbills and handkerchiefs were pointing to. There is a reason in the story for his getup—the Professor suffered from impetigo, "the country leprosy"—but why is Warren telling us a story in which there is a character who has a perfectly good reason for having his hands swathed in bandages?[3] It is not an unmotivated detail, but the motivation dwells within that realm of *Night Rider* in which it makes sense to talk about how Theban handkerchiefs answer Theban handbills. I am reading for plot, but one of the plots of this novel is the one in which such things as these are the leading characters.

In grappling with that last question we would do well to meditate on the sight of those white bandaged hands and to realize that what sent us off in this direction in the first place were some mysterious pieces of white cloth, the *hand*kerchiefs Warren drops into the story when it is time for Munn to leave. What Ball's peculiarity provides is another arrangement of the same elements that were present there: hands and white cloth. There are moments here when the text of the novel seems to speak in an allegory of its own construction, one of the most compelling of which appears at the beginning of chapter 5, the chapter in which Tolliver's letter appears and Munn discovers what is so fitting about the sentence that did not fit. Munn is thinking to himself about how he should have been able to read what was coming, the trap into which he was falling; but when he speaks of the way things were falling into place and of the necessity of getting beneath the surface, and most especially of hands and patches of white, it is remarkable how suggestive his words are of the desirability of getting beneath the surface of *this* text: "The signs of the future had been there . . . but he had lacked the key, the clue to the code, and had seen only the ignorant surface. Or those events of the future had appeared at that time like icebergs . . . patches of white cloud no bigger than a man's hand. . . ." He felt "as the loser feels when the cards of the last hand begin to fall . . ." (93). Munn uses precisely the same term he will use seven pages later—"it was the *key* of the letter"—to talk about what it was that could enable to him to read these signs correctly.

What may we read in the signs with which he allegorizes his situation? We could find that hands insist here, appearing twice, one compared to a sign in the sky (recall the Senator's hand held up in the air like his last word, and like the buzzard in the empty, cloudless sky),[4] and the other a hand a hand holds. We could find, too, that what is compared to a hand in the first of these is a patch of white: are we not once again in the realm of white-bandaged hands and white handbills and handkerchiefs? Why is it precisely such things as patches of white and hands that figure the future of Percy Munn? Is it not that they are precisely what is beneath the surface of the novel, like the "icebergs . . . which, with seven eighths of their enormous . . . bulk submerged, may be moving unpredictably toward a fatal conjunction"?

The fact of the matter is that the fatal juncture at which Munn arrives on the last page is one to which white bandages, Theban handbills, and handkerchiefs—and night riders' masks—will have led him. It was, after all, Professor Ball's white-bandaged hand that committed the crime for which Munn died. "It was perfectly clear to Munn how it had happened. And how Professor Ball had moved down the alley, erectly, almost somnambulantly, his white, club-like bandages hanging out from under the black sleeves. . . . He had lifted the rifle, clumsily to his bandaged, unaccustomed hands, and over there in the courthouse yard, in the clear daylight, the man had fallen" (319–20). It was suddenly perfectly clear to Munn that it was Ball who had assassinated the key witness in his son-in-law's trial, had done it with Munn's rifle from Munn's law-office window, and that that was the reason Munn's photograph was on handbills all over Thebes. But that realization did not come quickly. He had been hiding out at Proudfit's for some time, had been repeatedly going over every detail of that last morning he had spent in Bardsville in the effort to figure out what must have happened before Isabella Ball appeared on the stairs of his hotel to warn him he was about to be arrested. He had had to hide in a stable loft until nightfall, under the hay, "with a handkerchief over his face to keep off the dust" (305). But the facts did not yield to the interrogation of his memory. "Rather, the answer he finally had . . . came almost unsought, casually, at the moment of his waking one morning, before he had fully defined himself in consciousness. He woke, that morning, and . . . his mind seemed to say to him, You are lying here . . . because Professor Ball killed that man" (318).

The revelation comes just after the account of Munn's strange recurring dream. We are not told that the dream led him to the discovery of Ball's role in his predicament, but the Professor's bandage-wrapped hands do bear an astonishing resemblance to the dream's central, haunting image, a newspaper-wrapped bundle whose wrapping falls away to reveal a fetus. Given the identity Munn assumed in the beginning of the novel by becoming a member of the board of the Association of Growers of Dark Fired Tobacco, dreaming is perhaps the most important—and characteristic—thing he could do: " 'My boy,' the Senator announced, and approached him with an outstretched hand, 'we have come to tell you that you are a member of the Association board.' . . . He added, shaking the hand, 'To complete the unexpired term of Mr. Morphee' " (29). Munn is, in effect, the new Mr. Morphee (of whom no other mention is made except for the fact of his name and the reason Munn took his place: "When a Mr. Morphee resigned because of ill health, the members of the board appointed Mr. Munn . . ."; 29). He is, that is, the new Morpheus, son of Hypnos, god of dreams.[5] Thus, from the very moment he began his association with the tobacco growers, from the moment Munn, seduced by the gestures of Tolliver's fatherly hand, first became entangled in what would become a web ("They were all webbed together . . . coming together here, and becoming one thing"; 17) of increasing illegality and violence, he was also destined to dream, to create the one kind of text we are all capable of creating, the fabric by which the truth of underlying conflicts, as Warren once wrote in that early poem I quoted in the Introduction, are revealed: "... sleep, the dark wherein you all are piled, / Poor fragments of the day, until there come / Dreams to release from the troubled heart and deep / The pageantry of thoughts unreconciled."

Here is the dream:

> In the dream he saw May approaching him, slowly, as from a great distance across which he strained. Her pale hair was down, loose, and she held a bundle in her arms. On her face, as she approached him, there was a great sweetness, but a sadness, and she approached slowly, as though her feet were weighted with lead. Closer, she held out the bundle toward him. He saw that it was wrapped in old newspaper, stained and torn. Then, as he strained toward her and reached to take the bundle from her arms, the paper began to flake away from the bundle, as though disintegrating from its own sodden weight, hanging in shreds over May's hands and bare arms. He saw, then, what the paper had concealed. There on May's outstretched arms, was a body, a foetus like those which he had seen suspended in liquid in great glass jars at the medical school in Philadelphia, ill-formed, inhuman, dripping, gray like the ones in the jars, and with a stench like death. But May's face had retained the expression of sweetness and sadness, and his own arms had remained reaching toward her as though to take the bundle. Then, the last shreds of the sodden paper fell away from what was the face of that object in her arms. It was the face of Bunk Trevelyan, the redness of flesh and hair faded to grayness, but Trevelyan's face, and somehow, he knew that it was alive and strove to speak. But always, at that moment, May began to laugh. He could not hear the sound, but her face was contorted in a paroxysm of laughter that he thought would never end. Then, not in fury but with a coldness of calculation, almost with a slyness, he raised his clenched fist, thinking that he must stop her laughter, that if she continued to laugh like that all would be lost, everything would shrivel and be blotted out and devoured, and there would be nothing but that soundless ferocity of laughter and himself alone in the midst of it. Then he woke up.... (317–18)

There are "Poor fragments of the day" here to relate, too—events of the immediately preceding day that the unconscious seizes upon as raw material for the expression of a hidden agenda for which those fragments serve only as a cover, a clever disguise. "[I]n every dream it is possible to find a point of contact with the experiences of the previous day," Freud wrote in *The Interpretation of Dreams* (197); in fact, "the instigation to a dream is always to be found in the events of the previous day" (180). Yet, while this day residue will provide the catalyst to the dream and constitute part of its "manifest content," it cannot by itself reveal the "*latent* content . . . which is of far greater significance" (196). Dreams "pick up indifferent refuse left over from the previous day. . . . For reasons connected with the mechanism of association . . . the dream-process finds it easier to get control of recent or indifferent ideational material which has not yet been requisitioned by waking thought-activity; and for reasons of censorship it transfers psychical intensity from what is important but objectionable on to what is indifferent" (627–28). Thus the psychical intensity the dream *appears* to manifest—Munn's hatred toward his wife in this instance, the "clenched fist" with which he would have stopped her laughter—may in fact be indifferent to the dreamer. His real psychical investment may quite possibly lie elsewhere.

Warren in that early poem appears to be in substantial agreement with Freud. It is not the poor fragments of the day that the pageant of the dream is really about, but the "thoughts unreconciled." For the dream in *Night Rider* Warren has in fact set up a quite interesting context for dream analysis, one with a built-in day residue. The poor fragment of the day is itself another text, a ballad Adelle Proudfit sings and to which Munn pays only fleeting attention, but which, it is evident, serves as raw material for the manifest content of his dream. The story the dream tells—that of Munn being approached by his wife with a dead infant in her arms, together with the feelings of murderous hostility Munn feels toward his wife in the dream—was in fact first told in the ballad. And because it is not original to the dream, it is therefore not the real story his unconscious is telling but only the disguise for whatever that real story is. In the ballad a woman refuses a man's advances, even though he promises to marry her ("Walk with me, Pretty Polly / For we go to the church soon"). But he makes her accompany him into the woods anyway, and there he apparently takes her life: " 'But he took her by her lily-white hand / And led her far away.' Absorbed in his own thoughts, [Munn] scarcely followed the tune and the story of sadness and hinted violence in the woods" (316–17). The middle of the ballad is missing, because Munn's attention had wandered, but in the conclusion the man becomes a wanderer and dies at sea. Beneath the waves, in a kind of submarine afterlife:

> There he met his Pretty Polly
> All wrapped in gores of blood,
> And she held out her lily-white arms,
> An infant was of mine.

He had risen, and had walked away, across the yard. That night he had dreamed the dream. (317)

If what the dream ultimately has to tell Munn, and us, is not the story of an encounter between him and his wife and a dead infant—since that is what was already present in the day residue that the dream is using as the vehicle for saying something else—then what is that something else? In a self-referential way, the dream almost appears to present, tantalizingly, the key to the unlocking of this riddle. This self-referentiality actually takes more than one form, for not only does the dream, once it begins to recur, allude to itself—"Even in the dream now, he knew that it had been dreamed before" (316)—but also (and in this instance from the very first night) to the task of interpreting it. In the fetus that is gradually revealed, the dream presents an image of truth's unveiling—particularly for this dreamer, for Munn had already described the search for truth as a process of removing layers of wrapping. Speaking of young Benton Todd, he had observed that "It's all surface to him yet.... Getting older is breaking through the surfaces. Layer after layer. Peeling them off to find what's inside.... The chances were you never knew. Just kept on peeling. Like skin off an onion. And if you stopped you died, or rather, you were dead already" (86). Munn describes himself, too, as searching for what is hidden within a concealing integument: "as something concealed, precisely, at the center of his life, like the fruit within the rind, the meat of the nut within the gross and useless outer shell. What was the center of his life, he demanded of himself. He could not say" (130).

The newspaper wrapping around the bundle in the dream that gradually flakes away promises by its disintegrating disappearance to reveal the truth (or to desire that it be revealed, for "it was alive and strove to speak")—but does it? Is the face it reveals the answer or just another covering? And if it is the truth for Munn, is it also that for the reader of the novel? For we must acknowledge that the dream may function within the context of *Night Rider* in ways other than—in addition to—those in which it works in Munn's unconscious. It is in this light that we should consider the other instances in which what appears in the dream has already appeared, at least twice, in the novel.

At Bunk Trevelyan's trial, a newspaper-wrapped bundle was produced as a surprise piece of simulated evidence. "The prosecuting attorney unwrapped a newspaper-covered parcel and held up a knife. 'Was it a knife like this?'" (52), he asked of the merchant who had sold one to Trevelyan; it was. That Trevelyan had recently bought such a knife was a surprise to his lawyer, Percy Munn; the prosecutor's action was effective, for thus he established that Trevelyan owned a knife just like this, in a manner that would stay in the jurors' minds. What Munn did after that point was—like the Oedipus he would come increasingly to resemble—some detective work that would have disastrous consequences. After interrogating his client about the knife and being told that someone had stolen it from Trevelyan's house, Munn went out that night with some borrowed sheriff's deputies and, after a diligent search, discovered it in the cabin of a poor black sharecropper who had found it where Trevelyan had tossed it after he stabbed Tad Duffy. Munn won his case, and would realize only later that an innocent man was hanged for the crime.[6]

A somewhat more mysterious newspaper-wrapped package makes its appearance in chapter 11, when Munn rides out to a meeting at Professor Ball's house in which it will be decided to burn the Bardsville tobacco warehouses:

> Mr. Munn swung out of the saddle and dropped the rein. "Thanks," he replied.
> "Is you one of the gemmun gonna spend the night?" the negro asked.
> "Yes," Mr. Munn said. He fumbled in the saddlebags and pulled out a small packet, tied up in newspaper. (208)

I presume—given the question about spending the night—that the packet contains his clothes. The fact that it is never mentioned again, while in some sense it should be, gives it the appearance of being a kind of symmetrical counterpart to the handkerchiefs from Thebes that will be mentioned as though they had been mentioned before.

But where does that symmetry lie? Not, evidently, in Munn's dream; rather, in the larger dream in which it appears. Morpheus, after all, was not so much a dreamer as the bringer of dreams. Likewise, the dream to be analyzed here is not just the one Munn has, but the dream of the text, if I may speak so abstractly, in this novel put together like the text of a dream—the dream Munn (Mr. Morphee's replacement), through his dream, brings about. It is in this dream, endowed with both a manifest and a latent content, with puzzling details that call out for decipherment, that some of these other newspaper-wrapped bundles, hands, and patches of white, these seemingly indifferent fragments, promise to reveal their connecting strands.

The analysis of that larger dream, however, is best approached by a close reading of the one within it. What is it, then, about newspapers that they should envelop the mystery at the heart of that dream? Now newspapers in *Night Rider* have at least one clearly defined function, that of distancing the reader from real events with which he or she is directly connected. When Munn reads in the papers about the depredations in which he, as a night rider, had just participated, "he felt, almost always, as if he were reading of something in which he had had no part, of something that had happened a very long time before. The event, in the print there on the page, was meaningless and ghostly" (141).[7] Yet if appearance in newsprint can remove meaning, it can also reveal it—as it did when Munn, having puzzled the night before over the mysterious sentence in Tolliver's letter, was granted the sudden revelation that came "the next morning when he ... saw that very sentence in the newspaper" (101). Newsprint's ability to both conceal and reveal is at work in the dream as well, as it both hides and uncovers the object within.

But the most extended treatment in the novel of the essence of newspaperness appears in chapter 9, in the digression on Ianthe Sprague. It is a passage that would surely appear irrelevant to a reader interested only in what Warren has to say about the Kentucky tobacco wars or about his heroes' quest for identity or community. But to a reader interested in Munn's relationship with his father, and most especially to texts of paternal origin, it at least merits attention for the fact that it contains the only mention in all of *Night Rider* of Munn's biological father. Is it any accident that this single glimpse of the man for whom Tolliver is only a substitute should come through the medium of a text that the son inherited from that father? Munn "found that the name 'Ianthe' raised in his mind an image of great delicacy and beauty. *In one of his father's books* he read a poem with the title 'Ianthe': 'From you, Ianthe, little troubles pass / Like little ripples down a sunny river; / Your pleasures spring like daisies in the grass, / Cut down, and up again as blithe as ever' " (170; emphasis added).

Walter Savage Landor's poem (an attribution not spelled out in the novel, where it is more purely the father's text, even if only by the fact of ownership)[8] describes the elderly Miss Sprague pretty well too, for the most remarkable thing about her was her limited attention span. Munn, when he was a law student in Philadelphia, would visit her regularly; once, he thought he would read aloud to her and brought a sentimental novel but found that her attention wandered, so in the end he gave that up. "She finally said that what she would like to hear was the newspaper." But not "the long, important, consecutive pieces."

> What she liked was the short, flat statement that had no possible reference to her life, advertisements of merchandise which she could neither buy nor use, the notice of the death of an obscure citizen.... The novel had a direction ... it pretended to a meaning. Therefore she could not listen to it.... But the fragmentary, the irrelevant, the meaningless, such things she could receive and draw her special nourishment from.... [S]he was like some species of marine life that ... sustains itself on what the random currents bring, absorbing the appropriate

matter and ejecting all else, with a delicate and punctilious, but unconscious, discrimination. (172)

As I have already suggested in the Introduction, Ianthe's literally "unconscious" powers of discrimination bear a striking resemblance to the behavior of the unconscious itself, particularly to the way the unconscious selects what it needs to construct the text of its dream from apparently meaningless details, the "indifferent refuse," of memory. Freud quotes with approval the findings of an earlier observer:

> the remarkable thing is that dreams derive their elements not from major and stirring events nor the powerful and compelling interests of the preceding day, but from incidental details, from the worthless fragments, one might say, of what has been recently experienced or of the remoter past. A family bereavement, which has moved us deeply and under whose immediate shadow we have fallen asleep late at night, is blotted out of our memory.... On the other hand, a wart on the forehead of a stranger whom we met in the street and to whom we gave no second thought after passing him *has* a part to play in our dream.... (52)

What is especially relevant here, in the digression about Ianthe Sprague that might otherwise appear irrelevant in the story of Percy Munn, is the connection it suggests between the act of reading newspapers (or of reading them in a certain way, with an emphasis on the opportunity they provide for the random perusal of unrelated fragments) and the dreamwork of the unconscious. This is all the more relevant for the fact that Munn's memory of his Philadelphia experience with Ianthe is clearly evoked, albeit unconsciously, in the dream. For what the disintegrating newspaper revealed was something that reminded him of Philadelphia: "There on May's outstretched arms, was a body, a foetus like those which he had seen suspended in liquid in great glass jars at the medical school in Philadelphia...." (The city is nowhere else mentioned in the novel.) "Dreams can select their material from any part of the dreamer's life, provided only that there is a train of thought linking the experience of the dream-day (the 'recent' impressions) with the earlier ones," Freud argued (202), and the train of thought linking the recent memory of the ballad of Pretty Polly with the more distant memory of Ianthe Sprague is not hard to trace. For, like the dead child in the song (as well as the fetus suspended in liquid), Ianthe is best defined as an underwater creature ("some species of marine life . . ."). And Ianthe *listening* to Munn read the newspaper, using her unconscious powers of discrimination to take what nourishment she needed from what she heard, bears an astonishing resemblance to Munn himself as he hears the text of the ballad sung to him, and as his attention fades in and out ("Absorbed in his own thoughts, he scarcely followed the tune and the story . . ."). As a text, the ballad was more like one of the sentimental novels at which Ianthe's attention flagged ("he had not been reading for ten minutes before he knew that her attention was wandering"), but what Munn did in his selective perception, and hence memory, was to transform that tragic story into something more like the fragmentary newspaper pieces that Ianthe so eagerly devoured.

And of course those fragmentary newspaper pieces that constituted her unconscious nourishment are precisely what the dream embodies in a most literal sense when the newspaper begins "to flake away from the bundle, as though disintegrating from its own sodden weight." What they reveal in their disintegration is the face of Bunk Trevelyan, but can we believe that this is what Munn is really dreaming about? Not if, as Freud believed, "a dream is a (disguised) fulfilment of a (suppressed or repressed) wish" (194). For it to be fulfilled, it must be disguised; it must be distorted to get past the dream censor that would not knowingly allow such a wish to be expressed. Freud found that this disguise and distortion take the form of "displacement," the process by which an unconscious wish is transferred—displaced—from the real object of its desire to one that the dream censor would never suspect harbored an unspeakable wish. "The consequence of the displacement is that the dream-content no longer resembles the core of the dream-thoughts and that the dream gives no more than a distortion of the dream-wish which exists in the unconscious" (343). Freud compares the manifest content to "a transcript of the dream-thoughts into another mode of expression, whose characters and syntactic laws it is our business to discover by comparing the original and the translation." The manifest content is expressed in something like "a rebus," "a pictographic script" that must be translated into the language of the latent content if the dream is to be understood. "If we attempted to read these characters according to their pictorial value instead of according to their symbolic relation, we should clearly be led into error" (312).

Trevelyan's face, part of the rebus of the manifest content of the dream, is most likely, then, a disguise for something or someone else. But to make that disguise flake away, we cannot ignore the implications of Bunk Trevelyan posing as the fetus in Munn's wife's arms, as Munn's dead offspring. Trevelyan is, in fact, Munn's creation: Munn saved him from hanging and then made a night rider out of him (though not a very good one). In the eyes of Munn's colleagues, Trevelyan is "That boy of yours" (120), language that echoes what Senator Tolliver kept calling Munn: "My boy" (29, 30, 92). Munn had to destroy his creation when it was discovered that Trevelyan was engaging in extortion; and the repeated emphasis in the scene of Trevelyan's death on the fact that his corpse lay submerged in the water of the abandoned quarry into which he fell after Munn and the others fired their guns into him returns in the dream in its emphasis on the water in which the fetus floated, "suspended in liquid in great glass jars . . . dripping, gray like the ones in the jars" (and the seawater through which the dead infant in the ballad appeared to Polly's murderer). After the death of his "boy," Munn "thought suddenly of Trevelyan's face in the water," and then obsessively repeated, "In the water of the quarry . . . in the water. . . . A man would lie in the water and the water would be over him and inside of him and he would become a part of the water" (165).

The fact, however, that the fetus with Trevelyan's face is *May*'s child too, presented in her outstretched arms, makes it possible to begin the work of peeling off the layer of this disguise (in what is, after all, a novel about masked men, the night riders of the title). If the dream appears, because in the end it reveals the face of the man Munn killed, to bear the weight of the dreamer's guilt for that deed, might that guilt not in fact be more truly felt for the other man for whose death Munn was directly responsible, and whose death was totally unmerited (unlike that of Trevelyan, who really did deserve to die)—all the more likely if, as Freud maintains, a dream's manifest content is a mask for something else? I am referring to the man whose name Munn is obsessively trying to remember just two pages before the dream: "He would think of that negro man, the one who had had the knife, Trevelyan's knife. . . . Mr. Munn tried hard to remember his name. He would lie there, staring at the dazzling depth of the sky, and try to remember the name. It became almost an obsession with him. . . . He could see his face . . . the gray lips protesting. . . . But he could not remember the name" (315). That he had turned gray was something Munn noticed about Bunk Trevelyan in the dream. Not only was his fetal body "gray like the ones in the jars," but also the face that had been ruddy in life had been transformed in the dream to gray—at the same time as this face, like the man whose gray lips had tried to protest his innocence, struggled in vain to communicate: "It was the face of Bunk Trevelyan, the redness of flesh and hair faded to grayness, but Trevelyan's face, and somehow, he knew that it was alive and strove to speak." Now it would make marvelous sense, in the punning way dreams have with the truth they disguise, that Trevelyan's face should stand for the unnamable black's, for switching their identities is precisely what Munn is guilty of, as he made the latter Tad Duffy's murderer in the eyes of the jury. The dream does what Munn did when he pursued the trail of the knife that came into the courtroom in that newspaper-wrapped package and, through his too eager (too eager for the truth's sake) detective work, put the black's face on the murderer's body; but the dream does its switching in the opposite direction. If dreams are wishes, as Freud always maintained, then this dream can be read as the disguised expression of the wish that it had been Bunk Trevelyan who had been hanged for the crime he did in fact commit—that it be *his* gray lips that feebly protested.

That the fetus with Trevelyan's mask of a face is May and Munn's son ("An infant was of mine," as the ballad anticipates) contributes, too, to this reading of the dream. For May really has given birth to Munn's son, and the most striking fact about Munn's relation to this son is that he doesn't know *his* name, either. Recall that May's Aunt Lucille Burnham had already told him in a letter that May was pregnant and that he would never see his child. It was Sissie Proudfit, who on every baking day came up to the cave behind the house where Munn spent his daylight hours with "a couple of rolls wrapped up in a piece of white cloth," who told him the news:

> [S]he stooped to pick up the little square of white cloth, and smoothing and folding it in her hands, she said, "Mr. Perse . . . they's word yore wife's had a little baby."
> "That's true," Mr. Munn replied.
> "Hit's a little boy," she added, "ain't hit?"
> "Yes, Sissie."
> She laid the cloth between the palms of her hands, and held it there. Then she asked, "What's hit's name?"
> "I don't know," he said. (322)

It's as if the dream were coming true (this incident happens "toward the end of his stay," therefore after the first appearances of the dream). Now Sissie already resembles May because she, like Munn's wife, is a niece raised as a daughter. May had been brought up by her Aunt Lucille Burnham; Sissie, by Adelle and Willie Proudfit, her aunt and uncle. What would otherwise be a meaningless detail, given how minor a role Sissie plays in the novel, thus acquires some significance through the parallels the dream and its surrounding context set up between Sissie and May. May appeared in the dream bearing the newspaper-wrapped fetus; Sissie comes to Munn bearing not one but two things, each of which echo the other: something wrapped in a square of white cloth and the news of the birth of his son. The echoing takes place thanks to the dream in which his son appears wrapped in what were originally rectangles of white, and to the context of imagery in which handkerchiefs and other rectangles of white cloth (the night riders' masks) proliferate and in which certain handbills and handkerchiefs (the Theban ones) seem almost interchangeable.

Munn neither knows the name of his son nor can remember the name of the man who was hanged for Trevelyan's crime. But what is utterly remarkable in this novel in which names will prove to be of the greatest importance is that there is in fact a name attached to that man, and it is precisely the same name as that of the mother whose child it has entirely become. When Trevelyan finally told Munn about having bought the knife with which Duffy was murdered, he told him too that someone had stolen it from his kitchen table and that it must have been taken by a black man he had seen on the road near the house: " 'I recollect I seen one of them niggers up thar prowlen nigh on the road. One of them niggers lives over on *Mr. May's place,* or round thar. I seen him round, but I don't rightly know his name' " (55; emphasis added). Munn could not remember the man's name either, but it is more than likely that his unconscious, at least, had no trouble at all remembering the name that Trevelyan could associate with the man, the name that did enable Munn to locate the man when he went out that night to look for the knife, and thus that name *was* present in the dream when May appeared. And it was borne by the bearer of that name.

If I may digress for a moment, naming itself is a strong undercurrent in the novel, and it is perhaps wise to pay attention to how these names are distributed—especially in light of the fact that some of them are shared, with intriguing consequences. There are even two unusual *givers* of names, both of whom are fathers who name, and rename, their daughters: Professor Ball, who names all his daughters after Shakespearean heroines; and Bill Christian, who insists on calling his daughter "Sukie," even though her real name is Lucille, which she resents ("You needn't call me Sukie," she tells Munn. "My name is Lucille. . . . Do you see how he can make Sukie out of a name like Lucille?" [7, 8]), and who has the "touching habit," according to Lucille, "of naming dogs after young ladies he used to admire when he was young. It keeps his memory green" (136). One of the dogs is a Sukie.

If Bill Christian can call anyone Sukie (" 'I can make Sukie out of any name once I set my mind on it' " [8]), it seems that the novelist feels the same way about the name Sukie stands for in Lucille's case, for it has been given to three different characters: to Lucille Christian; to Lucy Burnham, the aunt who raised May like a daughter; and to the head telephone operator in whose presence the wires were cut on the night of the Bardsville raid and who testified at Dr. MacDonald's trial, Miss Lucy Mayhew. What logic might underlie this onomastic linkage?

Munn's first and last encounters with May's Aunt Lucy are characterized by moments that seem to return in his fetal dream. When he was "a boy just entering adolescence," he attended the funeral of Lucy's father, General Sam Burnham, and witnessed the "wild, pure cry wrung from her heart and saw her drunken lurching toward the open grave. He was to remember the moment, and much later was to try, puzzledly, to correlate its passion with the cold, trivial, foolish, and futile woman whom he grew to know" (181). Lucy's savage cry at the grave returns, perhaps, in the dream in the way May falls into a fit of uncontrollable utterance: "He could not hear the sound, but her face was contorted in a paroxysm of laughter that he thought would never end." And later, when Lucy Burnham, "with a ring, almost of long-deferred joy, in her voice," refused Munn access to his wife upstairs, he "thought how easy it would be to knock that rotten old head in with one blow of his fist" (186)—as in the dream, in the face of the "soundless ferocity" of May's scorn, "he raised his clenched first, thinking that he must stop her laughter."

At the graveside May had been present, too, a thin little girl of six or seven, and so Munn's "first sight of May" was accompanied by her aunt's wild cry of passion. This may account for why in the dream the two women seem to blend into one, as the dream recalls both the paroxysm of that cry and the fist Munn would later raise in Lucy's face. And it may account, too, for why it is that the mistress Munn takes in his wife's absence should be another Lucille, for thereby he possessed—in name at least—the other half of what his dream suggests he wanted, the other half of that adolescent encounter with the unintelligible mystery of the other sex, and of its voice. As a matter of fact, what first intrigued him about Lucille Christian was her name. After she and her father had bantered back and forth over whether it ought to be Sukie or Lucille, Munn curiously "did remember that it was Lucille, though certainly he had never heard Mr. Christian ever refer by any other name than Sukie to his daughter" (who had until then been living in St. Louis).

If the dream, as I suggest, brings together the Lucy he wanted to shake a fist at and the May who was his wife, then what are we to make of a name that combines them into one: *Lucy May*hew, the Bardsville switchboard operator (whose job it was to make connections)? What we make of it depends on what we make of the rest of her name. But thereby hangs a tale, for that last syllable is the exact homonym of a name that is spoken only once in the novel, and only at the moment its owner is being made to resemble the newspaper-wrapped fetus in the dream: " 'Then she said, Take off your coat, Hugh, so we can bandage up your hands. I burst right out laughing. For a fact. They they just bandaged me up, like the Professor. And they got one of the Professor's old long, black coats and I put it on . . .' " (270). It's Dr. MacDonald speaking, telling Munn how, disguised as his father-in-law whose hands were always enveloped because of a chronic skin disease, he slipped past the soldiers who had come to arrest him for his part in the Bardsville warehouse raid. We have seen how in the case of Senator Tolliver a strategically placed hand completed the illusion of paternity ("If the Senator had never laid a hand on his shoulder . . ."); similarly, here MacDonald accomplishes the feat of passing for his father-in-law by raising *his* hand as he rides past the soldiers: " 'I just lifted up my hand the way the Professor does when he meets somebody on the road, and prayed the Old Marster'd make those bastards notice the bandages and all. Well, they did.' " And the same gesture, minus the bandages, makes yet another son become the spitting image of his father: When Benton Todd, of whom I will soon have reason to speak in connection with the fetus in the dream, raised his hand to be sworn into the night riders, he looked just like Captain Todd when he raised his hand (as he "kept holding up one hand as though he wished to speak or as though, perhaps, to ward off a blow") during a meeting of the board: "Mr. Munn was to remember that scene—the Captain standing there with his hand raised a little—was to remember it very sharply ... when he saw, some six weeks later, Benton Todd advance ... and lift his hand for the oath. With his hand raised that way, he looked, somehow, more like the old man than ever" (146).

Lucy, May, Hugh: do they all figure in the dream? Is Lucy Mayhew the switchboard in whose name they all intersect? May is already there; Lucy (Burnham) is evoked when Munn raises his fist (a version of the raised hand by which sons become their fathers?); and Hugh, at the only moment he is Hugh, by his hands' resemblance to the wrapped fetus. But why should Munn dream of Hugh? What repressed or suppressed wish finds disguised fulfillment if Hugh is the fetus? The answer lies in the sudden discovery Munn makes upon waking up one morning during the period in which he kept dreaming the dream: that Professor Ball had killed Al Turpin, the most potentially incriminating witness against his son-in-law MacDonald, and that he had done it, knowingly or not, in such a way as to make it look as if Munn had pulled the trigger. Ball's bandaged hands, as we have already seen, figure prominently in Munn's reconstruction of the event. Ball had walked "almost somnambulantly" to Munn's office, "his white, club-like bandages hanging out from under the black sleeves" just as MacDonald's did when he assumed Ball's disguise. "He had lifted the rifle, clumsily to his bandaged, unaccustomed hands, and over there in the courthouse yard ... the man had fallen." The dream's white-wrapped, dead fetus evokes both MacDonald and Ball, and expresses the suppressed wish that they both be dead, since even at the moment he was dreaming the dream, even though he did not fully realize it until the light of day, Munn had figured out who was responsible for the fact that he was being hunted down for a crime he did not commit. His dream directs murderous thoughts against both of the white-bandaged men: one because the crime had been committed for his sake, and the other because he pulled it off, and in doing so framed the dreamer.

And yet Munn still cannot consciously express that hatred: "Later, thinking back on those things, Mr. Munn discovered that his bitterness was gone. If he should see Professor Ball, he himself, he decided, would be the one to feel guilty and ashamed, as though he had committed the wrong. . . . He had a momentary vision of Professor Ball's face as it would be if they should meet. . . . Involuntarily, shudderingly, he closed his eyes as against the actual sight, as one does at the obscenity of suffering" (320). Munn's conscious is even here blind to the true nature of this obscenity, for he prefers to see it as Ball's suffering for not having told the truth and exonerated Munn, when in fact it is the obscenity of a murderous desire that Munn cannot bring himself to recognize. The sight of such obscenity, it appears, can only be borne through the disguise of a dream.

But Munn knew long before he dreamed the dream that uncovering the truth is a matter of removing multiple layers of what appears to be depth but is still just surface. "It's all surface to him yet," he had said to himself as he observed Benton Todd becoming more and more infatuated with Lucille Christian, with whom Munn himself would soon be having an affair. Knowing that getting at the truth is like peeling an onion ("breaking through the surfaces. Layer after layer. Peeling them off to find what's inside . . ."), in Munn's estimation, distinguishes his manhood from Todd's immaturity. But it is precisely Munn's relation to Benton Todd and their mutual interest in Lucille that make it necessary to remove one more onion peel or layer of disintegrating newspaper from the fetus in the dream: *Night Rider* goes to extraordinary lengths in the plotting of its narrative to make it possible for the dream to be yet another disguised fulfillment of a repressed wish.

The groundwork is partly laid by the long, embedded tale of Willie Proudfit's journey west, told to Munn at the time he was dreaming his recurring dream. What is relevant to the analysis of that dream is the fact that Proudfit, too, had a dream, and that Munn had already acted out the drama his own dream may suggest on the site of that other dream. After years of shooting buffalo, and somewhat troubled by all that carnage, Proudfit had wandered alone into the high country of New Mexico. He fell sick, was taken care of by Indians, and in his fever had a dream in which he saw a long road coming down a green hill. "I taken a bend in the road, and thar was a little church, a white church" with a spring nearby. He drinks from the spring, and as he glances up he sees a young woman sitting there. When he woke up, his fever was gone, and his mind clearer, and he kept thinking about the dream until he discovered the name of the place he had seen. "I'd seen hit, I knowed I'd seen hit, but I couldn't give hit the name. Then I knowed. Hit was the road come-en down to Thebes, in Kentucky, when I was a kid thar, and the church setten thar whar it takes a bend" (340).

Thebes, the forgotten name in Proudfit's memory, may be the forgotten name in the memory of the novel, a fragment from the past—a prior past—that rises to the surface at the strangest times: when handkerchiefs whose prior mention is missing are mentioned; or now, when the ghostly double of Munn's dream is recounted. In both, the dreamer encounters his wife, for the girl at the stream will turn out to be Proudfit's future wife. Moved by the dream, he makes his way back to Kentucky, "to Thebes. . . . I taken the turn in the road, and thar was the church. New Bethany church hit is. And the spring. . . . And thar she set. Hit was Adelle" (341).

A reader of the novel would at this juncture have already heard of the New Bethany church, for it was the place where Benton Todd died on the night of the Bardsville raid, back in chapter 11. But that reader would not have known how close the church and Thebes were to each other until now. Given what we now know about Thebes—both its connection to the anomalous handkerchiefs and the handbills declaring (falsely) Munn's guilt, and to the crossroads where Oedipus slew his father—what difference might it make that that curiously named town and the New Bethany church should figure in the same landscape?

The New Bethany church was not only the scene of Proudfit's prophetic vision; it was also the scene where Percy Munn brought about the demise of Benton Todd, who died as the Bardsville raiders were being pursued by a posse from town, and who would not have died if Munn had not been so anxious to get to the crossroads at the New Bethany church. "If they could make it to the New Bethany crossroads with a decent lead, they could, Mr. Munn was sure, throw off the pursuers. They'd have a chance, a good chance in that tangle of lanes there in that locality and in the woods" (233). The crossroads were the key to the plan, because there "they could separate, and the pursuers would waver and hesitate and would not know what to do, for no man among them would want to be apart from the others" (234). But by now, on the level straight stretch before the church, they were already taking fire from behind. " 'Oughter bushwhacked 'em!' Mr. Simmons was yelling. . . . 'Them bastards kill me, Munn, and 'fore God, I'll hant you!' " Simmons had urged Munn to order the men to dismount and take cover behind the stone fence that ran alongside the straight stretch. There, they could have fired on the pursuers, maybe killed and wounded a few, and sent the rest packing. But Munn had resisted this sound advice, preferring to try for "the crossroads, the forked lanes towards the fords at the creek, the woods and the dense darkness" (235). They made it that far. Munn ordered his men to dismount. " 'If they come across that ford, cut down on them.' He stared toward the ford. The water glinted dimly there. . . . 'Don't shoot,' he told the men. 'Don't shoot unless they try the ford.' "

And Munn was right; their attackers left off the pursuit, just as he predicted they would. But they did sustain one casualty during that mad dash for the New Bethany church, the crossroads, and the ford: Captain Todd's young son Benton was bleeding to death from a wound in his thigh. "The blood welled out of the small puncture there, and flowed *darkly,* but *glintingly* over the white flesh" (238; emphasis added). That dark glint had already appeared when Munn first saw the ford: "He stared toward the ford. The water *glinted dimly* there" (235). And another detail ties Benton's fate to his own: "They plunged across the shallow waters of the ford, and the splashing from the horse next to him drenched him to *the thigh*. But he felt nothing."

Munn felt nothing because he was so intent on getting to the ford. But why? The reason is less tactical, despite what he claims, than personal—and beneath the level of conscious awareness. To hold them off at the ford held a symbolic value for Munn, and it did so precisely because of the esteem in which he held Benton's father, the Confederate veteran Captain Todd. If Tolliver is the bad father in Munn's psyche, Todd is the good one. Munn saw Tolliver's departure from the Tobacco Association as an act of treachery; but when Todd resigned, it was unquestionably a matter of principle. Tolliver had laid a paternal hand on Munn's shoulder; Todd never did, but was always there, in the background, as a model of courage and wisdom.

> He would study Captain Todd's face ... and wonder about his calmness ... his deep inner certainty of self.... Perhaps you could only get to be like Captain Todd if you lived through some firm conviction, some enveloping confidence, some time in your life; that is, if you were stout enough to come out on the other side of it afterward and still be yourself. Mr. Munn remembered that somebody sometime had told him how Captain Todd once down in South Tennessee held a ford on a frozen creek all night and half a day with just forty or fifty men against a couple of companies of Yankee cavalry. (39)

Munn evidently wanted to "get to be like Captain Todd." Lacking Todd's "firm conviction" and "enveloping confidence," he could at least hold off the enemy *at a ford*. Even his hasty rejection of Simmons's urging that they take cover behind the stone fence and "bushwhack" the posse had its roots in something else he knew about Captain Todd: Todd abhorred bushwhackers. " 'We hanged them,' the Captain admitted. 'Nobody else would so we did it. Blackguards and desperadoes,' " he added, speaking of how he "and some other men just out of the war took care of a gang of *bushwhackers* and guerrillas in East Tennessee" (145).

The irony of it was that in trying so hard to resemble that ideal father Munn killed his likeness. Indeed, that likeness is remarked upon more than once: Benton "did favor the Captain, he remembered" (78); "He did look like Captain Todd, still did. Probably would look more like as time passed" (83); "With his hand raised that way, he looked, somehow, more like the old man than ever" (146)—and caused him unspeakable grief.

Benton's death may be something other than irony, in this instance. The best-loved father may be the object of oedipal aggression, and things in this novel have been set up in such a way—thanks to what Proudfit and his dream contribute to the tale—that Todd dies on oedipal terrain: near a crossroads (Oedipus unwittingly slew his father at a crossroads), one of whose forks leads to Thebes. And as he lay dying, Benton Todd, who already resembled his father, came to resemble the newspaper-wrapped fetus in the dream, for, like Hugh MacDonald and Professor Ball, he was wrapped in white: "they packed handkerchiefs on top, and under the wound beneath, where the bullet had entered.... The handkerchiefs soaked up the blood soggily" (236).

There is still another layer to be removed from the fetal mask in the dream, but now no longer in the dream itself as the disguised fulfilment of a suppressed wish, but in the novel—*that* dream—where it becomes the sign of a wish undisguisedly fulfilled. There is someone wrapped in white whom Munn wants to kill; and, to the extent possible, he consciously acts on that desire. But that his victim would bear some resemblance to the fetus in the dream is not something Munn could have known at the time of his dream. That part of the plot of *Night Rider* functions not in Munn's unconscious but, possibly, in ours—or in whatever it is in a literary text that is structured like the unconscious, and that weaves its dreamlike text.

Part of that process is indicated by Munn's strange need for Theban handkerchiefs before he sets off on his journey. If there is any event that precipitated his sudden departure from the Proudfits' farm it would have to have been Lucille Christian's visit, immediately after which he decided to go. And if there was anything Lucille told him that made up his mind to kill Tolliver it was most likely the revelation that she had been the object of the Senator's desire, and that he had made unwelcome advances—appropriately, with his hands: " 'He'd put his hands on me every chance he got.' ... 'I hadn't thought of him in a long time,' Mr. Munn remarked, almost reflectively, 'not really.' Then he exclaimed suddenly, with cold ferocity, 'The bastard!' " (354). It is hard to say whether Munn was more upset about the sexual aggression those hands represented when placed on Lucille or about what they may have made him recall of their deceptively paternal touch on his own shoulders. Either would have justified his call for something from Thebes; that what he wanted was handkerchiefs is extraordinarily resonant, whether they recall those that bound up Benton Todd's wound or the bandages on Ball's or MacDonald's hands or the newspaper wrapping on the fetus in the dream—to which the matching Theban handbills, being in fact newsprint, link the Theban handkerchiefs in the subsurface imagery of the novel—resonant, that is, not even as much in Munn's own unconscious as in whatever it is in the novel that behaves in the same way.[9]

At the midpoint of Munn's journey cross-country to Tolliver's house, he stops to sleep in an abandoned cabin, where he finds a strange, ghostly fragment from his dream: "a glass jar, unbroken, sitting on the ledge of a window. In the bottom was a little accumulation of unidentifiable filth ..."

(362). Munn, who betrays no conscious recollection of his dream, may find it unidentifiable, but how can we not remember what had been in the "glass jars at the medical school at Philadelphia, ill-formed, inhuman, dripping, gray . . . and with a stench like death"? It is as if—unbeknownst to Munn— he were reentering his dream, or that he, the new Mr. Morphee, were making us experience his dream as the day residue for one of our own. We can see what is going on, but apparently he cannot. Are we dreaming? In that same room

> he made out a small huddle of clothing, lying as dropped there. He stepped to it, and on a momentary impulse leaned to pick it up gingerly. . . . A flat, *black* beetle, polished *clean* like a button, moved unhurriedly from the spot where it had been concealed, and disappeared beneath the bottom log. Mr. Munn held up the object. It was a man's jacket. . . . The fabric was unyielding and wooden in his hand. It had long since lost the shape of the figure it had clothed, and had stiffened earthily, once and for all, to the contour of the surface on which it had lain. (362; emphasis added)

If the glass jar is the glass jar, and the unidentifiable filth the fetus, of what is this article of male clothing the metamorphosis if not what had clothed the fetus in the dream finally completely removed, empty now of all save something clean and black that crawls out of it under its own power?

I believe that that black, clean something is the father's text. The text of the father, that is, is what is finally left when all the layers of disintegrating newspaper, all the disguises, all the hidden wishes of the unconscious, have been removed. The proof lies right there in *Night Rider* on the very next page, where what is precisely clean and black is the text of the father's name: "The house stood back from a rutty dirt road. He knew it was the place, because leaning over close to the mailbox he had been able to make out the name, "Edmund Tolliver." It was a new mailbox. The metal was *clean* and slick to the touch of his fingers, and the *black* lettering distinct upon it" (363; emphasis added).

Having identified Tolliver's house, Munn finds the man himself concealed by a double layer of cloth. First, the curtain that may not be a curtain but in fact a piece of cloth: "At first he thought the house was deserted; then, upon nearer approach, he saw that very dim light showed around a curtain at one window, or a cloth which had been hung there" (363). Second, the sheet that covers his body, the face not visible—as it was in the dream, where the face, too, was saved for last: "At the instant of his entering, he made out, by the unsure light of the turned-down lamp, the figure on the bed, covered only by a sheet, the face averted" (364).

Standing at the foot of the bed with his gun pointed at the man lying there, Munn announces, "I'm going to kill you, Tolliver . . . in a minute, when I've looked at you." He stands there for a long time in that position, elaborating on his purpose. " 'I'm going to kill you. . . . It'll be a favor. . . . If I didn't kill you, you'd lie here, in this house, and be nothing. . . . You've got a new mailbox, out there on the road, but . . . there won't be anything in it. Ever' " (365). The mailbox that bears the father's inscription, the paternal text that by its identification with the clean and black thing that emerged from the clothing on the floor shows itself to be what remains when the last layer of wrapping is removed, turns out now, if what the son claims is true, to be not the ultimate content but yet another container, and an empty one at that. But the father has a last trick up his sleeve, and it is what saves his life.

> Tolliver shut his eyes. . . . The faint rays of the lamp fell palely . . . shadowing the sunken sockets of the closed eyes. The wrinkles and tiny veining on the eyelids showed a little, like the veining of leaves. . . .
> "I'm going to," [Munn] repeated, "in a minute. When I've looked at you."
> He waited, the revolver unwavering.
> Then he commanded suddenly, "Open your eyes."
> The man on the bed gave no sign.
> "Open your eyes."
> "Why don't you, Perse?" the voice whispered dryly. But the man's eyes were closed.
> The revolver sank a few inches, uncertainly.
> "I thought," Mr. Munn murmured, as in reverie, "I could do it." (366)

Evidently, the reason he can't is that Tolliver won't open his eyes. What Munn had been waiting for, he had said, was to look at him. But as long as Tolliver keeps his eyelids closed that look will not be complete. By keeping them closed this father still keeps something concealed from the son's gaze, still keeps some of the wrapping on the mystery—just as he does in Warren's poem "I Am Dreaming of a White Christmas: The Natural History of a Vision": "No presents, son, till the little ones come." So the poet will always ask, "But tell me, tell me, / Will I never know / What present there was in that package for me . . . ?"

As we shall see in chapter 3, Willie Stark refuses to say to Jack Burden whether he really winked or not, so that Jack will always "have something to think about." And as we shall see in the next chapter, this son is not wrong to declare that the box with the father's name on it is, in essence, empty, for there the eyes of the dead will prove to owe their peculiar expressiveness to the fact that there is nothing beneath them any more.

Chapter 2

Unlocking
the Gate *At Heaven's Gate,* 1943

Chapter 1 Jerry Calhoun, former college football star, flies back from New York City where Bogan Murdock, a financial tycoon in a 1920s southern city that seems a cross between Nashville and Memphis, had sent him on business. Although Murdock's daughter, Sue, and Jerry are lovers of a sort, on the evening of his return she asks Slim Sarrett, a graduate student at the local university, to take her out to dinner. The governor, accompanied by World War I hero Private Porsum, dines at the home of Murdock, who proposes to donate a tract of mountainous land to the state on the condition it be named for his father, Major Lemuel Murdock, now in his dotage.

Chapter 2 The beginning of Ashby Wyndham's "Statement," which will take up alternating chapters for most of the novel. Wyndham is a religious fanatic from the hill country of the state who has wound up in jail and has been invited to write the narrative of how he came to be there.

Chapter 3 Jerry Calhoun's childhood: his father, strong but incompetent about small things, his mean-tempered and clubfooted Uncle Lew (his dead mother's brother), his blind Aunt Ursula; Jerry at college, poor but academically, socially, and athletically successful, is offered a job by Bogan Murdock upon graduation (which would mean abandoning his study of geology).

Chapter 4 Wyndham's upbringing: Orphaned early, he lived with his brother, Jacob. When a wagon with a sick old man and a young woman passes by, the brothers take them in; the old man dies, and Marie gets a job as a cook at the Massey Mountain sawmill.

Chapter 5 Jerry works in the financial department of Murdock's company for three years, getting sound advice and instruction in economics from Duckfoot Blake, an accountant in the firm. On a visit to his father, Jerry hears how Lem Murdock once assassinated Moxby Goodpasture when both were running for governor.

Chapter 6 Ashby Wyndham, returning from a visit to Marie at Massey Mountain, gets roaring drunk and kills her mule in a wagon accident. He tells Jacob he will go to work at Massey to get the cash to compensate her for the mule.

Chapter 7 Sue Murdock, who alternates between pretending to pay no attention to Jerry Calhoun and then demanding that he make love to her at potentially dangerous times and places, is playing Ellida in the college's production of Ibsen's *Lady from the Sea*. Bogan wants Jerry to marry his daughter so that he can be a better father to her than he has been.

Chapter 8 Marie is pregnant; Ashby wants to marry her and get Jacob to sell the homestead so that he can cash in his half. Jacob refuses, and Ashby strikes him down and walks away, with blood on his hands.

Chapter 9 Jerry takes Sue to visit his folks. She surprises him by announcing that they are to be married. At a country club party, where there is mention of labor troubles at Murdock's timber operation on Massey Mountain, Sue slips out. When she doesn't return, Jerry pays a man in a bar to call to see if she's come home, but she hasn't. He has the nightmarish fantasy that she has been kidnapped and murdered.

Chapter 10 Jacob has left, sold the homestead, and left all the money to Ashby.

Chapter 11 Sue had taken a taxi to town and arranged for Slim Sarrett to meet her there. He tells her what he claims is the story of his life: that his father was a New Orleans barge captain killed in an explosion (and that he had a recurring nightmare about seeing his father's head drifting toward him with "a hank of dirty white clothesline" attached), and tells of a succession of other "fathers"—chief among them the South American Almendro, whose seductive eyes Sarrett learned to imitate by practicing in front of a mirror.

Chapter 12 Marie gives birth.

Chapter 13 Sue returns home, accuses her mother, Dorothy, of leading an empty life, packs her bags, and leaves home. Her mother, suddenly feeling decisive, makes an appointment with Private Porsum to look at a horse he has for sale.

Chapter 14 Marie is sickly after the birth of Frank. Jason Sweetwater organizes a strike at Massey Mountain; Ashby supports him. Private Porsum, Ashby's "second blood cousin," comes to speak against the strike. Ashby's moral sense is offended in this debate when Sweetwater "takes a lie off a man" and doesn't defend his honor. When Sweetwater calls Porsum a liar, Ashby hits Sweetwater with a chunk of rock. Sweetwater is hauled off to jail.

Chapter 15 Sarrett is reading aloud to Sue from a paper on Elizabethan tragedy, sounding very much like Warren in "Pure and Impure Poetry." Description of Sarrett's coterie, which includes Sweetwater. Sue takes a dingy apartment, drawing on the interest of her grandmother's legacy.

Chapter 16 Ashby is laid off, as are all those who had first sided with Sweetwater. Their child, Frank, dies. Ashby hears Frank's voice tell him he died because he could not thrive on "the vittles of wickedness" (the money from the sale of the house) and that Ashby must go find Jacob and be reconciled with him.

Chapter 17 Murdock decides to send Porsum up to Massey Mountain to calm the strikers (an action preceding the events of chapter 14). Murdock gives Jerry a card on which he has written Sue's address. Jerry stops first at a drugstore to buy an envelope of condoms. Sue, persuaded that her father sent him, refuses his advances.

Chapter 18 Ashby and Marie leave Massey Mountain to look for Jacob. They pass from town to town, Ashby preaching his gospel, acquiring fellow travelers along the way, eventually living on a riverboat.

Chapter 19 Bogan comes to Sue's apartment to try to persuade her to come back to the family. Sarrett walks in, is insolent to Murdock, and boasts of his physical superiority. Bogan departs; that night Sue becomes Slim's mistress. At a Sarrett party, a Mr. Billie Constantidopeles shows up and mentions having recently spoken to Slim's father. Sue is furious, for Sarrett had told her his father died when he was a child. Another revelation is in store: Sarrett and Constantidopeles are caught in a homosexual embrace in the kitchen. Pandemonium ensues; Sweetwater escorts Sue home to her apartment.

Chapter 20 Ashby, drawn into a fight in Hulltown, is nursed back to health by Pearl, a prostitute.

Chapter 21 Jerry's father informs him that he is being foreclosed on; it's because Bogan wants to convert the area into a hunt club. Duckfoot tells Jerry that Murdock's company has committed some illegalities and that he's resigning before they're all arrested. The newspaper attacks Bogan's father concerning the park in his name and the "dumping" of the timber company and other holdings at enormous cost to the state. Bogan calls home to tell the black servant Anse to keep Bogan's father from reading the paper; Anse, however, neglects to do so. Lemuel Murdock, crazy and packing a pistol, hitches a ride to town on a mule wagon.

Chapter 22 Sue and Sweetwater are now lovers, although Sarrett keeps sending her published poems that he has dedicated to her. Sue tells Sweetwater she is pregnant, but he doesn't want to spoil his career as a labor organizer by getting married again. Sue says she'll get an abortion.

Chapter 23 Marie takes sick and dies. Pearl shoots a policeman and they all wind up in jail. A reporter comes to tell Private Porsum his cousin Wyndham is under arrest and asks what is he going to do about it. Porsum tries to get him out but Wyndham refuses. Flashback to Porsum wiping out a machine-gun nest singlehandedly (though with the help of a certain Percy) in the war.

Chapter 24 Porsum confronts Murdock with the letter he has given to the newspaper in which he apologizes for his role in the scandal. Dorothy Murdock claims that she and Porsum had an affair. Bogan draws a gun on Porsum, who (truthfully) denies it.

Chapter 25 Sarrett tries to talk to Sue; Sweetwater throws him out. Sue gets the abortion. Sarrett returns later and strangles her, stealing some $943. Though he also steals two rings and a bracelet, once outside he wraps them in a sheet of newspaper and thrusts them into the sewer.

Chapter 26 Anse has been arrested for Sue's murder. Duckfoot Blake visits Jerry, in jail for the Murdock financial scandal, to await the arrival of a bail bondsman. A crowd forms to lynch Anse. Porsum tries to talk them out of it; he is struck by a brick, and that disperses the crowd.

Chapter 27 Sarrett arrives in a hotel room in New York with expensive new clothes, does his calisthenics, and begins work on a poem. Jerry returns home to his father, ashamed of but aware that he has wished that Bogan were his father and that his real father were dead. Bogan, apparently recovered from the scandal (having benefited from public sympathy for the tragedy of his daughter's death), smiles for photographers in his living room, beneath a portrait of Andrew Jackson.

If the clue by which *Night Rider* provides access to the latent content beneath its surface is a sentence that doesn't quite fit—whether that sentence be the one about the Theban handkerchiefs or the one in Tolliver's letter—then its equivalent in *At Heaven's Gate* may be a certain hint about hieroglyphics. It appears when Sue Murdock realizes that she cannot really interpret the scars Jerry Calhoun's former unsophisticated rural background had left on him—for example, the clumsy way he held an unsmoked lighted cigarette and then knocked over an ashtray trying to put it out: "For a long time she tried to interpret those marks, to understand what life and meaning, what patience and strength and fortitude, lay behind them, but she did not have a key for the hieroglyphics." Jerry doesn't either, "for he had forgotten their true meaning or had put it from his mind." These hieroglyphics connote more than indecipherable writing. They are also, true to the original sense of *glyph,* carved into a surface, for in Jerry's case they can be erased through abrasion: "Then, after a while, the marks themselves were worn away, smoothed out by the daily abrasions of the world she knew, the world ... of her father" (59). Calhoun, in other words, was destined to lose his country roughness and agrarian integrity as he acquired the urban polish he needed to succeed in the business world of Bogan Murdock, his employer and the man he in the end admits he would rather have had for a father. Slim Sarrett, though not privy to this aspect of Jerry's life, nevertheless echoes these sentiments: "The successful man ... offers only the smooth surface.... In so far as he is truly successful, he has no story" (196).

That roughness and indentation are indicative of a hidden story is something Jerry would have already known from his college training in geology. "All I know is a little geology," he admits to Duckfoot Blake, who would show him the ropes. "Then you better forget it," Blake replies. "You don't want to let anything tarnish that profound and fruitful ignorance which is the *sine qua non* of your chosen profession" (72). What he needs to do well in this job is a smooth surface, a tabula rasa. He doesn't even need to memorize the pitches the other salesmen commit to memory "and run out quick to say ... to somebody before they forget it. But do they know what it is? Hell no," Duckfoot exclaims, about to make another hieroglyphic reference. "You might as well make 'em memorize the Rosetta Stone."

Yet Jerry's hieroglyphics will still be there at the end of the novel, as he will realize when he returns, after the disgrace of Murdock's financial scandal, to sleep once more in his father's house. Murdock had foreclosed on the mortgage in order to turn the area into a kind of Appalachian theme park (though its tenants were still allowed to live in it, for a while), and as a result the house had been "restored"—rebuilt from the inside, painted and papered. What Jerry discovers is that "Under the paper there was the old wall, secret, aware, with eyes to see the old Jerry Calhoun under the new" (386). Similarly, in the opening pages, as Jerry gazes down at the landscape from an airplane, he draws upon his geological expertise to recall that a prehistoric sea, with its slime and sediment, had once covered the kind of indentations he had been trained to read, and that those fossil imprints had retained their communicative power despite the weight of the mass of water and sludge:

> That great valley, and these hills themselves, had lain—how many years ago—under the suffocating mass, and undifferentiating tread, of water. It had been a lightless slime, receiving ... the sediments and wastage of a life above.... It had its history. He had seen the shell in the limestone which had once been slime; the print of the frond, its delicacy unimpaired. He

had chipped these things out of stone, with his hammer. He . . . had sorted and classified them. (10)

Like Ianthe Sprague in *Night Rider,* whose "delicate discrimination" made her resemble an underwater creature at the bottom of the ocean who sustained herself by "absorbing the appropriate matter and ejecting all else," Jerry in his student days could likewise draw a certain intellectual nourishment from whatever he found on what had once been an ocean floor, rejecting irrelevant matter by chipping it away with his hammer, sorting and classifying what remained with something like Ianthe's punctilious discrimination.

As he sat in that airplane, Jerry had the fantasy that the prehistoric sea had returned, though without altering in the least the delicate marks: "Now he looked down upon the valley, and the last light, layered, striated, and rippling, was like the substance of a crystalline sea which had risen again, on the instant, to drown out that valley, but had done so with such subtlety that not a single item of its cunning and laborious perfections had been altered" (10). If is as if at the moment he is about to reenter Murdock's world Jerry intuited Sue's perception of the danger that the marks of his original character could be rubbed out by the abrasive power of that business milieu, and as if his diluvial fantasy were an attempt to ward off the risk. Indeed, his Aunt Ursula's hands, which had nurtured him ever since the death in childbirth of his mother, and which were thus part of that original world whose marks Sue sought to decipher, revealed beneath their fleshly surface something very much like the "*cunning* . . . perfections" that, in his daydream, that sea could not alter: "Her hands, with the beauty and *cunning* of their bony structure scarcely concealed by the . . . skin which sheathed it . . ." (364; emphasis added).

Now the first thing presented to *our* view in the very first words of *At Heaven's Gate* is seen through a layer of light that bears an interesting resemblance to the one that caught Jerry's eye in the plane. Like the "light, layered . . . like the substance of a crystalline sea" through which he saw the earth below, it too is somewhat aqueous: "It was the brilliant, high, windless sky of early autumn. The blue was paler than the blue of summer, but not leached out, still positive, and drenched in sunlight as though treated with a wash which was transparent but full of minute gold flecks" (3). A painter's term, a *wash* is a thin layer of watercolor applied to the surface of an otherwise completed picture. Like the crystalline sea Jerry imagined covering the landscape beneath him and which the "last light, layered, striated, and rippling," embodied, this wash is a trick of the light; and, like the wash a painter would apply as his final touch, it would not fundamentally alter what it covered. Neither did the fresh paint on his father's house nor the new paper on the walls, as he was to discover when he felt the gaze of the eyes beneath the wallpaper.

Of these three instances of intervening, covering, yet ultimately unaltering layers—the watercolorist's wash, the primeval ocean, and the new paper on the walls of Jerry's father's house—it is through the last that this novel most clearly speaks the allegory of its own construction. The house is strangely the same and yet not the same. His father, uncle, and aunt had had to move out during its restoration (had in fact been evicted, but Jerry got Murdock to allow them to return temporarily). When they returned, "the objects which [his father] had so long been accustomed to were, though set in the old locations, in contrast to the new, discreetly gleaming walls, the even floors, the tight glass" (365). As Jerry was to find, there was something strangely familiar about the place, something that played with one's sense of place. What I hope to show in this chapter is that *At Heaven's Gate,* like that house whose new surfaces belie an essentially unchanged inner architecture and arrangement of furniture, is to a remarkable degree the same house Warren built when he wrote *Night Rider.* There is a certain identity of structure dissimulated beneath a new paper covering, in a house haunted by the same ghostly eyes.

Both novels are principally concerned with the decline and fall of a corporate enterprise—the Tobacco Association and Murdock's financial empire—and with what happens to a young man who has been seduced by a fatherly figure to hitch his wagon to the star of that enterprise when it descends into illegality and collapses. Percy Munn is hunted down and slain by agents of the law; Jerry Calhoun is arrested and imprisoned for being in Murdock's employ, and though Duckfoot Blake arranges bail and Jerry's father comes to take him home, his legal situation is by no means resolved at the end of the novel. It was when Senator Tolliver allowed the newspapers to print his letter of resignation that things began to sour for the Tobacco Association, and it is when Private Porsum denounces the machinations of Murdock's company through a letter to the newspaper first shown to Murdock (as the members of the board of the Association were likewise given the opportunity to read Tolliver's letter before its newspaper appearance) that the situation becomes irretrievable. Even the unnamed black from Mr. May's place who was hanged for a murder he did not commit returns in the person of the black servant, Anse, the Murdock family servant who is arrested (and will in all likelihood die) for Slim Sarrett's murder of Sue Murdock.

But it is the haunting that makes the *papered*-over walls in Jerry's old room such an evocative image; for what appeared to Percy Munn in a dream—the *paper*-covered bundle that was both his son and his father(s)—returns in a haunting way here. It begins to make its presence felt through another dream of a son about a father, the one Sarrett recounts to Sue when he tells her the story of his life. His father, he says, was a barge captain who died in a boiler explosion.

> "When I was a child I used to have a nightmare about his being blown to pieces. How his head—just his head, with something hanging out of the neck like a hank of dirty white clothesline—would come drifting through the air toward me, in the dark, dripping wet and muddy and with weeds in his beard and smelling of river mud and whisky. . . . And his face would be straining and twitching, so that I knew it was trying to tell me something. It would come close to me and put the mouth to my ear, but I couldn't hear a thing. . . ." (156)

The resemblance here to Munn's dream is astonishing: the head that tries to tell him something ("the face . . . was alive and strove to speak"), "dripping" and "smelling" ("dripping . . . and with a stench like death"), with "a hank of dirty white clothesline" attached (the white newspaper "hanging in shreds . . . the last shreds of the sodden paper fell away from what was the face"). Consider as well the fact that while Munn's dream was a dream of the father bearing the disguise of Bunk Trevelyan, this dream bears the disguise of the father. The dream itself, however, is a disguise: Sarrett, it turns out, is lying. His father is still alive, was never a barge captain, and is presently a washing-machine salesman in Miami, Florida—as Mr. Billie Constantidopeles reveals when he unexpectedly shows up at Sarrett's party (255).

A certain telltale element of Sarrett's dream makes a strange reappearance toward the end of the novel when Jerry contemplates *his* father's head:

> He looked at his father's face above the white shirt, the buttonless collar with the wisp of thread, the twisted tie. Looking at that wisp of thread, he saw with a horrible precision his father leaning over the open drawer, fumbling for the white shirt, dropping it in his haste, fumbling with the buttons, tearing off the button, his big knotted swollen hands shaking and his breath coming hard. And that scene was there before his eyes clearer than reality, and it was the last indignity, the last assault upon him, the last betrayal. No—it was more—it—(380)

Jerry is in jail, and his father has come to take him home. The wisp of thread ("Looking at that wisp of thread, he saw with a horrible precision . . .") is a hieroglyph of character (just like the ones Sue tried to read on Jerry), the sign of something peculiar to his father, his innate clumsiness with his hands. "That was the image of his father which had dominated his childhood, not the image of his father performing his casual and unprideful feats of strength" (41), but his incompetence at small tasks. "The stiff fingers could not hold the buckle, the wrench ... the face would work with the agony of its intenseness," though his father's typical response to this impasse was not fury but gentle acquiescence. But "Jerry, when he was a little boy and was often with his father on the farm, could scarcely bear those moments ... and, especially as he grew older ... this confusion ... might suddenly coagulate into a cold core of hatred, and he would suppress the impulse to hurl the object to the ground and strike out at his father or run away. At those times he felt as he did the time his setter puppy fell into the old well ..." (41). The puppy could not accomplish the task of climbing into the bucket he had lowered to save it. Its "thin, mechanical, gargling, accurately timed yelps ... strangely resonant" in the deep well, got to the boy, who, "involuntarily ... dropped the rope and watched it spin down to the water, and sink. He grubbed an old brick from the sod, and with the icy assurance of hatred, or something like hatred, hard in him now, leaned far over. . . . The one brick did it."

The trail of white thread beneath Jerry's father's head, then, is the sign both of his father's most characteristic trait, his incompetent hands, and of his son's long-standing desire to kill him, while hands themselves, though competent, were the sign of the father in *Night Rider:* Tolliver's hand on Munn's shoulder, Professor Ball's white-bandaged ones, the way in which Captain Todd raised his for silence. But a trail of white thread is also what ties this vision of a father to the dream Sarrett tells: to the "hank" of white clothesline that hung from Slim's father's head, as well as to "the white trail" of talcum powder Sue Murdock's hasty packing left across the carpet when she decided to leave home (178).

It is more probable that Sarrett made up the dream than that he dreamed it, since he tells it to Sue in the context of the lie about his father having his head blown off in an explosion. Fictive or not, it is a dream in the text and calls out for interpretation. Its telltale hank of white clothesline is particularly illustrative of Freud's discovery that each of the elements of a dream has "been determined many times over in relation to the dream-thoughts" (318), although in this instance the dream-thoughts do not, as they did with Munn, belong just to the dreamer but—appropriately, as a dream invented by a poet who bears such a strong resemblance to the author of the novel[1]—to the text in which the dream appears. The resemblance between the hank of white clothesline and the wisp of thread is part of the latent content of *At Heaven's Gate* and not of Slim Sarrett's psyche; so, too, is the white trail emerging from Sue's suitcase. Although, if Sarrett already knew what Constantidopeles was later to reveal about his father's current line of work—that he sold *washing machines*—then, as a piece of *clothesline*, this trailing white fragment could function in his dream to reveal some of the latent content of Sarrett's own psyche; for it is the perfect disguise for his father's real identity, alluding to the truth that is otherwise masked. In fact, it is precisely because the "something hanging out of the neck like a hank of dirty white clothesline" appears in the dream as something extra, something unaccountable, that it really is most likely to be a nagging indication of the truth behind the fiction of the death of the father. The dream is more accurate than the lie in which it appears, for even as the father's severed head emerges there as if fresh from the explosion that Sarrett says killed him, it brings with it evidence of his real profession and consequently gives the lie to the tale of his demise.

Freud found that dreams are profoundly linguistic, often employing ambiguous words and even downright puns to accomplish their decipherable disguises. He cites Alexander's dream, recounted by Artemidorus, of a satyr dancing on his shield at the time he was besieging Tyre; the conqueror was thus encouraged to pursue the siege to successful completion, because *sa Tyros* means "Tyre is thine" (131–32n). Sarrett's dream is no exception to this, provided we view it with regard to the latent content of the novel and of the one that precedes it, for it is perhaps no accident that he calls the white object hanging from his father's head a *hank:* no accident, that is, in the context of a latent content in which *handkerchiefs*—*hankies*—play such a significant role. There is a direct trail (white, like the one Sue left on the carpet) leading from this dream to Percy Munn's, from this hank of white to the newspaper shreds that hung from *that* father, and from those pieces of newspaper to Theban—and other—handkerchiefs. Even the square of white cloth napkin in which Sissie Proudfit wrapped the rolls (as well as the bread they enclosed) she brought to Munn reappears here, when, in the same narrative in which he tells the dream, Sarrett recounts how his mother "was in the habit of bringing me cake or something of the sort from the restaurant, wrapped up in a paper napkin" (159).

A most curious gesture near the end of *At Heaven's Gate* recalls the parallel roles of wrapping and concealment that handkerchiefs and newspapers play in these two novels, though it suggests even more. When Sarrett murders Sue Murdock, he rifles through her bureau drawers to find the money she had saved. "To perform these operations, he covered his right hand with a handkerchief" (362). He found as well two rings and a bracelet, which he took with him when he left her apartment and wrapped up in a sheet of newspaper he found on the street, but then—almost inexplicably—"thrust the mass of paper down through the grating of a gutter sewer . . . he congratulated himself on the idea. Nobody would ever find those things there" (363). What nobody would ever find is actually a remarkable double literary allusion—on the novel's part if not Sarrett's—to two plays already more or less explicitly evoked in *At Heaven's Gate*. One is Shakespeare's *Cymbeline,* from which the title comes ("Hark, hark, the lark *at heaven's gate* sings . . ." [2.3.20]), and the other is Ibsen's *The Lady from the Sea*, the drama in which Sue Murdock is playing the leading role— in more ways than she may realize.

Ibsen's play is the story of a dream—a nightmare—that comes true. Ellida, whose role Sarrett sees Sue act in a college production, has a recurring dream in which she sees standing before her the sailor with whom she had been romantically involved years before: "[H]e is drowned at sea. But the strange thing is that he has come home nevertheless. It's in the nighttime; and he stands there by her bedside and looks at her. He must be dripping wet, just as when they haul you up out of the sea" (251). We owe this vivid account not to Ellida but to Lyngstrand, a sculptor who is describing *to* her—without realizing that he is in fact talking *about* her—a sculpture for which he would like her to pose. He happened to have been on the ship with the man Ellida had once loved when that man, Albert Johnston, received the news that she had married someone else. Lyngstrand heard Johnston vow that, marriage nor not, Ellida was still his, and that she would have to follow him, "though I should have to go home and fetch her, as a drowned man from the bottom of the sea" (253). When she heard that, Ellida must have felt she was dreaming right then, for that scene was exactly the dream *she* had been having.

Sarrett watched Sue act out this scene in rehearsal, and he did so before he told her the story of his possibly fictive dream, so that *The Lady from the Sea* occupies a place in relation to his dream strangely analogous to the place the ballad of Pretty Polly occupies in relation to Percy Munn's—strangely so, because of the similarity of the stories they tell: in one, an abandoned woman comes back to haunt her lover at the bottom of the ocean; in the other, an abandoned lover comes back "from the bottom of the sea" to haunt the woman who left him. And, to hear Sarrett tell it, his father came back to him in quite similar fashion, "dripping wet . . . with weeds in his beard and smelling of river mud." Sarrett's words recall Lyngstrand's: "dripping wet, just as when they haul you up out of the sea." The words "dripping wet" appear in each of two translations widely available at the time Warren wrote the novel: the Archer translation (1912), cited here, and the Everyman Library edition (1910).

Now if Sarrett, litterateur that he was, was projecting his interest in Sue Murdock onto Ibsen's play, he must have been rather pleased to hear her tell him that the way she gathered sufficient courage to leave her fiancé Jerry Calhoun was by pretending she was in a play: "It was like when you rehearse something over and over in a play . . . in the end you didn't feel a thing, you just did something, and if you did it right you felt beautiful and empty, like a dream. It was like that" (151–52).

And this might help to explain Sarrett's strange gesture with the rings and bracelet. For in throwing them into the sewer, when they would be carried to the river (it was a city on a river—if Nashville, then the Cumberland; if Memphis, the Mississippi) and then to the ocean, he was enacting a parody of the ritual by which Albert Johnson had "married" Ellida years before she left him to marry someone else. It was a "marriage" that had the force of a lasting bond for him, despite its informality and the fact that it had not, then or later, meant the same thing to her: "He took a key-ring out of his pocket, and drew off his finger a ring he used to wear. Then he took from me a little ring that I had, and these two he slipped together on the key-ring.... And then he flung the large ring and the two small ones as far as ever he could into the deep water" (285–86). But the most extraordinary thing about Sarrett's gesture is that it accomplishes something else as well. In wrapping up those two rings and a bracelet in newspaper and thrusting the packing into the sewer, Sarrett, far from burying the evidence, has wrapped up allusions not only to Ibsen's *Lady* but to Shakespeare's *Cymbeline* too—a play that, like his fictive dream, features a severed floating head. And a stolen bracelet.

In *Cymbeline,* that stolen bracelet is the most tangible evidence Jachimo can use to persuade Posthumus Leonatus of his wife's unfaithfulness, which he is trying to do for a bet. Claiming that Imogen had given it freely, and providing descriptive evidence gathered from a night spent hidden in her room, Jachimo is able to trick Posthumus into believing he has lost the wager. Posthumus, the deceived husband, bears more than a little resemblance to Jerry Calhoun. Both were orphaned from their mothers at birth. While Posthumus was raised in a royal household as a kind of adopted son, Jerry was taken in by Bogan Murdock who, as head of the Massey Mountain empire, occupied a role in the region that could be described as monarchical. Murdock paid Jerry's college fraternity bills, offered him a job in the firm, and received him as a frequent visitor to the house. Here Posthumus's and Jerry's careers diverge, for while Murdock approved of the idea of Calhoun marrying his daughter, Cymbeline was forced by his wife to banish Posthumus from the kingdom.

But it is the fate of Posthumus's rival, Cloten, that resurfaces most intriguingly in *At Heaven's Gate:* "*Guiderius:* With his own sword, / ... I have ta'en / His head from him. I'll throw't into the creek / Behind our rock, rock, and let it to the sea, / And tell the fishes he's the Queen's son, Cloten" (4.2.149–53). Sarrett's nightmare of a head drifting through the air dripping from a watery catastrophe now appears to have, as does his thrusting the newspaper-wrapped bracelet and rings into the sewer, a double literary origin: the returning shipwrecked, wet ghost in Ibsen, the trunkless head in Shakespeare. His use of a gutter to dispose of something that had belonged to the person he just killed repeats the act of Guiderius, who tossed Cloten's head into the stream that probably passed for a sewer behind the cave where he, his brother, and adopted father lived.

That Sarrett should choose to wrap the rings and bracelet in newspaper may not be random either, in the larger scheme of things. He was, in a way, burying *Sue* in that sewer, disposing of those personal effects as carefully (if not as delicately) as if they had been her body. "Nobody would ever find those things there. Those things had belonged to Sue Murdock, and now nobody would ever find them" (363). At this juncture we might reasonably feel that we are in a strangely familiar place, as if we had turned a corner in *Heaven's* house and found ourselves back in *Night Rider,* where a dreamer could accomplish in his dreamwork the murder of his enemies and give them all a newspaper shroud. For not only is the newspaper wrapping in Percy's dream present once more, but the fetus, too: Sue had, until shortly before Sarrett strangled her, been pregnant.

The father of the fetus, Jason Sweetwater,

> seemed to see, as it would be there under his hand, the little hunched-up creature, blind, unbreathing, the tiny hands and feet like delicate carving.... He remembered fetuses in jars, the wizened, little, simian-wise faces, intent, and for all their wisdom, contorted in profound puzzlement. He remembered the Indian mummies he had once seen at Salt Lake City, how they were hunched, and the eyelids squinting because there was nothing under them any more, and the intent contorted faces. Those faces were like the faces of the fetuses, the same look, intent, contorted, the same invincible, painful abstraction. Before and after taking. (317)

Like the fetus in Munn's dream, the one inside Sue Murdock stands as much or more for death as for life. Even as Sweetwater places his hand on her stomach and imagines it beneath his touch, it is about to be placed under a death sentence, since he has already told Sue he will not marry her and a few pages later she announces that she will have an abortion (320). (Her death at Sarrett's hands takes place the day she returns from the abortionist.) It is touched by death, too, because the emblematic significance it has for Jason lies in its uncanny likeness to a mummy—with its oscillation between a look of wisdom and puzzlement, an intent expression suggesting both knowledge and ignorance but really due to neither. The eyes have such falsely expressive power because, in the case of the mummies, there is nothing under them any more (and, in the case of the fetuses, because there is nothing under them yet).

Fetuses and eyes appear in one of a series of poems, *Eleven Poems on the Same Theme,* published by Warren a year before *At Heaven's Gate.*[2] There they are said to resemble each other because both are hieratic, which is to say that they are both sacred (*hieros*) and hieroglyphic ("hieratic" in this sense is a term coined by the decipherer Champollion to describe a cursive form of hieroglyphic). In that collection of poems, what is hieratic is also clothed in white, and what is white-robed is also a sacrificial father:

> Of eyes hieratic like foetuses in jars . . .
> ("Crime")

> They sought a secret which, perhaps, the Moor,
> Hieratic, white-robed, pitiless, might teach . . .
> ("Terror")

> The first barbarian victor stood to gape
> At the sacrificial fathers, white robed, still . . .
> ("Pursuit")

In these poems, as Warren was to explain them later (in his Author's Note to Friar and Brinnin, 542–43), the white-robed Roman fathers and similarly clad Moor represent an ancient knowledge complete in itself but unable to speak to the needs of modernity, an unteachable secret (the "might" in those lines from "Terror" representing wishful thinking on the part of those who sought such knowledge) like, it would appear, the innaccessible, wizened wisdom Sweetwater saw in the fetuses under glass.

The construction of "Terror" centers around a juxtaposition that justifies the likening of Moorish with fetal knowledge and goes some distance toward explaining why both are characterized in the poetic sequence as "hieratic." The poem begins with a headline from an Italian newspaper announcing that American volunteers serving in foreign armies would not lose their citizenship, and, as Warren later commented, the "idea for the poem came" when he saw in the same newspaper (or another newspaper the same day) both that story, which referred to Americans fighting Russians in Finland, and "a report of the 'death' of the chicken heart which Alexis Carrel had kept alive for a long time in his laboratory and which had for popular-science writers the promise of a mortal immortality." In both the poem and his explanatory note Warren takes those volunteers to task for being so caught up in "passionate emptiness and tidal / Lusts" that their heroism had no meaning. Allied with the Soviets in Spain, they fought against them in Finland: "They fight old friends, for their obsession knows / Only the immaculate itch, not human friends or foes." These are the ones who sought a secret the Moor (glimpsed in Spain) might teach.

Carrel comes in on the heels of Onan:

> You know, by radio, how hotly the world repeats,
> When the brute crowd roars or the blunt boot-heels resound
> In the Piazza or the Wilhelmplatz,
> The crime of Onan, spilled upon the ground;
> You know, whose dear hope Alexis Carrel kept

Alive in a test tube, where it monstrously grew, and slept.
("Terror")

What was so monstrous about Carrel's project that the poet should, through such a juxtaposition, make him guilty by association with a form of self-abuse? Warren cites a popular-science writer's opinion that when disease and death are abolished the problem of evil will be solved; and Warren objects, particularly to the notion "that good and physical survival are identical." It's not natural, he says, to prolong the life of something that's already dead—hence his quotation marks around "death" when he speaks of the newspaper account—or to isolate something from its original context and to try to give it an artificial life-support system. This is of a piece with his condemnation of the American volunteers and his assertion that the Moorish view of things, adequate as it may have been for the Moors, is of no help to anyone today. "The Moor may have a secret ... which is enough for him—but not enough for us. (That is what the modern devotee of violence [the volunteer in Finland and Spain] is seeking. But it can't help him.)" The problem with the volunteers is that they, like Carrel, have isolated something from its original context and have tried to use it without reference to their present situation: "the devotion to isolated ideas or ideals (isolated because not related to some over-all conception of the human situation) [does] not suffice."

Thus Carrel's work was an experiment in onanism not only because it resembled Frankenstein's attempt to create life without its passing through the womb but also because, by tearing living tissue from its native site and trying to make it live, he was acting like those who pursue some abstract ideal without reference to the whole context of the human condition. And thus, too, the Moors, like fetuses, are hieratic: in the priestly sense, like the Roman sacrificial fathers, who embodied an ancient world view that lost its meaning with the barbarians' invasion; in the hieroglyphic sense, in that they are the living characters of a text no longer entirely readable.

It is strange, however, that Warren should condemn Carrel's procedure of removing tissue from its native environment to give it new life in one of his own making, for this is just what Warren has done in writing the poem. Like Ianthe Sprague, evidently, he is not immune to the pleasures of meditating on the various unrelated stories that happen to appear the same day in a newspaper. And, like her, he is quite able to find nourishment from what those random current events bring. Of course, there is a connection between the two news stories, as Warren takes the trouble to point out; they are both signs of the sickness of the age, the wrongful pursuit of isolated ideas. Yet there is a certain aptness here that adds to the pleasure the poem can give, even if it detracts from the force of its apparent message—and manifest content. And even if Warren should tell us that in generating a poem by juxtaposing (*his* term: "I don't mind making some remarks about the background ideas suggested by the two *juxtaposed* news reports . . .") these two newspaper items he was making explicit their implicit connection, that he was simply reconstructing their real underlying philosophical and political context, Carrel could have said the same in his own defense. After all, the object of his research was to discover what the actual life-supporting environment for such tissue was, to get at the truth of its cellular structure, and to do that he had to reconstruct that environment in the laboratory.

Warren's reconstructed context for these juxtaposed news items, the poem "Terror," itself appears in a sequence whose title (*Eleven Poems on the Same Theme*) asserts that it constitutes a context of its own, that the reader can expect to find implicit connections between "Terror" and the other poems in the sequence. If we were to read these poems as Warren read *Il Messaggero* of 27 January 1940, selecting those pieces that seemed when juxtaposed to bespeak some fundamental unity, we might well have come up with the string of quotations from "Crime," "Terror," and "Pursuit" in which hieratic fetuses lead to hieratic and white-clad Moors and sacrificial fathers. However, those echoes within the context of the *Eleven Poems* suggest that an even larger context supports their life in the Warren literary corpus—a context including the white (whether by handkerchiefs or strips of newspaper) sacrificial (in the other sense) fathers in *Night Rider* and the fetuses, both there and in *At Heaven's Gate*.

It is a combination that keeps reappearing. Bearing in mind that Sweetwater imagined the fetus inside Sue with features "formed like delicate carving" and looking like a mummy with intent eyes, consider the sight of Bogan Murdock lying under his sun lamp. And recall, too, that Bogan is the father Jerry Calhoun realizes at the end of the novel he wishes had been his:

> See, there is my father . . . looking unusually well and handsome and carrying his stick and smiling hospitably and look at me with his fine eyes. . . . That isn't your father, that's Bogan Murdock! . . . Where is your father? You better run, and you better run quick and find him. Before they say you killed him. Before the police come and dig in the leaves in the woods and drag the river and look in the old well where you hit the drowning puppy with the brick and pry under the hay in the loft. (388)

(The father to be looked for under the leaves here may be what the "mad killer" in the contemporaneous "Crime" has slain: "Envy the mad killer who lies in the ditch and grieves, / . . . He tries to remember, and tries, but he cannot seem / To remember what it was he buried *under the leaves.*" Pursued by his forgetfulness, he passes "among . . . rows / Of eyes hieratic like foetuses in jars . . ."). Bogan Murdock's body under the sun lamp had "an Egyptian delicacy of bone . . . like a carved figure on a tomb, or like a dead body laid out ceremonially . . . (182–83). As an Egyptian corpse, Murdock would have been, one presumes, a mummy. The observation Sweetwater made about the emptiness of mummies' eyes is one that will reappear in Warren; quite recently, in the *father's* eyes in "I Am Dreaming of a White Christmas . . .": "The eyes / Are not there. But, / Not there, they stare at what / Is not there."

The newspaper part of the combination of images that keeps reappearing is what brings about the denouement of *At Heaven's Gate* to which I alluded earlier when I pointed out the similarity between Tolliver's letter to the papers in *Night Rider* and Private Porsum's similar action here. Porsum's motivation leads us, interestingly enough, to a newspaper that plays a similarly pivotal role in the plot of Ibsen's *Lady from the Sea*. The denouement is not just the unraveling of Murdock's scheme to bilk the state but also the knitting together of the two narratives which, until chapter 22, had been vying in alternate chapters for the reader's attention, and which until Porsum's intervention seemed to have had hardly anything to do with each other.

The other narrative is the "Statement of Ashby Wyndham," a poor hill farmer who marries, has a falling-out with his brother over selling the family farm, gets religion, and wanders the earth to spread his version of the gospel. He makes his way down-river to the city where the rest of the novel takes place, is arrested when a member of his traveling church shoots a policeman, and is told in jail to write down his life story. In chapter 23 we pick up the thread of his narrative once again and at its conclusion discover that we have probably been reading it the whole time over Porsum's shoulder; he has been given the manuscript by a Mr. Tucker, a reporter for the local newspaper. Wyndham claims to be second cousin to the Private, whose roots are likewise in the mountains, and so Tucker puts Porsum on the spot and asks him what he is going to do about the jailing of one of his relatives. What the reporter is up to also has something to do with the controversy surrounding Murdock's scheme to unload his mountain properties on the state as a park bearing his father's name. Porsum, already a public figure because of his legendary heroism in the war, is president of one of Murdock's banks. In response to Tucker's question, he makes an equivocating, noncommittal statement, then asks to see what the reporter has written down on his note pad.

> His gaze met the brown uncommitting pupils of the muddy, flecked eyes which were now lifted to him.

>"Let me see that," Private Porsum commanded, and reached out his hand for the pad.
>
>The reporter passed it to him.
>
>He read it slowly.... Then, very deliberately, he tore the pages from the pad, dropped the pad, and tore the detached pages of notes into several bits.
>
>"For Christ sake," Mr. Tucker said.
>
>Private Porsum stood up. The bits of the paper scattered to the floor.... Then he said, "I'm going to the jail." (331)

When he does, he finds it nearly impossible to hold a conversation with Wyndham, who remains a willing victim wholly in the grip of his private religion. Yet his stubbornness does provoke Porsum to try to justify his own life in front of the man, particularly his role as Murdock's spokesman when he had gone to Massey Mountain to tell the strikers, including Wyndham, that the company really could not afford to pay them any more. Unable to persuade Wyndham to cooperate in his release from jail, Porsum returns home, relives the incident in the war that had brought him such honor and fame (and which he had cashed in when he went to work for Murdock, especially when he put his prestige on the line in the speech to the strikers), and then decides to make his damning statement about the company to the newspaper.

Duckfoot Blake had already told Porsum what was wrong with the bonds and how Murdock had unloaded the Massey Mountain property onto the state. But it took the encounter with Wyndham for the Private to come to terms with his own sense of what was right. Yet, on another level, it may take more than that for the novel to come to an end: certain other events must be recalled; certain other terms be met. In the stages of the process by which he comes to his recognition of what he has to do, Porsum touches base with certain symbols we have now come to recognize: a torn-up newspaper, a handkerchief, and a rectangle of whiteness.

The first occurred when Porsum tore the pages of the reporter's pad to bits. That note pad is not yet a newspaper story but is on its way to becoming one; as will later become evident, that the disintegration of a newspaper should here take the form of ripping apart a reporter's *pad*—a sort of newspaper ur-text—will make it possible for that pad to be part of yet another symbolic underpinning of the novel. The disintegration of newspaper—the sodden bits of the shroud in Percy's dream that fell away of their own weight—marked the beginning of a process of discovery for Munn; another kind of newspaper disintegration, more akin to what happened to the reporter's pad, took place in the scene in Ibsen's play in which Albert Johnston learns that his beloved Ellida has married someone else. His native tongue is English, and he had picked up an old, discarded newspaper in Norwegian in order to improve his command of that language. Lyngstrand recalls what happened: "When all of a sudden, I heard him give a kind of roar; and when I looked at him I saw that his face was as white as chalk. Then he set to work to crumple and crush the paper up, and tear it into a thousand little pieces; but that he did quietly . . ." (253).

When Porsum returns home after his meeting with Wyndham and settles into his easy chair to think back to the incident in the war, the remembered scene unfolds before his eyes and ours with absolute clarity. But we may not see the same things. What Porsum saw—his decision to assault the German machine-gun nest almost single-handedly, the dreamlike trance in which he shot twenty-two of the enemy, his weeping afterward, and his wish years later that he had not survived—together with his response to Wyndham's mad integrity, impelled him to act, to resign publicly from Murdock's empire, to denounce it to the newspapers, and to tell Murdock to his face what he had done. What *we* might see, however, in that scene from the war compels us to recognize once more the power of certain images to persist in Warren's texts. For Porsum did not quite accomplish his heroic deed alone; he was assisted by a man named *Percy* whom he instructed in the proper use of a *handkerchief*: "I told Percy to get behind the other tree across from me and put something on the ground, a handkerchief or something, to lay his clips on. I wanted him to have them where he could get at them fast and handy and I didn't want him laying them on the ground to get anything on them to foul if he got excited and fast. He did what I said" (338). As when he tore the note pad to bits, Porsum after his wartime recollection stands up once again, his mind made up to act: "He rose from his chair and stood there in the middle of the room, with his arms hanging limp at his sides. He switched off the reading lamp. . . . Now the moonlight made a rectangle of whiteness on the floor under the big window at the south end of the room. He walked to the window" (340). The whiteness beckons him, and he steps into that white rectangle that resembles both a sheet of paper and, in the immediate context of his recollection, a handkerchief, that may stand for both, as well as for the text he is about to enter—the text, that is, constituted by the union of the narratives separated until now, Ashby Wyndham's and the story of Calhoun, Sarrett, Sweetwater, and Sue; the text he is about to put together by confronting Murdock's crime with Wyndham's guilt; the text that is the novel itself.

Porsum, however, did not accomplish this combination entirely on his own. He had the help of Mr. Tucker, the reporter who put the text of Wyndham's story in his hands, thus serving as the catalyst to start the process that brought everything together, tucked in the loose ends of the novel, and made it possible for the alternating, though unequal, portions of the text to find their common ground at last. It is perhaps not unimportant that this man, who saw what possibilities lay in confronting Wyndham's world with Murdock's, should see the world through eyes that resemble the wash that colors the sky in the first lines of the novel and seem to have the right to color our reading of all that follows those lines:

> a wash which was transparent but full of minute gold *flecks* . . .
>
> His gaze met the brown uncommitting pupils of the muddy, *flecked* eyes which were now lifted to him.

Yet the reporter is not the only one with such eyes. One other character does; and the role he plays in both the story and the structure of the novel casts him as a distant double of Tucker, thereby confirming the importance of seeing that world through such eyes. Anse, the black servant Murdock was going to send to Columbia University, the young man who is made the scapegoat for Sarrett's crime (the absurdly proclaimed motive being his disappointment in not getting to go to Columbia) has "yellow *flecks* in the pupils of his large eyes" (180). Only he and Tucker share this peculiarity with the wash that covers the sky at the beginning of the novel. One might well wonder why.

The answer lies in yet another episode where a handkerchief and a newspaper are made rough equivalents, and where a confrontation is engineered from a distance (as Tucker engineered the confrontation between the Porsum and Wyndham—and, perhaps unintentionally, between Porsum and Murdock). Jerry Calhoun was in Murdock's office, and Bogan was trying to reassure him on the matter of the bonds, when a secretary tiptoed in to lay the afternoon paper on Murdock's desk. "She had dropped the paper, like an innocent catalytic . . ." (269). When Murdock saw the headline, he was furious: *"Murdock" Bill Passed.* Bogan had wanted to unload his unprofitable timberlands onto the state with the provision that it become a park named after his father, Major Lemuel Murdock. The newspaper seized upon the opportunity to dredge up an old scandal:

> Who is Major Lemuel Murdock?
> He is the man who, on April 4, 1892, in this city, shot and killed, willfully and of malice aforethought, Judge Goodpasture, a political opponent, who in the heat of a campaign uttered certain remarks which offended the vanity of Major Lemuel Murdock. Major Lemuel Murdock was tried and convicted in the courts of Mulcaster County. Upon appeal, the conviction was reversed. (270)

The Standard, Bogan was convinced, was trying to strike at him through his father, now senile and given to reenacting in his mind the day he shot Goodpasture at the train station. The scene shifts to the Murdock stables, where the old Major is telling the story once again to several of the black children on the estate. They already know what happened and are more amused by the telling than the tale. They want to make him cry. They act out the drama of that day, forcing him to rehearse the sequence of events over and over again. Old Anse, father of the younger Anse who answered Bogan's urgent telephone call, arrives at the climax of the drama, swoops down on the children, and sends them scattering. He leans down to comfort the Major, whose face is wet and quivering. "Old Anse fumbled with his free hand in the breast pocket of the black broadcloth coat and got the big, snowy linen handkerchief, initialed, and wiped the cheeks, and patted the eyes gently, like a child's, and held the handkerchief to the nose, muttering all the while" (274). The Major is still reliving the assassination, giving fragmentary and incoherent justifications for what he did, looking up into Old Anse's face as if for absolution. Old Anse wipes his eyes once more and casts about for another source of comfort, having done all he could with the handkerchief; thus, at a crucial moment in the story, a newspaper is substituted for a handkerchief, both offered as objects to assuage the grief of Lemuel Murdock: "You jes hush now. You hush, and it's about time yore paper git here. You got git yore paper and fergit all it. Maybe it in the box by now" (275). The paper is there. The Major reads the lead story, and it has its effect. He makes a strange sound in his throat, trembles, looks wide-eyed over the landscape, and goes up to the house. He finds a gun, and begins walking to town. Hours later, having hitched a ride on a mule-drawn wagon, he is found at the train station, gun in hand, wondering aloud why the band is not playing.

Evidently the younger Anse had not followed Bogan's order: he had not intercepted the newspaper. His nonintervention was surely intentional, and Bogan Murdock surely knew it: his revenge is allowing Anse to be imprisoned (and probably executed) for a murder he knew he could not have committed. Anse had his reasons, perhaps: Bogan had indeed promised to send him to Columbia University and had reneged on that promise. Several chapters earlier Anse is described as having been "puzzled by things he read in the newspapers, and ... books, which told what people had said and done a long time back and which told how the world used to be. He was puzzled by the way the world was now. He was puzzled by himself, and he did not know what he wanted in the world. But he knew the world was to live in. He knew that" (181). James Justus, in his book on Warren, complains that this passage is a "wasted closeup," as Anse "matters only in the final few pages because he is falsely accused of Sue Murdock's murder" (180). But perhaps, given the role he plays in the public humiliation of Bogan Murdock's father, this account of the inner workings of his mind is not, after all, without some relevance.

In any event, like the similar-eyed Mr. Tucker, Anse acts (or acts by not acting) to make sure that the newspaper plays its role, both in the plot of this novel and in the symbolic network it shares with its predecessor. These two know more about what is about to happen than do the other characters; that knowledge, and the way they intervene in the plot, suggest that they act in such a way as to reveal the hand of the author, who has perhaps let slip a clue by giving them eyes that resemble the transparent layer of light that colors our first look at the novel—that last touch of a colorist that serves at once to complete the picture and to put a layer of esthetic distance between the viewer and the world he might otherwise have thought was real.

That wash may be the first of several keys to *Heaven's Gate*. It alerts us to the significance of covering yet unaltering layers, beneath which we find ancient prints, hieroglyphics, and the inner structure of an older house. And what happens in the final pages of the novel holds out some hope that where there is a *Gate* there may in fact be a key.[3] For there, with the plot practically complete, if not resolved, we are presented with a sudden abundance of keys: the one the police discover Sweetwater had to Sue's apartment but which in the end does not implicate him ("they done let that white feller go what had the key" [365]); the jailer's key that alerts Jerry Calhoun to his father's presence ("he did not look up until he heard the chink of metal as the key was applied to the lock. There, beside the man with the key, was his father" [379]); the keys his father struggled with at the door to his house ("Old Mr. Calhoun fumbled with his keys ... finally opened the door" [383]); and the key pad from which Jerry detached his car keys so that Duckfoot Blake could return his car the next day: "Jerry took the key pad from his pocket and detached his car keys and held them in his hand.... Duckfoot ... reached over and lifted the keys from Jerry's hand as though he were taking them off a shelf" (383).

That last gesture repeats the one by which Murdock received the letter from Porsum that had already been delivered to the newspaper: "Bogan Murdock took one step toward him and grasped the paper, as if he were picking it up from a shelf" (342). What is paralleled here? What is the connection and what the analogy between the keys that came from Jerry's key pad and the signed confession that was provoked by a chain of events that began with Tucker's intervention? The answer, like the question, may lie in the precise use of words: Porsum's first awakening of conscience, his realization that he cannot evade his responsibility to visit the imprisoned Ashby Wyndham, seems to have come at the moment he tears the reporter's pad to bits. That small violence, which echoes so many other fragmentations of newsprint in these first two novels, is ambiguous enough to give rise to misinterpretation at first—is he not, Tucker surely thought, trying to destroy the evidence of his guilt? It becomes clear when Porsum stands up that it means something else. And in the context of subsequent events and the complex network of allusion that pervades the novel, it appears that it may mean even more.

Or rather, Porsum's destruction of the pad is part of an underlying symbolic and allusive framework that gives a different coloration to such pivotal moments in the unfolding of the plot. From the perspective of the eventual outcome of that awakening of conscience—Murdock's reception of the original news story that was to bring down his financial kingdom— and how that acceptance is reevoked by the way Duckfoot Blake picks up the keys Jerry holds out to him, there appears to be some distant connection between the reporter's pad and Jerry's. That connection is in fact based on an allusive analogy to the scene in the play Sue rehearsed, already reenacted by Sarrett's throwing the newspaper-wrapped rings into the sewer, in which the American sailor cast rings into the sea as a matrimonial rite. It will be recalled that they were linked by a key ring. The keys Jerry gives Duckfoot are linked by a key *pad,* and now we can see that by that act Jerry completes the allusion Sarrett had begun. The trail of internal allusion that links the key pad—through Bogan's reception of Porsum's statement—to the reporter's note pad sets up an equivalence between a newspaper and a device for linking keys, pad or ring. Thus, by uniting those rings for their descent into oblivion by wrapping them in a sheet of newspaper, Sarrett was linking them by what in Warren's text serves the same purpose as Albert Johnston's key ring; for, through a chain of substitutable links more akin to what one might expect to see in a poem than a novel, a key pad is a note pad is a newspaper.

One more key scene, and one more key pad, appear in the final pages of *At Heaven's Gate*. Sarrett, having successfully escaped detection for Sue's murder, and having wrapped her rings and bracelet in newspaper and thrown them away, is seen settling into a comfortable hotel room in New York. He too has a leather pad of keys, which he hands over to the bellboy so he may open his suitcase. That task completed, the boy moves to the window to make some final adjustments, "toying with the sash to bring it to the precise point . . . like an artist who, stepping back from the easel on the last day, picks up another brush and in a spirit of grateful reverence applies to the canvas the last, minute, fulfilling point of color, too precious for discernment by the vulgar eye" (376). Minutes later, after the bellboy's departure, Sarrett's body, glistening from the perspiration of performing his calisthenics, acquires a touch of the same hue that flecked the sky on the first page of the novel, "tinting the flesh from white to the merest suggestion of gold" (377). Could it be that momentary possession of Sarrett's keys gave the boy the power to apply that last fulfilling point of color?

Chapter 3
Willie's Wink *All the King's Men,* 1946

Chapter 1   The story begins in 1939 with a flashback to 1936, when Governor Willie Stark, Sadie Burke, Tiny Duffy, and Jack Burden (the narrator) drove to Mason City so Willie could visit his father, followed by a further flashback to 1922, when Jack first met Willie at Slade's pool hall in the capital. Twelve years after that first meeting Jack asked Willie if he had really winked at him or not, and he refuses to say. At his father's house, Willie gets word that Judge Irwin, a friend of Jack and his mother, has come out on the side of the wrong senatorial candidate. Stark, with Burden in tow, drives that night to Burden's Landing to scare the Judge out of his decision, without success. On the way back, Stark tells Jack to dig up some dirt on Irwin.

Chapter 2   This tells how, back in 1922, then Mason County Treasurer Stark was vindicated when the bricks in the new local school turned out to be rotten and some children were killed: Willie had objected to the way the bids were let. Because of Willie's newly acquired popularity with the rural population, in 1926 gubernatorial candidate Joe Harrison had the idea of getting him to run in order to split the vote of his opponent, MacMurfee. Tiny Duffy approached Stark. Unaware that he is just a patsy, Willie runs in earnest but is a terrible orator—too many facts and figures. When he discovers the truth, he throws away his prepared remarks at the Upton barbecue, makes a sensational denunciation, in down-home terms, of the Harrison outfit, and in the process sends Duffy pin-wheeling off the platform. He withdraws in favor of MacMurfee, who wins. Stark runs for governor in 1930. Jack Burden quits his newspaper job because he can't bring himself to support Stark's opponent, but when he's elected, Willie hires him on. In this chapter we are introduced to Jack's friend Dr. Adam Stanton, to Adam's sister, Anne, with whom Jack was once in love, and to Jack's father, Ellis Burden, who left his family to do missionary work in the slums. Some say it was because he couldn't satisfy Jack's mother.

Chapter 3   In the spring of 1933, Jack visits his mother, who has had several husbands since Ellis Burden left. At a social gathering in Burden's Landing, Jack defends Stark's politics of taxing the rich to provide social services for the poor. When he arrives back in the capital, "hell has popped": state auditor Byram White has been caught with his hands in the till and is about to be impeached. Willie saves White's hide in order to prevent his enemies from scoring a victory. But then they try to impeach Willie, who fights them off by rousing the populace to his defense and by blackmailing a sufficient number of legislators.

Chapter 4   Recalling Willie's words when he told Jack to dig up something on Judge Irwin—that there is always something to find in everyone's past—Burden tells the story of how when he was a graduate student in history he had researched the life of Cass Mastern (a maternal uncle of Ellis Burden), who in the 1850s had an affair with Annabelle Trice, the wife of a friend. The friend committed suicide, as the slave Phebe discovered when she found—and gave to her mistress—the wedding ring Duncan Trice had removed before what had, until then, seemed a gun accident. Annabelle sells Phebe downriver because she knows the truth; Cass tries but fails to find her. Mastern frees his own slaves but joins the Confederate army in hopes of dying, and does. Burden tried to leave Mastern's journal and letters and his own manuscript behind him, but his landlady forwarded it, and thereafter the brown-paper package keeps following him.

Chapter 5   As Willie commanded, Jack digs up the dirt on Judge Irwin. He decides to find out if there ever was a time when the Judge was in dire need of money. He asks his father, in his slum mission, and from Ellis Burden's inarticulate but impassioned response concludes that there must be something to find out. He eventually learns that when Irwin had been state attorney general twenty years before, he had taken a bribe from a power company and in the process had driven Mortimer Littlepaugh, whom he replaced at the company, to take his own life.

Chapter 6   Stark wants Adam Stanton to be the director of the yet-to-be-built Willie Stark Hospital, and gets Jack to persuade him to do it. Given that Willie knows one must use evil to work for good, Jack finds it strange that he is adamantly set against Tiny Duffy's desire to let contractor and MacMurfee friend Gummy Larson build the hospital. Jack learns that Anne has been having an affair with Stark.

Chapter 7   In the wake of that revelation, Jack gets in the car and drives west to California, reliving his memories of Anne: how he almost made love to her late one summer when he was twenty-one and she nineteen but held back for some reason; how they drifted apart when he returned to college. He recalls his marriage to Lois, whose body he loved but nothing else. Burden takes comfort in "the Great Twitch": "the dream that all life is but the dark heave of the blood and the twitch of the nerve," and begins to drive back home.

Chapter 8 On the return trip, Jack picks up an old hitchhiker with an unconscious twitch on his "mummy's jaw" that bears out his discovery about the Great Twitch. A Hubert Coffee tries to bribe Adam into giving Larson the hospital contract; indignant, Adam wants to quit the directorship, but Jack persuades him to stay on. A Sybil Frey, whom Willie's son Tom had been seeing, has become pregnant, and even though there are other candidates for paternity, MacMurfee is using it against Stark so that he can run for the Senate. Stark tells Jack to force Judge Irwin to lean on MacMurfee. Jack confronts him with the Littlepaugh documents. Irwin kills himself, and Jack then learns from his mother that the judge was his father.

Chapter 9 With Irwin dead, Stark must give Larson the hospital contract in order to stop MacMurfee. Tom Stark is crippled in a football accident. Wanting now to name the hospital for his son instead of himself, Willie, not wanting to allow any "evil" to enter into its construction, reneges on his promise to Larson (and Duffy). Adam, whom someone had telephoned to tell about Anne and Stark, shoots Willie, who dies a few days later.

Chapter 10 Jack interrogates Sadie Burke and finds out that she told Tiny Duffy about Willie and Anne, and told him to tell Adam—knowing what Adam would do. Jack does not blame Sadie, since she acted out of jealous passion, but he does blame Duffy, who brought about Stark's death in cold blood. Duffy offers Jack a job in his administration, but he angrily refuses and tells him he knows of Tiny's role in Stark's death. But in the end Burden does not act on this knowledge, even though he later could have brought about Duffy's death by telling it to Willie's devoted chauffeur, Sugar-Boy. After Tom dies of complications, Jack visits Lucy Stark, who has adopted Sybil's baby, convinced it is Tom's. He marries Anne and lives for a while in Irwin's house, caring for the gravely ill Ellis Burden, until the mortgage is foreclosed.

The relationship between Willie Stark and Jack Burden began with an empty, indecipherable sign. Back in 1922 when the narrator of *All the King's Men* first met the future governor, then a mere county treasurer, in the back room of Slade's poolhall, Burden could have sworn, at the moment of the handshake, that Stark gave him a wink. "Then looking into that dead pan, I wasn't sure" (15). It's an ambiguous sign that Willie gives young Burden, all the more difficult to interpret because its author refuses to acknowledge authorial intent. Twelve years later, Jack asks him if it had been a wink or not.

"Boy," he said, and smiled at me paternally over his glass, "that is a mystery."

"Don't you remember?" I asked.
"Sure," he said, "I remember."
"Well," I demanded.
"Suppose I just had something in my eye?" he said.
"Well, damn it, you just had something in your eye then."
"Suppose I didn't have anything in my eye?" (16)

Had Willie intended the wink[1] it would have meant something: "maybe you winked because you figured you and me had some views in common about the tone of the gathering"—a gathering that included the kind of corrupt politicos Stark would later campaign to throw out of office. But as Stark refuses to say whether or not it was an expressive wink, it means something else. It is a gift—a paternal one, to judge from the adverb that qualifies his smile—and to comment on it further would be to take it away: " 'Boy,' he said, 'If I was to tell you, then you wouldn't have anything to think about.' "

So Jack had something to think about; and so perhaps do we. For the problem Willie poses bears an interesting resemblance to the one that Jason Sweetwater, in *At Heaven's Gate,* thought about when he meditated on the fetus in Sue Murdock's womb and the mummies who, like fetuses, had peculiarly expressive eyelids. Paradoxically, their apparent fullness of meaning is due to actual emptiness ("because there was nothing under them any more"). They are as empty as Tolliver's mailbox in *Night Rider,* though, like the eyelids Tolliver refuses to open, they hold out the possibility of something more within, some meaning still to be grasped, some text to be read.

Willie Stark's closed eye is paradoxical too, but the terms of the paradox are now reversed. With the mummies and the fetus the eyes seemed to contain meaning because they were empty. But it is precisely if Stark *had* had something in his eye, some speck or cinder that made him blink, that it would have been meaningless, an involuntary physiological response. Whereas if he had shut his eye without having anything in it, as Burden suspected but could never confirm, it could have been a wink—and hence, perhaps, have meant something.

It is remarkable that each of Jack's three fathers do as much blinking (if not winking) as they do. Willie Stark, about to address the crowd in Mason City in chapter 1, could be seen "blinking his big eyes a little, just as though he had just stepped out of the open doors and the dark hall of the courthouse behind him and was blinking to get his eyes adjusted to the light. He stood up there blinking . . ." (8). The first time we see Judge Irwin, who Jack does not realize is his biological father until his death, Jack says that he "stood there blinking into the dark outside, trying to make out my face" (41). Likewise, when Ellis Burden, Jack's legal father and putative biological one, first appears, he too "did not recognize me, blinking at me in the darkness" (195).

Amid all this blinking there is yet another staging of the paradox of the wink-that-might-have-been. It comes from the old hitchhiker Burden picks up in New Mexico, who tantalizes him with the hint of a wink to come.

> The only thing remarkable about him was the fact that while you looked into the sun-brittled leather of the face, which seemed as stiff and devitalized as the hide on a mummy's jaw, you would suddenly see a twitch in the left cheek, up toward the pale-blue eye. You would think he was going to wink, but he wasn't going to wink. The twitch was simply an independent phenomenon, unrelated to the face or to what was behind the face or to anything in the whole tissue of phenomena which is the world we are lost in. (313–14)

The characteristic is all the more related to the tissue of phenomena we have examined here, for the mummific quality of the old man's leathery face puts him in league with the mummies in *At Heaven's Gate,* whose eyes, like his, seem to mean something but don't. It is likewise related to the wink that might have been just a blink, for the twitch in the jaw is a good example of what Willie's action would have been if it were wholly unintentional.

The important aspect, of course, about what Willie's eye does is that he refuses to say whether it was intentional. Jack has been given food for thought by this creation of something out of practically nothing, by this something that seems to exist only in order to cast doubt on the possibility of its existence. It is not pressing too hard to say that Willie's wink is like a text whose only decipherable message is that it may not *be* a text, for the paradox is stated in just such explicitly textual terms elsewhere in Warren. In "Aspen Leaf in Windless World" (from *Being Here: Poetry 1977–1980*), it is what one can read on a beach:

> Look how sea-foam, thin and white, makes its Arabic scrawl
> On the unruffled sand of the beach's faint-tilted plane.
> Is there a message there for you to decipher?
> Or only the joy of its sunlit, intricate rhythm?

This is a persistent question in Warren; and in the fiction, as I mean to show, it takes the form of a text a father may or may not have left a son. The textuality of Willie's eye movement is not as immediately evident as are later instances—the handbill in *World Enough and Time* that Jeremiah Beaumont thinks came from Colonel Fort, or the poem in *Wilderness* written by Adam Rozenzweig's father whose worth Adam will spend his life searching for. But an important clue in *All the King's Men* for interpreting Stark's enigmatic eyeblink—Jack Burden's discovery "that the reality of an event, which is not real in itself, arises from other events which, likewise, in themselves are not real" (384)—does have explicitly textual echoes in something else Warren had written not long before. In the critical essay "Pure and Impure Poetry" (first published in 1943) he makes a quite similar statement about where poetry comes from: "Does this not, then, lead us to the conclusion that poetry does not inhere in any particular element but depends upon the set of relationships, the structure, which we call the poem?" (24). Both of these statements address the paradox of the origin of something out of practically nothing. There is no reality in any particular event, no poetry in any particular element of a poem, but the reality and the poetry somehow arise out of combinations, out of structures, out of relationships among events that are not in themselves real, among elements that are not in themselves poetic.

These echoing statements point to a way of investigating the problem Willie's eye poses. They suggest that the place to look for an answer is not in the phenomenon of Willie's wink or blink but in its relationship to other events in the novel—which is to say, since the novel is both a collection of events and a literary text, in its relationship to other poetic elements. And it should not be forgotten that we are reading not only *All the King's Men* but the larger narrative, or poem, of which this novel is itself a part.[2]

One of those other events, in this novel, is the mummy-jawed hitchhiker's involuntary twitch, the unintentional hint of an imminent wink that never came. Another, in *At Heaven's Gate,* is what Sweetwater saw in mummies' eyes, whose paradoxical expressiveness anticipates Burden's paradox about reality emerging from unreality. Still another is the way Bogan Murdock, by resembling an Egyptian corpse, anticipates the way Willie Stark would look when he underwent his mysterious transformation from inarticulate country bumpkin to stemwindingly eloquent politician. Murdock, asleep under the sunlamp, displayed "an Egyptian delicacy of bone . . . like a carved figure on a tomb, or like a dead body laid out ceremonially." The night when Willie discovered the truth about how he had been set up by the Harrison gang to split the MacMurfee vote, got dead drunk, and fell asleep, he struck a significantly similar pose: "the hands were crossed piously on the bosom like the hands of a *gisant* on a tomb" (83). During the deathlike sleep, an almost miraculous metamorphosis occurred. Until then Stark had cut such a comic figure that Burden had had to stifle his laughter with a pillow when he heard him pacing the floor next door, rehearsing his earnest but ludicrous speech. But Willie awoke from that cadaverous sleep a changed man. The speech he gave that afternoon at the Upton barbecue was electrifying. He made a big show of throwing away his prepared speech and spoke from the heart as a hick to hicks, pointing an accusing finger at Tiny Duffy and revealing that he had been set up to run with no hope of winning, just to split the opposition. Stark dropped out of the race for governor, but now possessed the style he would exploit to such perfection in the next election. He had become Willie Stark.

It is one of the most entertaining moments in the novel and should be cherished for that fact. But it is also a moment when Warren's text allows us a glimpse of the mystery of origins, and we are beginning to realize that that is one of the things the larger narrative is chiefly about. Where did the Willie Stark who would become governor come from? How did the boy, "Cousin Willie from the country" (51), become a man? How did he become Jack Burden's father instead of the object of his condescension?[3] Clearly, it happened because Stark decided to stand on his own two feet and speak his own language. But, the way the story is actually told, it must have had something to do, too, with the mysterious *gisant* pose in which he passed the night before the Upton barbecue.

As a *gisant* Stark is both corpse and statue. So, too, it happens, was the fetus Sweetwater pictured in Sue Murdock's womb that reminded him of certain fetal mummies, for it had "tiny hands and feet formed like delicate carving" (the word "carving" echoes the "carved figure on a tomb" that Bogan Murdock becomes in the same novel). When Willie awakes from his petrified slumber, from the chrysalis of his metamorphosis, the first sign of a return to life is curiously like that ambiguous eye closure he made in Jack's presence the first time they met. Here, his eyes, the only moving parts in a body still frozen in that carved *gisant* pose, seemed almost to speak: "his hands still crossed on his chest, his face pale and pure.... His head didn't turn, but his eyes swung toward me with a motion that made you think you could hear them creak in the sockets" (86). The creak is surely impossible, yet something in the movement of the eyes makes Jack think he can hear it. It will happen one more time, when Stark lies dying in the hospital: "Finally, the eyes turned toward me again, very slowly, and I almost thought that I could hear the tiny painful creak of the balls in their sockets" (400). Together, these two instances of creaking, speaking eyes frame the existence of the real Willie Stark.

There is another significant wink in the novel—though it is not entirely real either, since Jack only imagines it. He imagines it coming from Tiny Duffy, whose destruction and recreation is a measure of the power that Willie Stark acquired the night he slept like a *gisant* on a tomb. The image comes to him after Stark has been assassinated and Duffy offers Burden a job in his new administration.

> It was as though the scene through which I had just lived had been a monstrous and comic miming for ends I could not conceive and for an audience I could not see but which I knew was leering from the shadow. It was as though in the midst of the

> scene Tiny Duffy had slowly and like a brother winked at me with his oyster eye and I had known the nightmare truth, which was that we were twins.... We were bound together under the unwinking eye of Eternity.... (417)

If Willie's original wink (or whatever it was) was the first instance of his ability to fascinate Jack Burden, as well as a sign in the symbolic network of Warren's novels of the father's power to produce an indecipherable text, then why should the despicable Duffy be able to wink at Burden, even if only in Jack's imagination? Duffy, it is important to recall, was the agent of Harrison's setting up Stark to run in that first hopeless race; it was Duffy whom Willie pointed his finger at and under whose nose he fluttered the abandoned manuscript of the speech he wasn't going to give at the Upton barbecue, a gesture that started Duffy careening backward in a pinwheeling dance that took him right off the speaker's platform. Like Humpty Dumpty, he had, literally, a great fall.[4] And what all the king's horses and men could not do for the character in the nursery rhyme is precisely what Willie *could* do for Duffy. It was, in fact, in order to display this creative and repairing ability that Willie kept him in his entourage despite the fact that it was Duffy who had lied to him and framed him to run for governor on Harrison's behalf. Stark had "busted Tiny Duffy and then he had picked up the pieces and put him back together again as his own creation" (97), making him highway commissioner, and later lieutenant governor. "In a way, the very success which the Boss laid on Tiny was his revenge on Tiny, for every time the Boss put his meditative, sleepy, distant gaze on Tiny, Tiny would know, with a cold clutch at his fat heart, that if the Boss should crook a finger there wouldn't be anything but the whiff of smoke. In a way, Tiny's success was a final index of the Boss's own success" (98). Stark, who knew how to create good out of evil—"Goodness.... You got to make it.... If you want it. And you got to make it out of badness.... Because there isn't anything else to make it out of" (257)—put Duffy back together again as his own creation in a way that bears a certain parallel to divine creation in the theological perspective of Ellis Burden, the man Jack grew up thinking was his father. Here, too, successful creation out of imperfect material is an index of the greater glory of the creator: "The creation of man whom God in His foreknowledge knew doomed to sin was the awful index"—note that Jack had used the same word in saying that "Tiny's success was a final *index* of the Boss's own success"—"of God's omnipotence. For it would have been a trifling and contemptible ease for Perfection to create more perfection.... The creation of evil is therefore the index of God's glory and His power" (437).

What Stark does with Duffy is thus no trifling matter. Its centrality to the novel is underlined by both its allusion to the title and its allusion, through that echoing *index,* and its parallel to Ellis's discussion of Creation itself. And although Ellis Burden looks to be a ridiculous man, Jack was to find himself in substantial agreement with at least this one article of his faith: "later," he will say of the passage just cited, "I was not certain but that in my own way I did believe what he had said" (437).

Jack had been troubled early on by Stark's decision to sign up Duffy, his enemy's former henchman. It seemed a totally unnecessary gesture. "I used to wonder why Willie kept him around. Sometimes I used to ask the Boss, 'What do you keep that lunk-head for?' Sometimes he would just laugh and say nothing" (97). What seems troubling at that point becomes tragic—that is, fated and inevitable—in the end; for Tiny Duffy in fact arranges Willie's death. He tells Adam Stanton that Stark has been having an affair with Adam's sister, Anne, knowing what will happen, and knowing that by setting that train of events in motion he can avenge all those years of humiliation. He also knows that, as lieutenant governor, he can accede to the throne of his slain oppressor. Stark could have let Duffy fade into oblivion at the beginning of his own success, but he preferred to hold on to, and carry with him throughout his meteoric career, the man who, transformed by him into a thing, turned out to be his own death warrant.

That Duffy can indeed be likened to a deadly piece of paper whose contents are unknown to the bearer—Bellerophon or Uriah—is suggested by one strand of the symbolic network of the novel, a chain of fateful letters and bundles with insistently similar wrappings. In an episode that parallels Stark's decision to keep Duffy on, Willie's response to the news that state auditor Byram B. White has been caught with his hands in the till and is in danger of impeachment is to defend him to the utmost, even at the cost of his own impeachment. There were sound political reasons for not throwing Byram to the wolves, reasons less inscrutable than Willie's ultimately fatal decision to hire and keep on Tiny Duffy. Yet Stark's decision to keep White in his administration gives rise to an evocative metaphor with deeper resonance than one might have expected from an instance of cool political calculation: The White case becomes "a tidy package of disaster lying on the scales with the blood seeping through the brown paper" (145) when it leads to the possible impeachment of the governor himself. Stark fights fire with fire, in a way, countering that brown paper package with a brown paper envelope containing the names of the sufficient number of legislators whom he had coerced into voting against impeachment. It is Jack Burden's job to deliver it to the leader of the opposition: "He opened the door . . . didn't recognize me at first, just seeing a big brown envelope and some sort of face above it. But I withdrew the brown envelope just as his hand reached for it" (148). And this "big brown manila envelope" (148) bears a strong resemblance to the "brown manila envelope" he will first give Anne Stanton to peruse (252) and then be forced to deliver himself to Judge Irwin (345), containing the fruits of his historical research into the Judge's past. It will prove to be fatal; soon afterward Irwin shoots himself in the heart.

Jack's other piece of historical research eventually finds its way into a similar package, for when he abandons his work on Cass Mastern and leaves behind those letters and diaries and what were at that time "the complete works of Jack Burden"—his unfinished manuscript on the story—the landlady of the apartment where he had intentionally abandoned them wraps them all up and mails him the bundle Collect. "The parcel, unopened, traveled around with him from furnished room to furnished room . . . a big squarish parcel with the brown paper turning yellow and the cords sagging, and the name *Mr. Jack Burden* fading slowly" (190). Jack lugs this burden around with him in rather the same way that Willie Stark keeps on the excess baggage Tiny Duffy or the blood-tinged brown parcel that was Byram B. White. Like the brown envelope Burden handed the leader of the impeachment forces, and, like the one he gave Judge Irwin, this brown package contains bad news. It takes nearly the whole length of the narrative for Jack to open it—the deaths of Irwin, Stark, and Adam Stanton compel him to. For in acknowledging the fact of his "having killed the father" (Irwin, his biological father) and "of having delivered his two friends [Willie and Adam] into each other's hands and death" (436), Jack comes to realize just how much he has in common with Mastern. On the last page he tells us that he is still going to live in his father's (Irwin's) house for a while, until the bank forecloses, and to spend what was left him in the Judge's estate "to live on while I write the book I began years ago, the life of Cass Mastern, whom once I could not understand but whom, perhaps, I now may come to understand" (438).

Jack can come to understand him now because Mastern bore a similar burden of guilt, having provoked his best friend into suicide by having a clandestine affair with his wife and caused his mistress's slave to be sold into prostitution, and seeking death on a Civil War battle field convinced that the world was one immense spiderweb of inescapable relation and responsibility. Jack Burden, before the events recounted in the story of Willie Stark and his involvement in his administration, could not understand such an expression of the utter unity of existence, "for to him the world then was simply an accumulation of items, odds and ends of things like the broken and misused and dust-shrouded things gathered in a garret. Or it was a flux of things before his eyes (or behind his eyes) and one thing had nothing to do, in the end, with anything else" (189).

What the world was like to Burden before his ultimate illumination is what the novel at hand, or any novel of Warren's, is to the reader for whom there is a clear demarcation between action and description, or between the foreground of the plot and the supporting background detail of subsidiary events and scenery, and for whom what is on the far side of that line is not much more than accumulation of items, odds and ends. But something resembling Jack Burden's enlightenment at the end of the novel is available to that reader, and it takes the form of a dawning awareness that more and more of that flux of things is not background but foreground (or that it is becoming increasingly difficult to distinguish figure from ground), as the reader discovers that more and more of what seemed unrelated is in fact part and parcel of the principal movement of the novel.

Such is the case with these envelopes and parcels, whose insistently similar brown wrapping suggests that the reality of their similarity may be more significant than the reality of any one of them considered separately— that they may be an example of Burden's paradox, according to which "the reality of an event, which is not real in itself, arises from other events which, likewise, in themselves are not real." Considered together, these two packages and two envelopes reveal a certain dynamic of their own: the blood-tinged package that is, figuratively, Byram White leads Stark to devise an appropriate response; the brown envelope contains a text Stark has written (and had to engage in considerable political chicanery to compose) and has Jack deliver. The second brown envelope (that containing the truth of Irwin's past) Jack also delivers, but this time he comes up with the text (and had to perform considerable historical spadework to do so). This letter bears a certain relationship to the other package: both are the fruits of Burden's historical research, and the consequence of his delivery of the envelope (the Judge's suicide) contributes to his eventual ability to reopen the ubiquitous package (by generating the guilt that motivates him to write the book on Mastern).

We know what was in the two brown envelopes and the second brown package, but what exactly lay hidden in that "tidy package of disaster lying on the scales with the blood seeping through the brown paper"?—butchered meat, to judge from the scales. Yet that reading does not entirely account for the feeling of dread that "package of disaster" connotes. What it contains may still be alive. If the package is Byram White, as it appears to be, it may contain the fetus Byram seems to become when he hunches over the desk to write the text Stark dictates, his undated letter of resignation, "drawing himself into a hunch as though he wanted to assume *the prenatal position* and be little and warm and safe in the dark" (132; emphasis added). Byram waiting in that position for the words Willie will tell him to write resembles Burden listening in anticipation as Stark is about to deliver a speech in Mason City. In both scenes, the listener turns fetal as Willie Stark gets ready to deliver his text. As he stepped before the crowd, Willie "stood there blinking . . . gave his head a twitch," and we are reminded of the old hitchhiker's twitch that presaged a wink which never came. There is a "glitter" in his eyes.

> *It's coming,* I thought.
> You saw the eyes bulge suddenly like that, as though something had happened inside him, and there was that glitter.... It was like the second when you come home late at night and see the yellow envelope of the telegram sticking out from under your door and you lean and pick it up, but don't open it yet.... [Y]ou feel there's an eye on you, a great big eye looking straight at you ... and sees you huddled up way inside, in the dark which is you, inside yourself, like a clammy, sad little foetus you carry around inside yourself.... But the clammy, sad little foetus which is you ... lifts up its sad little face and its eyes are blind, and it shivers cold inside you for it doesn't want to know what is in that envelope ... but you open the envelope, you have to open the envelope, for the end of man is to know. (9)

What the yellow envelope contains seems as deadly as a Bellerophontic letter[5]; exactly what it contains is not clear, but in the context of similar imagery in the rest of the novel we may, perhaps, be allowed to guess.

We recall that the package with Burden's name on it—the Cass Mastern papers—was "turning yellow" as he carried it around. It is also by now apparent that the fetus here finds a counterpart in Byram White, both as a creature of Willie's who has been frightened into a fetal position and as a blood-tinged brown paper bundle of suspicious contents, and that that parcel itself finds an echo in the brown package that Burden carried around for years without opening. By this chain of reappearances, therefore, both the fetus and the yellow envelope in Burden's allegorical fantasy eventuate in the yellowing brown burden Jack can only open after all the unsettling events of the novel—the deaths of Irwin, Stark, and Adam—have occurred. At the time of the daydream about the fetus and the yellow telegram, Burden, like the fetus, does not want to know what is inside that paper covering; during his delay in opening the telegram transpire the events narrated in the novel. What he learns when he is able at last to reopen the Cass Mastern package, or what he has to learn in order to want to reopen it, is that to a certain degree he *is* Cass Mastern—that, like the "foetus you carry around inside yourself ... which is you," the brown bundle he has been carrying around for so long is really him. Thus the message the yellow envelope contains may be what Burden eventually learns, which is something the Burden who imagined that allegory already knew, that the fetus he has been carrying around inside him is him (though the dark in which it dwelt was him, too).

Whatever parallels the plot offers between Tiny Duffy and that tidy package of disaster that was Byram White may allow us to fill in more of the picture. Chief among them is the fact that Duffy and White are both employees of Stark whom he might have dismissed (or never hired, in the case of Duffy) had he not been so imbued with his Machiavellian philosophy of creating good out of evil in the absence of purely good raw materials. In that regard, Willie behaves as God does in Ellis Burden's theology, using his ability to create good out of evil as an index of his own power. He broke Byram White by an imperial display of omnipotence, transforming him into a cowering, fetal amanuensis with eyes "as numb and expressionless as . . . oysters" (133) by making him transcribe his own undated letter of resignation. He broke Tiny Duffy the day he made him fall off the stage at Upton. He "busted" that Duffy-Dumpty[6] and then fixed him by putting back together the pieces as his own creation. And, like Byram, Tiny had an "oyster eye"—the one Jack imagined winking at him (417). There, perhaps, the resemblances end, for Duffy also "became, in a crazy kind of way, the other self of Willie Stark," the part of himself that Willie heaped contempt on "because of a blind, inward necessity" (98). This was an honor to which Byram White could not aspire; yet some of the imagery of Jack's fetal allegory attaches itself to him, displaced from where it might really belong—with Tiny Duffy. For it is Duffy that Stark carries around with him ("I used to wonder why Willie kept him *around*") like the fetus "you carry *around* inside yourself," and like the brown parcel of Mastern papers Burden carried around for so long without opening. And just as the Mastern bundle of guilt is, as Jack eventually realizes, his own guilt, and the package thus becomes him (even more fully when he transforms it into his own text by writing the book on Mastern); and as the fetus "is you" in Jack's allegory, so is Tiny Duffy, once broken apart and put back together by Willie Stark, the other self of his creator. Duffy is to Stark as the Mastern bundle with his name on it is to Jack Burden: the fetus that becomes his text, a text with a dangerous but inescapable message.

But perhaps Tiny Duffy had always been a text for Willie Stark—or at least the bearer of one. For one more thing should be said about Duffy and the wink Jack could imagine him sending his way. It is the father who winks (and blinks; viz. Stark, Irwin, and Ellis Burden) in this novel. But what is fatherly about Tiny Duffy? When Jack imagines him winking, it's not as a father but "like a brother," a twin. Yet in fact Duffy *is* a father, *Willie's* father. Because back when Willie was a child, politically speaking, before he assumed his manhood on the speaking platform at the Upton barbecue, it was Duffy who got him to run for governor and who guided his first boyish steps into the arena of state politics, managing his campaign. And in the beginning it had been Duffy who drove up to Mason City and spoke with the voice of God to persuade Willie that he could save the state. "The Lord was calling Willie" (66) and Tiny Duffy was the messenger. "For him to deny the voice of Tiny Duffy would have been as difficult as for a saint to deny the voice that calls in the night" (69). As will so often happen in Warren, a paternal authority figure has given the son a text to interpret and to live up to, a text that in this instance came from an impeccable source.

So Stark's decision to keep Duffy around does not arise out of, or just out of, vengeance against a man who had made a fool of him. By keeping Duffy, Stark maintains a tie to his past, to his political infancy. Duffy, in fact, is the degraded corpse of the father. In breaking apart and putting together Tiny Duffy, Willie Stark destroys and recreates his own father. This makes him an even more powerful father for Jack, for it means he knows how to pass through the oedipal ordeal a boy must undergo to become a man. And Duffy was Jack's brother, his *twin* ("I had known the nightmare truth, which was that that we were twins"), because Jack, narrator of the story of Willie Stark, becomes Willie's father too. It is clearly a situation fraught with possibilities for Warren: "I am the father / Of my father's father's father," he would write two decades later in "The Leaf."

Stark breaks Tiny Duffy apart and puts him back together as an author breaks apart and puts back together whatever it is that he transforms into a text. And while Burden is not the author of *All the King's Men*, though on its last page he *is* on his way to becoming the author of a book on Cass Mastern, he is the closest thing we have to one in the novel. The voice of its narrative is Burden's voice, a constant and unmistakable wise-guy sneer that is a large part of the novel's charm and for which nothing in its two predecessors had prepared us. The necessity for this breaking apart and putting back together was evident as far back as *Night Rider*, when Percy Munn discovered what a poor storyteller he was. He tried to make a narrative for his wife out of his experiences in the Tobacco Association and to find a way of having it make sense to himself; he failed miserably at both. "He had thought that, if he could tell her the story exactly as it happened, the meaning would become clear too," but as he attempted to do this he found that "the story was going to pieces in his hands" (42).

To convey the meaning of events it is not enough to tell things exactly as they happened; to arrive at meaning one has to approach the history of those events as Ianthe Sprague dealt with texts, preferring to the ready-made continuity of a novel the broken fragments of nonconsecutive and apparently unconnected newspaper items. Jerome Meckier has observed that the story line of *All the King's Men*, which rapidly shifts in the first chapter from 1939 to 1936 to 1922, and from 1933 to 1896 to 1854 in chapters 3 and 4, is "seemingly told in fragments" and "at first examination, seems to be in itself a sort of Humpty Dumpty that has shattered into several pieces" (69). Indeed, the fragmenting and reassembling of that famed fallen egg is what, it seems, the story is all about—whether we follow the narrative of Willie Stark's busting and repiecing of Tiny Duffy and its eventual tragic result or the story the novel tells of its own production.

These jumps in time are not the only form this fragmentation of experience takes. Jack Burden found that his mind kept making "crazy wild leaps" at a most inappropriate moment, in that key scene of sexual fiasco when the teenaged Anne Stanton was removing her clothes in an upstairs bedroom of his mother's house: "my mind kept flying to peculiar things— to a book I had started and never finished . . . to a scene . . . I tried desperately to locate out of my past" (294). And when she lay down totally nude on the bed and straightened out, her hands across her chest and her eyes closed, it happened again, though this time a very specific image came to mind: "And at the instant when she closed her eyes, as I stared at her, my mind took one of the crazy leaps and I saw her floating in the water, that day of the picnic three years before, with her eyes closed and the violent sky above and the white gull flashing high over, and that face and this face and that scene and this scene seemed to fuse, like superimposed photographs, each keeping its identity but without denying the other" (295). This experience of split vision has a very specific consequence for young Jack Burden. Although his body was "tumescent," he was suddenly seized with the conviction "that everything was wrong, completely wrong, how I didn't know," and he had to say to Anne, who was surely expecting to hear other words than these, "it wouldn't be right."

There is no single explanation for what happened here, for this impasse is surely an instance of what Warren was talking about when he wrote, in the introduction to the Modern Library Edition of this novel, that "in fiction one should never do a thing for merely a single reason (not if he hopes to achieve that feeling of a mysterious depth which is one of the chief beauties of the art)" (95). Understanding, for example, how Jack was distracted from the business at hand by seeing double is complicated by the fact that he had used the same language of superimposed images a few pages earlier to talk about what it is like to be in love:

> [Y]ou create yourself by creating another person, who, however, has also created you. . . . So there are two you's, the one you yourself create by loving and the one the beloved creates by loving you. . . . [I]f you loved and were loved perfectly then there wouldn't be any difference between the two you's or any distance between them. They would coincide perfectly, there would be a perfect focus, as when a stereoscope gets the twin images on the card into perfect alignment. (282)

What is here the image of perfect love—the alignment of two photographs in a stereoscope—just a few pages later becomes the very thing that prevents the fulfillment of love. The double vision Jack experiences, despite its potentially sexual overtones of perfect union ("that scene and this scene seemed to fuse, like superimposed photographs"), seems to describe a more general category than love; true love, with its perfect focus and alignment of twin images, is only a special case of that larger category.

The stereoscopic experience that figures so prominently both in Burden's description of true love and in his inability to achieve its bodily fruition could be described not only as the fragmentation of experience—the breaking apart of a single moment into the troubling coexistence of that moment and a memory it conjures up—but as its opposite, or the phase that follows it in the model Willie Stark's treatment of Tiny Duffy provides: putting the pieces back together. Although love itself is a kind of creation in which two images coalesce, what Jack found that night when Anne lay on the bed was that such a coalescence of images can serve another purpose than love's, and in doing so interfere with love's progress. Jack, though he did not consciously want to, was at that moment engaged in putting together some of the pieces of his own experience, one of which was the image of Anne in the water that had haunted him from long before, an image that "would have been there if I had never fallen in love with her, or had never seen her again, or had grown to detest her" (119). This image had nothing to do with loving Anne; rather, it was a personal mystery, one "of the true images . . . the kind which become more and more vivid for us as if the passage of the years did not obscure their reality but, year by year, drew off another veil to expose a meaning which we had only dimly surmised at first" (118). What he saw when he looked at Anne lying on her back on the bed had lifted another veil from that original image.

Warren's novel is constructed in such a way as to allow us to experience that sense of revelation and stereoscopic vision, too. For a number of other images from the novel come to superimpose themselves on Anne's, and although Jack Burden is the narrator through whom we learn about them, he does not seem to be aware of their existence. We could not expect him to be, for his concerns are different from ours: he is trying to make sense of his experience; we are trying to make sense of the novel. In that effort we might well have reason to wonder exactly what certain striking but eccentric details have to do with the rest of the story—what purpose, for example, do George, whom Jack's putative father, Ellis Burden, took under his charitable wing, and his wet-bread angels serve in the larger scheme of things? In what is surely one of the least commented-upon scenes in the book, Jack begins his search for the skeleton in the Judge's closet by paying a visit to Ellis, the "Scholarly Attorney" who had been his mother's husband at the time of Jack's birth and whom he always had every reason to believe was his father. Ellis, who left Jack's mother when he discovered her liaison with Judge Irwin (but whose departure had, for Jack, always been a mystery), is now living in a poor section of the city, devoting his time to helping the disadvantaged and to writing religious tracts. When Jack finds him, Ellis is picking up "a largish brown paper bag full of something" from the restaurant below his apartment (195). Knowing what we now know about brown paper parcels in this novel—of which one, the Mastern package, had made its appearance just a few pages earlier at the conclusion of chapter 4 (190)—we cannot fail to be interested in the contents of that sack.

They happen to be bread crusts, and Ellis is going to give them to George, an "unfortunate" he has adopted, who chews them briefly to get them wet and then makes statues out of them: "The figure of an angel, with wings and flowing drapery, had been executed in bas-relief in what looked like putty" (197). All he makes is angels, in memory of his wife, who was an angel in the circus. "She fell down a long way with white wings which fluttered as though she were flying," but one day something went wrong with the apparatus, and George never got over her death. He has transformed her into a graven image, and he remakes her daily out of the contents of that brown paper bag, parodying Burden's definition of true love: "The person who loves you has picked you out of the great mass of uncreated clay which is humanity to make something out of ... the poor lumpish clay" (282). He also parodies what happens to Jack when he is paralyzed by images of Anne at the very moment when the real Anne is more available to him than ever before; for George, who is also in a state of near-paralysis, can do nothing but multiply images of his angel wife. At least that is one conclusion we might draw from the way that certain details encourage us to see Anne Stanton in that angel: Jack tells us that she looked like an Egyptian bas-relief (104) (George's angel "had been executed in bas-relief"), and when Anne dove from the great height of the hotel diving tower, she hit the water "as though she had dived through a great circus hoop" (288).

Jack had come to see Ellis Burden to ask about Irwin, specifically, if there had ever been a time when the Judge was in dire need of money. Ellis would not answer, refusing to touch ever again the "foulness" of the past. Jack thus came away from the interview with very little. "But I got one thing. I was sure that he had known something. Which meant that there was something to know" (203). In fact, his confidence that there was something usable behind Ellis's horror at the mention of the Judge's name is probably a misreading of his reaction, since what Ellis was most likely responding to was Irwin's affair with his wife and not his profiting from extending preferential treatment to the American Electric Power Company when he was state attorney general, nor the fact that he had indirectly caused the suicide of Mortimer L. Littlepaugh. For Ellis could not possibly have known about these things. Jack is in fact in error to think that he learned something about the Judge from his supposed father, but that error is a fruitful one, for it starts him on a quest that eventually leads to the truth. Ellis's one-word response to Jack's questions—"Foulness . . . foulness"—is, like Willie Stark's ambiguous wink, a paternal text whose message is unknowable, perhaps nonexistent. But, like the wink, it gives Jack Burden something to think about.

And we are given something to think about, too, in Jack's encounter with Ellis and George, for what George does with what Ellis brings him in the brown paper bag ought to remind us of, of all people, the Judge. Irwin had a collection of military toys in his library, and when Jack was a boy he used to come over and help assemble them. At a dinner party one evening, when Jack was working for Stark but before Willie had given him the assignment of digging up dirt on the Judge, Irwin began to regale the guests with a history of warfare before the invention of gunpowder and, to illustrate his narrative, brought out a miniature ballista.

> Then he didn't have anything to shoot. So he rang for the black boy and got a roll. He broke open the roll and removed a little hunk of the soft bread and tried to make a pellet of it. It didn't make a very good pellet, so he dipped it in the water to make it stick. He put it in the carriage . . . and tipped the trigger.
>
> It worked. The pellet was heavy with a good soaking and the zip hadn't gone out of the ballista with the passage of the years, for the next thing I knew there was an explosion in the chandelier and Mrs. Patton screamed and spewed mint ice over her black velvet and bits of glass showered down over the tablecloth. . . . (121–22)

Jack's response to all this, especially when he discovered that the twists on the ballista were brand-new, that the Judge's interest in those toys was therefore not casual but passionate, was to feel "sad and embarrassed." But if he felt that Irwin looked ridiculous then, what would he have thought if he could have seen the parallel between the Judge's use of soaked bread and George's manipulation of the same material? Surely there is something going on in the narrative of which the narrator—Burden—is unaware. This reuse of the same material can be very suggestive, to us if not to Jack. Burden was saddened and embarrassed by the Judge's apparent reversion to childhood; such a return to infancy is even more pronounced in the case of George, who has fallen into a state of total dependence, scrambling to the floor for a piece of candy from Ellis's hand. Yet, pathetic as he is, George put his moistened bread to a better use than did the Judge; he did it for love, and the result was art, at least in someone's eyes, while Irwin was toying with an engine of death.

Just how deadly the Judge's bread pellet could be is suggested by certain undertones in the scene in which Jack speaks with the surgeon who has just extracted Adam Stanton's bullets from Willie Stark. Like the Judge's ballista, Adam's weapon had been a toy, "a little toy target pistol" (397); like the Judge's alimentary ammunition, Adam's bullets are termed, likewise *pellets* and, through the doctor's irony, are given a nutritive value: "Dr. Simmons picked up a little envelope from his desk, and emptied the contents into his hand. 'No matter how strong they are they can't take much of this diet,' he said, and held out his hand, open, to show me the two little pellets resting there. A .25-caliber slug is small, all right, but these looked even smaller and more trivial than I had remembered" (399). That the doctor took the pellets out of an envelope has a certain resonance in this narrative about envelopes and packages out of which something baleful comes: the envelope Jack in his fetal allegory does not want to open but knows he must, the brown parcel of Mastern material that follows him around, the envelope he gave to the Judge that made him commit suicide, and the bloodstained, tidy package of disaster that was, figuratively, Byram White. Up to this point Ellis Burden's brown paper bag with George's bread inside has not connoted any catastrophe. Yet through the perspective of something like the stereoscopic view of which the narrator speaks, but with three pictures in place of two, it can and will, if we line up these scenes linked by a common vocabulary, each of which centers around one of Jack's three fathers.

We were first introduced to that stereoscopic view when Jack saw superimposed on the naked, reclining body of Anne Stanton his memory of her floating on her back in the water. And we found that we could experience a feeling of déjà vu akin to his in contemplating the spectacle of Anne's diving into a circus hoop splashdown at the same time as we imagined what it must have looked like for George's late wife to make her dramatic descent to the circus floor. Anne is clearly meant to suggest Poe's Annabel Lee when Jack tells us that he, Anne, and her brother Adam were once "children by the sea" at Burden's Landing, and that stormy weather "didn't chill us or kill us in the kingdom by the sea" (103). And so, when we subsequently learn that the name of Cass Mastern's mistress was *Annabelle* Trice, we are prepared to see something of Anne/Annabel in her (though Mrs. Trice's maiden name, Puckett, points in another direction: Sadie Burke, whose name was attached to Sen-Sen *Puckett's* before it was to Willie Stark's [73]).

But there is one more image that Anne supine on the white counterpane of that bed invokes, one that, could Jack have seen it, would have offered a more powerful reason for his inability to continue with that seduction than the reason and image he does acknowledge. Before she lay down Anne, standing unclothed in the darkness, "hunched her shoulders a little ... she stood ... hunched slightly forward, perhaps shivering, her knees slightly bent and pressed together" (294–95). Now this by itself recalls two other earlier images (earlier in the novel, though not in time): one, the hunched fetal position of Byram White ("drawing himself into a hunch as though he wanted to assume the prenatal position"), the other, an image of Anne herself, when her pressed-together legs once reminded Jack of certain Egyptian bas-reliefs: "her small legs . . . accurately together, thigh to thigh, knee to knee, ankle to ankle. There was, in fact, always something a little stylized about her—something of the effect one observed in certain Egyptian bas-reliefs" (104). Ultimately, in the wider context of other Warren texts, Egyptian statuary evokes both tombs and fetuses, as we saw when Willie's wink and the old mummy-jawed hitchhiker's twitch recalled Bogan Murdock's "Egyptian delicacy of bone" and how he looked like "a carved figure on a tomb, or like a dead body laid out ceremonially." These lines of Warren's symbolic network are strengthened by what happens after Anne hunches over in that quasi-fetal way: She "lay back on the white counterpane, then punctiliously straightened out and again folded her hands across her bosom, and closed her eyes." She looked, that is, like a corpse, or a figure carved on a tomb. In particular, she looked like the *gisant* that would be Willie Stark, whose hands would be "crossed piously on the bosom like the hands of a *gisant* on a tomb in a cathedral."

Nor is this the first time that Anne Stanton is made to look like Willie Stark. A few pages earlier, Burden had described the process of falling in love—specifically, of Anne Stanton falling in love—in terms that recall the process of transformation Willie underwent the night before the Upton barbecue. The miracle of his metamorphosis transpired when he was lost in a slumber in which he took on the appearance of that *gisant* on a cathedral tomb. Jack Burden, thinking of Anne Stanton going up to her room to delight, as he was delighting, in the sensation of discovering that one is in love, evokes the image of a metamorphosis invisibly in process beneath an outward appearance of stillness, inside a chrysalis as hard and quiet as the funerary stone effigy of Willie Stark: "Maybe she went up there to be alone, absorbed in herself the way a child is absorbed in watching a *cocoon* gradually part in the dusk to divulge the beautiful moth" (281–82; emphasis added).

Can *All the King's Men* be read as Jack Burden's attempt to solve the riddle of Willie Stark's wink, that paternal text whose only clear message is its absence of meaning? Yes, to the extent that what Jack learns in the course of the novel is not only the reality of the interrelatedness of things—that, as Cass Mastern had already learned, the world is "an enormous spider web" (188)—but that reality itself arises from that interrelatedness: "that the reality of an event, which is not real in itself, arises from other events which, likewise, in themselves are not real." For that is what Willie prepares Jack to learn, by forcing him to read the text he gave him with neither authorial nor parental guidance, by making him realize he could never know for sure if the text had been real. What Jack learns is that that particular reality can never be known, nor even come into existence, except in its relation to other events whose own reality may be in doubt. What Willie does is make Jack become a stereoscopic reader of a literally one-eyed text, force him to learn to read the reality that arises from the juxtaposition of images and events. Hence the recurrence of superimposed double images in the text. Hence, too, that curious remark Jack makes to Tiny Duffy as the end of the story, when he knows about all there is to know: "My name is Jack and I'm the wild jack and *I'm not one-eyed*" (414; emphasis added).

This may also account for the action of the other character in the novel who is equipped with a kind of stereoscopic vision, Lucy Stark, who has a real stereoscope, the kind with cards, which Jack does not fail to notice on more than one visit (333, 335, 373). She adopts Sibyl Frey's baby in the firm belief that it is Tom Stark's, even though she is aware that Sibyl had had intercourse with other men besides her son and that its paternity is by no means assured. It is, in fact, like the nature of the wink, unknowable. Secure in that faith, she names the baby Willie Stark, and when she gives it to Jack to hold, his response to the touch of the child suggests that even he, perhaps without realizing it, sees in it something of the Humpty Dumpty heritage of a Willie Stark creation: "I hefted him, while I carefully tried to keep him from falling apart" (426).

Both Lucy and Jack have a kind of stereoscopic view; they read an uncertain paternal text with both a certain faith and a certain ability to see one image superimposed upon another. Lucy's certainty is partly based on her ability to perceive a superimposed image that no one else can see.

> "It looks like Tom," she said. "Don't you think so?"
> Then before I could get an answer ready that wouldn't be too horrendous a lie, she went on, "But that's silly to ask you. You wouldn't know. I mean he looks like Tom when he was a baby.... I know it's Tom," she declared fiercely to me, "it's got to be Tom's, it looks like him." (427)

" 'I named him for Willie because ... Willie was a great man.... You see, Jack,' she said, 'I have to believe that' " (426–27). Burden will tell us that he had to believe it too. But at the same time he tells us that, in the end, there is nothing left of Willie Stark but *a wink:* "I must believe that Willie Stark was a great man. What happened to his greatness is not the question.... Perhaps he piled up his greatness and burnt it in one great blaze in the dark like a bonfire and then there wasn't anything but dark and the embers winking" (427).

Cass Mastern, too, had a vision of the nothingness that is left when a father dies. Jonathan Baumbach convincingly demonstrates that it was his father:

> Since Duncan Trice, who is considerably older than Cass, initiates him into vice, he is, in effect, the father of Cass's adultery with Annabelle. What Cass has learned from Duncan he had put into practice with Duncan's wife. Therefore, Cass's crime, Warren suggests, is implicitly incestuous, for if Duncan, the man whose death he effects, is his "substitute" father, Annabelle as his wife is a sort of symbolic mother. This is essentially what Cass understands when he proclaims himself " 'the chief of sinners and a plague spot on the body of the human world.' " (139)

To this it could be added that Annabelle, too, is significantly older than Mastern, and that she takes care to emphasize that age difference when she begins her seduction: " 'Seven years ago you were a child, Mr. Mastern. . . . But I wasn't a child.' " (168) Her name as well shows how the Mastern story could be projected onto the plot of *All the King's Men:* Annabelle née Puckett becomes both Anne "Annabel" (as the Poe allusions confirm) Stanton and the Sadie once attached to a Puckett—both of whom were Stark's mistresses, while Duncan becomes Stark and Cass becomes Jack, who loved Anne and made futile passes at Sadie and felt he had caused the death of Willie Stark.[7] So the vision Cass suddenly has as he is carrying Duncan's coffin has a powerful resonance in a Warrenian context:

> The coffin which I carried seemed to have no weight, although my friend had been of large frame and had inclined to stoutness. As we proceeded with it, I marvelled at the fact of its lightness, and once the fancy flitted into my mind that he was not in the coffin at all, that it was empty, and that all the affair was a masquerade or mock show carried to ludicrous and blasphemous length, for no purpose, as in a dream. . . . I had the impulse to hurl the coffin to the ground and see its emptiness burst open. . . . (172)

Cass Mastern's impulsive desire anticipates, in an illustratively grotesque and graphic way, the yearning Warren was later to express in "I am Dreaming of a White Christmas . . . ," to open the package to which the parent denies access, and suggests that what it contains may be the dead, but missing, father.[8] But it would be premature, at this stage, to say we now know "What present there was in that package for me. . . ." For there is still more to discover in the logic of the dream.[9]

Chapter 4
The View from the Attic

The Circus in the Attic and Other Stories, 1947

"*The Circus in the Attic*" The story chronicles the life of Bolton Lovehart (b. 1880), of Bardsville, Tennessee, son of a Confederate veteran who died when Bolton was a boy and of a monstrously overprotective and hypochondriacal mother. At sixteen, Bolton briefly escapes to a circus and later finds solace in a miniature circus he spends most of his life constructing in the attic. His mother's supposed heart condition (she dies of it, but not until she's eighty-seven) has kept him from attending college; well-instructed in high-school Greek, he runs Professor Darter's prep school for a while and courts his daughter Sara, who abruptly leaves town for a better life after seducing him on her late father's sofa. In the eyes of the community, Bolton is a promising young writer engaged in writing a history of the county, but this is just a cover for his devotion to the attic circus. In middle age he marries Mrs. Parton, a widow, and inherits a son, Jasper, who dies in World War II. Bolton donates his circus to be broken up and sold to raise money for the Red Cross ("The death of Jasper had brought the secret circus out into the world to live, to be enjoyed, to be used and broken in the end"). His wife dies in a car accident in the company of a Captain Cartwright; they had both been drinking. The story of Bolton Lovehart is preceded by the accounts of the ignominious but locally mythologized deaths of Cash Perkins and Seth Sykes, who supposedly defended the town against Union invaders in 1861.

"*Blackberry Winter*" The narrator, Seth, a young boy on a farm in middle Tennessee, goes outside barefoot during a cold spell in June even though his mother tells him not to. A tramp approaches the house wearing inappropriately urban clothes and carrying a newspaper-wrapped parcel. The mother gives him some work to do; the boy goes out to the creek to inspect the damage from the recent flood. There he finds his father, who lifts Seth up onto the saddle of his horse so he can see better. After that Seth goes to visit his black playmate, Little Jebb, but Jebb's mother, Dellie, is ill and slaps her son for making too much noise playing with Seth near her bed. Seth goes to talk to Old Jebb, who suggests that it's too late for blackberry winter and that the weather is so cold because the earth is tired of feeding sinful men. Seth returns home, where his father is telling the tramp that he has no more work for him and can only pay him for half a day. Angered, the stranger spits near the father's boot; had he spit closer, there would have been trouble. As the tramp walks away, the boy follows him until he threatens to cut his throat if he doesn't stop. In an epilogue, the narrator says that his parents have since died, Little Jebb is in the penitentiary, Dellie has passed away, but Old Jebb is probably over a hundred and still living. Recalling the threat the stranger had made to him, the narrator says, "But I did follow him, all the years."

"When the Light Gets Green"   A brief sketch about the narrator's grandfather on the family's tobacco farm in 1914. He used to tell the boy stories about his experiences in the Civil War. The title refers to the way the sky looks just before it is going to hail; it looked that way, and then hailed, just before the grandfather collapsed and had to be dragged into bed. He thought he was going to die and said so, and that nobody loved him, to the narrator, who replied, " 'Grandpa, I love you' . . . knowing all of a sudden it was a lie, because I didn't feel anything." He didn't die until four years later, when the narrator no longer lived there—"and it didn't matter much."

"Christmas Gift"   Ten-year-old Sill Alley shows up at a small town's general store one wintry day to ask where the doctor lives, because his half-sister's going to have a baby. As the son of Milt Alley, described in "Blackberry Winter" as "poor white trash," he is the object of some sarcastic remarks made by the men lounging in the store but is defended by the proprietor, who offers him some red-striped candy as he leaves. He finds the doctor's house, and in the buggy on the way back home Dr. Small rolls a cigarette and then passes the tobacco and paper to the boy, who reciprocates with half a stick of candy.

"Goodwood Comes Back"   The narrator reminisces about Luke Goodwood, a local boy whose major league pitching career was cut short by his love of drink. The title is somewhat ironic, as it was originally a newspaper headline announcing his short-lived return to the majors; Goodwood had to come back to his hometown because the comeback cited in the headline never occurred. The narrator had played baseball with Goodwood when they were boys, but didn't like catching because of the danger of getting hit in the head with the bat; they used to go hunting together too. He had admired Goodwood's earthier approach to life. On his return, the former pitcher is the object of pity from the men lounging about the blacksmith shop, but accurately throws a rock at a distant telephone pole to show he still has control. He eventually meets a violent end in a domestic dispute.

"The Patented Gate and the Mean Hamburger"   In Cobb County, Tennessee, Jeff York, about fifty, has broken the curse of his Appalachian ancestry and managed to put together, piece by piece, a decent farm of sixty acres. He is especially proud of his patented gate, which can be opened without getting off one's horse. On market Saturdays in town, he treats his young wife and children to the hamburgers they delight in at Slick Hardin's Dew Drop Inn Diner. When Hardin jokes to Mrs. York that anyone who likes hamburgers as much as she ought to own her own hamburger stand, she takes him seriously. In fact, he does want to sell out, and within two weeks she has gotten her husband, we do not exactly know how, to sell the farm in order to buy the diner. He helps her get it set up, gives it a fresh coat of paint, and is later found dead—hanging from his patented gate.

"A Christian Education" Jim Nabb, a well-to-do farmer, has two sons. The older one, Silas, is retarded. His parents have given him "a Christian education," teaching him to turn the other cheek. The other boys give him lots of provocation, but it isn't until they are in a rowboat on a Sunday school picnic that Silas finally strikes back, with a pocketknife. In the ensuing struggle, Silas falls out of the boat and is drowned. The narrator, a good swimmer, might have been able to save him, but is unable to react. Later, the men row back out so he can try to find the body, but he can't. The younger son, Alec, grows up without being taught to turn the other cheek, and winds up in the penitentiary at age twenty-two for killing a man.

"The Love of Elsie Barton: A Chronicle" In Charlestown, Tennessee, Elsie Barton is now a withered old woman who lives alone in the house where she was born, eating her supper out of cans. She has a daughter, Helen, who was a beauty (and will reappear in "Testament of Flood") but moved away from town. When she was young, Elsie had been seduced on a drive in the country by Benjamin Beaumont, a tobacco buyer from Kentucky. She became pregnant, so they married at Christmas and went away to his father's farm, where she had the baby away from the prying eyes of her hometown. Beaumont later died in the company of liquor and fast women in a Nashville hotel.

"Testament of Flood" The title refers to Elsie Barton, who "was like those bits of straw or trash lodged innocently in the branches of creek-bottom sycamores as testament of long-subsided spring flood—a sort of high water mark of passion in the community." The story is told from the point of view of Steve Adams (possibly the son of the Thomas Adams who unsuccessfully courted Elsie in the previous story), who has a crush on his fellow high-school student Helen Beaumont. Helen, however, is being courted by Frank Barber, who is older and has a car.

"The Confession of Brother Grimes" This story is an elaborate joke. Brother Grimes is a preacher who spends a number of sermons trying to justify the ways of God to man after the tragic automobile accident in which his daughter died. Her husband, Archie Munn, was driving, drunk, and at fault—as he had been in many car wrecks before this one. Munn survived,

but Grimes's wife died soon afterward, even though she hadn't been in the accident. After preaching at her funeral, Grimes didn't come out of his house for weeks; when he finally did, his black hair had turned white. He sermonized that all had been for the best, since Archie had reformed. But subsequently Archie kills two more victims by running into a horse-drawn wagon and is sentenced to the penitentiary. In his next sermon, Brother Grimes says that it was all his own fault, divine punishment for the sin he must now finally confess, that of having dyed his hair black all these years.

"Her Own People" Mr. and Mrs. Allen's black maid, Viola, whom they have brought up to Tennessee from Alabama, quits just as they are getting ready for a party. To make matters worse, in order to get more money from Mrs. Allen, Viola claims that a black couple, Jake and his wife, Josie, are charging her more for her board than in fact they are. Mrs. Allen fires Viola and tells her to go back to "her own people" in Alabama, but she refuses to get up from her bed at Jake and Josie's.

"The Life and Work of Professor Roy Millen" Life had never been easy for Roy Millen; he had worked at many unpleasant jobs before getting a college professorship, and that only through marrying the department chairman's daughter, who has recently died after a long illness. When student Tom Howell comes to his office for a letter of recommendation for a scholarship for France, Millen at first says he will write him a good one, and after the boy leaves begins to dictate it to his secretary. But, jealous of the student's easy grace and good fortune, he breaks off the dictation and later writes a negative letter in his own hand.

"The Unvexed Isles" Professor George Dalrymple and his wife, Alice, are having a drink at their home with Phil Alburt, one of his students, just before the Christmas break. Phil, evidently from a wealthy family, is going to Bermuda, the "unvexed isles"; Alice would like to spend Christmas with her well-to-do Baltimore parents, but Dalrymple is too poor to afford the train fare and plans to spend the time getting up a note on Chaucer. George notices that Phil's cigarette bears lipstick stains—Alice's. Dalrymple, whose origins are humble—he comes from a Nebraska dirt farm—will never advance beyond this "sad, pretentious little college" in Illinois.

"Prime Leaf" This story begins with the visit of Mr. Wiedenmeyer, a tobacco buyer, to the farm of Joseph Hardin and his son Thomas; also present are Thomas's wife, Edith, and son Tommy, as well as Tommy's black playmate, Alec. The Hardins have joined the tobacco association and tell Wiedenmeyer that he will have to buy from the association. Mr. Hardin brings down a chicken hawk after Tommy tries a shot and misses. That winter Joseph Hardin tells his son he's getting out of the association because he objects to what the night riders within it—particularly Bill Hopkins—are doing. He argues with his son, telling him that if he disagrees he ought to become a night rider himself. Thomas changes his mind and decides to join his father in leaving the association and selling their crop privately. Then their barn is burned. Thomas cuts across a field to ambush the night riders and shoots Hopkins off his horse. Hardin telephones the sheriff to say that his son is coming into town to turn himself in. But on the way in someone shoots and kills him.

When Bolton Lovehart's father collapsed from a fatal stroke on the brick walk in front of his house, Bolton's mother saw him fall and ran to him uttering "wild cries of anguish that might have been wild cries of triumph . . . for no one knows the meaning of the cry of passion he utters until the flesh of the passion is long since withered away to show the austere, logical articulation of fact with fact in the skeleton of Time" (28). This image of Time's skeletal articulation of fact with fact itself has a long afterlife in Warren's oeuvre, reappearing some thirty-five years later in "Youthful Picnic Long Ago: Sad Ballad on Box" (*New and Selected Poems: 1923–1985*). The voice of a girl strumming a guitar by a Tennessee campfire "confirmed the sweet sadness / Young hearts gave us no right to. / / No right to, yet. Though some day would, / As Time unveiled, / In its own dancing parody of grace, / The bony essence of each joke on joke." In that poem what Time would reveal was some genuine grief to incarnate the sadness the girl named in her song but had not yet experienced: the name exists before the thing it names. Within the sequence in which the poem appears (*Altitudes and Extensions*), the contiguity of this poem with the immediately preceding "Winter Wheat: Oklahoma" reveals even more. There a grieving widower wonders "How flesh would peel off cheekbones in earth out yonder" in her grave, while in "Youthful Picnic," the poet, having first spoken of how Time unveils the "bony essence," then thinks of the youthful singer who may well be dead by now, and wishes he could once more see "Flame reveal the grave cheek-curve. . . ." The echo in "Youthful Picnic" between what flame can no longer reveal and what Time will inevitably unveil is thus itself an echo of the cheekbones that peeling flesh could show in the poem just before—could show, that is, if one could see into what cannot decently be opened.

To read one poem through the one alongside it in the sequence, which may be a larger poem, might also be to look where one shouldn't; but it is a risk worth taking.[1] In "History during Nocturnal Snowfall," the poem immediately after "Youthful Picnic," the pulse and wrist that belonged to the youthful strummer—"delicate / Was the melancholy that swelled each heart, and timed / The pulse in wrist, and wrist, and wrist"—now belong to the woman sleeping beside the poet with whose heartbeat he seeks to match his own: "I reach a finger laid light / To a wrist that does not move . . . / And wonder if I might devise the clever trick / Of making heartbeat with heartbeat synchronize." In both poems the poet attentively listens to a woman's beating pulse, timing it, and thereby encouraging the reader to do the same, to "synchronize" the two poems lying side by side in the sequence of the text. That way we might learn something about Time and what it can eventually reveal.

One thing revealed by the passage of time between the original appearance of "History During Noctural Snowfall" in the Fall 1983 number of the *Sewanee Review* and its 1985 reappearance in *New and Selected Poems* is that the poem has undergone two changes that make it better able to synchronize with its neighbor in the sequence. Originally its first line had read, "Dark in the cubicle curtained from snow-darkness of night," but later *curtained* becomes *boxed,* so that it echoes the subtitle of "Youthful Picnic Long Ago: Sad Ballad on *Box*"—the box being the instrument on which the fireside singer played her pulsing beat with fingers and wrist, "in their delicate dance / On the strings of the box." The other revision changes "In the synchronized rhythm of heart, *or lungs*" to "the synchronized rhythm of heart, *and heart,*" with the result that the line is more closely aligned to the repetitive "pulse in wrist, and wrist, and wrist" that throb in the poem just before.

"Could one guess the other's buried narrative?" the poet asks when he puts his finger to that wrist. In light of what lies buried in these poems, in a series of connected echoes leading back to what is in fact buried in "Winter Wheat," one might well wonder if some buried narrative lies hidden in the sequence, too—especially in light of these poems' tendency to name, perhaps surreptitiously, what it is they are collectively doing (synchronizing pulse-beats, for example). There is, as the narrator of "The Circus in the Attic" suggests, a certain logical articulation of fact with fact, of detail with detail (of a cheekbone in a grave with a grave cheek-curve), that comes to light only after the warmth of the original expression has died away. Such a suggestion is of a piece with Jack Burden's insight that "the reality of an event ... arises from other events which, likewise, in themselves are not real," and with Warren's own idea that "poetry does not inhere in any particular element but depends upon the set of relationships, the structure, which we call the poem." It depends on what we call the poem—the individual poem in a sequence or the sequence itself.

All these observations are particularly relevant to the short-story collection *The Circus in the Attic,* which resembles Warren's poetic sequences in that it is made up of texts that already have separate claims on the reader's attention. And there are, as I hope to demonstrate here, enough connections of detail with detail among these stories to conclude that this collection may also make such a claim. Furthermore, just as the poems can speak, in evidently self-referential terms, of the synchronization they actually enact, so can a statement, like the one in the title story about how time eventually reveals the "logical articulation of fact with fact," speak beyond its immediate context (the wild cries of Bolton Lovehart's mother) to address what may happen when this story is placed alongside "Blackberry Winter" and the other twelve.

Indeed, the word *articulation* in itself speaks a great deal. Its double sense of "utterance" and "jointed connection" articulates (in both senses) the linkage between enunciation and connection, between passionate expression and dispassionate analysis of skeletal connections in the text. I could start by pointing to a connection, the same story in this instance, between this word and the toy circus to which its title alludes. Bolton Lovehart spends his life assembling the circus in secret. He is supposed to be writing a book of local history, a project that merely serves as a cover for his real passion. When the paints for his carved wooden animals arrive, for instance, he tells his mother they are for a multicolor county map; when people pass by the house late at night and see his attic light burning they marvel at his authorial industry. The circus is Bolton's escape from responsibility and the meshes of an overpossessive mother as well as a substitute for the actual circus he tried to run away to as a child.

Though assembling the toy circus is presented as what Bolton does when he is supposed to be writing a book, given more of the context of the story, it could be read as a kind of writing, in particular as writing a history of the county. It is when the narrator gives us a glimpse of that history that we see just how close Bolton's attic perspective comes to capturing the spirit of the place. On 16 December 1861, "Bardsville had its home guard, a few middle-aged men and a rag-tag-and-bobtail of young boys who could ride *like circus performers* and shoot anything that would hold powder and to whom the war was a gaudy picnic that their tyrannous mothers would not let them attend" (6; emphasis added). Bolton could have done worse than to have debunked local mythology and portrayed the mock heroics of the town's defenders as the circus stunts they were. Thanks to the narrator's manipulation of events, to the way he allows us to see the resemblance between the home guards and the circus Bolton ran away to join, Lovehart almost seems to be doing that, though it would never occur to us that he intended his toy circus to be read as a revisionist reading of history. His circus is something more like a cry of passion, a way of bolting—as his first name suggests—the attic door against a domineering mother ("nobody knew what went on up there, behind the always bolted door" [41]).

It is in the connection of Bolton's circus pastime with other facts of the story that the skeletal, structural logic of the narrative emerges. It was on the near-anniversary of the battle of Bardsville—"One day in middle December" (40)—that Bolton had passed by the local hardware store and seen the model circus that was to inspire his efforts. He would not have grasped the irony of this fact, but we can, and we can see, too, that in playing with his model men and animals he is rehearsing, not only the circus antics of his father's generation that gave them the illusion of escape from their mothers, but also the ludic manipulation exercised by that same maternal tyranny. For Lovehart also bears a resemblance to his trapeze artists and ringmaster and cleverly constructed elephants with jointed—that is to say, *articulated*—legs ("He had managed, after two weeks of experiment and effort, to make legs that would bend" [41]). For his mother is said to have created and governed him, possessing him "with a thousand invisible threads controlling the slightest movement of his limbs and lips and spirit like a clever puppet" (16).

Like "History During Nocturnal Snowfall," these stories already come to us at some remove from their first appearance, some distance along on that passage of time that leads from one kind of articulation to another; all appeared earlier, separately, in print (listed in Grimshaw, 228–30). An author's note hints that in one sense the book is a new creation and not merely a reprinting, for the order of the stories no longer coincides with that of their first appearance: "The earliest story in this book was written in 1930, the latest in 1946, but the order here is not chronological" (i).[2] Given that Warren's poems (though from a later date than *Circus*) can acquire new meaning through the order in which they appear, and this is especially true with contiguous poems, an incident in "Blackberry Winter" takes on a certain tinge of irony when we discover that we have already seen its ghostly inversion in the immediately preceding story—if we read the stories in their sequence in the book. The boy Seth has wandered out to gaze at the flooded creek. Among the crowd of onlookers he sees his father on horseback.

> the first thing that happened was, I remember, the warm feeling I always had when I saw him up on a horse. . . . I heard his voice calling, "Seth!" . . . I did not look up at my father until I was almost within touching distance of his heel. Then I looked up and tried to read his face, to see if he was angry about my being barefoot. Before I could decide anything from that impassive, high-boned face, he had leaned over and reached a hand to me. "Grab on," he commanded. (73–74)

Whatever misgivings the boy will have about the unseasonably cool weather or the tramp with the knife or the way Dellie slaps her son, his father will remain an undiminished source of confidence and love. He won't be angry, as Seth's mother was, about the bare feet. " 'You can see better up here,' " he will say when he swings the boy up to the saddle. But the reader who can recall a strangely similar event in "The Circus in the Attic" will not so easily share this faith in a father's affection, for he or she will have remembered what happened to another Seth when he approached a man on a horse. Though a monument was erected to his memory, Seth Sykes did not exactly die a hero's death in the battle of Bardsville. He was simply objecting to the Union cavalry's expropriation of his corn.

> Seth Sykes came on and the troopers watched him. He grabbed the lieutenant's near leg, the left leg, and shouted, "Hit is my cawn!"
> The lieutenant leaned over and struck him about the head with his gauntleted fist. The horse shied and the lieutenant almost reeled from the saddle.
> But the nearest trooper was on them now. He leaned from his saddle, seized Seth Sykes by the long, uncombed, matted hair, jerked his head back, and carefully put the muzzle of a pistol against the head, just above the ear, and pulled the trigger. (11)

It is the small details that are troubling. The father "had leaned over and reached a hand"; the lieutenant "leaned over and struck ... with his ... fist." Seth Sykes had grabbed the lieutenant's leg; the younger Seth gauges how close he had come to his father by the fact that he was "almost within touching distance of his heel." And then, of course, there is the fact of the name: Although we are at the midpoint of the story, it is only when the boy hears his father's voice calling "Seth!" that we learn his name; in fact, the name never reappears in "Blackberry Winter"—almost as if the boy were fully Seth only at the moment he and his father repeat those gestures of the Seth Sykes's martyrdom.

Now as it happens, Seth's namesake in the other story, the unfortunate Sykes, appears only in the version printed in the book, for the shorter version of "Circus" in the September 1947 issue of *Cosmopolitan* omits about four thousand words (18 percent) of the text, including the entire Seth Sykes episode (pp. 4–12 in the book). It is less likely that the Sykes anecdote was added to the book version than restored there, for the magazine text repeats the story's later mention of the Sykes monument (*Cosmopolitan*, 83; *Circus*, 42) in a way that really makes no sense (since it assumes an acquaintance with Sykes that the reader could not have had) and cannot be accounted for except as a slip on the part of whoever— editor or author—shortened the story to make it conform to magazine length. Nevertheless, the presence of this episode in the book makes the experience of reading the first two stories in the collection a rather different one from that of reading them separately in their first published version. And so to the two ways the fullness of time brings new meaning to light— recurring details and the order of the stories—we can add a third: textual differences between their separate and later collective appearance.

Many of these differences are relatively minor. Elizabeth Beaumont, in "The Love of Elsie Barton: A Chronicle," becomes Helen Beaumont (her original name in the earliest, though unpublished, version of the story, the untitled novel Warren wrote in 1933–34), with the result that the continuity between this story and its immediate successor in the collection, "Testament of Flood," where Helen Beaumont also appears, is assured. Sill Alley, the boy in "Christmas Gift" who goes to fetch the doctor for his pregnant half-sister and who is "one of Milt Alley's kids" (98), was Sill Lancaster when the story appeared in 1937.[3] Milt Alley owned the cow that drowned in the flooded creek in "Blackberry Winter," and a boy who asks if it might be edible was "the kind of boy who might just as well as not have been the son of Milt Alley" (76); this change of name thus draws the two stories into closer orbit.

The telltale presence of the monument to Seth Sykes in the magazine version that otherwise omits all mention of his name suggests that he had been there all along, like Sara Darter's seduction of Bolton Lovehart in the same story, which, once she performed it, "seemed like something which had always had its existence, waiting not for her doing but for her recognition. It was done, but it had always existed, even before her doing" (36–37). The intriguing thing about the aptness of these words is that they, together with the seduction scene itself, are also missing from the magazine version of the story. By contrast to the change of names in "Elsie Barton" and "Christmas Gift," both the execution of Sykes and the seduction of Lovehart promise to be rather more meaningful revisions, for what happened to Sykes can change the way we read "Blackberry Winter," and what Sara Darter did may somewhat alter our picture of Bolton (at least he had *one* sexual experience in his youth, though he still cuts the figure of a man easily manipulated by a woman, whether it be Sara or his mother). A greater significance, however, may lie in what connection that missing seduction scene may have with other stories in the volume. For if the Sykes episode is any indication, passages missing in the magazine versions but present in the book may serve to alert us to ways in which the book functions on its own as a unified work of art—how, to quote from still another missing yet now self-referential passage, it "slowly achieved its perfect form, like a crystal growing, according to its ineluctable pattern" (147). What such statements as this and the one cited earlier in this paragraph, themselves present only in the book, hint at is that the stories in their first appearance already contained within them the inner logic of these episodes and their accompanying imagery, and that their later "crystallization" in the book was nothing more than a drawing out, or recognition, of what was already there in that ineluctable pattern.

Sara's seduction of Bolton Lovehart falls into this category, for when her submerged desire breaks the surface it takes the form of a striking image that will have resonance later in the book:

> That last encounter with him had not been part of the plan. Or if it was a part, it was a part that had not showed itself above the surface of the stream, where the trivial debris and drift moiled and spun in the light, but wallowed in the dark central depth of the current, like an old log, black and waterlogged, sucked up from the mud, and borne in secret to the rock-tossed, rapid narrows where the waters boiled over with a last fury into the placid reaches below, and wherein that final, funneled rush the unwieldy inner burden heaved and lunged upward, black, blunt, big, and dripping. . . . (36)

Given Bolton's almost feminine passivity,[4] it is perhaps appropriate that his only sexual partner (until he marries a widow at age fifty-nine) should evoke such usually masculine imagery, her desire expressing itself in the symbol of a big, blunt, dripping log. When it heaves and lunges upward out of chthonic darkness, it is almost as if Sara Darter, not Bolton Lovehart, were the one equipped with male apparatus.

It is curious that the first-person narrator of another story in the collection, "Goodwood Comes Back," who is also in certain respects depicted as feminine and passive, should be frightened and feel endangered by an object resembling that phallic, blunt, and menacing log. That story opens with Luke Goodwood pitching and the narrator catching but afraid to stand very close to home plate "on account of the boys flinging the bat the way they did when they started off for first base" (109). His fear is not ungrounded; he does get hit in the head with the bat, and Goodwood, whose surname has the virtue of calling our attention once again to the strength of ligneous imagery, takes away his catcher's mitt and sends him to the outfield. Other details in that story reinforce the masculinity of Goodwood and the femininity of the narrator. The "Goodwood house was a man's house," with hunting coats and flyrods and shotguns scattered even on the bed and the six men outnumbering the women, keeping them "going back and forth to the kitchen with sweat on their faces and their hair damp from the stove" (109). The narrator's house was just the opposite: "At my house everything was different, for men there always seemed to be just visiting" (110).

Later, when he has grown up and come back to town to visit, the narrator stays at another woman's house, his sister's, and on one occasion again assumes a passive and receptive role. He sees Luke Goodwood coming up the street and stopping to chat with some workmen installing a culvert just in front of the house. Instead of coming out to greet his childhood friend, the narrator chooses to hide and listen: "there were still enough leaves on the vine on my sister's porch to hide me from the street, but I could hear every word they said" (114).

Now the roles that vines play in three other stories in *The Circus in the Attic* enlarge upon the femininity attached to them here: in one, they do precisely what they do in "Goodwood," provide a feminine house with a protective screen; in the other two, they take up the woman's side in the battle of the sexes, playing the part of entwining and endangering parasites to masculine wood. In "The Love of Elsie Barton," passersby "would know that Miss Elsie was sitting on her porch behind the screen of moonvine. What she did behind the moonvine or in the house, they didn't know or think about" (143). A passage present only in the book reinforces the feminine associations of these porch vines, showing us Elsie's daughter Helen leaving a boy standing at the gate to go in and "join her mother behind the moonvine" (145). In a passage in "The Circus in the Attic" present only in the book, a "single scrofulous cedar, weathering to earth" above the house that was once Seth Sykes's is depicted as "surrendering to the clawing hands of vine and briar" (4), and in a parallel scene on the next page the monument itself to Sykes is obscured by vines ("If you tear away the love vine . . . you can read the words" [5]). One is reminded of the "thousand invisible threads" with which Bolton Lovehart's mother controlled his slightest movement like a puppeteer (16). In "The Patented Gate and the Mean Hamburger," Jeff York is proleptically described on the first page as having wrists that "hang out from the sleeves of the coat, the tendons showing along the bone like the dry twist of grapevine still corded on the stove-length of a hickory sapling" (120)—proleptically, because York, whose face resembles the wood of the weathering and vine-affected tree next to Sykes's house to the extent that it looked like "a piece of hewed cedar which had been left in the weather" (120), was yoked to a wife whose emblematic coat had "a scrap of fur at the collar which looked like some tattered growth of fungus feeding on old wood" (124). The rope around York's neck at the end of the story is, on a metaphorical level, the crystallization of an inner logic present from the beginning, whether we first see it in the parasitical, wood-devouring collar his wife wore or in the combination of twisted vine and sapling to be found in his own wrists.

Luke Goodwood made it to the major leagues as a pitcher, but love of liquor shortened his career, and when he returned to town he seemed a shadow of his former self. "I noticed Luke's arms had got pretty *stringy*," the narrator observes (113; emphasis added), echoing the description of Bolton Lovehart's feeble appearance when he tried to apply for work with the circus: " 'You don't look stout,' the old man said, eyeing the *stringy*, tallish boy with the perspicacity and contempt of a horse trader inspecting an inferior animal" (25; emphasis added). Despite his weakened state, Goodwood demonstrates that he still has control, if not strength, by scooping up a rock and throwing it square at a distant telephone pole (114). That pole, of the same general shape as the bat that used to strike the ball for which this rock is a substitute, as well as the blunt log that stands for Sara Darter's sexual drive when she has her way with Bolton Lovehart, reappears a few stories later, in "The Confession of Brother Grimes." That story begins with a man driving his car into the rear of a parked truck that had "a pole sticking out behind," thereby killing his wife, the pole going through her "like the toothpick through a club sandwich" (170).

Thus, in the way that certain objects in these stories have of reemerging in other stories, the surfacing log that gave Sara Darter the power to attack Bolton Lovehart becomes the bat that frightens the narrator of "Goodwood Comes Back," which becomes a telephone pole later in the same story. The pole in "The Confession of Brother Grimes" does its deadly work in an automobile accident that, except for the pole, is a duplicate of the one near the end of "The Circus in the Attic" that killed Bolton Lovehart's wife. Her adulterous lover had been at the wheel, and "had driven at high speed into the back of a heavy truck parked on the shoulder of the highway" (60); in "The Confession of Brother Grimes," Archie Munn drove his "new Ford coupe through the back end of a parked truck that didn't have any lights on" (170).

It is thus in light of these logs and poles (including the one that functioned like a toothpick) that we might read the way Elsie Barton "stuck the needle neatly into the white cambric she had been sewing" (155) as she accepted Benjamin Beaumont's invitation to go for a ride in the country. For what is about to happen is another seduction scene, and though Beaumont believed himself to be the seducer, Miss Barton knows what she is doing. And when it is over, something in the way she so casually stops on the porch to pick up her sewing before disappearing into the house, "which under ordinary circumstances would have been so natural, seemed to be a monstrous attack upon himself" (158). It is no longer so clear to him who is in charge. Given what we have, by this point in the book, already read about how Sara Darter's lust could take the form of a lunging log, we might give the edge in this balance of power to Miss Barton, seeing in the thrust of her needle a sign of her exercise of the same power Sara displayed, and seeing in Beaumont's almost uncanny apprehension at her return to her sewing some confirmation of the significance of that gesture. If these stories were a dream, then Elsie's needle would form part of the chain of transforming symbols that include both Sara's log and the toothpick which the pole in the truck became. And if *The Circus in the Attic* is a dream, then it is possible to look for, in Freud's words, the repressed wish of which we have now seen the disguised fulfillment.

One plausible candidate can be found by returning to the title story. The death of Bolton's wife in that accident seems a kind of poetic justice in the context of his collection of stories where what Sara did to Bolton finally comes back in the form of a highway accident that is a stand-in for the one in a later story in which a woman is decisively penetrated by a log.[5] And a later addition to Elsie Barton's story tightens the resemblance between Elsie and Barton's seductress: "Her passivity, her silence which he could not force her to break, her acquiescence, her clenched hands thrusting him away after consummation, all in all, the undecipherable compound she presented to him left him always baffled and confused . . ." (159). For these clenched hands and this undecipherability echo a moment in "The Circus in the Attic" when Bolton Lovehart was unsuccessfully trying to woo Sara Darter (four pages before she counterattacked by surprising him on the couch): "Sara Darter wept often now, and Bolton tried to comfort her. But once when he put his arms around her and tried to kiss her, she struck him savagely on the chest, with clenched fists, and screamed at him with furious words which he could not interpret" (32). Four pages earlier, Bolton's mother had uttered similarly undecipherable words, the "wild cries of anguish that might have been wild cries of triumph"—the cries that the narrator tells us no one could know the meaning of until the flesh of passion had withered away to show the logical articulation of fact with fact in the skeleton of Time.

We have already seen how the mother's cries are emblematic of the way the story collection lends itself to a different kind of reading than do the stories by themselves. That they should be uttered by another character is emblematic as well, for certain other gestures persist from story to story, independently of the characters who perform them. Piecing together such repeated gestures (as well as repeated names, images, and even household objects) is part of the work of tracing the logical articulation of fact with fact. Allen Shepherd has observed of the title story that "Warren's structural-thematic technique is much like that in his novels: alternatives, opposites, and contraries are examined, arranged, and rearranged like pieces in a jigsaw puzzle" (11). The undecipherable cries that two characters independently speak in that story are a good example of this, but Shepherd's description is equally applicable to the whole collection.

One of the most striking of these reiterations grows out of the almost obsessive attention given to the mechanics of how many of the characters in these stories walk. The narrator's grandfather in "When the Light Gets Green" has such small hips and backside that when the boy notices them he says "I felt a tight feeling in my stomach like when you walk behind a woman and see the high heel of her shoe is worn and twisted and jerks her ankle every time she takes a step" (88). In "Her Own People" we actually see this twisted step in the gait of the black maid, Viola: "The Negro moved across the porch and into the house, her bowed legs setting the feet down on the boards with a sort of painful accuracy, so that the heels twisted over at each step" (185)[6]—so that one is tempted to continue the associative leap begun by the narrating grandson that linked his grandfather's legs to a woman's awkward heels, and to muse on what ironic connection there may be between that Confederate veteran and this descendant of the slaves he fought to keep.[7] But the associative network is larger than that; the way Viola was "setting the feet down" with "painful accuracy" can remind us of how the boy Bolton Lovehart walked, who "set his neat little booted feet . . . with the motion of prinking precision and appealing weakness" (16), or even of Luke Goodwood, who "looked to be setting his big feet always carefully on the ground" (110).

To make sense of all this we should return to the scene in "Blackberry Winter" where young Seth approached his equestrian father and dared not look up at him until he "was almost within touching distance of his heel." He was a little afraid of what his father's response would be (having already read the oddly parallel scene in "The Circus in the Attic," we might share that apprehension, for reasons of our own), and the reason for that fear had to do with his own feet: "Then I looked up and tried to read his face, to see if he was angry about my going barefoot." When "Blackberry Winter" began, the boy narrator was consumed by the desire to go shoeless: "I was standing on the hearth, almost into the chimney, hunched over the fire, working my bare toes slowly on the warm stone. I relished the heat which made the skin of my bare legs warp and creep and tingle, even as I called to my mother, who was somewhere back in the dining room or kitchen, and said: 'But it's June, I don't have to put them on!'" (63). It may be June, but it's also blackberry winter, or so his mother says. Seth gives us, if not his mother, a very specific justification for going barefoot:

> You do not understand that voice from back in the kitchen which says that you cannot go barefoot outdoors and run to see what has happened and rub your feet over the wet shivery grass and make the perfect mark of your foot in the smooth, creamy, red mud and then muse upon it as though you had suddenly come upon that single mark on the glistening auroral beach of the world. You have never seen a beach, but you have read the book and how the footprint was there. (64)

If Bolton Lovehart's circus was a kind of writing, all the more so is Seth's footprinted mark, which as soon as he makes it assumes writing's characteristic quality of appearing to have been made by someone else. This moment of defamiliarization, in which a mark made, a letter mailed, or a word spoken takes on an identity of its own divorced from its maker, as if someone else had made or written or said it, as if it were now a text in its own right, is repeated in other stories in this collection. In "When the Light Gets Green" the boy narrator tells his grandfather he loves him, "feeling like it hadn't been me said it, and knowing all of a sudden it was a lie, because I didn't feel anything" (95). He realizes he only said it because his grandfather had said he wanted to die because no one loved him. The boy seems to be realizing for the first time how it feels to make a fiction, a lie, to say certain words for the effect they have and not because he means them. His response to this realization is to go outside and do what Seth took pleasure in doing in the immediately preceding story—"rubbing my bare feet over the slick cold grass" (95)—thereby affirming the link that story had already made between this process of defamiliarization and bare feet.

One could take this a step further and explore the hypothesis that *The Circus in the Attic* seriously entertains a connection between walking and writing. One clue that points in this direction is what happens in "Goodwood Comes Back" when Goodwood is said "to be setting his big feet always carefully on the ground," for in the same paragraph the narrator also talks about the way Goodwood wrote: "The only good grades he made were in penmanship.... He could make his writing look exactly like the writing at the top of the page, a Spencerian hand tilted forward, but not too much like a woman's" (110). Writing too well, it appears, would run the risk of appearing feminine. It makes all too much sense: in the small-town culture of western Kentucky and Tennessee that is the setting for these stories, the kind of writing for which Goodwood's Spencerian penmanship is a metaphor is commonly perceived to be a womanly activity. Goodwood, for all his virile qualities, had both a womanly walk and an almost womanly handwriting. The combination appeared in Bolton Lovehart, too, for Bardsville's "most promising young writer" (an appelation earned for his desultory work on local history), when he was a boy, "set his neat little booted feet [down] with the motion of prinking precision and appealing weakness."

Helen Beaumont, who—in narrator Steve Adams's imagination—undergoes the same process of defamiliarization with an actual piece of writing that Seth experienced with the mark his foot made, is, obviously, a woman; less obvious, yet accessible to the reader who will track down a literary allusion, is the fact that the narrator of "Testament of Flood" sees her as a double of himself. Near the beginning of this short narrative, Steve Adams remembers something he never saw but "felt as if he had observed," Helen mailing a letter:

> So long as the letter remained between the fingers, it was intimate and part of herself. When the letter plunged into the black cavity and the lid clicked, the inscribed sentiments were abstracted, only connected with her being by a signature which he might recognize in precise backhand like the "Helen Beaumont" on her school papers. The letter with the signature "Helen" would no longer belong to her; it would belong to the world, to almost anybody.... (164)

The reference to a schoolroom signature recalls the association established in "Goodwood" between school penmanship and feminine writing; the abstracting of sentiments and the fact that the letter would no longer belong to its author recall the intentional forgetting by which Seth could pretend that his footprint had been made by someone else (in fact, by someone else in a book). At the close of the story the narrator undergoes a similar experience. Thinking of Helen Beaumont seated somewhere behind him in the classroom as he reads from a book about Webster's *The Duchess of Malfi*, he comes across the line "*Cover her face: mine eyes dazzle: she died young.* His lips, moving stiffly . . . formed the words. . . . Did he really speak the words out loud; he could never remember . . . [H]e discovered that he felt himself far away from her [from Helen], and much older . . ." (169). As Seth could look at the track in the mud and imagine it wasn't his and as Helen, in the narrator's postal fantasy, could write and mail a letter that was no longer hers, here that narrator, at the same time as he incorporates Webster's poetic line, can doubt whether he actually spoke the words or not. In the double context of the story and the play, the line yields two meanings. In the story it is preceded by the contextual note (from the book Steve Adams is reading) that these words are spoken "when the brother looks at the sister slain to avenge the family honor." Repeating the line with Helen in mind would then amount to a murderous wish on Steve's part—and getting even through writing does occur elsewhere in *The Circus in the Attic,* for the abstraction of sentiment the postal system affords makes it possible for the protagonist of "The Life and Work of Professor Roy Millen" to act out, with no apparent guilt, the hostile intent of a Bellerophontic letter. The plot there turns upon the professor's taking his revenge against a student's youth and good fortune by writing a damning letter of recommendation; mailing it would be the most casual of acts: "He would, he remembered, pass a postbox on his way home" (198).

The distance Steve Adams could now feel stretching between himself and Helen after he mouthed Webster's line—"in the resultant quietude he discovered that he felt himself far away from her, and much older"—seems to be achieved by making of her a text, sending her back in time to become the dead duchess. Like Webster's Ferdinand, who was angered because his sister had secretly married beneath her, Steve, frustrated in his desire for Helen because of her affair with Frank Barber, an older man,[8] wishes to make her inaccessible by giving her a literary death. That he is already at this point able to reduce life to literature is suggested by the way his eyes reduce a three-dimensional scene to a plane surface, through a window that takes on the two-dimensional quality of a page: "Beyond the window a man followed a plow, seeming in the false perspective rather to ascend the pane than retreat across the field toward the green haze of woods" (168).[9]

But the presence of that line from *The Duchess of Malfi* is susceptible of another interpretation, too, one that has a different sort of resonance with the earlier scene at the post office: The reason why Ferdinand's eyes dazzle and he wants his sister's face covered is, at least in part, that she died young, as the next lines he speaks make clear:

> She and I were twins:
> And should I die this instant, I had liv'd
> Her time to a minute.
> (4.2.267–69)

Ferdinand is sufficiently superstitious to imagine his twin sister's fate is linked to his. But in the context of "Testament of Flood" the possibility that Steve Adams might, by implication, be Helen's twin throws a new light on the earlier scene that cast Helen in the role of writer—or, rather, a familiar light, since it has already become apparent how the distancing effect Steve experiences at the end of the story parallels the one he imagines Helen undergoing when the letter that had been "part of herself" is abstracted into a text "only connected with her being by a signature." In acknowledging this twinship, if in fact that is what he is doing by quoting Ferdinand, the narrator affirms that Steve's transformation of Helen Beaumont into a text is not just the work of a reader but a writer. And to be a writer is to be, if not a woman, at least woman's twin.

When Seth makes his footprint in the mud of the auroral beach of the world in "Blackberry Winter," he is in fact rehearsing what will happen in the book in which his story appears; for when we see this barefoot print again (and the mud has dried to dust) it will appear as the mark of another, indeed, of a black companion like the Friday Seth was thinking of: "Alec devoted his attention to making elaborate and *perfect* footprints in which the dust outlined the creases of the skin and stood up beautifully in the spaces between his toes" (216; emphasis added). We might remember that Seth too had been interested in perfection: "and make the *perfect* mark of your foot. . . ." Alec is Tommy's black playmate in "Prime Leaf," a role analogous to that of Little Jebb in "Blackberry Winter," and a measure of the subtle precision of the structural connections underlying the *Circus* stories is a coincidence of names like the one of the two Seths that links Alec to Jebb through another Alec who bears a resemblance of his own to Jebb. "A Christian Education" concludes with a note on the fate of Silas Nabb's younger brother, who did not have to undergo Silas's "Christian education" (with its injunction to turn the other cheek): "Alec turned out to be a terror. . . . When he was about twenty-two he got in a row and shot a man with a .38. The man died. Alec is over in Nashville in the pen now, and I guess he'll be there a good long time" (142). "Blackberry Winter" closes with a remarkably similar epilogue: "As for Little Jebb, he grew up to be a mean and ficey Negro. He killed another Negro in a fight and got sent to the penitentiary, where he is yet, the last I heard tell" (86).

The hearth Seth had stood on in his bare feet before he went outside to make his footprint in the mud likewise reappears in "Testament of Flood," as that story's boy protagonist "crouched on the tile hearth and stared at the disintegrating embers. He heard his mother's voice from the next room" (166). The hearth also reappears in "Prime Leaf," where it is joined by some other significant details from "Blackberry Winter": a father on horseback and a son who tries, as Seth had tried, to read his father's thoughts by reading his impassive face. As Thomas Hardin, both a father (to the younger Tommy) and a son (to his father Joe Hardin), fixed his gaze on the family hearth, "his eyes stared into the depth of the embers like those of a man who sees something he desires but may not have. Then his wife laughed" (247). One thing he desires but cannot easily obtain—but which his father seems to possess—is his wife's admiration and love.

> "You and Papa are mighty different" [she says to her husband]. I don't know which one of you I like the best."
> "I know which one. It's him."
> "Maybe so, maybe you're right." And then she caught sight of her husband's face. "Why, Thomas! ... I do believe you're jealous of your own father. You ought to be spanked like Tommy."
> He turned and stared directly at her with the same look in his eyes as when he had been staring into the center of the fire. (247–48)

The immediately preceding story, "The Unvexed Isles," might have alerted us to expect a scene of jealousy around a fireplace. There, Professor Dalrymple had reason to be suspicious, for he happened to notice that the cigarette his student guest had laid on the ashtray was stained with lipstick. The young man had "a kind of aimless vitality that seemed to make the fire burn up brighter and the *bulbs* behind their parchment shades glow with more assurance" (200; emphasis added). Now, in "Testament of Flood," Steve Adams, whom we may presume to be the son of the Thomas Adams who unsuccessfully courted Elsie Barton in the immediately preceding "Love of Elsie Barton,"[10] had been consumed with desire for Elsie's daughter, Helen, thinking about her incessantly as they both sat in the schoolroom. As he did, stoking his desire for that which he could not have, he stared at the "swollen *bulb* of the stove" that glowed with heat. "At noon recess the older girls sat near the stove to eat their lunches. Heat flushed their cheeks and their voices harbored a subdued excitement" (165). In "The Love of Elsie Barton," when Elsie threw over Thomas Adams for Benjamin Beaumont, she would sit with her girlfriends as they teased her about him "with a secret, sweet thought in her head, like the piece of candy a child holds on its tongue and secretly sucks . . . and a little spot of color would glow in either of her cheeks" (153). Both of these girlish glows and groupings reaffirm what was already evident in the swollen bulb of the stove that glowed like their cheeks (from "red" to "tint of rose" as it cooled at the end of the schoolday [166])—the sexuality of their subdued excitement and his. Thus, the linkage of fire and glowing bulbs in the observation in "The Unvexed Isles" concerning the effects of the student's "aimless vitality" is no accident. All of this comes to a head in a remarkable scene involving the professor, his wife, the student, and the fireplace:

> Alice Dalrymple gave her gaze to the fire, where flames scrolled ornamentally upward to the black chimney throat. The brass dogs gleamed, the hearth was swept to a sharp border, the flames sprouted upwards like flowers from an accurate parterre. . . . Alice Dalrymple held her head at right angles to the young man's chair; her profile was clean and delicate, with a careful dyspeptic beauty. The young man himself was looking into the fire. (203)

Alice's posture allows us to see her in profile, and a closer look focuses on her throat: "When she laughs now she holds her head up so the skin won't sag in her neck. Craning her neck like that, she looks like a cigarette advertisement" (205). Her throat invites a cigarette, or nourishes the thought of one, as the "black chimney *throat*" of the fireplace draws the flame. The right angles of her pose, the clean look of her profile, and the "accurate modulation" of her laugh (205) from that throat recall, respectively, the "sharp border" and clean-swept look of the hearth and its appearance of being an "accurate" bed for sprouting flames. If Alice is the hearth, the student with his aimless vitality supplies the flame—as does the elder Mr. Hardin in "Prime Leaf" when he "got down to his knees and began to blow Edith's remnant of coals back to flame" (267). And it is with reason that the coals bear her name, for Edith is as closely connected to that hearth as Alice was to hers. When she sits at her fireplace, a sense of order prevails in the surrounding disorder, as if things were now in their right places; her robe falls to the hearth and almost makes her one with that hearth: "She . . . wore a blue flannel robe which dropped loosely from her shoulders to the stone of the hearth and crumpled there to give a strange impression of arrangement in the cold disorder of the room" (264).

The drama in "Prime Leaf" of the struggle between father and son is played out on the stage of that hearth. What is at issue is participation in or denunciation of the tobacco farmers' association's strategic shift from boycott to terror. The elder Mr. Hardin had resigned from the board of directors to protest this new direction and said he would leave the association itself the first time it burned a barn. When he does decide to leave, and to write his letter of resignation from the association—a moment in the story exactly parallel to Senator Tolliver's letter to the Tobacco Association in *Night Rider*—the first (and only, as it turns out) mark he makes with his pen on the letter has enormous resonance in the larger context of Warrenian narratives in which the relationship between a father and son is determined by what the father writes. Here, the text is a single line, and it obliterates the son: "Mr. Hardin got another sheet of paper from one of the pigeon-holes before him and laid it on the desk. Across the top of the sheet ran the business caption: *Cedardale—J. C. Hardin & Son—Tobacco Growers and Stock Breeders*. Carefully he drew a single line through the "& Son" of the caption, but he did not begin to write again" (258).

The day the younger Mr. Hardin had stared at his wife the way he stared at the fire, with the eyes of a man who sees something he desires but may not have, and the day his wife accuses him of being jealous of his own father, the senior Hardin arrives with the evening paper and its news of the night riders' burning three barns. The newspaper was in his pocket when the older man came in to sit by the fire opposite his son, "propped his stick against the stonework of the fireplace, and began filling his pipe." After the first few puffs, he takes out the paper and hands it to his son. Tom Hardin stares at the paper as intently as he had gazed into the fire, and when he turns a page, "the paper crackled sharply in the silence, like a new-lit log at night." Thomas holds fire in his hands, both for the simile that makes the paper sound like a crackling log and for the incendiary news it brings. Perhaps in another sense as well, if we pay attention to what happens in the background as he reads: "His father watched him; he still held the pipe fixed between his teeth while he watched, but no more puffs of smoke came from it" (251). Some kind of fire has passed from father to son, or so at least the son hopes, if, as one might suspect, his principal motivation is to possess the vital fire that would command his wife's allegiance and desire, to steal it away from his father.

How appropriate it is, then, that when he finishes the article and begins to argue with his father about the association he should get up from the stool and step "to the center of the hearth." The hearth is more than high ground; it is the prize for which the battle is fought. Simply to occupy it gives Thomas an immediate apparent advantage over his father: "The father, sitting in the chair with the newspaper on his lap, looked very small before him" (242). But Thomas's moral disadvantage is very real: his father had been among the first to oppose the oppression of the tobacco buyers by joining the association, and had persuaded his son to come along. Now it appears that it is just as heroic to oppose the oppression of the association's terrorist tactics, and the father has been the first to make a moral point of leaving. Standing on the hearth, the son accuses his father of endangering the family farm by having made a mistake he can't correct: "You helped start this association. You got us in it and you got a lot of other people in it. You've started something and you can't stop it, so you're getting out. You made your mistake when you got off the board. Papa, you're on horseback now, you're on horseback, and it's a wild piece of horseflesh" (253). The image Thomas adopts here is curious, and perhaps premonitory, for after much discussion and his eventual turnabout decision to leave the association with this father and sell out their crop together, he will try, fatally, another heroic tack. Their own barn is burned that night and, too late to prevent that disaster or even for the act to be justified as self-defense, Thomas will go out with a gun and shoot a night rider off his horse. When he returns to the house to tell his father what he has done and the elder Hardin begins to telephone to find out who was hurt, Thomas's victorious pose on the hearth takes on a look of almost sexual triumph: "Thomas stood on the hearth, rigidly erect, and never shifted his eyes from his father's face. The face was inscrutable and tired" (272).

If we have the feeling that in aiming at the night rider Thomas was also aiming at his father, it may be not only because he had just accused him of being on horseback but also because at that moment he was reenacting a sequence of events we have seen enacted before in "The Circus in the Attic" and "Blackberry Winter." The outcome was very different, but when Seth approached his father on horseback and came almost close enough to touch his heel, he had "tried to read his face," that "impassive" paternal face. Likewise, Thomas never shifts his eyes from his father's "inscrutable" face. There was a persistent focus on the horseman's leg in both "The Circus in the Attic" and "Blackberry Winter": it was when Seth Sykes grabbed the lieutenant's left leg that he made his fatal move (and Bolton's own father, Simon Lovehart, was flung from his horse in another Civil War battle by a wound in his *left* leg [17]);[11] the other Seth thought about how close he was to touching his father's heel. That focus continues in "Prime Leaf," for we are twice made to focus our gaze on the legs of the man Thomas shot. It was Mr. Hopkins, whose "thick, booted legs almost gave the look of deformity" (240)—an almost obsessive reiteration of the earlier sentence, "His thick legs were ridiculously short, and the boots which he wore almost gave the look of a deformity" (228).

Fathers are not alone in their inscrutability; mothers, too, are capable of difficultly decipherable utterance. Bolton Lovehart's mother made those passionate cries that could be misread as anguish at the death of her husband; only time could show that they were really cries of triumph. But her cries are now always as susceptible of interpretation as that, for when Bolton later tried to persuade her to see a specialist for her heart condition "she uttered again the wild, undecipherable, ambiguous, untranslatable cries which she had uttered by the fallen body of Simon Lovehart" (34). They are made more difficult to decipher by the narrator's claim that they are the same cries, for the situation is entirely different. How could now they be cries of either anguish or triumph? More likely than either is that they articulate nothing but the fact of their articulation, phatic sounds uttered in order to keep Bolton off balance, to convince him of her otherness and of his inability ever to interpret her. And if their second articulation is made more difficult to interpret by a changed context, what are we to make of the fact that they appear on yet another occasion divorced not only from that context but from that speaker as well? When Bolton tries to steal a kiss from Sara Darter, she too "screamed at him with furious words which he could not interpret." If what the narrator says is true about having to wait until the flesh of the passion has withered away to interpret such articulations, to wait until instead of hearing them we see with scrutinizing eyes the logical articulation of fact with fact, then perhaps not only the passion but also the speaker is unimportant. Perhaps what matters is less that Bolton's mother or that Sara Darter uttered those cries than that they were uttered at all, that Bolton finds himself in the position of being unable to interpret them—the same Bolton Lovehart who found himself unable to write the history of his county and constructed a soft pine circus instead.

Professor Dalrymple finds himself in a similar position of remoteness from the world in "The Unvexed Isles":

> As he turned about and traversed the excessive distance across the blue carpet, he felt that all these objects accumulated around him—table, chair, blue carpet, rug, lamp—were unfamiliar to him, and not for the first time might, if he so chose, be construed in their unique and rich unities. After he had adjusted the tray, with special care, on the stand, he gave to its design a lingering and analytic regard. Lingering ... as if his attention to the intricacies of the design might postpone the need to inspect those people whose voices, somewhat remotely, impinged upon him. (201)

If Bolton Lovehart found a distraction in objects of his own making, Dalrymple is distracted by everyday, preexisting objects that for others, and for himself before this moment, were mere background details of no importance. Suddenly they demand his attention, and in their unfamiliarity, their opacity, acquire a rich density of their own. We may be so accustomed to valuing engagement with the "real world," that we can too easily assume that when the choice of such a disengagement as Bolton or Dalrymple experiences appears before us in a work of fiction we are being exhorted to beware their evil example. Yet what Dalrymple does is precisely what Warren's story collection encourages us to do, and what we have been doing in these pages—to read these narratives less for their passion than for their connection of fact with fact, for the way in which they succeed in making such homely things as bulbs, stoves, hearths, shoes, legs, and limps uncannily unfamiliar. There is a certain remoteness attached to this critical activity that has more to do with Dalrymple's discovery of the esthetics of everyday objects and the intricacies of their design than it does with the kind of vicarious desire for intervention that we might nevertheless have wished that the professor had exercised. But he never intervenes in the drama or farce that he thinks is being played out between his wife and the student guest, and, serene to the end, lingers downstairs alone after she goes up to bed.

"Somewhere on the upper floor a light burned, splaying shadow and angular patches of illumination into the lower section like a gigantic, ghostly pack of cards" (209). This light from the upper reaches of the house illumines more than Professor Dalrymple realizes, for it appears to one who has read the immediately preceding story in the collection, "The Life and Work of Professor Roy Millen"—likewise about a professor and a student of whom he had reason to be jealous—as the ghost of an image that the reader could have remembered from the first page of that story, the professor's recollection of "long tranquil evenings at the bridge table with the light glinting subduedly on the exciting and rich designs of the royal cards" (190). Dalrymple had been struck by the rich unities and intricate design of what he saw in the household furnishings; we have reason to be struck by the rich unity of these two passages, and to suspect an underlying intricacy of design. By design or not, the presence of this image in two so similar and contiguous stories should be cause for reflection. Yet it is not exactly the same image, for the playing cards at the beginning of the first of these two stories are real, their designs revealed by the glinting light, while their counterparts on the next to last page of the second story are imaginary, brought into existence only by the trick of the light from upstairs, gigantic ghost cards occupying the space that had earlier been inhabited by those everyday furnishings that had first attracted Dalrymple's gaze.

Perhaps the cards' significance is in that difference, a movement from the real to the imagined, a movement in the same direction of greater remoteness from the world that Dalrymple was pursuing when he was distracted by impinging voices from what he could construe of the design that surrounded him. Like Bolton's circus constructions, the second set of cards is no longer something merely perceived, like the furniture, but Dalrymple's own creation, a trick of the light that would not have worked without his participation. And, like the circus in the attic, they are playthings, flat surfaces as subject to playful manipulation as the tigers and trapeze artists of Bolton's upstairs menagerie. Representative as they are of the kind of double images Warren's *Circus* provides, where so much happens more than once, in different contexts, for different reasons, and with different actors, the second pack of cards in particular seems especially indicative of the kind of reading this book (as opposed to its stories separately considered) invites—a reading imbued with the attic perspective that takes pleasure in contemplating the rich, separate existences of these images, their intricate design, and the underlying logic of their reappearances, that takes the risk of seeing them as a hand dealt a reader fully aware of the possibility that they may only be tricks of that upstairs light.

Chapter 5

Beaumont's Dream
World Enough and Time, 1950

Chapter 1 Jeremiah Beaumont was born in 1801 in western Kentucky. His father, who taught him to read from a primer he wrote himself, did not prosper, and died. Young Beaumont went to a school run by the eccentric physician Dr. Leicester Burnham. He spent several summers with his maternal grandfather, the wealthy Morton Marcher, but they had a violent falling-out when he tried to make Jeremiah renounce his father's name in order to inherit Runnymede, Marcher's estate. Later, the boy briefly came under the spell of the preacher Corinthian McClardy; in the aftermath of one revival meeting, he ran into the woods in his enthusiasm and lost his virginity to a snaggle-toothed hag who was crouching there. When the boy was seventeen, Burnham introduced him to Colonel Cassius Fort, who offered him an apprenticeship in his Bowling Green law office.

Chapter 2 In Bowling Green, Jeremiah becomes friends with Wilkie Barron, who tells him about Rachel Jordan, a young woman whom Fort had seduced, and who gave birth to a stillborn fetus. Beaumont breaks with Fort and tries to court Rachel, who at first rebuffs his advances.

Chapter 3 Wilkie introduces him to Percival Skrogg, a man devoted to "pure idea" and the editor of a Frankfort newspaper dedicated to the Relief party (those in favor of changing the debtor laws for the sake of the indebted). They induce him to join them on election day at Lumton, and manipulate him into taking part in the traditional violence at the polls. His persistence with Rachel finally pays off: she at last takes him to the grave of her stillborn child and says she will marry him if he swears to kill Cassius Fort.

Chapter 4 Jeremiah writes to Wilkie asking if he would serve as second in a duel with Fort. Barron asks him not to attack Fort because of his usefulness to the Relief faction. Beaumont goes to Frankfort, tells Fort that Rachel wants him dead, and tries to provoke him into a duel, without success. Fort leaves town the next day and Jeremiah can't find him. In Lexington, Wilkie introduces him to Senator Madison, who reminds Jeremiah of Morton Marcher. Mrs. Jordan dies; touched by Jeremiah's apparent tenderness with her dying mother, Rachel kisses him for the first time; they make love that night and marry without Beaumont killing Fort.

Chapter 5 Jeremiah enters into a partnership with Josh Parham to survey and purchase western lands. The political situation heats up, the Reliefers wanting to unseat the state court that has ruled the replevin law unconstitutional. Rachel announces that she is pregnant. Jeremiah reads in the newspaper that Fort has returned from a long absence in the East, which reawakens his determination to kill him, even though Rachel now says that was never what she wanted. Beaumont has a dream in which he struggles in vain to identify certain trees and sees a murdered body whose face he cannot identify but which he knows must be Fort's. Wilkie and Percival come to tell Jeremiah that Fort has gone over to the anti-Relief side and to persuade him to run for the legislature. To do this, Beaumont must give up his partnership with Parham, an anti-Reliefer. While campaigning, Jeremiah is handed a handbill that accuses Fort of having seduced Rachel; he burns it. Beaumont loses the election. Rachel's pregnancy ends in stillbirth when she reads another handbill, purportedly from Fort, claiming that the father of the first stillborn child had been a slave on the Jordan farm.

Chapter 6 Wanting to find out who had brought that handbill, Jeremiah asks at the local tavern what messenger had come to his house on a sorrel horse in his absence, for the man had dropped his handkerchief on the front porch (a detail Beaumont has invented to justify his inquiry) and he wants to return it. A Tim Adams had come with the letter, though he owned no handkerchief; a stranger had asked him to deliver it. Rachel, blaming her premature delivery on the handbill and its upsetting contents, now again wants Jeremiah to kill Fort. He gets Captain Marlowe and his wife to look after Rachel and the farm and sets off for Frankfort. There, he takes a room at Caleb Jessup's and, after dark, lures Fort out of the house he was staying in, and stabs him to death, making sure before he strikes that Fort recognizes him. He escapes capture, returns to Jessup's, and the next day begins the trip home. He triumphantly tells Rachel the deed is done.

Chapter 7 Four men come to take Jeremiah back for questioning. They have a handkerchief bloodstained from a nosebleed that he inadvertently left at Jessup's but someone planted at the murder scene. Beaumont secretly destroys it in a fireplace during the journey. Madison agrees to represent him and the court of inquiry begins.

Chapter 8 A Sugg Lancaster, who falsely claimed to have heard Jeremiah utter threats against Fort, has come up with two handkerchiefs, a bloodstained one to replace the one Beaumont burned and a clean one of the same design. He tries to bribe Marlowe into testifying that the clean handkerchief is one Beaumont had lent him. But Marlowe informs Jeremiah, who instructs him in a letter to Rachel to play along with Lancaster in order to discredit him at the trial.

Chapter 9 At the trial, Beaumont's lawyers' skill in casting doubt on the false testimony of Jessup, Lancaster, and others at first makes it appear that he will be acquitted. But Marlowe produces the letter in which Jeremiah had told him what to say, and Wilkie Barron appears as a witness for the prosecution to report Beaumont's threats against Fort. The jury finds him guilty. When he returns to his cell, Rachel is there.

Chapter 10 Rachel had been arrested for complicity in Fort's murder, but after her appearance in the court of inquiry the proceedings are stopped. Beaumont gets the idea that if he confesses and makes public the handbill in which Fort had claimed that a slave was the father of the child the governor will pardon him. He confesses to his lawyers, and they try to find a copy of the handbill, even looking in his house for the one he received, but cannot. In their prison cell, Jeremiah and Rachel fall into a "black honeymoon" of lust, interrupted only by his writing the story of his life and her composing poems. The jailer, Munn Short, tells the story of how, back in pioneer days, he "died" and was brought back to life by Perk, the older man whose young wife he had seduced.

Chapter 11 Dr. Leicester Burnham arrives in Frankfort for a last glimpse of his former pupil. Jeremiah persuades him to procure him some poison, but his and Rachel's double suicide attempt is unsuccessful. Crawford, one of the false witnesses, comes to apologize and to tell them One-Eye Jenkins, Percival Skrogg's former bodyguard, can come up with a copy of the missing handbill for the right price. Wilkie Barron and One-Eye's brother, Lilburn, suddenly appear and rescue Jeremiah and Rachel from jail.

Chapter 12 Lilburn Jenkins escorts them on their flight west and delivers them into the swamp kingdom of the old humpback river pirate La Grand' Bosse. There Rachel goes mad and Jeremiah drifts into a stuporous, though tranquil, existence. He begins to sleep with the Bosse's former mistress (and inherits his venereal infection); Rachel adopts the infant the Bosse had sired upon her. One-Eye Jenkins shows up with the news that he has the handbill. Lilburn steps in the door and aims his pistol at his brother, who kills him with a knife when Jeremiah interferes. Rachel stabs herself to death. Jeremiah and One-Eye set out for Frankfort, though Jeremiah does not really expect a pardon, only "expiation." On the journey, One-Eye tells him that Wilkie Barron and Percival Skrogg wrote the handbill, and that only one copy was ever printed—except for the proof copy he rescued from the fire. The next morning, Jeremiah pulls a gun on Jenkins and ties him up before moving on, but

One-Eye catches up with him, with Barron's help kills him, and takes his head to Frankfort as a trophy. Wilkie marries rich and prospers but keeps Beaumont's autobiographical manuscript and, because of the truth it contains about his own conduct, eventually commits suicide.

It is no secret that *World Enough and Time,* Warren's fourth novel, is based on actual events. In 1825 in Frankfort, Kentucky, Jereboam Beauchamp murdered Colonel Solomon Sharp for the seduction of Ann Cook. Though Beauchamp pleaded innocent, he was convicted of the crime; while he lay in jail awaiting execution he wrote a *Confession,* published in 1826, in which he told how and why he did it. It was in 1944 or 1945 that Warren says Katherine Anne Porter, who had an office near his in the Library of Congress, one day gave him a copy of Beauchamp's *Confession,* which he "had vaguely heard of ... before" but had not read until that day (*RPW Talking,* 62). Leonard Casper correctly observed that "Warren's ... version borrows all the details offered in the *Confession*" (143). Not only is Jereboam Beauchamp Jeremiah Beaumont, Solomon Sharp Cassius Fort and Ann Cook Rachel Jordan, but even the mysterious Sugg Lancaster is based on an actual person, Patrick Henry Darby, Caleb Jessup on a Joel Scott, William J. Garrison (whose name Beaumont announces, but as William *K.* Grierson, when he lures Fort outside) on a John W. Covington (whom Beauchamp similarly announces, but as John *A.* Covington), Hilton Hawgood (as the man who comes up to Beaumont and says he has made more accurate measurements of the footprint at the murder scene) on a George M. Bibb, and Jackson Smart (the "Scylla" whose house Beaumont had to pass on the way back home from Frankfort) on a Thomas Middleton. Furthermore, there really was a rumor that the stillborn child to which Ann Cook had given birth was black and therefore not his, one of the four men who came to take Beauchamp back to Frankfort really did lose the dirk, and Beauchamp really did burn the falsely incriminating handkerchief.

So close are the two versions of the story that the differences are likely to prove especially meaningful. The most obvious change is that while Beauchamp was hanged on schedule, Beaumont is rescued and escapes, for a while, to the West. Another difference, equally important but less remarked upon, is that while Sharp claimed the baby was black, Fort did not—though Beaumont thought he had and therefore murdered him. (Beauchamp, like Beaumont, had first tried to provoke Sharp into a duel but could not; it was only when he got news that Sharp was saying the dead child was fathered by a slave that he, like Beaumont, was goaded into killing him.)

Warren's relationship with his material in the case of this novel, as with regard to the facts about Huey Long in *All the King's Men*, bears an interesting—and enlightening—resemblance to the relationship of Percy Munn's dream in *Night Rider* to the ballad of Pretty Polly he had heard sung just before he dreamed it. Like day residue—the "Poor fragments of the day"—that provides the raw material for a dream and is transformed into another story according to the hidden agenda of the unconscious, so these histories and stories undergo a transformation to become part of the ongoing dream that Warren's successive novels tell. That it is an ongoing dream is evident from the dream Jeremiah Beaumont has (and Jereboam Beauchamp did not), for it is remarkably similar to the one that came to Percy Munn:

> That night he had a dream. He dreamed that he stood at the edge of a big woods, a forest, toward night, and the forest was full of shadow. It was fall or winter, for the trees were nearly bare. He seemed to recognize the place as some place he had seen in the West, but it was different, too, from any place he had seen in Kentucky, and he did not know the names of the trees. That fact was terrible to him, and he struggled in his mind to know their names.
>
> Then he saw the form on the ground before him. He saw it with no surprise because at the moment of perception he knew that he had already known it there. It was a strong man's form, naked, lying on the back, and bleeding from a wound in the chest. He could not make out the face, no matter how hard he tried, but he knew that it was the face of Cassius Fort. He knew that if he could only make out the face, he would feel the great joy that all had been done for, but when he looked, there was only a patch of grayness that swam in his sight and made him think of the gray growth on the eyes of the blind and made him fear that it was coming on his own. So he would look quickly away to be confirmed in his vision.
>
> Looking up thus, he saw Rachel, more beautiful than in life. She was kneeling on the ground, beyond the head of the bleeding form, and was staring at him with horror and reproach. He was compelled to speak to her, to justify himself, and tell her that now they could be happy. But the words would not come, though he thought he would strangle with the effort of speech.
>
> Then, as he looked, he saw that her face was changing. The brown spot on her cheek was enormous and each instant was larger and more devouring. It was Rachel's face and was not Rachel's face. It was Rachel's face but it was also the face of the old woman, her mother, peering at him, spying on him from

the shadows. Then it was all discolored, but was still Rachel's face and the mother's face, but was another face as well, and he knew its name, but like the names of the trees it would not come to him.

Then she lifted her hands to her face, where the horror was increased by the fact that he saw Rachel's white bosom beneath. She said, staring above her hands, to him, "Look, what you have done to me."

At that he knew that there was something which could be said to make all clear, but speech would not come, though the agony of effort grew greater. He felt cold, and a great desolation overcame him.

He woke at this point, with desolation still on him. (188–89)

Munn, too, had dreamed of a supine corpse whose face was, at least at first, invisible; and when it did become visible it assumed the identity of the man Munn had killed—as here, even without the face, Beaumont knows it belongs to the man he is supposed to kill. The face in Beaumont's dream belongs, as do several of the eventual multiple identities of the fetus in Percy's dream, to a father figure, for Fort clearly plays a paternal role in his life. When Jeremiah discovers the handbill purportedly from Fort claiming Rachel's first stillborn had been black, he says he felt "the gratitude of a good son to a father" (209). When in the dream he looks at where the face should be, Beaumont sees only grayness; the fetus at which Percy Munn gazed was also gray, "gray like the ones in the jars." Munn's wife was in his dream, presenting the dead fetus to him in her arms; Beaumont's wife is in his dream, calling his attention, with horror and reproach, to the corpse by which she kneels. The face of the fetus strove to speak; here, speechlessness belongs to the dreamer.

What these dreams make evident is that it is through the medium of a dream—Beaumont's—that the parallel between Warren's literary creation and the dreamwork of the unconscious most clearly surfaces—a dream, that is, within a dream; and a recurring one, as it already was—for Munn—the first time it appeared. Colonel Sharp's murdered body becomes Colonel Fort's in order to be the one in Jeremiah's dream so that the dream of the dead father may return once more, as it first had in Munn's dream, where its fetal quality masked the paternal identity. Sharp's and Beauchamp's story serves as raw material for what it is the unconscious in Warren's texts is forever trying to say, and once more finds the occasion of trying to say in *World Enough and Time*.

But in this instance the raw material (Beauchamp's *Confession*) becomes part of the recurring dream in yet another way. Not only is it plundered for fragments to be reassembled for other ends, but because one of those other ends is the recurring story of a prior text, it also appears in the reassembled story in the form of just such a preexisting text—specifically, as a Bellerophontic one. Beauchamp's *Confession* was published in the same year he was hanged, but in Warren's version Beaumont's manuscript falls into the hands of Wilkie Barron, who secretly carries it with him until it kills him by making him kill himself. In this regard, though more fatally, the manuscript parallels the brown paper package of Cass Mastern papers that Jack Burden unwillingly carried around with him and refused to open for a long time.

The narrator of *World Enough and Time* acknowledges its existence, but only as the fictive manuscript in Beaumont's hand that Wilkie secretly preserved, not as the printed *Confession of Jereboam O. Beauchamp* that appeared in 1826 and was sold on the streets of Frankfort, Kentucky. "Here are the diaries, the documents, and the letters, yellow too, bound in neat bundles with tape so stiffened and tired that it parts almost unresisting at your touch" (3). This is, of course, as it should be, although Warren, when speaking in his own voice, readily acknowledged Beauchamp's existence and that of his *Confession*. But the perhaps the most intriguing thing about the relationship of the novel to that earlier text is that it is in a dream—the kind of text where what is hidden can come to the surface—that we are given a hint of the existence of what the novel represses.

I am referring to the part of the dream that seems unmotivated by what is on Jeremiah Beaumont's mind—the only part that has, to all appearances, nothing to do with his intention to murder Fort or with Rachel's conflicting feelings about whether the deed should be done. It is almost the first thing he recalls from the dream: "He seemed to recognize the place as some place he had seen in the West, but it was different, too, from any place he had seen in Kentucky, and he did not know the names of the trees. That fact was terrible to him, and he struggled in his mind to know their names." In the dream it functions (as something mentioned early on in a poem that is recalled again at the end functions in that poem) to form a parallel with the other face that came to coexist with Rachel's mother's face (which had already come to coexist with Rachel's face). It, too, had a name: "he knew its name, but like the names of the trees it would not come to him." And we may, and will, speculate on whose face that is. But why trees? And why names known but impossible to recall, as if repressed? And repressed by whom?

Much later, in that part of the novel most clearly not part of Beauchamp's story, Beaumont's flight to the West, Jeremiah and Rachel are led by their rescuer shortly before dawn "into a constricted valley, then up the stream where the valley narrowed like a gorge, with dank stone walling each side. Then suddenly, there was a little open space, with grass and a few trees like great blobs of denser blackness. From the shape, Jeremiah decided that they must be beeches" (417). This time, unlike what happened in the dream, Beaumont has no trouble identifying the trees, despite the darkness; the trees are indeed darkness itself, more densely black than the night sky. But from the shape of things, the dream seems to have anticipated this identification scene: here he is on his way west, traveling from his Frankfort prison cell to the land of Boz on the banks of the Mississippi; while in the dream, the trees with the forgotten names seemed to be in "some place he had seen in the West."[1]

Yet dreams do not predict the future—unless it is a future that is already past, as it is for the real maker of Beaumont's dream, who has also devised it so that in his youth Jeremiah actually became, for a moment, the tree he will recognize on the flight west and which, it appears, he will not be able to remember in the dream.[2] It happened after a night of frost and freezing rain:

> Next morning there was brilliant sun that made the whole landscape glitter. Beyond the door of the house was a big beech tree, "all shining and with the wide boughs brought low with ice." He went to the tree and reached to pluck an icicle to put in his mouth. At that instant he thought how God made all things, and "my own strength seemed to pass away through my fingers into the very tree. I seemed to become the tree...." (29)

Why should Jeremiah Beaumont become a beech?

Because in his earlier, historical incarnation he was a Beauchamp—a name that, in a state where the second syllable of Versailles, for example (a city between Lexington and Frankfort) is not pronounced *sigh* but *sales,* was pronounced in the same way that the name of the falls the beech glade and cave overlook in Warren's subsequent novel *The Cave* is spelled: *Beecham's Bluff* (139, 376). (There is a Beacham, too, in Warren's last novel, of which more later.) Jeremiah, it turns out, can read but cannot correctly pronounce the language from which his name, and that of his historical prototype, derives; he certainly cannot recognize it when it *is* correctly pronounced. This becomes apparent when he enters the kingdom of the Gran Boz (La Grand' Bosse) and asks a French-speaking boy what that name means. "'Eel-eel,' he said, and that is the way Jeremiah transcribes it for us ... 'eel bow-sue.' 'And what the devil is that?' Jeremiah asked sharply" (425–26). When he later gets to see the Gran Boz and his enormous hump, Jeremiah tells us:

> I suddenly knew what was the name of the creature, what Jenkins and the other had meant by the name Gran Boz. I remem-

bered from my days with Dr. Burnham that in the French tongue the word for hump is *la bosse,* and therefore knew that what they meant to name him was The Big Hump, and that what the child had said was not gibberish but *il est bossu,* he is hump-backed, the defect of understanding being in my ear that did not well know the language in the living mouth." (430)[3]

Jeremiah's memory of the day he became a beech is an insistent one, returning twice in the narrative. When he is crouching outside the house in Frankfort, waiting for Fort to appear so that he can murder him, "he remembered how . . . he had touched the bough of the ice-ridden beech and had felt his being flow out into the shining tree . . . and down the trunk into the secret earth. . . . That memory was important to him now, for it seemed to verify him, to say that all his past was one thing . . . that all had moved to this moment" (238). And when he is first brought into his underground prison cell "he thought of that morning in his youth, long back, when . . . he had touched the bough of the ice-ridden beech and had felt all his being flow into it, into the tree, and into the earth downward . . ." (315). Could it not be said that it was when he came closest to being Beauchamp—at the moment just before he committed his crime and began to enter upon the punishment which Beauchamp, at least, would not escape—that Beaumont felt "verified" by the memory of his kinship with a beech, felt that all had moved toward the moment when, under the guise of fulfilling his personal destiny, he was actually fulfilling his fictive one?— that, by a powerful twist of textual irony, he was becoming someone else at the very moment he thought he was being most himself?

That last recollection triggers another one on Beauchamp's part that might deepen our understanding of what it means for Jeremiah to feel himself flowing down the trunk of that beech into the secret earth. The rekindled feeling of wanting to extend his roots down into the earth, having become a tree, reminds him of his childhood exploration of caves and in particular of the time he had crawled into a narrowing passage until he could go no farther. He had lain there and taken some delight in, as he put it, the "inward smell of earth's bowels" (315). He found it " 'a smell cleanly and rich, not dead and foul but pregnant with a secret life, as though you breathed the dark and the dark were about to pulse.' " It is not difficult to imagine that this is a voyage deeper into the past than he may realize, that the pregnancy and pulsing secret life is that of his prenatal existence.[4] His insistence on the cleanliness of this space makes it possible to interpret his comment earlier in the novel, when he first ventured into the house of his maternal grandfather, Morton Marcher, that he felt a great homesickness "and wanted to be in the clean room of his mother" (16).

That visit to Marcher's Runnymede was characterized by enormous conflict between the opposing claims of mother and father, for his grandfather will offer Jeremiah his estate on the condition that he renounce his father's name. The scene in the cave that he recalls in the dark of his prison cell places him in the same kind of conflict, allowing him in that instance to retreat from the demands of his father by taking refuge in something like the dark interior of his mother. " 'And while I lay there,' " Jeremiah recalls, " 'I thought how I might not be able to return, but would lie there forever, and I saw how my father might at the moment be standing in a field full of sun to call my name wildly and might run to all my common haunts to no avail' " (315). The same disposition of players—the paternal figure above, in the realm of light, and the son below, crouching in subterranean darkness—appeared when Marcher first spoke to Jeremiah: "We leaned down at the boy as though 'Peering down a well.' . . . Then he prodded the boy with the stick as he would prod an animal. 'Git in the light,' he ordered" (17). Throughout this episode, Marcher will brandish his gold-headed cane (as Jeremiah's defense attorney, Madison, whom he thought bore a strong resemblance to his grandfather, would later brandish his), the apparent symbol, together—as we are about to see—with power over fire, of his authority. It is precisely these two emblems—the phallic rod and the flame of a sperm candle—that come into play when Jeremiah and Marcher square off over the issue of whether Beaumont's recently deceased father was, as Marcher puts it, a worthless blackguard and bankrupt.

The old man had leaned back to puff on his cigar and " 'stared at the flame of the sperm candle in the candlestick' " (21) before he announced to his grandson that he intended to make him master of Runnymede after his death, that he considered him worthy of such a bestowal, but that if a suitably hot-blooded heir had not been found he would have sooner " 'burn down with his own hand the house he had built in his strength and let his bones rest in the ashes.' " The proper use of fire keeps coming up in this passage, prefaced by Marcher's threat to go after the cook with a beech bough[5] because she burned the dinner, and culminating in a struggle at the hearth. Before it begins, we are told that Jeremiah's father had had the weakness to die overcome by something like fire, "the fever that burned him up in his strength" (20), wherein we may catch a proleptic echo of the words Marcher will use to say what he would do if he had no one to leave Runnymede to.

Marcher had hated Jeremiah's father because he had stolen away his daughter. " 'He stole her,' he cried, and leaned at me over the table, 'away from her home and proper kind. Had I been in Lexington I had whipped him down the public street' " (22). Now this is precisely what Jeremiah later threatens to do to Cassius Fort, toward whom he will feel such filial gratitude: " 'I will horsewhip you in the streets of Frankfort, tomorrow, before the eyes of the town' " (131)—thereby carrying out the father-punishing gesture his grandfather had first proposed, and against which he had originally recoiled in horror. No doubt Fort became the object of Beaumont's oedipal hatred, replacing his own beloved father, yet he later confesses that " 'Men have laid low their fathers only because they were fathers' " (462). In the scene with his grandfather Marcher, when Jeremiah declares that if he were not his grandfather he would show him he was his father's son, Marcher strikes him with the gold head of the cane, which the boy wrests from his grasp. The grandfather then " 'picked up the heavy silver candlestick before him, so that the lighted candle fell from it to the table' "—a pivotal moment, the fall of the lighted candle coming just before the older man's ultimate defeat at the hands of his younger adversary. Beaumont's narrative continues: " 'and reached as to strike me with that, but I brought the stick down on it just above his hand so that he dropped it.' " Now this, too, will find its echo in the confrontation with Fort. When Jeremiah's intended victim emerged from the house, the narrator notes, "Fort was carrying no candle. If Fort had had a candle Jeremiah would have struck it from him" (239)—as if it were important that the patricidal stroke be preceded by an almost ritualistic removal of the flame, of the power over fire, from the hands of the father to be destroyed.

Jeremiah Beaumont, who as Rachel's lover sought to enact a just vengeance and as a Reliefer sought to make his society more just, seems, in his relation to the paternal flame, to be a failed Prometheus. He can knock the fire out of Zeus's hand but cannot hold on to it himself, much less bestow it on his fellow beings. Freud, in his essay "The Acquisition of Power over Fire," saw in Prometheus, who gave fire to humankind rather than keeping it for himself, someone who could renounce his instinctual drives, since "The warmth radiated by fire evokes the same kind of glow as accompanies the state of sexual excitation, and the form and motion of the flame suggest the phallus in action" (297). Now Jeremiah seems peculiarly aware of fire's eroticism, ever since seeing the picture of a young woman martyr about to be burned at the stake that first excited his sexuality. She was tied

> cruelly to a post "so that the bonds seemed to crush her sweet flesh and her face lifted up while the flames rose about her. . . . Sometimes looking fixedly upon it, my breath almost stopped and my bowels turned to water. Sometimes the strange fancy took me that I might seize her from the flame and escape with her. . . . At other times it seemed that I might throw myself into the fire to perish with her for the very joy. And again, my heart leaping suddenly like a fish, and my muscles tight . . . I myself flung the first flaming faggot and could not wait to see her twist and strive . . . to utter a cry for the first agony. . . . Then when I grew to be a big boy and knew the early stirrings of manhood, it was the picture come alive in my mind which disturbed my

slumbers or made me stop bemused by the trail or roadside in broad day." (10–11)

One viewing was especially memorable: " 'I held the old book on my knee and leaned over to study the picture by the light of the fire, for the candle was not yet lit. I stared at the page and felt the heat of the fire make the flesh of my face creep and tingle' " (11). He did not hear his mother come into the room. She laid her hand on his shoulder and asked what it was he was looking at so intently. " 'At her touch and words I felt a hatred for her and for myself' " and leaped from his chair, flinging the book into the fire.

Another mother and another hearth provoke a feeling of horror in young Beaumont when he witnesses the easy familiarity with which his friend Wilkie Barron hints at his sexual escapades to *his* mother. Mrs. Barron was sitting by the fire, "munching an apple," when the young men returned late one evening. Wilkie's winking answer to her asking where he had been so late elicited a teasing response, and after she tossed her apple core into the fire, mother and son " 'fell to bussing and tickling,' " Jeremiah observes, " 'as if she had been one of the loose sluts of his pleasure.' " Later that night Jeremiah lies awake thinking about how Wilkie's mother " 'had known him returned hot from his pleasure. . . . The thought was horrible to me' " (41). The apple in this objectionable mother's hand not only connotes Edenic temptation but the particular temptation into which Jeremiah had once fallen in a moment of hot religious ecstasy, which did not prevent him from literally tumbling into his first experience with a woman. He had run screaming into the woods, as had so many other worshipers from a religious revival, proclaiming the joy of salvation. But at length he stumbled and fell—right into the arms of an ancient crone from whose hideousness the darkness had at first spared him. The apple connection lies in what the narrator twice tells us about the "snaggle-toothed hag" was unfortunately *not:* "if the unresisting partner had been a buxom, apple-cheeked girl . . ." but "it was no apple-cheeked girl or pleasant wife" (31).

A certain oedipal configuration emerges, principally in Beaumont's murderous attitude toward some of the fatherly men in his life—Marcher, Fort, Madison—but also, as the dream makes apparent, in the way his wife's face fades into another, more maternal one, and then into one he claims not to be able to recognize ("It was Rachel's face but it was also the face of the old woman, her mother, peering at him, spying on him from the shadows. Then it was all discolored, but was still Rachel's face and the mother's face, but was another face as well, and he knew its name, but like the names of the trees it would not come to him . . ."). There is not much doubt that the face must be *his* mother's; the only mystery is why Beaumont doesn't seem to realize it. When he first saw Mrs. Jordan's face it was in a mirror, a "peering face, hung back in the shadows as though belonging to no body but floating motionless in the medium of the shadows like something drowned.... Covertly studying the face in the mirror, he relished the fact that it belonged to the dark house and unexplored rooms ..." (102). The house itself is clearly part of what Beaumont desires. When he first arrived there to court Rachel he paused before knocking, marveling at the great quiet and imagining her to be under some "terrible enchantment" and that he would find her "in the innermost dark of the house" (64), as if her connection to that house were part of his interest in her.

Beaumont's fascination for interior space soon finds some satisfaction when he notices, upon entering, that the hall "was wider than he had anticipated from the exterior of the house," and his esthetic sense is aroused by the way "the stair curved gracefully 'toward the upper region where my interest lay.' " That upper region undergoes a shift in meaning, for on this first visit it is Rachel's realm, from which she does not descend to greet him but sends word that he is welcome to avail himself of the library in her absence; while later, as they begin to spend long evenings by the fire alone in the downstairs library, the upstairs becomes the domain of Mrs. Jordan, from which she will sneak down to spy upon them in the mirror, and in the end the place where she will retire to die. In dying she will come to resemble, strangely, the bewitched, paralyzed captive that Jeremiah had first imaged Rachel to be, in that moment in which he had paused before entering the house. Rachel, then, would have lain in the innermost part of the house "with eyes closed and breast scarcely moving with breath" (64); while as she lies dying Mrs. Jordan likewise imitates *la Belle au bois dormant*—it was "as though a statue tried to talk" (143). Jeremiah will even, impulsively, kiss the dying Mrs. Jordan and say, "I love you." When, on the next page, he repeats these words to Rachel, he does so twice, with the apparent proviso that the Jordan house is somehow a concomitant of that love: " 'nobody ever loved anybody in this house, not here. . . .' He grasped her firmly. 'I love you,' he said, 'And in this house. . . . I love you. And in this house' " (145). He possesses her that night in the library, Mrs. Jordan is soon buried in the beech grove, and Jeremiah marries Rachel and moves into the house, the estate becoming a substitute for the inheritance he had missed acquiring when he could not agree to his grandfather's terms, his mother's ancestral home.

The Jordan house changes its identity for Jeremiah in a way that parallels the sequential fading of faces in his dream, for the deepest recesses of the house at first enclose Rachel, then her mother, and at last his own mother, to the extent that by possessing the house he succeeds where he had failed six years before in the struggle that concluded with his breaking his grandfather's cane on the stone of the dead hearth. In the dying Mrs. Jordan he in fact reports catching a glimpse of "his own mother 'come from the long past and far places to lie dying at last in the arms of a pious son' "

(143), a mother who after her death had lived on in her son's memory as if she were merely farther back in the house, out of sight, as if she had gone " 'into a farther and colder room to give me peace' " (39).

If the Jordan house is a new Runnymede for Jeremiah, so is the Gran Boz's island, where he not only finds the peace of "the 'black inwardness and *womb* of the quagmire' " (439; emphasis added), but where he also feels " ' that I had previously lived that moment. . . . Then I knew what echo had risen from the hallowness of memory. I had felt thus on that day long ago when I had first entered the house of my Grandfather Marcher . . .' " (423).

The scene of the battle at the hearth, where Jeremiah wrestled his grandfather's cane from his grasp and caused him to drop both candle and candlestick, reverberates throughout the novel, as if nearly every encounter with an older male were a variation on that original struggle. Like Morton Marcher, the attorney Madison had a gold-headed cane, and when he first met him Jeremiah "was suddenly reminded of the day when he had first met his grandfather. . . . He almost expected Mr. Madison to tap him with the gold-headed stick" (132). When Madison travels to Beaumont's house (the former Jordan house) to look for the handbill Fort was supposed to have written, Jeremiah is troubled by the thought of him "in that dark house" with Rachel. "He had been in the house with her," he repeats, as if it were a mystery he could not fathom. Madison brandishes his cane in suggestive ways, on one occasion "intently tracing the whorls of a knot with the point of his stick" (355), and on another "leaning toward [Rachel] over his firmly planted stick . . . while a flush grew under his swarthy skin" (356).[6]

While Beaumont awaits trial in the relatively relaxed confinement of the first of his two jails, the Marton house in Frankfort, a Captain and Mrs. Marlowe occupy his own house, on his invitation, to care for Rachel and the farm. It is reported that Marlowe would sit by the fire of an evening with the two women and that he "spat in the general direction of the burning log and half the time fell short and fouled the hearth" (300). This gesture was to be repeated by the jailer Munn Short, who "clumped across to spit in the dead fireplace" (313) of the Marton house on the morning when he came to announce that Jeremiah had to be put in a real jail, the underground cell that would remind him of the caves he had explored as a child—and that because of those associations joins the list of reincarnations of maternal space, a site that is both the mother's womb and final resting place. But it is curious that his first "jail," the Marton house, whose hearth Munn Short befouled in the same way that Marlowe had defiled the Beaumont/Jordan hearth, should have a name composed of an inversion of the two middle syllables of Mor*ton* M*ar*cher's name, as if it, too, were another version of the original Runnymede—of that maternal space.[7]

Jeremiah Beaumont had had no choice on his way home after murdering Fort but to pass by what he called his "Scylla," Jackson Smart's house by the side of the road. Hospitable to a fault, Smart would let no man walk past his front porch without inviting him in for a drink, no matter how inconvenient to the traveler. In his haste to get back to Rachel, Jeremiah had no desire to stop and be interrogated on the latest news from Frankfort. But there was no road around the place, and though Jeremiah tried to slink by unnoticed on the far side of the road, he was hailed and tried to put the best face on an awkward situation. The Jackson Smart episode is an instance of something it could be taken to stand for in the novel: the need for the story, no matter where its own inner drive may want to take it, to return from time to time to the historical narrative it has adopted as its origin, its need to negotiate its own passage by referring at times to certain preexisting coordinates, certain landmarks along Beauchamp's original journey. Thus Jereboam Beauchamp, too, did in fact have to pass, as he put it, "through the straits of Scylla" (36), the house of an inconveniently hospitable Thomas Middleton, on his way back from Frankfort. Yet at the very moment when the narrator of the novel pretends to be quoting the original text, the true nature of the novel's relationship to that original can be most revealingly glimpsed: "long before he came abreast of the porch he saw that it 'accommodated a congress as numerous as a flight of wild pigeons settling in a beech wood'" (247). Beauchamp had said nothing about beeches.

When beeches appear in *World Enough and Time* they ultimately lead to origins, whether they define the final resting place of the woman whose house Jeremiah sought to possess—the grove where Mrs. Jordan was buried (as if the beech grove were that "more distant room" where Jeremiah's mother, for whom Mrs. Jordan comes to stand, could in the end be found, the uterine origin to which he would like to return)—or the place in his dream with trees whose names he knew but could not remember until he journeyed west and discovered they were beeches. Or they might evoke the tree from his childhood he remembered both at Fort's door and in his prison cell, which ultimately led him to recall the bowels of the subterranean chamber that had a cleanliness like that of his mother's room for which he longed on a visit to Runnymede. Here, too, at Jackson Smart's house, we are brought into contact with an origin, one the novel perhaps seeks to conceal at the same moment as it appears to call attention to it, the Beauchamp whose name it hides in both the name of its protagonist and the name of the tree.

But there is yet another set of coordinates to be reckoned with here, for the novel appears to be aligned not only with its historical pre-text but with the novels that precede it. Like the *Circus* stories, the novels make a somewhat different, and perhaps larger, sense when considered together rather than separately; together, they constitute, I think, a text of their own, something like a buried narrative. We have seen, for example, how *Night*

Rider's interwoven handbills, handkerchiefs, and fragmented newsprint reappear in *At Heaven's Gate* and how the fetus in Percy Munn's dream reappears not only there but in *All the King's Men*. So it is not surprising that handkerchiefs and handbills should play as significant a role as they do in Warren's next novel, *World Enough and Time*. What is rather remarkable is that there were already handkerchiefs and handbills aplenty in the Beauchamp *Confession* (and the contemporaneous *Vindication of the Character of the Late Col. Solomon P. Sharp*), which Warren claims not to have read until some five years after the publication of *Night Rider*. Not that one would want to dispute that claim, rather to marvel at his good fortune in finding an inspirational text that spoke so well to the unconscious agenda of his novelistic production.

In both Beauchamp's account and Warren's novel, the assassin is convicted of a murder he did commit by a piece of falsified evidence, a handkerchief[8]—bearing drops of blood not from the murder but from an innocent nosebleed—that had been inadvertently left in the room where he spent the night in Frankfort but was planted at the scene of the crime by those anxious to secure a conviction. (And in both narratives there is a second handkerchief, which Beauchamp/Beaumont bound around his forehead to relieve the discomfort caused by the smoke of a large brush fire through which he passed on his way to Frankfort, and which he wore also to help secure his mask when he committed the murder.) *Night Rider's* symbolic underpinning is in part based on the equivalence set up there between certain handkerchiefs and certain handbills (both from Thebes); here, Warren accomplishes a similar equation, for if a false appearance of a handkerchief can send his protagonist to the gallows, a false handbill that mysteriously appears on his doorstep can, he hopes, save his life. They are equally false, and they hold equivalent powers of life and death.

Before Beaumont's murder of Fort, when Jeremiah and Rachel were expecting the birth of their child, domestic happiness (and the passage of time since the occasion upon which he had unsuccessfully tried to provoke Fort into a duel) had allowed Jeremiah to neglect his vow to kill her seducer. But one day, in Jeremiah's absence, a stranger came by the house to deliver a handbill, purporting to be written by Cassius Fort. It claimed that the stillborn child of Fort's seduction—a seduction already alluded to in another handbill that had surfaced in the recent election—was not Fort's at all, as the child was black, its real father being a slave in the Jordan household. The shock of reading this printed fictional account causes the stillbirth of the child Rachel is now carrying. As their servant, Josie, later recounts, it was soon after she gave the handbill to Rachel that she heard her scream and fall to the floor. Josie ran upstairs and got her into bed, and then "It done come. . . . A-fore its time. Hit warn't nuthing. Nuthing but a pore little piece of meat" (204).

The arrival of the handbill, with its horrible aftermath, was enough to awaken Jeremiah from his domestic torpor and steel him to the long-delayed task. "The night when Jeremiah stood in the dining room holding in his hand the broadside with Fort's name at the bottom, all was clear to him.... He was ready to seize horse, and ride, and on the instant" (207). This handbill is, for Jeremiah, a paternal text,[9] though what he doesn't yet know is that it is one of doubtful authenticity. He was grateful to Fort with "the gratitude of a good son to a father. He was grateful because Fort, with the last outrage, had showed him the truth" (209). Yet it was not the truth, for Fort had not written it. Percival Skrogg and Wilkie Barron had, and printed only one copy (save for the proof-sheet that One-Eye Jenkins rescued from the smoldering hearth), their object being to provoke Beaumont into assassinating Fort, who had betrayed their cause when he deserted the Relief for the anti-Relief side. Jeremiah is thus tricked into playing the role Adam Stanton played in *All the King's Men*, when Tiny Duffy called him up to let him know about Willie and his sister, Anne. Stark and Fort share a similar fate, as the fact that their names mean the same in German and French strongly suggests.[10]

Mistaking the handbill for the public text it pretends to be, unaware that it is actually a message meant only for him, Beaumont is trapped in an error that symmetrically matches the contrastingly accurate interpretation Percy Munn made of Senator Tolliver's letter in *Night Rider*, for what Munn correctly saw was that it was a public text disguised as a personal one. And in his effort to determine who had brought the handbill to his house, Jeremiah Beaumont repeats the gesture *Night Rider*'s narrator performs and that makes the text of that novel subject to the same analysis Munn made of Tolliver's letter. (What alerted Percy to the realization that the text of the letter was not what it appeared to be was the fact that it contained a sentence that "didn't fit" with the rest; and we have seen that Warren's first novel, likewise, was to contain a phrase that didn't fit—the reference to handkerchiefs from Thebes presuming an earlier mention that was never made.) Like the narrator, Beaumont, too, drops a handkerchief:

> Jeremiah tore himself from the bedside for an afternoon, and rode to Tupper's tavern. Somebody had kindly brought a message to his house three days before, he announced casually, when he wasn't home, and the messenger must have dropped his handkerchief, for one had been found on the porch. He wanted to return it, he said, and thank the man for his neighborliness. Did anybody know a man with a small sorrel horse? Then he exhibited a handkerchief, a big checked cotton handkerchief, rather worn and frayed. Or did anybody recognize this? They passed it from hand to hand. (210)

Any reader who looks back to find the earlier mention of the handkerchief that this passage seems to presume will be disappointed, for it isn't there. Of course, it is more likely that Beaumont made the whole thing up in order to justify his visit to Tupper's tavern. The excuse of wanting to return the handkerchief precluded his having to reveal the content of the message. That he did make up the story is apparent from the answer he got from the tavern regulars. Tim Adams had a small sorrel horse, they said, and had recently been seen talking to a stranger, but he "never had a snot-rag in his life . . . and if he takes a notion to blow his nose he don't hold with the foolishness of a handkerchief . . ." (210).

Nevertheless, a few pages later the handkerchief does show up, described in terms that make it impossible to mistake, yet the fact that it is the same handkerchief is not acknowledged (as, in some sense it could not be, given that the first one was, at the time of its appearance, a fiction): "a big, checked cotton handkerchief, quite old and faded with a stain at one corner" (229). Except for the stain, it answers to Beaumont's description. In fact, it is the handkerchief in which Beaumont had packed his belongings when he went to Frankfort and negligently left behind in the room at Jessup's where he stayed the night of the murder, and which his enemies planted at Fort's doorstep on the morning after the murder to make it appear that Jeremiah had dropped it there the night before. By a kind of poetic justice absent from the historical model (for Beauchamp, of course, mentions neither a mysterious messenger nor a handkerchief dropped at his door), the novel has Beaumont trapped at his trial by the same lie he introduced.

Warren's novel improves upon the historical material he had to work with by taking a real handkerchief—since Beauchamp, too, was framed by the fiction of one dropped at his victim's door—and connecting it, by Beaumont's parallel and premonitory fiction of a dropped handkerchief, to a handbill that was only marginally present (marginally, because it does not appear in Beauchamp's *Confession* but in a document by another hand) in the original story but assumes a greater significance both in this novel and in the larger story pervading Warren's fiction. Beauchamp makes no mention, at least in print, of any handbill; what he does say is that he heard in "a letter from a gentleman," whom he refuses to name (Kallsen, 20), that Colonel Sharp was claiming the child was black. The *Vindication of the Character of the Late Col. Solomon P. Sharp,* a highly suspect document written by Sharp's brother, however, quotes Beauchamp's jailer, John McIntosh, to the effect that Beauchamp had spoken to him of having received "an anonymous letter enclosing a handbill" (Kallsen, 355) in which Sharp made such a claim. Here indeed is a prior mention of a handbill;[11] as with the handkerchief, Warren did not invent it, but he did adapt it to suit his needs, among which is that, apparently (whether he realized it or not), of making these two elements fit into a symbolic network established in his first published novel linking handkerchiefs with handbills and fetuses. But the most significant difference between the historical narrative and the novel is that the handbill did not become for Beauchamp what it became for Beaumont, his last and best hope of escaping punishment for the crime of which the handkerchief helped convict him. " 'We'll not die,' " Jeremiah tells Rachel as they wait out the days until his execution. "And he began to explain very carefully how once the truth was known they would live, they would be pardoned, the Governor would pardon them, for he would not stand against the will of all good men, who would know how he, Jeremiah Beaumont, had acted in justice, how Fort had betrayed her and in the end had printed the handbill laying fatherhood to the black man and how no husband could suffer that" (364). Then begins a mad but fruitless search for another copy of the handbill. Surely there are others to be found elsewhere in the state, Beaumont reasons, not realizing that, as a personal message disguised as a public text, only one copy was ever printed. Only much later, on the way back from the Gran Boz's wilderness kingdom, will he learn the truth, when One-Eye Jenkins tells him what really happened that night in Percival Skrogg's print shop.

Like the only remaining copy of the handbill, the handkerchief with which it is linked is also burned in a hearth, when Jeremiah surreptitiously steals it from a member of the posse transporting him back to Frankfort for trial and burns it in a fireplace when no one is looking. This remarkable episode actually took place in Beauchamp's account, too; but by inventing the story of Percival Skrogg's printing of the phony handbill and its partly burned double (the proof-sheet One-Eye rescued from the fireplace), Warren gives a resonance to that fragment of history which it never had before, and could only have in his private universe.

The same can be said with respect to another detail from Beauchamp's text. Beauchamp had burned the silk mask he wore for the murder in the hearth of the room where he stayed in Frankfort, and charred remnants were recovered and displayed at the trial. He does not say what he did with the second handkerchief (the one he wore on his forehead when he passed through the brush fire on the way to Frankfort and was still wearing when he committed the murder), though it appears that he effectively disposed of it somehow, for no mention was made of it at his trial. Warren's version reverses the fate of these elements: Beaumont burns the green silk handkerchief (which, like Beauchamp, he wore through the brush fire and likewise as part of his disguise when he killed Fort) in the fireplace of the room where he spent the night in Frankfort, and gets rid of the mask by throwing it in the river. So in Warren's retelling it is yet another handkerchief, together with the only other copy of Percival's handbill, that gets burned in a fireplace—yet not so consumed that, like the handbill's proof-sheet, it does not have some afterlife. In the novel it is thus the charred remains of the silk handkerchief, not the mask, that are presented in evidence at the trial, in a scene that reenacts word for word the scene in Tupper's tavern where Beaumont had displayed the other handkerchief, the one he claimed the bearer of the handbill had left behind on his doorstep: "They passed it from hand to hand" (210); "Nathan Gregg gave it to the jury. The men passed it from hand to hand" (322). This echo heightens the irony of Jeremiah's lie about the handkerchief, which is already apparent when we learn that the handkerchief he allowed the tavern customers to pass from hand to hand is to be the very one that will, by a parallel lie, incriminate him at his trial. That scene at Tupper's comes back to haunt him—or us—at the trial when the other handkerchief retraces the hand-to-hand journey of the first, fictive one. On a level of which only the reader can be aware, that reenactment tends to strengthen the suspicion fostered by these echoing moments from Warren's several plots that ultimately we are talking, in all these instances, about the same handkerchief.

And about the same fetal wrapping, whether it be the newspaper enveloping the moribund child Percy dreamed of or the handbill a similarly named Percival printed that contained a (fictive) description of one fetus and brought about the death of another. For the silk handkerchief that was passed around at the trial survived to tell its tale only because, after he burned it in the fireplace in his room at Caleb Jessup's, Jeremiah had, rather carelessly, thrown some dirty water onto that hearth (after having washed out the socks he had worn, shoeless, in Fort's yard) before the charred remnants of that handkerchief had been entirely consumed. Beauchamp had made the same mistake, except that it was his mask that was thus incompletely destroyed. However, the addition of a small but eventually significant scene in the novel's version of Beaumont's arrival at the Jessup house makes Jeremiah's premature throwing of water on the hearth not only a reenactment of an event in the historical original, but a repetition of that earlier scene in the novel: He saw a young woman "changing . . . a baby on her knees, flinging the soiled cloth to the hearth where it steamed most abominably" (226–27). The novel will use this verb again in telling how Jeremiah "*flung* the water into the fireplace" (243; emphasis added), thereby unintentionally saving the silk handkerchief from complete extinction. So the cloth that wrapped an infant comes to occupy the same place that the handkerchief he left behind him would occupy—as though Beaumont were acting out, unconsciously, the insistent logic of the dream.

Chapter 6
Decomposing
Angels *Band of Angels*, 1955

Chapter 1 The story is told by Amantha Starr, who cannot remember her mother's face but can recall the gravestone inscribed "Renie 1820–1844." She has been raised by her father, Aaron Starr, and her black mammy, Aunt Sukie, on a farm near Danville, Kentucky. She remembers the doll Bu-Bula and Old Shaddy, the slave who made it for her, and how her father suddenly sold him when it was discovered that the way he held her in his lap and told her scary stories was about to lose its innocence. In August 1852, when she was nine, her father took her to Cincinnati, where she met "Miss Idell"—actually Mrs. Hermann Muller—who helped her father buy a new wardrobe for her imminent arrival at Oberlin College, where she would begin her formal education.
Chapter 2 Amantha spends seven years at Oberlin, where she must defend her slaveholding father's reputation against the abolitionists, and where she develops a crush on Seth Parton, a theological student. Seth gives her some instruction in Hebrew, that "holy tongue," and takes her out into the woods to "redeem" a spot made sinful by another couple's lust, though nothing overt transpires. Amantha learns of her father's death when Seth shows her a newspaper account of it; he died in Cincinnati, and Seth explains that Aaron Starr had been having an adulterous affair with Miss Idell, whose husband was in prison for embezzlement. Amantha rushes back to Kentucky, arriving at the conclusion of the funeral. She is shocked to see that he has not been buried, as he had said he would be, next to her mother.
Chapter 3 Her mother was a slave, it is now revealed, and Amantha therefore is one too. She is sold for debts—her father had gone bankrupt—and is put on a steamboat bound for New Orleans. She survives a feeble attempt at suicide.
Chapter 4 Hamish Bond, who walks with a limp and carries a big, silver-headed, blackthorn walking stick, buys Amantha at auction and takes her home, where she is very well cared for by another slave, Michele, and has no duties. Michele is married to the groom Jimmee, whom

she suspects of having fathered a child on Dolly, another household slave, though it may have been Rau-Ru, whom Bond brought over from Africa and put in charge of his plantation at Pointe du Loup.

Chapter 5 Amantha is introduced to Rau-Ru, who speaks an indecipherable tongue with Bond and is treated by him as a son. She also meets Charles de Marigny Prieur-Denis, a frequent visitor at Bond's house who tries to teach her French. She decides to escape on a boat leaving to Cincinnati but crosses paths with Rau-Ru in the street, and comes back. Amantha accuses Hamish of setting him to spy on her. Bond comes to her room later that night to announce that he's booked passage for her to Cincinnati, and that she'll be free. Still later, a dramatic thunderstorm breaks; the windows are blown open and rain rushes in. Hamish comes back to repair the damage and put her back in bed. He joins her there.

Chapter 6 Bond puts Amantha on the boat the next day, accompanying her as far as Pointe du Loup; he gives her a brown envelope containing money and her manumission papers. As he is disembarking, she runs down the gangplank after him, having decided to stay. They live for a while at Pointe du Loup, where Prieur-Denis tries to court her with riding lessons. One day when Hamish is away, Prieur-Denis tries to force himself on her but is prevented by Rau-Ru, who strikes him. Rau-Ru flees, knowing the punishment for hitting a white man. When Bond returns, he tries to kill Prieur-Denis under the guise of a duel, but Amantha prevents it. In Rau-Ru's absence, disorder sets in at Pointe du Loup. Hamish and Amantha return to New Orleans. Fort Sumter has been fired upon; the war has begun.

Chapter 7 As Federal troops approach the city, Bond tells Amantha the story of his past: born Alec Hinks to a mother who claimed to have come from a wealthy slave-owning family and an ineffectual father, he left Baltimore to join the illegal slave trade by signing on with a swaggering captain whose ship and name he stole six years later. He recounts stories of Africans' barbarism and complicity in the slave trade in order to argue that bondage in the American South is an improvement over their original condition. He recounts how he saved the infant Rau-Ru from death in a wartime tribal raid and raised him as a son.

Chapter 8 Hamish definitively sets Amantha free, again giving her the brown envelope with money and freedom papers; she takes a room elsewhere in the city and earns her living embroidering corset covers. A Captain Tobias Sears in the Union army rescues her from an abusive corporal; Seth Parton, now a lieutenant and Sears's best friend, happens upon the scene at the same moment. Sears courts Amantha, successfully; Bond reappears and proposes marriage, but she weds Tobias— even though Parton felt obliged to tell his friend about Amantha's past. Miss Idell, now married to a Captain Morgan Morton, shows up at the reception.

Sears takes command of a black regiment; Amantha teaches school to recently freed slaves.

Chapter 9   Rau-Ru returns as Lieutenant Oliver Cromwell Jones, and is often a guest of Tobias Sears now that the war is over. At issue is whether blacks will be given the vote gradually or immediately. Radicals in favor of the latter are planning to hold a state constitutional convention of their own; unreconstructed rebels threaten violence; Tobias tries to find a middle way. Seth Parton tries to force his affections on Amantha but she fights him off. He informs her that what he had told Tobias about her past was not the fact of her black ancestry, which he has only just learned from Miss Idell, but the scandal of her father's adulterous affair with the latter. Miss Idell pays a visit and reveals her own gold-digging past, asks Amantha not to tell Tobias about Seth's attempted rape, and says she is going to run away with him (and that she is not really married to Morton). Amantha tells Tobias the truth about her mother, explaining that she thought he already knew. He appears to take it well, but when she later sees his fingers bloody from anxious nail-biting, Amantha angrily says she hates him and tells him to go away. She then goes out to find Rau-Ru and asks to see the scars on his back from the flogging he had received when he was captured after defending her from Prieur-Denis at Pointe du Loup.

Chapter 10   A parade of black freedmen marches to join the convention, which is then attacked by the police and rebel sympathizers; many are killed, still more wounded. General Baird's troops should have protected the convention but did not. Rau-Ru, angry at the betrayal, and particularly at Sears for his attempted role as compromiser, tells Amantha she has to be on the side of her own people now, like it or not. He places her out of harm's way in a room she can bolt from the inside. After her solitary confinement there for some twenty-four hours, during which she felt "out of time and out of life" and saw images of her past flow by in a confused but somehow logical way, Jimmee comes—his head wrapped in a turban like the one Old Shaddy wore (from a similar head wound) when he was being sold off her father's estate—to take her into the swamps where Rau-Ru and his men are. After gazing at Amantha, Rau-Ru announces that there is something he has to do. He leaves with some of his men; Amantha manages to sneak away to follow him and finds herself at Pointe du Loup, where Hamish Bond is about to be lynched. Amantha pleads with Rau-Ru to spare him; Hamish laughs and jumps off the wagon to his death. Rau-Ru points out to Amantha that if she hadn't intervened he might not have gone through with it, nor would Bond have leaped.

Chapter 11   Rau-Ru and his men are captured, but Amantha is allowed to escape. She makes her way back to New Orleans, where it turns out that Tobias has been in the hospital with wounds from the convention melée and is unaware of her escapade with Rau-Ru. She never tells him. In the coming years they live in St. Louis and a succession of miserable Kansas towns, as Tobias struggles to make a living as a lawyer. He publishes poetry and, more importantly, *The Great Betrayal,* a book in which he denounces the materialism of the Gilded Age. His rich New England father cuts him out of his will "because [he is] unaware of the obligation which wealth entails." In 1888, Amantha thinks an old beggar who has suddenly begun to appear on the street corner in town is Rau-Ru, because she recognizes the herringbone pattern of the scars on his back—until she realizes that she never did get to see those scars on Rau-Ru. The beggar dies in the shack of a local black garbage collector, Uncle Slop, whose wealthy son Tobias aids in locating his father. Amantha visits his grave, wishing she were free of the hold Rau-Ru has on her, then realizes no one can set her free but herself. As Tobias recounts how he helped Uncle Slop's son to honor his father by buying him new clothes and cleaning him up, Amantha suddenly realizes that her father really did love her, and that the reason he had never drawn up her manumission papers was that he could not "declare me less than what he had led me to believe I was."

Band of Angels is not universally admired. For James Justus it is an "aesthetic failure" (236), whose narrator "is mediocre . . . an inept raconteur, short on art but long on ego" (32). For who could really care what happens to this whining narrator? And, he adds, the ending is weak: "too sudden and too unrealized dramatically" (246); it is "forced, hurried and derives from no logical or psychological precedent," according to Allen Shepherd (82). Even Warren has joined this negative chorus, admitting to an absence of sufficient "richness and depth in the experience of the narrator" (*RPW Talking,* 188).

I must confess to a similar disappointment when considering the book only on its own terms. But when read in the context of Warren's previous novels, and particularly with an eye to the ongoing story they tell, it is not at all disappointing. In this regard Amantha Starr, inept narrator that she is, unwittingly provides a clue to how to read the book: "When you try to tell somebody about a dream, you find in the telling that you are simply having another dream" (3–4). What we have discussed so far in Warren—most recently in Jeremiah Beaumont's dream that seemed to disguise, and thus revealed, what the novel itself was repressing—has taught us to see the analogy in his fiction between dream and narrative and the way each flows into the other. And this statement by Amantha certainly reinforces that analogy, since it declares that to narrate—in this case to narrate a dream—is really to dream. Her words form a regret that a dream cannot be communicated, as its transformation into yet another dream by the telling of it gets in the way. But the truth of this statement could be expressed in another way: within every dream is another dream, and it is in telling the first that the second is revealed.

This may not be what Amantha had in mind, but it is true of the book in which she appears, and of the books that precede it. It is another way of saying what Jack Burden once declared, that the reality of an event is not in the event but arises "from the relationship of that event to past, and future, events." It is in the relationship of Amantha's narrative to past and future Warren narratives that the reality of the other dream can be perceived. So there is a narrative dreamed here other than the one about the Amantha Starr who was sold into slavery and was rescued by Hamish Bond and later Tobias Sears, who "failed westward" with the latter and eventually faded into obscurity and middle age in Halesburg, Kansas. And there is a story here other than the one with the false and sentimental resolution.

In the context in which Amantha makes her opening statement, the two dreams—the one she had dreamed and the one she finds herself telling—resemble, or become, two places: an imagined "picture of a grassy place, a place with sun, maybe water running and sparkling, or just still and bright" (3), a spot associated with a feeling of "being light and free" (4), and a real place, the site of her mother's grave, "a grassy place, no dream.... At the head of the grave there is a little stone, and on the stone folded wings carved, and the word *Renie,* and the dates 1820–1844." Like the dream and its recounted version which is yet another dream, the imagined place and the real one have a certain sameness: "Sometimes this real spot and the spot of my imagination, of my dream of freedom and delight, seem to become the same spot.... Why ... do the two images, with such poignant excitement, sometimes merge in my heart?"

It may be here, when Amantha senses that there is something going on of which she is only partially aware, some mystery connected with the workings of her own imagination, that the reader ought perhaps to wonder if something like that will take place in his or her own mind, some parallel blending of images and places that, if it could be discerned, would make it possible to dream that other dream of the narrative. Something similar happened in *All the King's Men* when Jack Burden stared at Anne Stanton as she lay naked on the bed and was reminded of her floating on her back in the water—as we were reminded of Willie Stark laid out like a *gisant* with his hands on his chest in parallel pose. Jack spoke of a kind of stereoscopic vision and of how reality arises from the combination of events and not the events themselves; Amantha Starr had her own encounter with Burden's paradox when she witnessed "the task of creation" (13) in the glow of Old Shaddy's hearth as he assembled her beloved Bu-Bula. Like poetry, by Warren's own definition, which "does not inhere in any particular element but depends upon the set of relationships, the structure, which we call the poem," Amantha's favorite doll visibly came to life from inanimate, meaningless fragments: "[P]erhaps one reason I loved her was that I had seen her come into existence. She had been a chunk of white pine, the hank of tow, the snippets of cloth, and I had seen these things take shape, grow together, and suddenly glow with her being." And in the same way that Warren's ideal of a poet could make a poem out of anything—"granted certain contexts, any sort of material ... might appear functionally in a poem" ("Pure and Impure Poetry," 24)—Old Shaddy "knew everything and could put it into a tale" (13).

The reader who awaits an experience akin to Amantha's merging of images will not be disappointed if he or she is still waiting for it near the end of the novel, for in those closing pages Amantha stands at a grave in Halesburg, Kansas, that is in several respects the analogue of her mother's, at whose edge the novel began. Like the first grave, whose headstone bore carved folded wings (as if, like the paradise with whose image it blends in Amantha's imagination, it were guarded by cherubim), this one also enjoys angelic protection: "There were a couple of stone gate-posts, each surmounted by a decomposing angel" (361). This Kansas counterpart to Renie's Kentucky grave is not as well marked; it bears an empty inscription, a "scrap of paper" tacked onto a stick saying "in a pencil scribble: *Old man, colored, no name*" (362). Yet the inscription on Amantha's mother's grave is in fact comparably ambiguous, and negative; for what it contains is, as Amantha puts it, not the *name* but "the *word* Renie." Renie in fact *is* a word, the second-person singular imperative of the French *renier*, to deny. Not only is this grave part of a double image (of which the other half is Amantha's dream of her spot of paradise); it is itself a double image, its inscription apt to give its reader double vision, as it transforms itself from a name into an injunction, a text that is almost self-destructive in its ambiguity—for what does it ask its reader to deny but itself?

The project of determining how the Kansas grave may be analogous to the Kentucky one now assumes added importance, for it may make it possible to fathom the ambiguity of that one-word text. The nameless old man in the Halesburg cemetery had been the object of false recognition on Amantha's part, for when she saw him hunched over in the street she was sure he was Rau-Ru, come back to haunt her after all those years. A quarter-century earlier, she had known him as the mysterious *k'la* of her owner, Hamish Bond, the infant he had rescued from a burning village in Africa and made a kind of adopted son, putting him in charge of his plantation at *Pointe du Loup*. It was the "neat herringbone pattern" of whip scars on the beggar's back, barely visible through the gaps in his torn shirt, that had convinced Amantha he was Rau-Ru, for she knew he bore such marks because of a flogging he had received defending her honor against a white man's advances. Rau-Ru had been the most insistent reminder of the negritude she inherited from her mother (she was so light-skinned that even Tobias Sears did not know about it when he married her), as the following exchange (which takes place in chapter 10, when Amantha seeks out Rau-Ru to see his scars) indicates:

> "Well," he said, "whose side are you on?"
> I kept staring at him.
> "Well," he said, "if you can't say it, I'll say it for you. You are on the nigger side."
> I felt something closing in on me, to suffocation.
> "And," he said, "I'll tell you why."
> He leaned at me, grinning suddenly with an implacable, glistening, glittering malevolence. "It's because you haven't got any other side to go to." (300)

So these two graves, like the two decomposing angels on either side of the gate to the Halesburg cemetery, appropriately frame the novel; their occupants share the power to tie Amantha to her blackness.

Rau-Ru, of course, cannot exactly be said to be her father (as the woman in the other grave was her mother), yet she does have more than one father, and these other fathers are at times, as Rau-Ru nearly was, her lovers. Hamish Bond, who was himself a father to Rau-Ru, is the chief example; but even Seth Parton, who eventually marries Amantha's father's former mistress but once courted Amantha herself, is confused with her father in her imagination: "I shuddered with a chill, and shut my eyes, and saw Seth dying on that white bosom—no, it was my father dying there" (236); and later: "I suddenly saw in that same instant, her head on an arm . . . over Seth's arm—no, that couldn't be—over my father's arm" (278).

But it's the scrap of paper at the grave of the man Amantha imagined was Rau-Ru that most intriguingly connects him to her father. Its brief inscription is in fact the last in a series of scraps of paper that are for Amantha what Willie's wink was for Jack Burden: an ambiguous, doubtful parental text. Even Amantha appears to begin to make this connection when, on the same page where she speaks of it, she uses the same turn of phrase to describe, disparagingly, the manumission papers Bond gave her: "Hamish Bond—oh, I could hate him for his kindness!—giving me a *scrap of paper* in the end, offering me love in the end . . ." (362–63; emphasis added). The precision of this repetition may signal the presence of two other more extended echoes of the language used to describe the "scribble" on the "scrap of paper" at the grave that had held Amantha's interest because of her misreading of what was imprinted on the body it contained: (1) Seth Parton tells Amantha she ought to learn Hebrew and writes down the name of a textbook: "He was *scribbling* something on a *scrap of paper*. He thrust it at me. 'Get this book,' he said" (47; emphasis added); (2) on the night

Bond makes love to her for the first time Amantha realizes that his leg is not as lame as she had imagined: "somewhere back in my head there was the detached thought: *He walks pretty well*. That thought was lying there in my head like something *scribbled* on a *scrap of paper* and flung down in a dark closet" (132; last emphases added).

The first instance finds Amantha in a position she will be in twice more, that of being confronted with a language she does not understand. Infatuated with Seth Parton, the religious farm boy who spoke with a prophetic accent at Oberlin—Seth of the "high, hieratic head" (44)—Amantha found that "the under-music of that desire was pitiless even as my mind strove to grasp the thorns of the holy language" (48). When he gave her the scrap of paper with the scribbled name of the book, he also gave her a sample of that sacred tongue, a rush of rhythmic but undecipherable sounds, phatic words that conveyed nothing to her but the fact of their existence: "with no meaning ... except the exalted intensity" (47). Despite the lessons, Amantha confesses that she has "never known the meaning of those words," but later, in memory, could see Seth's "bony face lifted into autumn sunshine of Ohio, and ... be on the verge, if I could only attend more closely, only strain a little more my intellectual ear, on the verge of knowing the inwardness of that grand, infatuate gabble" (47–48). The combination of hearing the stream of undecipherable words and staring at the high, bony face for some clue to their meaning recalls two moments in *The Circus in the Attic*: the "wild, indecipherable, ambiguous, untranslatable cries" Bolton Lovehart's mother twice uttered in the title story, and the effort of another Seth to read his father's face ("I looked up and tried to read his face ... that impassive, high-boned face"). In both instances, the text to be deciphered is a parental one; the line between lover and father will eventually blur for Amantha in the case of Seth Parton, as we have seen, when he becomes the lover of her father's former mistress, Miss Idell.

Hamish Bond, whose age and role as protector project him into a paternal role, but who on a particularly stormy night will also cross that dividing line, spoke, like Seth, a language Amantha could not fathom: the African dialect in which he chatted with Rau-Ru, an "outlandish gabble, much like the racket of the provoked master of a turkey flock" (119). Amantha's pejorative characterization of that tongue seems to stem from the fact that Hamish spoke it as a father to his adopted son (whom he had greeted with an "immemorial gesture of fatherly affection"), and that the "secret gabble ... made me feel rejected and cut off," a daughter displaced in her father's affections by an elder brother who shares with that father a secret knowledge she cannot attain. But despite the abuse she heaps upon what she here terms gabble, her very choice of that word underscores its ultimate connection to the "grand, infatuate gabble" Seth Parton spoke.[1]

The other instance of foreign-language instruction in Amantha Starr's life involved Charles de Marigny Prieur-Denis, and the language is French.

Like Jeremiah Beaumont, Amantha had known that tongue only in its written form: "my ear was so unused to the spoken language despite my long study of it" (91). Prieur-Denis's pedagogical method involved the recitation of a memorized phrase ("Je viens doucement comme la rosée de l'aube") that may have become for Amantha the Gallic equivalent of the rhythmic flow of Parton's burst of unintelligible Hebrew, a string of sounds she could hear herself say ("I heard my voice saying . . ." [122]) yet not, at first, understand. What significance might this French instruction have for Amantha beyond Charles's use of it as an aid to seduction? If she had known French better, she might have been able to give her mother's gravestone another reading than what it appeared at first to say; from being a name, *Renie* could have become a message from the tomb, a command, a directive to do perhaps what she was in fact already doing—an act of prior denial Charles's own name might have taught her to recognize—to deny her past.

Or at any rate, deny something. But what? The message itself? Is this a text that asks its reader to cancel out its existence in the very act of reading it? What Amantha does in the Halesburg cemetery near the end of the novel suggests that this may be true, for she cancels out the empty inscription on that other grave: "before I left I had leaned over and torn the scrap of paper off the stob at the grave-head, and let it go, and the wind had taken it off across the prairie" (365). She does this having realized, despite what she first thought, that this is not Rau-Ru's grave after all, that the old man she had seen in the street "crouching on his hams with arms forward over the hunched-up knees and the head bowed forward to rest there in a posture of the last weariness and despair" (354) was not Rau-Ru, even though she had glimpsed "on the half-exposed shoulders and upper back the neat herringbone pattern of old welts and scars." For standing at the grave Amantha discovers that although the image of Rau-Ru's scars had preoccupied her for a quarter of a century she had never actually seen them. She had left her husband in the middle of the night in the midst of the New Orleans riots of 1866 to go to Rau-Ru and ask to see the whip marks he had received for having defended her virtue against Prieur-Denis's attempted rape, but he had not complied. "I had only dreamed the scars" (365). So that, in tearing away the negative epitaph (". . . no name") and letting it whirl away across the prairie into oblivion, she could enact the negation for which she had so longed, the death of Rau-Ru: "Perhaps if I could drive a stake down six feet into the earth, through the old black heart, then I would be safe . . . then I would be free" (362). Yet, paradoxically, this removal of the inscription—which gives her some semblance of peace, if not safety: "I felt quiet. . . . Well, that was something, to be quiet at last" (365)—can be done only when she knows the grave is not Rau-Ru's, transpires only as the negation of a negation. Something like this paradoxical logic governed her earlier conviction that the man in the street was Rau-Ru: "Even at the instant my brain was making denial of the identity of the creature. No, he was larger than this. No, there must be a thousand old Negroes left with scars on the shoulders. No, there is no resemblance in the face. . . . But the assertion was there, deeper than denial, manifesting itself in the very denial, and as yet, only in the denial . . ." (354–55). Convoluted as this logic may appear to be, it makes perfect sense in the perspective from which Amantha's meditation at the grave of her mother invites us to read the nameless epitaph. For what Prieur-Denis's instruction in French could teach Amantha was to see that her mother's tombstone did not bear a name but an assertion manifesting itself in the form of a denial—a denial prior to anything else Amantha could remember. And because the inscription lay at the very origin of her life, the brightest vision of future delight Amantha can conjure from it is the once-lost paradise of which this marker is both the sign and the gate, entry to it denied by those folded wings.

To understand Amantha's gesture at the grave of the unknown black, it may help to compare it to a similar removal, a few pages earlier, of a memorial to a nameless deceased, her husband's poem "The Dead Vidette." Tobias had succeeded in getting it published in the *Atlantic,* and Amantha had cut it out, framed it under glass, and hung it on the wall, pleased to point it out to guests. Its subject, and that of Sears's other Civil War poems, was the "hero of the hundred names, or namelessnesses, who had died into the hundred graves" (354) of the war. Embarrassed, perhaps, by this indulgence, and by a poetic career that had not lived up to its promise, Tobias removed it one night, for the next morning Amantha noticed it was gone—its absence made almost tangible by the "pale rectangle" (342) it left on the faded wallpaper. Tobias's choice of a title for the poem is intriguing, perhaps revealing, for *vidette* (a common nineteenth-century misspelling for *vedette*) is, like *Renie,* a French funerary inscription rich in meaning. The unknown soldier in Tobias's poem is a sentry, from the Italian *vedetta,* "observatory," deriving from *vedere,* "to see." The videttes Sears thus memorializes are observers, *seers;* the first line (aside from the title, all we know of the poem) confirms this punning identification of the poet with his subject: "I who, alone, through night and cedarn glade" (345).[2]

Yet another incident in which a person is reduced to a piece of paper and then discarded may make it possible to find the ultimate connection between what Tobias does to "The Dead Vidette" and what Amantha does to the paper epitaph at the grave of the unknown former slave. Seth Parton, arguing with Amantha at Oberlin about the immorality of her father's owning slaves, had reinforced his point with a theatrical gesture that would resonate later in the novel. He held his arm up against the sky, and his hand opened: "all at once, at the end of his gesture, as though it released something, and flung that thing away. I had the distinct image that the hand flung my father away, my father so little and shriveled and pitiful that he was crumpled in the palm of that hand, like a wad of paper, to be flung away, to whirl across the snow, forever" (37). It is not difficult to see that what Amantha later does in the Halesburg cemetery is very nearly the same thing: "I . . . let it [the scrap of paper] go, and the wind had taken it off across the prairie." But did she mean to imitate Seth's gesture, and, if so, was that graveside gesture directed, as was his, against her father? The context that immediately surrounds the death of the man whose epitaph she flung away suggests that it was. The beggar she had seen crouching in the street and who she thought was Rau-Ru had shared lodgings with a local character named Uncle Slop, Halesburg's garbage collector. The beggar's death coincided with a spectacular instance of filial piety that Amantha envied but knew she could not imitate (or could not imitate at the moment she stood at the grave). Uncle Slop had, years before, "abandoned his son, going West, to freedom, to success, to gather garbage" (373). But that son, Joshua Lounberry, succeeded in tracing him down and came to Halesburg to restore him to his affections and a considerable fortune. Amantha's response was to compare that paternal abandonment to the one she had suffered from "my father, how he had betrayed me and how I hated him. . . . I suffered a dry, gnawing envy of Mr. Lounberry, who could honor his father."

Aaron Starr's abandonment of his daughter had been quite shockingly revealed to Amantha when she stood at his grave in Danville, Kentucky, and Cy Marmaduke claimed her in payment for her father's debts. First the sheriff asked if she had any *papers*.

> "Papers?" I echoed, in question.
> "Yeah, papers!" the Sheriff said. "Papers yore pappy give you. Didn't he ever give you papers? Spent all that money and sent you up North and all, and he's bound to give you papers." A trace of outrage was coming into his tone. (58)

No wonder Amantha's anger toward her father—and her displaced revenge at the grave at the end of the novel—took the form of reducing him to a piece of paper and then flinging that paper away. It was a kind of poetic justice for his not having bothered to write out the piece of paper that would have spared her the horror of being sold into slavery at the foot of his grave. And no wonder she saw the love which Hamish Bond tried to offer her in compensation for an inadequate father as "a scrap of paper." The whole problem of her existence was this missing text from the father, the manumission papers Aaron Starr never had the heart to draw up, as they would have acknowledged the truth his love for her made too hard to bear. What Aaron Starr did to Amantha was make her identity dependent on a nonexistent text. It is a remarkable variation on what we have learned to recognize as a consistent theme in Warren's fiction: the text from the father with which the son (or daughter) must come to terms in order to live his (her) life, even though the very existence of that text is placed in question. It is certainly in question here, since Aaron never wrote it; yet it does have a kind of negative existence, for everyone, including the sheriff, assumed that he had written it. And this variation on the theme is joined in *Band of Angels* by another parental inscription, the *Renie* left by the mother (though it was presumably the father who had it carved), which appears to be a simple statement of fact but may be more.

Perhaps we are now in a position to better understand that other instance of something scribbled on a scrap of paper, Amantha's realization that Hamish Bond "walks pretty well" after all, that thought "lying there in my head like something scribbled on a scrap of paper and flung down in a dark closet." When he had rescued her from the auction block on the Rue Royale, she had noticed that "he had some kind of a limp, a stiffness of the right knee, and that in walking he set the blackthorn down with deliberation for each step" (89). Whatever irregularity there might have been in his stride was countered by the "metronomic precision" (90) with which he set down his walking stick as he walked. That Amantha should be intrigued by the question of whether or not Hamish had a genuine limp is more than a little like Jack Burden's wondering if Willie Stark winked at him or just had something in his eye. Willie's eye did close for a moment; the question was whether he meant anything by it. Hamish behaves as if he has a limp, tapping his stick metronomically wherever he goes; the question for Amantha is whether he does it for show or for real. It is an ambiguous message from a fatherly figure in the same sense Stark's was—is it a sign or not?—and Amantha's response is, curiously, to compare her awareness of it to a text of her own, scribbled on a scrap of paper and flung down in a dark closet. Whether or not the limp originally was a sign, a text she was meant to read, it is one now. What happens to Hamish's limp may be what Amantha fears happens to a dream when you try to tell it: "you find in the telling that you are simply having another dream"—it may take on a reality it did not originally have. But, then, reality, after all—as Jack Burden learned, and as Amantha witnessed when Old Shaddy made Bu-Bula—arises from the combination of events that are not in themselves real.

Still, there is something real behind Bond's limp, though that prior reality is itself a kind of inscription akin to the hieroglyphic marks of herringbone lines Amantha thought she could read on Rau-Ru's back even though she never actually saw them. There is the scar on his thigh made by the African amazon from whom he rescued the infant Rau-Ru—the scar Amantha discovered after she noticed that Hamish walked pretty well after all, when she awoke with him asleep in bed with her the night they first made love. Amantha learns to read another mark in Bond's house, the hieroglyphic "wavy line looping between the peaks" (103) under the letter *B* on his napkins. And she even learns how to inscribe, to embroider, that mark herself, under Michele's tutelage. "It is the sea," Michele tells her, as her finger traces the wavy line, alluding to the years Hamish spent on shipboard. Amantha "looked down at the bold initial, as though it might divulge something." The hieroglyph may divulge more than Michele allows or Amantha acknowledges, for though the reader is never given a definitive answer to the puzzle it poses, its combination of peaks (or points) and loops ("the wavy line *looping*") makes it almost a rebus for the name Bond chose for the plantation he entrusted to Rau-Ru's care, *Pointe du Loup*. (Here I assume an Americanized mispronunciation akin to that which made beeches out of Beauchamp.)

But the initial may have yet another connection to Hamish's *k'la;* for what Amantha was to imagine all those years as written on Rau-Ru's flesh, a text that she had invented out of whole cloth and that caused her to misread what she glimpsed through the tattered shirt on the half-exposed back of the hunching beggar, does not escape a certain resemblance to the hieroglyph she learned to replicate in Hamish Bond's house. For what she thought she recognized on that back was another kind of embroidery stitch, a "neat herringbone pattern"—a transmuted version, perhaps, of the pattern she had tried to imitate ("I plied my needle, trying to imitate Michele's meticulous art, tracing out, thread by thread . . . some sort of wavy pattern" [99]). Having learned to reproduce that puzzling pattern at will, Amantha may have projected it onto a surface she had never seen for reasons she did not fully understand.

There is more, however, to the Halesburg beggar and his herringbone back to justify Amantha's false recognition scene, to us if not to her. When she had first described what she thought must be on Rau-Ru's back, years before, she twice made reference to its *humped* quality: "I saw it in my mind, the healed-up scars . . . humping out, interlacing mathematically . . . [the] humped, corded scars" (271–72). Beyond anything Amantha could have known, the peculiar way in which Rau-Ru's back is humped recalls another, more genuinely humped back: the Grand' Bosse's in *World Enough and Time:* "The shoulders were very large and the head was thrust forward from the pillows by a swelling or hump, not unlike the hump of the bull of the buffalo. . . . He was hump-backed" (429–30). Jeremiah Beaumont at that moment remembered that Dr. Les Burnham—who had appeared propped up in a wagon in a way that likewise reminded him of a buffalo . . . propped in the lashed-down chair that was big as a bed" (395–96)— had taught him enough French to recognize that *bosse* meant hump, though Jeremiah had trouble realizing it when he heard the word spoken. In response to a bystander's question "That yore pappy?", Jeremiah had remarked that Burnham was "like a father to me." That the Grand' Bosse could be a grotesque double of this paternal figure may explain why he and Rau-Ru are linked through their association with humped backs, for just as what Amantha saw in the hunched beggar was Rau-Ru, what she saw as she stood over that nameless grave was her father. *Band of Angels* renews the inquiry into the word Jeremiah first found so puzzling—*bosse*—by offering a meditation on its English version, for underlying Amantha's confusion is a linguistic connection linking her description of Rau-Ru's humped back with her description of the beggar's hunched posture ("He was crouching on his hams with arms forward over the *hunched-up* knees"). Despite the fact that the beggar was not humpbacked, there is a certain substitutability between hunch and hump, for the hunch is in fact "to arch into a hump," a hunch can be a hump, and a hunchback and a humpback are really the same thing. So there is good reason for Amantha's feeling that she had seen that hunch before.

We have seen it, too, and her false recognition scene prompts a recognition for the attentive reader of Warren's novels that I hope is not false. Would we be as misled as Amantha if we thought that in the "hunched-up" figure in the Halesburg street we saw "the little hunched-up creature" that Jason Sweetwater imagined under the mound of Sue Murdock's abdomen and that reminded him of "the way certain primitive tribes buried their dead. Hunched up like that"? Would it be wrong to suppose that the mysterious figure Amantha encounters here is actually the fetal mummy that haunts Warren's novels?—that her moment of false recognition is meant to provoke one of our own? that the attempt to tell the dream of her narrative makes us dream one too?

Percy Munn had his dream of a fetus, Sweetwater his daydream of one, Jack Burden his vision of the "sad little fetus" within, Rachel her stillborn ones—and Amantha Starr her Bu-Bula. In the unpublished, unfinished novel "God's Own Time," Warren, listing the prizes available at a rural carnival, once dwelt on dolls' fetal qualities (and at the same time placed Indians and fetuses side by side, a juxtaposition Sweetwater was subsequently to make with his recollection of fetally crouched American Indian mummies): "leather pillow covers with the imbecile profile of an Indian in warpaint, great foetal baby dolls sitting with outstretched arms in the gloom" (35–36). "[H]ow," Amantha wondered in the opening pages of her story, thinking of the way the paradisiacal place of her imagining and the actual site of her mother's grave strangely merged in her heart, "can that be, when the place in my dream is a place of beginnings and the place in my true recollection has a grave, the mark of endings?" (4). Warren's linking of birth with death in the figure of the fetus poses precisely this question, and Bu-Bula's very name incarnates one of the two terms of that merger, as we are reminded at the foot of Amantha's father's grave: " 'Yes, there's a will,' he was repeating, 'and you gentlemen know how a will begins—you all being the kind of gentlemen having estates to set in order before taking out for the *Beulah* shore'" (58–59; emphasis added)—Beulah Land being, in a Bunyan-influenced topography, the Elysian rest at the end of life's journey.

Bu-Bula's creator, Old Shaddy, shares with Rau-Ru the distinction of being "recognized" by Amantha when he's not there at all. Twice she sees him in the person of Jimmee, a slave in Bond's house, the second time really believing it is him: "the head preternaturally big with swathing of white cloth, like a turban, all familiar, terribly familiar. Then I knew. Shaddy, it must be Old Shaddy, Shadrach, with his broken head bandaged like a turban.... [T]hey had broken his head, and now he had come back to me, he would show me the head" (310). Amantha's déjà vu will be matched by ours, if we remember how Slim Sarrett claimed that his father had come back to show him *his* head, one that also had a piece of white cloth attached: "How his head," Sarrett said, "just his head, with something hanging out of the neck like a hank of dirty white clothes-line—would come drifting through the air toward me." Shaddy was in fact a father to Amantha (and, like her other fathers, a seducer as well), who became in his cradling arms a kind of double for the doll he made: "I would be holding her," Amantha said of the doll, "and he would be holding me.... Now and then he would joggle me and Bu-Bula, the way you joggle a baby" (13).

As for Jimmee, there was a certain paternal mystery attached to him: was he or was he not, Amantha long wondered, the father of Dollie's baby (120)? He was husband to Michele, as Old Shaddy had been to Aunt Sukie back in Kentucky; in these two triangles Amantha might have seen in the appropriately named Dollie a double of herself, the childlike woman with whom Jimmee/Shaddy may have committed adultery, with his wife's knowledge. For it was in carrying his games with Amantha a little too far that Shaddy got his turban: "It was an old game, with a thousand variations, but one night it was, all at once, different.... Aunt Sukie ... just looked quiet at Shaddy and said: 'That chile gittin too big, you to fool her up that a-way'" (14). When Amantha's father found out, he sold him downriver; it was in trying to escape that Shadrach received the blow to the head. Seeing him being carted off, Amantha "could see a big bandage about Shadrach's head, like an untidy turban" (16). When Jimmee appears in *his* turban, he has come to take her to Rau-Ru, who at this juncture in the story has fled to the swamp to escape prosecution in the wake of the New Orleans 1866 riots.

Just as Jimmee's turban reminds her of someone else, so does the posture he instructs her to assume on her journey across the water recall the hunched-over position in which the Halesburg beggar crouched: "Jimmee ordered me to cover my head against the gallinippers. 'Git yore dress up,' he said, 'up over yore head, jist so you kin breave.' I bowed forward and drew the skirt up over my head, holding it close to create my own airless, inner darkness, and be safe in it" (315). Byram B. White had found a similar safety in his inner darkness, "drawing himself into a hunch as though he wanted to assume the prenatal position and be little and warm and safe in the dark." And Jack Burden could imagine himself in something like the same situation, faced with a yellow envelope that he didn't want to open— and that presaged the yellowing brown paper package of Cass Mastern papers as well as the brown manila envelope containing the truth about Judge Irwin: "huddled up way inside, in the dark which is you, inside yourself, like a clammy, sad little foetus you carry around inside yourself.... [I]ts eyes are blind, and it shivers cold inside you for it doesn't want to know what is in that envelope." Amantha Starr, however, does not assume this position because she wants to hide from anything, but because she was told to do it, and her assuming it in the boat in the swamp has more to do, perhaps, with images of death (with Jimmee as Charon in this ferry crossing) and watery (re)birth.

Yet Amantha is, like Jack Burden, trailed by a brown envelope that she keeps putting off reopening—and, like Jack's, it is consistently brown. ("He withdrew a big thick brown envelope" [137]; "From the drawer he took a metal box, unlocked it, and took out a brown envelope" [217].) It is the one piece of paper Hamish Bond can offer her that will do her some good, the missing text her father should have provided but did not, the manumission papers: "I went to rummage in a valise and take out the papers, the manumission papers, that Hamish Bond had made out so long ago.... They had been in the brown envelope.... But that first night at *Pointe du Loup,* I had laid the envelope on the table in the hall. That was the last I ever saw of it until the morning in May.... He gave me the envelope then" (209). Amantha's forgetfulness is understandable, for to pay attention to those papers would have been to acknowledge something she would rather forget. The fact that her father had neglected to write them out in the first place was due to a similar desire to deny, as she finally realizes at the end of the novel: "[I]t was, in a funny, sad, confused way, his very love for me which made my father leave me to be seized at his grave-side. He had not been able to make the papers out, or the will, that would declare me less than what he had led me to believe I was ..." (373).

Amantha's early reluctance to hold on to the brown envelope Bond gave her reemerges at the novel's close in the dislike she ascribes to her husband of carrying a package in public: "Tobias could bring a parcel home. No, I couldn't make him do that—not with his face the way it always was when he had to walk down the street carrying a sack of groceries, his face stiff and averted" (355–56). The ultimate significance of this otherwise trivial household concern becomes clearer when she applies this observation to how she imagined he must have felt when he drove Uncle Slop and his newly discovered son into town in his surrey: "I thought how his face must have been stiff and distant above the leers of Main Street, the same thing as when he had to carry a parcel, but worse" (369). The manner in which the mysterious, sudden appearance of the Halesburg beggar is intertwined with the story of Lounberry and his father encourages a completion of the comparison: Tobias's shame at carrying a parcel home resembles his "shame" at being "a Jehu to coons" (369), though this shame exists only in Amantha's mind, in the projection of her own shame onto her husband, for as Tobias later reveals, he really took considerable delight in playing the role of intermediary in the Lounberry matter. This "shame" of Amantha's itself recalls her horror of being discovered by Rau-Ru, of having any connection to the man whose scars she left her husband in the middle of the night to inspect—her shame, in short, of acknowledging the burden of her past. If Uncle Slop is a parcel for Tobias, the man with the herringbone-humped back is a parcel for Amantha that, like the brown envelope she kept leaving behind, she does not want to carry.

A curious anticipation of this episode took place when Amantha first laid eyes on Tobias Sears on the New Orleans street where a Union officer claimed to have found her in violation of General Order Number 28 (which forbade women to make insulting remarks to occupying troops), and from whose insolence Tobias rescued her: "I was carrying a parcel in my hand. The parcel contained some fine linen undergarments, two corset-covers, to be exact, which I was to embroider.... [T]he corset-covers I carried were to conceal the rigor of whalebone that held in place the loyal Unionist bosoms of ladies of Federal officers" (205). How remarkable that the eventual contents of the coverings of which this parcel is the package should be a variation on the pattern Amantha thought she saw on that rejected "parcel" in the Halesburg street, the bony innards of "fish"—whalebone for herringbone.

But even more remarkable is the way this scene of her first encounter with Tobias Sears seems teasingly to allude to the origins of her husband's first name. The first Tobias was the biblical one in the Book of Tobit in the Old Testament Apocrypha. Given the evocative associations of other names in Warren's fiction (we shall later see how significant a choice "Perse" was for his first novel's protagonist), it is not surprising that this name should recall some of the circumstances of the story in which his namesake was involved. Tobias Sears is indebted to the virtues of something that comes from inside a "fish" (a whale) for the chance to meet the woman who becomes his wife, for to embroider the undergarments that depend on that commodity for their support was the reason Amantha was on the street that day. Now the original Tobias was likewise indebted to what comes out of a fish for the chance to meet *his* wife—specifically, to the viscera of a fish that leaped out at him from the Tigris River and that the angel Raphael instructed him how to use to win the hand of the woman God had planned for him to marry.[3]

The Book of Tobit abounds with blindness and burial. Tobias's father, Tobit, was almost obsessively devoted to burying corpses no one else would touch; it was in undertaking one such burial that he lost his sight. Ritually unclean from having touched the corpse, he could not come home until he had purified himself at sunrise. Thus he spent the night out-of-doors, sleeping on his back near a courtyard wall where birds had perched, whose droppings consequently fell into his open eyes; a strange but necessary detail of the story is that he evidently slept with his eyes open—as fish are said to do because they have no eyelids. What Tobias, at the angel's instruction, later finds inside the fish eventually restores his father's sight and wins the hand of the bride. *Band of Angels,* which begins and ends with a graveside meditation, is also concerned with the proper care of the dead: Amantha had always wondered why her mother's grave was not near the rest of the family and when her father died was scandalized, until she learned the truth, to see that her father was not being interred where he belonged. "My first awareness was not the renewal of grief, it was an impulse to cry out, 'No—no—that's the wrong place—come over here—over here to the cedars!' For that was where my mother lay. She lay there because there she would be closer to the house, and to him, my father had said, and he should be buried there with her" (55). A similar concern for proper burial is apparent at the end of the novel, when, like father Tobit (or like the elder Tobias, in the Latin Vulgate version, where both have the same name), Tobias Sears assumes responsibility for the burial of the nameless black beggar, the one Amantha thought was Rau-Ru. It was Tobias who discovered the body and who arranged for the coroner to take the remains to the Bended Head Undertaking Parlor. They found almost enough money on him, thanks to Amantha's generosity when she had passed him on the corner, to pay the expenses; Tobias evidently made up the difference.

A remarkable parallel lies in the fact that Amantha had at one point thought that, like his biblical namesake, Tobias had been temporarily blinded. It happened when she returned to him after the time she spent with Rau-Ru in the swamp during the convention disturbances in 1866. Tobias had been seriously wounded in the riots, and when she first sees him in the hospital, she says, "I thought he was blind—one of the blows had been to the head—and with the awfulness of that thought I had some fleeting, submerged sense, like the white flash of a fish-belly in deep water, of fulfillment, of vindication: I should lead him, always, by the hand" (336). The principal elements of the biblical scene are amazingly reunited here: blindness, the fish, Amantha leading Tobias—as did the angel—by the hand.

The poetic structure of the biblical text of the Book of Tobit is erected on an uncanny resemblance between the father's obsession with putting the dead below ground and the son's panic at seeing a fish leap up from the surface of the water; both would rather such things stayed below, where they belong. Now it happens that this equivalence of fish and corpse is reenacted at the Halesburg cemetery in the person of the corpse with the herringbone marks. What Amantha most fears as she stands at the grave is that its occupant may rise and reappear, and that, in the very act of drawing breath, she will have to recognize her identity with what was buried—a fear she expresses by gasping for air like a fish out of water: "I stood there a minute or two, looking down at the grave. Well, there it was, and I had seen it, for whatever reason I had had to see it: to prove to myself, perhaps, that it was dead, was under the earth, that I was free.... I took a gasp of breath, like a fish" (362).[4]

Chapter 7
The Fictive Fetus in the Cave *The Cave,* 1959

Chapter 1   It is June 1955. Monty Harrick, of Johntown, Tennessee, in a beech glade with his girlfriend, Jo-Lea Bingham, silently regrets that his older brother, Jasper, is more able than he to live up to the reputation of their father, Jack, as a virile hell-raiser. He sees Jasper's boots and guitar propped up at the mouth of a cave that Jasper has gone into partnership with its owner, Isaac Sumpter, to explore and exploit as a potential tourist attraction. Monty and Jo-Lea have been there for some time, in gradually increasing stages of undress, before Jo-Lea suddenly realizes that Jasper must be trapped in the cave, for he would not have left his guitar outside all night to be ruined by the dew.

Chapter 2   Nicholas Papadoupalous—Nick Pappy in Johntown—had met his wife in a striptease establishment and married her because she looked like Jean Harlow, but now she is no longer blonde or slender. He had begun to impose himself sexually on similarly blonde-haired Dorothy Cutlick, a nineteen-year-old waitress who lived in the back room of his restaurant, but she left to become a bookkeeper in Timothy Bingham's bank. When Nick goes to see Bingham, with some apprehension, about the loan he never seems able to pay off, he is agreeably surprised to hear the banker ask for his help in securing the services of an abortionist.

Chapter 3   In 1916 Jack Harrick had made Mary Tillyard pregnant, and then had run off to World War I after getting into an argument with his former drinking and whoring partner, MacCarland Sumpter, who has since become an ordained Baptist preacher, over whether Miss Tillyard had been a willing partner. In Harrick's absence Sumpter marries Mary and is happy later when she ejects the stillborn fetus his friend had fathered. But when his own son, Isaac, is born, Mary dies. Isaac does quite well in college in Nashville until he wins—and loses—the love of Rachel Goldstein. Demoralized, he flunks out of graduate school but does not tell his father. Back in Johntown, his only hope is to make a financial killing on the cave.

Chapter 4   Old Jack Harrick, dying of cancer, looks back on his life, remembering his courtship of Celia Hornby, his wife, who cured him of his hell-raising ways. Nick Pappy asks his wife if she knows how to perform an abortion; he assumes the woman Bingham wants it for is Dorothy Cutlick.

Chapter 5   Jo-Lea runs into the Harrick house with the news that Jasper is stuck in the cave. Isaac is fetched and persuaded to go in after him, since he knows the cave. Nick Pappy drives him there, and on the way he points out to the restaurateur that there is a lot of money to be made off this situation, for countless gawkers will come to wait out the rescue and they will have to be fed. He proposes a partnership in which Nick will invest his own money, not only to set up a food service for the crowd (Isaac will persuade the police to keep competitors out), but to get a phone line set up for himself so that he can talk to the press.

Chapter 6   As people gather at the cave entrance—including Jack and Celia Harrick, Timothy Bingham and his daughter, Jo-Lea, townsfolk, and even some out-of-towners—Monty Harrick picks up his brother's guitar and sings an impromptu ballad about his trapped brother. Isaac emerges from the cave to announce that Jasper is still alive.

Chapter 7   Isaac manages to keep anyone else from going in—even the police, whom he convinces Jasper cannot be reached through the passage he crawled into, but only by digging from above. He is persuasive because he has the envelope upon which Jasper had in fact written the compass readings and distances to the fourth chamber—where Isaac says he is—before transferring that data to his notebook. With equipment he has had Pappy procure, Isaac begins to tape dramatic eyewitness news accounts of the event and relay them to a Nashville radio station.

Chapter 8   Isaac allows Jebb Holloway, a friend of Jasper's, in to help him run an electric line for a heating pad for Jasper. Some distance into the cave, by a stalagmite that Jebb finds strangely reminiscent of a beech tree, Jebb waits while Isaac goes the rest of the way in to Jasper. On his return, Isaac brings a message from Jasper to "his girl." Jebb asks if it is Jo-Lea, whose panties another boy found outside the cave (where she dropped them in chapter 1). Isaac tells him he can speak in front of the TV cameras this time and say he spoke to Jasper, which Jebb does, then finds himself hoping that Jasper will not come out alive to contradict him. On a later emergence from the cave, Isaac tells the public that Jasper sends word to his girl that he would have loved the baby.

Chapter 9   We learn that Isaac had not found Jasper in the cave. He had intended to tell the truth the first time, but the words just wouldn't come out. He was convinced that Jasper was dead and that therefore he was free to invent his fiction.

Chapter 10 Jo-Lea's mother is scandalized by the fact that her daughter's name is mentioned in the newspaper as having first discovered that Jasper was trapped in the cave and that the same front page carries the story of his supposed unborn child and its unnamed mother— this, compounded by the fact that Jo-Lea has gotten pregnant (by Monty) and refuses to name the father. At the mouth of the cave, Isaac's father, MacCarland Sumpter, is preaching, praying, and imploring the poor girl carrying Jasper's child to come forth and confess her sin. The boy who found Jo-Lea's panties presses them into her hand and asks her if they are hers. In response to Sumpter's appeal, even though it isn't true, Jo-Lea jumps up and confesses that she is the mother of that child.

Chapter 11 Isaac and Jebb emerge from the cave once more; Jebb relays the news that Jasper is dying. Isaac's father goes into the cave before anyone can prevent him and returns to announce that Jasper is indeed dead, but that his dying words were that he had never made anyone pregnant. Isaac publicly accuses his father of not having had the courage to go all the way into the cave, and of lying. Although convinced that Jasper is dead, the crowd refuses to believe that Jo-Lea isn't pregnant with his child.

Chapter 12 MacCarland Sumpter tells his son that when he found Jasper he was dead but the body was still warm and that he was not where Isaac had said he was (which proves Isaac was faking). Isaac, in effect, killed Jasper by preventing his rescue. Sumpter claims that he lied about Jasper's last words in order to counteract the effect of Isaac's more harmful lie and adds that he went back and got the heating pad and placed it by the body to cover for his son. Isaac drives to the Nashville airport to fly to New York to collect the money he has earned from the national media for the story, and presumably to begin the writer's career that his fiction about the cave has opened up for him.

Chapter 13 Back home in Johntown reconciliation is almost general. MacCarland Sumpter confesses to Jack Harrick that he had been glad when the son Jack fathered on Mary Tillyard was born dead; Harrick counters with the confession that he wanted his son Jasper to die, in the hope that his own life would be spared. Timothy Bingham gathers up the courage to tell his shrewish wife that he is going to divorce her; he will bless the marriage of Jo-Lea and Monty Harrick, the actual father of her unborn child, and will pay his way through college so that he can have a career to provide for her future happiness.

The Cave, James Justus has observed, "is the only one of Warren's novels which lacks a true protagonist" (274). Told from multiple points of view, the novel finds a certain obvious unity in the cave around which its principal characters gather as they participate in or await the outcome of the supposed rescue of the man trapped inside;[1] it finds a subtler and more far-reaching unity in the use it makes of some of the elements that recur in the symbolic structure of Warren's five earlier novels.

Some of these connections are stranger than others. *World Enough and Time,* for example, as we have seen, links beeches and caves for reasons of its own: it was Jeremiah Beaumont's memory of a beech tree that prompted him to recall the "deeper, truer" memory of a cave, of how he used to love to lie in caves and breathe the clean smell of the pregnant and pulsing dark. *The Cave* could not be expected to exploit, as does the earlier novel, the echo of the name of the tree, for Jereboam Beauchamp has no role to play here. Yet it does seem to insist on the same linkage, for its cave is entered through the roots of a beech—its mouth "the little hole in the ground under the roots of the biggest beech" (376), an opening "flanked by the great humping gray roots of the biggest beech" (208)—and inside it is something that could be mistaken for another beech tree, as when Jebb Holloway "leaned against the rough surface of the stalagmite [and] felt its roughness, but its funny sort of smoothness too, through the coveralls. It was like a beech, that was what it was feeling like. If you leaned up against this thing in the dark, durn it, you'd think it was a beech" (260). Even stranger is the fact that the cave is located near a place whose name precisely evokes the sound of the name at which it seemed the persistent beeches in Jeremiah Beaumont's story were hinting: "Beecham's Bluff Falls" (139).[2] It is as if the cave-beech-Beecham/Beauchamp connection had taken on a life of its own, severed from its contextual origin in *World Enough and Time;* as if it had acquired, mysteriously, some autonomous reality and meaning through the context it creates for itself; as if it were yet another illustration of the truth of Jack Burden's insight that "the reality of an event, which is not real in itself, arises from other events which, likewise, in themselves are not real." As it happens, the plot of *The Cave* turns upon just such a creation of meaning out of practically nothing, out of a fiction, a lie—a *bluff.*

Although it is true that the novel seems to consist of the various personal histories of Jack Harrick, MacCarland Sumpter, Isaac Sumpter, Jo-Lea and Timothy Bingham, Dorothy Cutlick, and Nick Papadoupalous, and that the story appears at times almost arbitrarily fragmented as it shifts among their different points of view, it is also true that there is one character, and only one, who acts in the present, who is not the mere sum of his past actions, and whose present actions have some effect on the other characters in the novel. Madison Jones has recently suggested that although *The Cave* "has no clear protagonist at all ... Jack Harrick, the aged and dying blacksmith ... comes nearest to that role" (51). But the elder Harrick, though both hero and villain of much that occurred before the summer of 1955 when the novel takes place, and clearly a character who elicits the reader's sympathy, is less the protagonist of the present than its victim. With one exception, the only person who actually does anything of any significance within the time frame of the novel is Jasper Harrick; but even his having got himself trapped in the cave is a fact in the recent past with which the novel begins, and he never appears, as Justus has noted, "except in the flashbacks of other characters" (275). He is absent from the novel, though he is the absent center around which the plot unfolds. The exception, the best candidate for protagonist because he does act in the present in which the novel transpires, is Isaac Sumpter, who bluffs his way to riches and fame by pretending to relate to Johntown, and to the world, the hour-by-hour decline of the trapped Jasper, to whose dying words he has acquired exclusive copyright but which he has in fact invented.

The cave is on land Isaac inherited from his grandmother, and he and Jasper Harrick, an experienced caver, had entered into a partnership to exploit the cave as a tourist attraction. Jasper's interest in caves was in fact an obsession, interpreted by his mother as a desire to escape from his father. "You made jokes with him," she said to Jack Harrick. "You'd wink at him.... That's why he crawled in the ground. To get away from everything. To get away from the hands on him. To get away from the jokes and the winks.... To get away from ... you" (298). The hands were those of the Johntowners who had congratulated Jasper as he was about to depart for Korea, telling him he was a chip off the old block, for his father had won a medal in World War I and had emerged victorious in countless backwoods brawls. The paternal winks were given in the hope Jasper would live up to the other half of his father's reputation, that of having seduced half the women in the country. Like Jack Burden in *All the King's Men,* Jasper Harrick was troubled by a paternal wink; what troubled him, however, was not that he couldn't interpret it but that he didn't want to live up to what it meant. Jeremiah Beaumont in *World Enough and Time* provides a closer parallel, as Jasper succeeded in doing what Jeremiah could only fantasize about, definitively escape from his father into a cave. What Jasper's mother says about how he took refuge in caves to run away from his father recalls how Beaumont described the delight he took in crawling into subterranean passages, how he could breathe there "the limey, cool, inward smell of earth's bowels ... a smell cleanly and rich, not dead and foul but pregnant with a secret life, as though you breathed the dark and the dark were about to pulse. And while I lay there, I thought how I might not be able to return, but would lie there forever, and I saw how my father might at that moment be standing in a field full of sun to call my name wildly ... to no avail" (315).

Yet the similarity between Jeremiah and Jasper should not be allowed to obscure a greater one between Jeremiah and Isaac: like Beaumont, and

Burden as well, young Sumpter is trying to make sense of a difficult paternal text, even at the risk of substituting his own interpretation for his father's. What functions for young Sumpter as the equivalent of the handbill that Fort never wrote but to which Jeremiah responded with "the gratitude of a good son to a father," certain now at last that he had reason to avenge Rachel's dishonor, or the equivalent of Willie Stark's wink which the Boss always refused to acknowledge (or of the manumission papers Aaron Starr never wrote), is the name Isaac's father gave him: " '[W]hy did you name me Isaac? . . . There wasn't any reason to. There wasn't any Isaac in the family, ever. I have looked at the family Bible' " (95). The Reverend Mac-Carland Sumpter's answer was straightforward enough: " 'For Sarah conceived, and bare Abraham a son in his old age.' " But this could not satisfy Isaac, who was certain there was more in that name to interpret, and was especially troubled by the rest of the biblical paradigm. "Abraham," he countered, "was so glad that he took the bloody little miracle out in the country and tied him up and was going to cut his bloody little miraculous throat." This was not what his father had had in mind at all, but he knew the proper biblical response: " 'God in his mercy put the ram in the bushes,' the old man said, 'caught in a thicket by his horns' " (96). Jasper Harrick, trapped in the cave on Sumpter's Ridge, becomes that sacrificial ram, for he dies there for Isaac's sake, and at the same time MacCarland Sumpter saves his son, Isaac.[3] He saves him, that is, by covering for the fiction which Isaac had concocted for public consumption and his own glory, and which had in fact prevented a real rescue from taking place. In particular, Sumpter carries the heating pad Isaac had carelessly tossed aside back to where Jasper's body lay, so that it would look as if Isaac had indeed gone all the way into the cave to comfort Jasper and hear his last words.

Yet Isaac persists in his own reading of the text of his name, interpreting even this fatherly mercy as the ultimate filicide: "[I]t was as though there had been a knife, after all. The old fool had saved him. The old fool had done that and he could never escape that fact. That fact was like a knife blade plunged between your shoulder blades, and you take a step away, and another, and another, waiting to fall" (359).

In this latter-day twist on the biblical tale, it is not God who tests Abraham, but Isaac. "I was just remembering how the story goes," young Sumpter had said to his father when he first asked him about the name, taunting him, almost daring him to live up to his role. "Wondering how you'd do. Personally, I don't think you'd be up to it" (96). It is only in retrospect, perhaps, that Isaac Sumpter's role in the botched rescue of Jasper Harrick takes on the appearance of a biblical Isaac obediently going up the mountain to test his father's ability to save him; at the time, the sequence of events had seemed to Isaac to conform to some other "inner logic" of their own (285).

> It was an accident that Mrs. Harrick had not been willing for Monty Harrick to go in [the cave where Jasper was trapped]. . . . And it was an accident that . . . Bingham had suggested that he, Isaac Sumpter, should go in. . . . And from those words which, upon coming out of the cave, he had heard his own voice, from no intention of his own, saying to the assembled people, all else had followed, step by step, by its own logic. He had planned nothing. (292)

It was with a sense of obedience to that logic that Isaac was able to seal Jasper's fate with a clear conscience: "He was nothing, merely the guiltless instrument of a power, but that power, which was not himself, somehow conformed to his will, so that his will was, guiltlessly, achieved and he was filled with the exultation of power" (285).

But that inner logic has another sense as well, for yet another drama is being reenacted here. Nearly forty years earlier, Isaac's father and Jasper's had been linked in an awkward alliance that bears an interesting resemblance to their sons' joint exploitation of the cave. Isaac and Jasper would not normally have been friends, though they may have had more in common than they realized, in that each in his own way felt the need for escape: Jasper, into caves; Isaac, to the greater world beyond Johntown, from which he had returned in disgrace after being thrown out of college but to which he is desperate to return. Isaac cultivated Jasper's acquaintance for purely financial reasons; he needed the money for his escape. "He thought how maybe the cave might pay off. But . . . it meant associating with that Jasper Harrick. Suddenly he couldn't bear the thought of Jasper Harrick" (132). Years before, their fathers had been temporary companions in hell-raising but parted company when MacCarland Sumpter got religion and began preaching hellfire theology to a Baptist congregation. However, one indissoluble connection remained between them, Mary Tillyard, whom Jack Harrick first entered and knew in the biblical sense, but whom in the fullness of time MacCarland came to possess. Jack left to fight the Germans after he knocked Sumpter unconscious for striking him in remonstrance for Jack's too cavalier account of how he had seduced her; MacCarland took advantage of his absence to marry the girl himself, and was later overjoyed, though not without guilt (a guilt it took him forty years to realize), to see that he would not have to be the legal parent of the child Jack had fathered on Mary: "[T]hat night when Mary Tillyard had suddenly seized her middle and fallen to the floor, and brought forth the dead child, his heart had leaped with joy. . . . [I]t had been joy, he now knew, in the fact that what would have been the son of Jack Harrick was dead, was nothing, nothing but a bloody package of offal, and would never stand before him to remind him" (90–91).

Similarly, Jasper Harrick had been the first to find the cave and do the preliminary exploration, while ownership rested with young Sumpter. They would exploit it together, reaping the financial reward, charging admission, developing it into a tourist attraction that would include the nearby and scenic Beecham's Bluff Falls. Jasper's disappearance would leave Isaac the sole proprietor of not only the cave but the venture; Isaac's improvisatory response to that disappearance, however, the "inner logic" he felt constrained to obey, would bring him still greater reward. Isaac had a flair for writing that he displayed when he wrote a newspaper column while still in college, and he knew enough about the media to react quickly to the news of Jasper's entrapment, could see that if it worked in the Floyd Collins case it would work for him. He had a telephone line installed at the mouth of the cave, procured a tape recorder, made a deal with a television station, even opened a bank account in New York where they could send the money. He finagled the exclusive rights to take food to Jasper as well as tell his story and distracted the authorities by producing an envelope on which Jasper happened to have jotted down the coordinates of his position, thus instructing them to dig from above, away from the mouth of the cave.[4]

The uterine quality of Warren's caves is at work here and strengthens the analogy between the woman whom the fathers both knew and the cave that brought the sons together. It does so in imagery specific to the plot of *The Cave:* Mary Tillyard died in childbirth—Isaac's. Specifically, she bled to death: she "ejected from her body the burden that was to be known as Isaac Sumpter, and then nobody could stop the blood" (83). The cave is a virtual fountain of blood, leaving its mark on those who venture into it or are otherwise caught up in its imagery: when Jasper's younger brother, Monty, ran home with the bad news, his mother noticed that the red dust of the cave floor where he had crawled in to look for Jasper had rubbed off from Monty's face onto her own when he kissed her, "to give the impression of rouge smeared crazily, drunkenly, on one cheek in wanton dissymmetry" (187–88). This could have reminded her, as it should the reader, of another red facial smear, a genuinely bloody one, the one she had noticed on Jack Harrick's face the first time she saw him with the carcass of a bear he had shot: "a smear of blood on the man's face as the man yelled in joy," an image that appears three times in the novel (204 [quoted here], 160, 375). And when Jebb Holloway, whom Isaac tricked into becoming his spokesman in front of the television cameras and into pretending that he, too, had been in contact with Jasper, leaned against a stalagmite that seemed peculiarly like a beech tree, he began to get the feeling that he was "bleeding to death. It was like blood running out of him from a secret wound . . . and nothing could staunch the wound. He was just bleeding away into the dark beyond the edge of the light made by his carbide lamp" (261).

All this blood has not gone unnoticed. Charles Bohner finds that

"Every man is diminished by the death of Jasper, and this ebbing of vitality is symbolized in the novel by the recurring image of bleeding," but complains that "the very profusion of imagery seems a mechanical and calculated intrusion rather than an integral part of the action" (139). If one interprets the bleeding as an ebbing of vitality caused by the death of Jasper, then perhaps it will seem excessive. But there are other reasons for its pervasiveness, and ultimately they have a great deal to do with the action of the novel.

Nicholas Papadoupalous, in a passage Bohner cites, "felt like he was bleeding away in weakness" (267); what was on his mind, however, was not Jasper Harrick but the fear that some of the people running the food service Isaac encouraged him to set up to feed the crowds that came to gawk at the cave would steal him blind: "He knew he ought to go check receipts, before somebody stole a million dollars off him.... It looked like a man could not help things slipping away" (267). Later, when he realized he would not make any money after all off the abortion Timothy Bingham was going to arrange for his daughter, he had the same ebbing feeling: "It was like bleeding to death" (326). Nor was Jasper Harrick on the mind of Giselle Fontaine, the future Mrs. Papadoupalous, in that scene in an Indianapolis strip joint when the blood on Nicholas's knuckles (he had just bloodied his fist against the jaw of another patron) "reminded her of the blood in her handkerchief, her own blood," the blood she had been coughing up lately, since this scene from their courtship occurred long before Jasper was stuck in the cave. In that instance blood was the point where sex and death came together (her blood and intimations of mortality; Papadoupalous's dream of a resurrected Jean Harlow)—a potent compound, for the ecdysiast Fontaine abandoned her art for this ardent admirer, hoping "that his blood might mystically replace whatever blood she had lost, or might lose; that blood-taken-in might, by a mystic homeopathy, cure the disease of blood-going-out" (47).

The promise of such a cure for the hemorrhaging Mrs. Papadoupalous feared (and would continue to fear [174]) has at least a proleptic function in the novel, for a kind of mystic hemotherapy will take place at the mouth of the cave where Jasper is trapped. Isaac's father will preach to the gathered multitudes (the occasion providing him the same opportunity it does his son to exercise his talent for creative discourse) and many will confess their sins and be saved, singing "Rock of Ages," a hymn that puzzles Papadoupalous, who "hadn't never got the words straight in his mind except at the beginning. He could not quite make out what the other words meant, about the water and the blood stuff" (266). His interpretive quandary is really our own, for though we might understand the fountain of blood imagery of evangelical Christianity better than he (Papadoupalous was from up north, and a Greek), we might with reason suspect that Warren has not simply borrowed that metaphor without giving it a significance and a context of his own. Central to that context specific to *The Cave* (and to the imagery that so consistently appears in his work) is the bloody stillbirth (Jack Harrick's illegitimate issue: "a bloody package" [91], "a bloody nothing" [380]) and death in childbirth (Isaac's birth, his mother's death: "nobody could stop the blood") of Mary Tillyard.

These two events are at the root of a great deal that happens in the novel. The stillbirth of Jack Harrick's son was associated with a fall, which in the passage already quoted appears to have been incidental to an already premature birth: "Mary Tillyard had suddenly seized her middle and fallen to the floor, and brought forth the dead child." But in another account of how it happened, the fall is revealed as the cause of the death of the fetus: "Ole Mac Sumpter . . . had married Tillie Tillyard ["Mary Tillyard, whom everybody had called Tillie, but who, to MacCarland Sumpter, had always been Mary" (83): the doubleness of her name will not be without significance] and they were about to have a baby but she had a fall or something and spilled the works right on the floor" (138). In any event, when it happened, MacCarland Sumpter's "heart leaped with joy" that he would not have to be a father to Jack Harrick's child. In a strangely proleptic analogue to this scene (a scene which transpired years earlier but appears in the narrative twelve pages after its analogue), Timothy Bingham is overcome with joy, too, when he sees his daughter Jo-Lea fall down in the street in front of his bank window: "He knew enough to know that a man had better not mess with joy. A man better have no truck with joy, for there was no telling where it might end" (78). It's an almost inexplicable joy, though at first it seems to come from the superposition of another image upon that of Jo-Lea falling down in the street, Bingham's memory of how she would dry her hair in the sun: "Jo-Lea Bingham had, for a fact, fallen, right there on Main Street, in Johntown, and right now was there on hands and knees, her head hanging forward and her hair, jerked loose from ordinary moorings, flung forward over her head. . . . It seemed, preposterously enough, that the girl had chosen that spot of all spots to sun her hair, the way girls do after washing it" (77). But in retrospect, in light of the joy Brother Sumpter will experience a few pages later when he sees Mary fall and the fetus aborted, and in light of the fact that the abortion Timothy Bingham had been asking Nick Pappy to help him arrange in the pages immediately preceding Jo-Lea's fall was for Jo-Lea herself (and not, as Pappy first thought, for Bingham's employee Dorothy Cutlick), it would seem that the superimposed image is only a cover for the reason for Bingham's happiness. If a fall can abort an unwanted fetus, as it may have done in the case of Tillie Tillyard, then Bingham might well have reason to rejoice, though he gives no sign of realizing it aside from his vaguely expressed fear of pursuing the real reason for his satisfaction: "a man had better not mess with joy."

But perhaps the ultimate realization of the reason for Bingham's joy, the fetus behind the scene, should rest with the reader. For if we take seriously his fear that "there was no telling where it might end," taking his hint that it does lead somewhere, if we pursue the echoes of these scenes of falling, we are bound to learn things he could never know. Bingham is not aware, for example, of what Jack Harrick had told MacCarland Sumpter about the way he seduced Tillie Tillyard. According to Harrick, her surrender was premature: " 'I wasn't even prowling for a hand-holt. . . . I wasn't doing nothing worse than counting her verti-bry a little and breathing in her hair, and she of a sudden said, oh, God, and give a moan-like, and it looked like a strut done busted in her. Her knees plain gave down and . . . [s]he would have fallen in the road. If you can call that old grass track a road now' " (87). It was Harrick's insistence that Tillie had fallen of her own accord that made Sumpter hit him, which made him knock Sumpter unconscious, which made Harrick leave town to go to war, which left a pregnant Tillie Tillyard behind for Sumpter to console. So the fall was at the origin of it all—a fall so destined to resemble Jo-Lea's fall on Main Street that it had to happen in a road, too, "that track up by the old Folsom farm" (86) ("if you can call that old grass track a road").

Neither could Bingham know that when he spread a handkerchief on a rock to sit on outside the cave and then, when he saw his wife Matilda approaching, "quickly retrieved his handkerchief from the rock, as though to destroy evidence" (271) he was reenacting a gesture Giselle Fontaine had made when she found there was still more blood on her handkerchief (that, despite marrying the bloody-knuckled Papadoupalous, the homeopathic cure had not taken) and denied the fact in her mind, "crammed the fact down to the bottom of things in her head, like the dirty handkerchief crammed down in the bottom of the laundry basket" (50). A metaphorical handkerchief also appeared in the scene where Papadoupalous first laid eyes on Giselle Fontaine: "Time . . . had stopped, because some mysterious element in the scene . . . made an old forgotten fantasy come alive. It came alive out there on the handkerchief-size patch of floor, in the stunning, shattering, noiseless collision of the dimension of Time and non-Time, Dream and non-Dream, which is what we call Truth with a capital *T*" (43).

Something about Giselle reminded Nick of Jean Harlow. Yet "Giselle Fontaine" was already someone else, and in telling us that, the narrator reminds us that there are some things about a person that even the person does not know: "standing in a pocket-handkerchief-size patch of open floor . . . the artiste Giselle Fontaine—whose real name was Sarah Pumfret, and who was descended, though she did not know it, from a long line of learned New England divines and talented Pequot-killers" (43). Two other characters in *The Cave* have two versions of their names: Mary/Tillie Tillyard and Nick Pappy, "which was what Johntown had decided was a good enough name for Nicholas Papadoupalous" (41). As we have seen, the play on beeches and Beauchamp in *World Enough and Time* suggests what significance can arise from the way in which the inhabitants of Warren's native region mispronounce proper names. What, then, might underlie Mr. Pappy's name and the fact that these three characters (Sarah/Giselle, Mary/Tillie, and Papadoupalous) are thus related?

Isaac's insistence on a literal reading of his own name may provide a clue. He had never known his mother since she died at his birth, but were he the biblical Isaac he claimed his father made him, his mother would have been a Sarah. MacCarland Sumpter nearly said as much when Isaac asked why he had given him that biblical name: "speaking as though to no one, not even to himself, the man said: " 'For Sarah conceived, and bare Abraham a son in his old age' " (96). Now Isaac never knew that Mrs. Papadoupalous's original name could have fit his fantasy and perhaps would not have cared; but we should, knowing how the blood she couldn't stop coughing up could, without medical intervention, have killed her as surely, though not as quickly, as the hemorrhage that killed Isaac's mother. "The time came when Giselle Fontaine's fear at what she saw in her handkerchief overcame the fear-prompted denial of the thing seen"—the denial she enacted by cramming the bloody handkerchief out of sight in the bottom of the laundry basket—"and she went to a doctor" (52). But, though treatable, the disease exacted its price; she lost her figure and the color of her hair and became "Sarah Pumfret, who had been Giselle Fontaine" (53).

If Giselle became the Sarah she had always been, bearing the name of the mother Isaac seems to have always wanted (to become the Isaac his interpretation of his name made him think he ought to be), then it makes sense that her husband's name should undergo a change in Johntown that would make it the equivalent of the local patois for *father*—as the word appears, for example, in the song Jasper's father sings at the end of the novel: " 'I'm coming, son, I'm coming, take your Pappy's hand' " (402).[5]

The other woman who had to be spared the sight of a handkerchief, Timothy Bingham's wife, has nothing unusual about her name, except that it echoes—as does Mrs. Pappy's, via the biblical source—Isaac's mother's. If, that is, the bestowal of two names on a character should sensitize us to the possibility that that character may have a connection to another character which is worth exploring, then the persistence of the first syllable of Isaac's mother's original surname in the nickname by which everyone but his father knew her—the *Till* of *Till*yard, repeated in *Till*ie—should make us wonder if Ma*til*da Bingham might have something in common with the former Tillie Tillyard. Strangely enough, there is a link between them, discoverable through one of those offhand narrative remarks, easily forgotten until we suddenly remember them, which patiently await our realization of their significance: Timothy Bingham "had got married young, to Miss Matilda Bollin, a sickly, pertinacious, culture-hot and cold-bellied girl several years older than he, who had delivered him first a stillborn son and then a beautiful daughter . . ." (37). Matilda's firstborn, like Tillie's, had been a dead fetus.

In an exchange that would seem to have served no purpose except to keep alive the notion that the novel is full of local color, Mr. Pappy is confused with Jasper Harrick. It happens because one of the participants in the conversation has been distracted by Jo-Lea's panties, which she left behind back in chapter 1 when she got up from a sexual embrace with Monty Harrick to run to the mouth of the cave and call out to Jasper, having suddenly realized he was trapped inside.

> The boy wadded the garment up and stuck it into his hip pocket.
> "You might as well keep on admiring and mirating," Jebb Holloway said. "The wrappings is all you got."
> "There is that Greek," Jebb Holloway said.
> "I bet it was that Jasper pulled them things off her hen house," the slick-faced boy said.
> "He is shore dark-complected," Jebb Holloway said.
> "He ain't dark-complected," the boy said.
> "The hell he ain't. He is nigh nigger–complected. Jes you look at him."
> "You durn fool, how can I look at him when he is stuck in the ground?"
> "Who is stuck in the ground, you durn fool?"
> "Jasper Harrick is stuck in the ground, and I bet it was him pulled them things offn' that—"
> "Durn," interrupted Jebb Holloway, with high contempt, "if you'd jes git yore mind out of that hen house, you could follow a conversation and a man's line of thinking and know I was talking about that Greek." (222)

Jo-Lea's panties are indeed a distraction, and for another reason than the one that troubled the slick-faced boy who thought Jebb was talking about Jasper when he was really talking about Pappy. He was concerned with finding out if they indeed were hers, and if it had been Jasper who pulled them off; and this will in fact become a question of considerable importance, fueled by a fiction Isaac Sumpter will invent about Jasper, and to which Jo-Lea will contribute a fiction of her own.

But before that happens, this wadded undergarment has a part to play on a stage of the drama of Warren's fiction inaccessible to either Jebb or the boy. This piece of cloth that Jo-Lea "flung aside" (210) in her haste to get to the mouth of the cave, having "stumbled and almost fallen flat" (34) in her haste to extricate herself from them, and which she left by the beech tree, finds a counterpart in the envelope on which Jasper "had scribbled" the compass readings and distances of his path into the cave and which, when he transferred the data into his notebook, under the same beech, he "had wadded up" and "idly tossed" away (134). The panties will remain in their *wadded* state ("The slick-faced boy held something wadded in his hand which he was showing to the other boys" [210]; "he wadded something soft and silky into her hand.... 'Yores, they's yores, huh?' " [323]), a persistence that, along with the fact that both the wadded envelope and the panties (both "wrappings," as Jebb Holloway would say) were tossed and flung aside under the same beech tree, makes it legitimate to wonder what it is that connects them in the symbolic underpinning of the novel or in that of the larger fiction that all of Warren's novels, when read in light of each other, have the power to tell. *Band of Angels,* too, had its "wad of paper, to be flung away" (37) and its "something scribbled on a scrap of paper and flung down in a dark closet" (132). Both of those were texts with paternal connections: the wad of paper to which Seth Parton symbolically reduced Amantha's father and Amantha's soon-to-be-forgotten mental note that her substitute father, Hamish Bond, walked better than his limp would suggest, respectively.

Now what Jasper idly tossed away later served Isaac in good stead, not to find the way back beyond the fourth chamber where Harrick was trapped, but to distract the official searchers away from the fiction he was constructing around the event. In a moment of brilliant improvisation, he faked a call of nature to walk over to the beech to retrieve the envelope he suddenly remembered Jasper had tossed there and returned to present it to Lieutenant Scrogg in order to persuade him that it would be unnecessary to send surveyors into the cave, that the figures scribbled on the envelope gave Jasper's precise location, and that it would be best to dig from above. It was a Skrogg, by the way, in *World Enough and Time,* who had penned the apocryphal handbill that Beaumont took to be a text from the man who had been a father to him. As we remember the paternal resonances of equivalent pieces of paper in *Band of Angels* and *World Enough and Time,* we might well want to ask what could be paternal about this scrap of scribbled notes Jasper Harrick left behind, and which Isaac, by intentionally misinterpreting them, puts to such profitable use? The misunderstanding that for a moment confuses Jasper with Pappy (in the mind of the slick-faced boy who held Jo-Lea's panties, the equivalent of the scrap of paper Jasper left behind) points the way to an answer; the ultimate fiction Isaac is about to invent confirms it.[6]

If MacCarland Sumpter could preach to the crowds gathered at the cave's mouth a gospel of salvation through blood and rebirth, his son is even more persuasive when he announces from within the cave the touching news of a birth to come: "Jasper just said, 'Tell my girl I love her and would have loved the baby. Tell her I was not going to run out on her. Tell her I was exploring this cave hoping to make a little money for her and the baby'" (274). This is great copy. It galvanizes the media and the public, those assembled at the mouth of the cave as well as those following the story on television and in print. One newspaper even gets the idea of raising money, and thereby its own circulation, for the unborn child. But the announcement is false, for Isaac had only pretended to have been in contact with Jasper.

Yet Isaac in his creative journalism had unwittingly stumbled upon something else that *was* true, and that had been hidden from the public until now: someone really was going to have a Harrick baby. His father's Baptist preaching to the crowd assembled at the mouth of the cave helps to bring out the truth of the matter. "He said that whoever lives with a guilty secret lives in a dark cave and cannot breathe for the weight of sin.... He implored that poor girl to come from the darkness where she lay with the weight of her sin" (320). Moved by this exhortation to confess, and having just been confronted by the slick-faced boy who had found her panties, Jo-Lea Bingham—who was pregnant with *Monty* Harrick's child—stood up and "said she was the one that had lain down in the dark and had in her that baby that Jasper Harrick had put there" (324). When Sumpter, having figured out that his son was lying about Jasper's condition and that Jo-Lea's confession had been artificially induced, slips into the cave to discover the truth and finds Jasper dead, his body yet warm—which compounds his son's guilt, for it means that Jasper could have been saved had Isaac not misled the rescuers—he emerges to announce that Jasper's dying words were that he had impregnated no one, countering his son's lie with one of his own. But the crowd, aided by Isaac's tearful suggestion that his father has not had the courage to crawl all the way to Jasper, refuses to believe this second, more truthful, falsehood. "'Look at him! ... Him a preacher and lying!' ... 'Yeah, lying—fer that girl—she said it was her!' ... 'Whoop-ee! And she ought to know!'" (336–37). As Lieutenant Scrogg sums it up later, "It is a lot more fun to believe that that Jo-Lea is knocked up.... Folks believe what they want to believe" (350). The upshot is that Isaac's fiction is more telling than his father's, and more powerful than the truth.

But the power of fiction is such that, in the larger fiction of the novel—in the context, that is, of the complex intertwining of the novel's characters around all its fetuses, double names, misplaced referents,[7] and reenacted gestures—Isaac Sumpter's fiction comes to be a variation on the story his father keeps telling, an unconscious parody of the exhortation to rebirth that was the essence of his preaching at the mouth of the cave. For if the cave which was for the sons what Tillie Tillyard was for the fathers can stand for Isaac's mother, and if the man inside it can, for an apparently fortuitous but in the end revealing moment, be taken for a Pappy, then Isaac's attribution of paternity to Jasper completes his new fictive family circle. By inventing this unborn child he not only succeeds in acquiring enough money and fame to get out of Johntown, but he reinvents himself as well. What gets reborn is Isaac Sumpter, who leaves to begin a new life in New York and a whole new career in a field where his peculiar talents for playing with the truth can be appreciated—"in the world of Big Media" (371).

He has adopted the cave for his mother, has had the unusual opportunity of choosing his own father, and has unwittingly created, in the fictive fetus that results from that combination, the kind of doppelganger Jack Burden spoke of in *All the King's Men* in his meditation on the "sad little fetus you carry around inside yourself . . . the . . . fetus which is you." Two texts that confront Isaac on his way out of town in the aftermath of what happened at the cave serve as signposts along his flight, which in their combination will remind him, and us, of that fact. The first is, quite literally, a sign:

> He saw a highway sign saying:
> SMYRNA, TENNESSEE
> See the Historic Home of
> Sam Davis
> Boy Hero of the Confederacy
> "Ikey Sumpter," he said aloud, "Boy Hero of the Confederacy." His heart bubbled with gaiety. (367)

The reading of the second sign, however, is preceded by a strange, almost unaccountable sense of fear and loathing. In the airport lounge

> his glance fell on an old man, poor, dirty, derelict, with a parcel tied with string, who was sitting over there on a bench. What the hell would such a guy be doing on a plane? That thought—the man's age, his dirt, his poverty, his paper parcel—was a personal affront, a diminution of his triumph, a smear on his pleasure. Then the old man leaned over and picked up from the dirty floor a discarded newspaper. The old man opened the mixed-up sheets, idly, and fixed on something. The sheet held up to the view of Isaac Sumpter was the front page of yesterday evening's *Press-Clarion*. There was the headline:
> WOMEN OF STATE RALLY
> Mother's Committee Formed to Guard Sweet-
> heart and Unborn Child of Trapped Hero
> Fund Tops $20,000
>
> (368–69)

The derelict with the paper parcel who seemed to Isaac so disturbingly out of place in an airport lounge has already created a place of his own in Warren's fiction. We saw him at the end of *Band of Angels* in the hunched-over old beggar whose presence so troubled Amantha Starr, and in the tramp with the newspaper-wrapped parcel in "Blackberry Winter," whom the narrator "did follow . . . all the years" (87); in *Meet Me in the Green Glen* he will become the protagonist himself.

If Isaac's reaction to the first of these two signs along his way is a pleasurable but unjustifiable identification with its content, his response to the apparition that preceded the second is distaste at having to be accompanied on his journey to a new life by this objectionable stranger with a paper-wrapped parcel. But Isaac, too, will have to carry some baggage into his bright future. Like Percy Munn's dream in *Night Rider* of a fetus wrapped in newspaper (395), this second sign along Isaac's escape route, the one the old man holds up to his gaze, is a fetus in a newspaper, too, for whose presence there Isaac is ultimately responsible.

"Crime," from *Eleven Poems on the Same Theme,* tells a similar tale. A "mad killer" cannot remember who it was he murdered, but carries

> His treasure: for years down streets of contempt and trouble
> Hugged under his coat, among sharp elbows and rows
> Of eyes hieratic like foetuses in jars;
> Or he nursed it unwitting, like a child asleep with a bauble.

Though Isaac's "heart *bubbled* with gaiety" in response to the first sign, the second's uncomfortable message is that, like the objectionable stranger, he will not be traveling alone, that he will have to take along something like this *bauble,* this hugged object that in the poem leads to thoughts of fetuses in jars, as did the newspaper-bundled infant in Percy Munn's dream. "Hieratic" eyes will be upon him even in his "high, spacious office" in New York "with a suffering and *hieratic* canvas of Rouault smoldering on one wall" (370; emphasis added). And he will one day read the news that Rachel Goldstein, whose rejection of him had sent him back to the Johntown from which he had gone to all this effort to escape, had eventually—like his mother—died in childbed (372). It was Jeremiah's Rachel in *World Enough and Time* who gave birth to a dead child after the shock of seeing a printed handbill whose author arrogated to himself, as Isaac Sumpter did in the case of Jo-Lea, the right to invent the paternity of a fetus to which she had earlier given birth.

There may be no escape from the meshes of this recurring fetal dream that persists throughout Warren's writing. In *The Cave,* it is the pivot upon which the plot turns, a plot that may be said to be a story about fiction's own creation—certainly Warren's.

Chapter 8

Moses in
the Wilderness   *Wilderness*, 1961

Chapter 1   It is 1863 in a Jewish community in Bavaria. Adam Rosenzweig's father, Leopold, has just died. He had, in the eyes of his older brother, deserted the faith of his fathers to fight for the secular ideal of human liberty in the Berlin uprising of 1848. He had, in the eyes of his son, deserted that idealism when, at his brother's urging, he renounced his hope in the improvement of the human condition to return to strict observance of the Mosaic Law six months before his death. Adam, who suffers from a deformed left foot, had, coincidentally, conceived at the very moment of his father's recantation the idea of a "clever" boot that would conceal his deformity, thus enabling him to join the fight for human liberty—specifically, to get past the examining officers and join up with the Union army in the American Civil War. Despite his father's repudiation of his secular hope, at least Adam still has the text of the poem his father wrote about his desire to "be worthy of what he loves"—which proved truer to those ideals than did its author.

Chapter 2   On a ship bound for America with recruits for the Northern forces, Adam's deformity is revealed when the ocean's surface "twitches" and he loses balance. The recruiting officer, Duncan, is especially irate because his own bad leg is revealed when the ocean twitches again. He accuses Adam of trying to steal free passage, knowing he would not be accepted into the army.

Chapter 3   Duncan tells him he won't be allowed to disembark with the rest but will have to work off his passage without pay and be thrown off the ship on its return to Europe. Later, a sailor explains to Adam how he can jump ship in America without getting caught.

Chapter 4   On the streets of New York City, Adam, bearing the address of Aaron Blaustein, a friend of his uncle's, is caught up in the draft riots. He sees a black man hanged on a lamppost. He falls into a cellar about to be flooded to drown other blacks inside, and loses consciousness.

Chapter 5 Adam is rescued and brought to the richly furnished houses of Aaron Blaustein, who had come to America forty years before to ply the trade of a Jewish peddler. Now quite wealthy, he has lost his son, Stephen, in a Civil War battle and asks Adam to become his adopted son. Adam declines, asking only for his help in getting to the front lines.

Chapter 6 Blaustein has rewarded Mose Talbutt, the black man who was trapped in the flooded cellar with Adam and who rescued him, with a job under peddler Jedeen Hawksworth, and has granted Adam's wish to get to the scene of battle by doing the same for him. The three are rolling south through Pennsylvania on two wagons.

Chapter 7 They camp for several days near the farmhouse of Maran Meyerhof and her dying husband, Hans, in whom Adam sees his own father, for he too had fought in Germany in 1848 for revolutionary ideals. Adam is tempted to stay on with the Meyerhofs as a hired hand and perhaps succeed Maran's husband when she becomes a widow.

Chapter 8 But he continues with Hawksworth and Talbutt as they make their way south. They stop to view the Gettysburg battlefield and share a jug with a Mordacai Sulgrave and some others charged with the task of reburying the dead, by states. Jedeen reveals to Adam that when he was run out of North Carolina for defending a black man in court he had done it to spite his father.

Chapter 9 Encamped in Virginia, where Hawksworth is sutler to the army, Adam is teaching Mose how to read and write. He learns from a newspaper that Aaron Blaustein has died.

Chapter 10 Mollie the Mutton, a camp prostitute, is being flogged on the bare rump for plying her trade, and Adam finds he cannot watch. The commander of a black regiment recognizes Mose Crawfurd, a.k.a. Talbutt, as a deserter. Hawksworth covers for Mose but confirms the truth of the accusation by discovering the brand of a *W* (for "worthless") on his thigh.

Chapter 11 The next morning, Adam discovers that Mose has murdered Jedeen and stolen his money belt; he secretly buries the body. The camp is breaking up and heading out for the Battle of the Wilderness. Adam at first joins the wagon train but then drops out.

Chapter 12 Lost in the woods, Adam stumbles upon the cabin of Monmorancy Pugh and his wife, where he bargains for lodging and for Pugh to guide him to a ford in the river. He says he wants to catch up with the army to sell them things from his wagon. The next day the woman takes him aside, gives him an unloaded pistol, and warns him that Pugh may try to kill him on the way to the river.

Chapter 13 Pugh's wife was right, but Adam successfully disarms him and compels him to take him to the ford. Once across the Rapidan, Pugh discovers that the pistol was not loaded, but does nothing about it. Adam pays him and he leaves.

Chapter 14 Alone in a glade in the woods, Adam listens to the distant sounds of battle.

Chapter 15 Eight rebel soldiers burst into the glade and raid Adam's wagon for food. One steals his boots, and is dismayed when he finds the left one impossible to wear. Union soldiers suddenly appear and kill or chase off the rebels—except for the one Adam himself shoots with a rifle one of them has dropped. Adam is again alone and rejoices in the knowledge that "We always do what we intend."

Warren's seventh novel tells the story of a son who tries to live up to a precept his father abandoned just before he died. Leopold Rosenzweig "had told his son that there was no nobler fate for a man than to live and die for human liberty" (7), and had nearly given his life to that struggle in the revolution of 1848, having fought at the barricades and suffered imprisonment before returning at last to his family in broken health. But to his son's dismay, Leopold, in the end, had capitulated to his brother's importunate demand that he return to the Mosaic Law, which held that it was blasphemy to engage in secular politics, to invest one's efforts in the hope for a better world (or, for that matter, to join the goyim in such a struggle) instead of trusting in God's plans for a messianic future. Leopold's deathbed assent, in his son's view, "undid the meaning of his . . . life and martyrdom" (14). But this retreat from idealism, this withdrawal of "the gift given long ago to the son" (9), this death of the father ("The father's body had needed six more months to die [after his recantation], but Adam knew that the father's self was already dead") made possible the birth of the son: "when his father's self had died, his own self had been born. . . . [W]hile the father was bearing the pain of his death, the son had borne the pain of his birth" (9, 17). Despite the considerable gulf between Isaac Sumpter's selfish savoir faire and Adam Rosenzweig's altruistic naïveté, *Wilderness* picks up where *The Cave* leaves off, with the rebirth—the birth of the self—of its filial protagonist, and his ensuing journey: Isaac to a career in New York, Adam to the New World.

That continuity is underscored by a fresh allusion to the biblical event that had so disturbed Isaac Sumpter in *The Cave*—Abraham's obedience to God's command to bind Isaac upon an altar and sacrifice him—articulated in the prayers said over Adam's father's grave: " 'O Thou who speakest and doest, of Thy grace deal kindly with us, and for the sake of him who was bound like a lamb.' He said the words aloud, and wondered what they meant to him, to Adam Rosenzweig" (5). In trying to determine what relevance these words might have to his own situation, Adam continues on to the end of the prayer—"Have mercy upon the remnant of the flock of Thy hand, and say unto the Destroying Angel, Stay thy hand"—and sees himself as that remnant, standing "where my father once stood." Indeed, he is, as throughout the novel he will seek to do what his father, before that deathbed renouncement, would have done, standing where he once stood, on the front lines of human freedom. But the rest of the allusion to Isaac is surely lost on Adam Rosenzweig, for the father's sacrifice of his son has no particular resonance in his life or his father's when considered only in the context available to Adam. It need not, however, be lost on the reader who comes to this novel fresh from *The Cave;* for what is alluded to here, I believe, is not just the biblical Isaac but the one from Tennessee, who found a way to a new life, like Adam's, the long-delayed birth of the original self ("Little Ikey . . . could at last be totally himself"). Isaac, too, tries to make out the meaning of a difficult paternal text (his own name), and then sets out on a journey in which he is not as totally alone as he had intended, for Isaac Sumpter's solitude on his journey to rebirth is spoiled by the presence of the old derelict in the airport waiting room with the paper parcel and by the mixed-up newspaper pages that confront him with the textual outcome of his fictive inventiveness (the public fuss made about the unborn child that never was); later, hieratic (which is to say, fetal) eyes will stare down upon him from the wall of his Big Media office. To pursue the parallel, then, and realizing that immediately after Adam's birth on the occasion of his father's death he, too, will set out on a journey to America to fight for freedom in the Civil War, we need to ask if he is accompanied on that voyage by anything like that which dogged Isaac's steps.

Adam Rosenzweig, naive young innocent that he was (at twenty-nine), surely could not have been hugging under his coat some "treasure" akin to the forgotten guilt of the mad killer in "Crime" whom Sumpter so resembled; nor is it possible to imagine him trailed by anything like the mysterious old man and his newspaper-borne account of a fetus emblematic of the murder Isaac had committed in order to invent that unborn child. On the contrary, Adam's problem is that for the longest time he seems incapable of doing wrong to anyone; only in the final pages of the novel can he bring himself to kill an enemy soldier, and when he does, it comes as a complete surprise. Yet some parallel does exist, for Adam does carry some baggage on his journey, the satchel given him by the uncle who had persuaded his father to return to the Law, a satchel containing a text Adam never opens and nearly forgets about until the end of the novel. It is the *seddur,* the prayer book that, in this context, stands for another text, the Law of Moses for whose sake his father betrayed his secular hope.

As his father's text—the Law his father came finally to own up to owning—in the possessive, not the objective, genitive sense, the prayer book in the satchel is a kind of paternal text. What parallel there is to Isaac in *The Cave* encourages us to look for some equivalent to the paternal text of his name, the one-word text his father gave him and that he spends what we see of his life trying to decipher. Adam's first name is as much a text from the father as is Isaac's, and in a symmetrically opposite way; for, just as Isaac had been puzzled by his father's choice of a name bearing not only a hint of filicidal intent but also being a strangely Jewish name for a Christian boy (it had that effect on Rachel Goldstein, who first thought he was a coreligionist [123]), so Adam was aware, if not puzzled, by the implications of *his* father's choice: " 'Adam,' " he told Mose Talbutt, " 'means, simply, man. . . . But it is not a usual name for Jew to be called. My father gave me that name because he loved mankind and wanted men to be fully man. . . . He gave me that name that I might try to be a man in the knowledge that men are my brothers' " (91–92).

Yet there is another paternal text in Adam's possession, not just the prayer book from the Mosaic paternal text (more grandfatherly, as we will see, than paternal), but a text his father actually wrote. It was a book of poetry that expressed his never-satisfied desire to live up to an ideal that was to characterize his son's encounter with the world and his memory of his father. When Adam repeated the prayer said over his father's grave and wondered what the words about Isaac ("him who was bound like a lamb") could mean to him, he also murmured the opening lines of his father's poem:

> If I could only be worthy of that mountain I love,
> If I could only be worthy of sun-glitter on snow,
> If a man could only be worthy of what he loves.
> (5)

The poem sums up the book, and the thrice-spoken *worthy* sums up the poem, in Adam's consciousness. For his whole voyage to America and his hope of engagement in the Civil War with its struggle for human liberty is a quest for worthiness. When, for example, he gazes on the mutilated corpse of a black man hanged from a lamppost in the New York draft riots by those who were unwilling to be conscripted to fight for the sake of blacks, he finds to his dismay that "He had not been *worthy* of the pain. Ah, that was his guilt" (57). And when he tells Mose Talbutt about why his father gave him his name, he asks him to call him Adam (which Mose refuses to do, preferring to call him "Slew," on account of his foot) to "help me be *worthy* of my name" (92).

With this poem we have, at last, a paternal text in a very real sense—not one falsely attributed to a father (Scrogg's handbill), nor one the father should have written but did not (Amantha Starr's manumission papers), nor one so delicately poised on the verge of intentionality as to consist of a gesture whose only message is to call into question whether it is in fact a text (Willie Stark's wink), but a real text, one we can read and try to interpret, one we can watch the son trying to interpret and live up to.

Already in the opening chapter we find Adam Rosenzweig interpreting these lines by trying to obey their specific call to worthiness, refusing to return to the room where his father's body had lain, refusing to honor him according to the custom his uncle wants him to observe, preferring to "look at the mountain to honor him," the mountain his father loved. The novel itself begins with that mountain, its first words anticipating the words of the poem: "If the mountain had not gleamed so white.... If the sky above that glitter of snow.... If none of these things had been as they were, he, Adam Rosenzweig, might have fled inward into the self.... He might have been able to go back into that house behind him" (3–4). Instead, he went to America, hoping that despite his twisted left foot he could march, fight, and maybe die to set men free.

His crippled foot, on the face of it, already made Adam unworthy, for it rendered him technically ineligible to enlist in the Union army. He tried to make up for that lack, and conceal it, with a special boot he had invented and commissioned to be made, for which "the idea had come to him that very instant ... his father had repudiated his own life," the pain the boot would inflict in its straightening effect being the "pain of his birth," begun "while the father was bearing the pain of his death" (16–17). But his encounter on shipboard with Sergeant Duncan, whose job it was to swear in the enlistees who had been given free passage to America in exchange for their military service, effectively removed that disguise. By a strange symmetry, Duncan himself suffered from a lameness in *his* left leg which he, like Adam, wished to conceal and which was the sign of unworthiness— only more genuinely so. For Duncan had broken and run at the first battle of Manassas, receiving a knee wound ignominiously from behind, in mid-flight. When the surface of the ocean just happened to heave, to give "a little mysterious twitch" (20), as the narrator puts it, at the moment Adam was to step forward, it threw him off balance so that "his left foot came out in that twisting motion which, during all those months, he had so painfully conquered" and the "ingenious" but useless boot was left dangling for all to see. "At that moment the ocean twitched again," and it was Duncan's turn to display to all the assembled hands and enlistees what was wrong with *his* left leg by falling down into a sitting position, "ass-flat on the deck." From the way the story is told, it appears that Adam might have passed muster if Duncan's impairment had not also been so embarrassingly revealed, or at any rate if Duncan's cowardice had not made him "so sensitive about Adam Rosenzweig's special deformity." Given the profits to be made in supplying willing cannon fodder for the war effort, Adam's lameness alone might not necessarily have kept Duncan from allowing him to enlist.

"If all these things had not happened in their unique pattern, then things might have been all right, after all" (22).

What had to happen was that the previously calm sea should just happen to break its rhythm, twice, at those particular moments, and that Duncan should be so hypersensitive about his wound, that his sudden anger at Adam is partly prompted by the irrational fear that he is mocking him. But although the narrator speaks of the unique pattern of these conspiring events, another voice, speaking through the narrator's, hints at a more pervasive pattern, one discernible only in the larger context of Warren's novels. For there is an extraordinary insistence in the narration on the ocean's "little mysterious *twitch*," a word that occurs seven times in three pages here, often enough to remind us of its locus classicus in Warren, the scene in *All the King's Men* that led Jack Burden to his doctrine of The Great Twitch.

The original twitch belonged, we remember, to the face of the old man Burden picked up on the highway in New Mexico, a face "which seemed as stiff and devitalized as the hide on a mummy's jaw [where] you would suddenly see a twitch in the left cheek.... You would think he was going to wink, but he wasn't...." And we may recall, too, that Jack was encountering a reenactment of the event that had been troubling him: Had Willie Stark really winked at him in Slade's back room back in 1922 or had it just been an involuntary twitch? The reason we should be reminded of it here is that, while the whole point of the hitchhiker's twitch was that it seemed to be leading up to a wink that never came, what happens in *Wilderness* is that this "mysterious twitch" should by rights have likewise been followed by a *wink*: "There was, in fact, no logical reason why Meinherr Duncan should have been so outraged by Adam Rosenzweig's physical defect. He knew that the examiners did not really examine. He knew that he himself had *winked* at, and passed farther along, some rather poor specimens" (22; emphasis added). Bear in mind that in both instances it is the simile of a hide that does the twitching—"the hide on a mummy's jaw" in the case of the hitchhiker, a "mysterious twitch like the twitch on a horse's hide" (21) in the case of the ocean. So, if the hitchhiker was repeating the paternal gesture Stark had or had not made, then does Meinherr Duncan in some way play a father's role for Adam (as another Duncan—Duncan Trice—had done for Cass Mastern)? If so, then he is not the only father figure Adam will encounter on his journey. Aaron Blaustein, who tries to adopt Adam as his son, clearly falls into this category; so does Hans Meyerhof, by whose deathbed Adam will feel "as though, again, he sat beside a dying father ... but who, in dying ... would not repudiate the old truth" (120). That some of the other men in Adam's story—Jedeen Hawksworth and even Mose Talbutt/Crawfurd—are also stand-ins for his father is less apparent but will be the burden of this chapter to prove. What Ernest Jones, drawing upon Freud's *The Interpretation of Dreams* but speaking less of dreams than of the way myths and literary works behave like dreams, calls "decomposition" seems to be at work here. In this process "various attributes of a given individual are disunited, and several other individuals are invented, each endowed with one group of the original attributes. In this way one person of complex character is dissolved and replaced by several, each of whom possesses a different aspect of the character which in a simpler form of the myth was combined in one being.... A good example ... is seen by the figure of a tyrannical father becoming split into two, a father and a tyrant" (131).

Adam's father is, to be sure, a character of some complexity. He represents an ideal that may well be unattainable and places a perhaps impossible demand on the son: the call to worthiness that he himself renounced by returning to the Law, and, by denying the poem he wrote in favor of the more ancient text of his fathers, a denial of authorship to become a mere reader again. Like the inscription on the mother's gravestone in *Band of Angels* that seems both to negate and affirm, to deny at the very moment it names, Leopold Rosenzweig's life sends a mixed message to his son. And even if Adam, as he seems to do through most of the novel, were to base his interpretation on the text his father left behind rather than on the final moments of his life that contradicted it, he would find that the paternal call to worthiness is betrayed by the other gift his father left him, the imperfect foot that will prevent him from legally enlisting in the Union army to carry out those inherited ideals. "*And my father*, he thought, *he betrayed me*. He looked down at the twisted whiteness of his poor foot. He stared at it. *My father*, he thought, *that is what he gave me*" (303). But it only keeps Adam from battle because of the intervention of Sergeant Duncan, and only then because of the intervention of two twitches and a wink that never occurred (which is to say, by the intervention of a greater force field than that of his own story). Duncan's tyrannical withholding of the wink is thus in line with that part of the paternal complex that makes it impossible for Adam to live up to what another part of that complex demands of him. It is important to note that Adam's realization that his father betrayed him by giving him an imperfect foot comes only at the end of the novel; it is only then that he feels "that he was on the verge of a great truth ... that everything he had ever known was false" (303). Until that moment he does not see his father as a tyrant making an impossible demand (thus allowing Duncan to play the part of the father who says no); instead, from the moment Leopold renounces his idealism he merely ceases to exist: "The father's body had needed six more months to die, but Adam knew that the father's self was already dead."

Adam's encounter with Aaron Blaustein seems in certain respects to bear out the observation Jones goes on to make in the passage quoted above: "The tyrant who seeks to destroy the hero is then most commonly the

grandfather, as in the legends of the heroes Cyrus, Gilgam, Perseus . . ."
(131). Blaustein is not Adam's grandfather, only a friend of his uncle's, but
their meeting recalls in a number of ways an earlier meeting in Warren
between a young man and his maternal grandfather, Jeremiah's encounter
with Morton Marcher in *World Enough and Time*. It will be recalled that
Marcher wanted to adopt Jeremiah as his heir, but only on the condition
that he renounce his father's name. A struggle ensued, in the course of
which Jeremiah warded off his grandfather's silver candlestick with the cane
he had wrested from the older man's grasp, but only after "the lighted
candle fell from it to the table," as if the flame ("the flame of the sperm
candle" into which Marcher had stared before he said he wanted an heir
worthy of the estate) embodied the paternal virility that now would not be
passed on. There is no hostility evident in Adam Rosenzweig's visit to Aaron
Blaustein's home, where he shows up after his arrival in New York and his
brush with death in the draft riots, but something like a variation on that
earlier drama is played out before "the great gilt mirror above the screened
fireplace" (recalling the "great mirrors streaked black and with peeling gold
frames" [16] which Jeremiah saw when he entered Runnymede) and "the
great bronze of Perseus meditatively holding the head of Medusa" (67). That
even this statue may allude to the Greek myth is suggested by the fact that
Perseus killed his grandfather, Acrisius (accidentally, with a discus; in an
analogous scene in Warren's last novel, the younger protagonist will find a
life-size copy of a matching statue—the Discus-Thrower—in the home of
the grandfatherly Dr. Stahlman [61]), and that Acrisius tried, as did Morton
Marcher, to keep his daughter Danaë away from prospective suitors (thus
her insemination by Zeus had to take the form of a surreptitious golden
shower). "He stole her," Marcher exclaimed to his grandson, calling Jeremiah's father a blackguard and a bankrupt—words that whipped Jeremiah
into an almost murderous fury, leading to the aforementioned struggle with
cane and candlestick, and culminating in the extinction of the candle and
Beaumont's breaking his grandfather's cane on the dead hearth. Now Jones's
commentary on the myth of Perseus, as it happens, draws out aspects of the
story that parallel in a remarkable way the generational struggle Warren
recounts:

> [The grandfather] opposes the advances of the would-be suitor
> . . . and even as a last resort locks up his daughter in an inaccessible spot. . . . When [the] grandfather's commands are disobeyed or circumvented his love for his daughter turns to
> bitterness and he pursues her and her offspring with insatiable
> hate. When the grandson in the myth . . . avenges himself and
> his parents by slaying the tyrannical grandfather it is as though
> he realized the motive of the persecution, for in truth he slays

> the man who endeavoured to possess and retain the mother's affections, i.e. his own rival. Thus in this sense we again come back to the primordial father, for whom to him the grandfather is but an *imago* . . . (136–37)

The counterpart to Marcher's sperm candle, whose fall and extinction presage the extinction of his paternity, is Aaron Blaustein's cigar, whose extinction and replacement and eventual definitive extinction parallel the rise and fall of his hopes of persuading Adam to take the place of his dead son.

It was when the conversation turned to conscription, to the necessity of drafting unwilling men into the Union army to replace the first, now dead, wave of eager volunteers, that Blaustein first lit up. "Aaron Blaustein lighted his cigar, shut his eyes and inhaled the comfort of the smoke. 'And,' he said, 'when the heroes are dead, you have to fill the ranks some way. Even with ordinary mortals' " (70). The apparent connection between the pleasure of smoking the cigar and the salvation to be found in such drafted replacements continues. He "closed his eyes, and let the smoke float from his nostrils. 'Yes,' he said, opening his eyes, looking down at Adam, 'only conscription can save us. Conscription and—' He paused, then took a step toward Adam. 'What ship did you come on?' he demanded" (70). Conscription and what? The sudden gaze at Adam, the step in his direction, and the question that seems to change the subject all suggest that in fact the subject has not changed at all, that the request Blaustein is going to make—that Adam take the place of his dead son—is what he was not able to express in the blank following "and—." Indeed, he will not make the request for a few pages more. Before he broaches that subject this cigar will die, prematurely. " 'I really am not that bitter,' he said, looking at his cigar, now dead, but not making any motion to relight it" (73). He continues to hold it in his fingers, neither relighting it nor throwing it away, until he comes to the point of revealing to Adam that his son, one of that first wave of heroes, had fallen at the Battle of Chancellorsville.

> He flung the twisted, crumpled cigar to the red carpet, and stared down at it.
> "My son was killed," he said dully. He sat down. . . . "I did not think I could live."
> He looked down at the broken cigar on the red carpet. "You know," he said, and lifted his dark face beseechingly to Adam, "I cannot die." (75–76)

If the cigar's fall parallels his son's death, then his decision to replace it with another prepares the way for the delicate request he is about to make.

> Very carefully, he took out his cigar case, and prepared and lighted another cigar.

He drew in the smoke, exhaled it. He inspected the cigar. "These cigars are very expensive," he said. (76–77)

He then reveals to Adam, who earlier that evening had glanced admiringly at himself in the mirror of his room, dressed in a coat Aaron had lent him, that the coat he is wearing was his dead son's. With a "cold terror," Adam suddenly realizes that he had known that already, and "felt a thousand filmy strands being cast over him," that he was about to be caught in the trap Blaustein had so carefully prepared. Aaron then popped the question, and "dropped to one knee before Adam, letting the cigar fall from his fingers. . . ." This time the fallen cigar is still burning, like this would-be father's hope offered in all its vulnerability, the hope that his paternal line will not die out; this fatherly desire is laid bare at last, but in such a way that it must risk the son's rejection:

> Adam, sitting there in his sickening disorientation, stared at the cigar on the floor. He saw the red carpet about the lighted end of the cigar scorch to brown, then to black. . . . He saw the red *winking* of the blackened strands of the fabric as they were consumed and parted. . . . Adam rose abruptly from the chair. He thrust his left foot forward from under the touch of the old man crouching there, and ground his boot on the cigar and the smoldering spot of the carpet. (78–79; emphasis added)

Adam's abrupt and violent gesture is untypical of his otherwise passive character and, though clothed perhaps in the guise of protecting the carpet from further damage, is nevertheless the definitive stamping out of the winking paternal flame. This rejection of an enfeebled father's pleading offer provides an interestingly symmetrical counterpart to the rejection Adam himself had suffered at the hands of the tyrannical father (Meinheer Duncan) who would not give him the wink of acceptance. Adam realizes the ultimate violence of his gesture here near the end of the novel, when he sees that he was responsible for Aaron's death from a heart attack a few months later: "he thought how, if he had stayed with Aaron Blaustein, Aaron Blaustein would not have died" (301). And thus what happened that evening in the shadow of the bronze Perseus was, in the end, as violent, indeed, more so, than the struggle between Jeremiah Beaumont and his maternal grandfather. Marcher, as it happened, did not soon die and may in fact have had a subsequent heir to fill the place Jeremiah refused; for he subsequently married "a sluttish wench from the inn" and gave his name to a son that, though he might not have been his, did have a long line of descendants, including an associate professor of French at a midwestern university.

But if Adam plays Perseus to Aaron's Acrisius, in what way does he live out the episode enacted in the statue itself, which depicts the conquering hero "meditatively holding the head of Medusa"? Before severing that head from its body Perseus could not look at it without risking being turned to stone, and had to have recourse to Athene's shield, because of whose polished surface he was able to accomplish the task by looking at the reflection of that horrible face. Freud saw female genitalia in the petrifying head of Medusa, both because "becoming stiff means an erection" and because "To decapitate = to castrate. The terror Medusa induces is thus a terror of castration that is linked to the sight of something. . . . [I]t occurs when a boy, who has hitherto been unwilling to believe the threat of castration, catches sight of the female genitals, probably those of an adult, surrounded by hair, and essentially those of his mother" ("Medusa's Head," 212). The statue's proximity to the mirror and the hearth puts it in touch with the elements of its own story, if in the mirror we can see the reflecting surface in which Perseus stole a glance at Medusa and in the hearth, the womb, the feminine genital space that Freud saw, ultimately, as the mother's. Jeremiah Beaumont's furtive glimpse of Mrs. Jordan, Rachel's mother, who stood in the shadows of the hallway in such a way that she was just visible out of the corner of his eye in the mirror above the fireplace, in *World Enough and Time,* seems now, in retrospect, a glance at Medusa, as before it had seemed a vision of his own mother. Later, when Mrs. Jordan lay dying and she did remind him of his mother, he saw her lips move, soundlessly: "It was, he thought, as though a statue tried to talk"—as though, now that the presence of the statue of Perseus and the head of Medusa in Aaron Blaustein's drawing room and the parallels between Adam's confrontation with Aaron and Jeremiah's with Marcher have clarified the analogy between Beaumont and the slayer of Medusa and Acrisius, she had become a very particular statue, one that in life had had the power to turn whoever gazed at her into stone.

Which is to say that Medusa appears in Warren's texts already transformed into art, of which the bronze in Blaustein's drawing room is one instance and the bare rump of Mollie the Mutton another. Not that the Irish prostitute's backside, "big . . . fer them legs," was a work of art, but the treatment it receives in the novel is such as to arrest our attention, for it functions for Adam as the equivalent of what Perseus could only gaze at indirectly. Tied face down over a length of log, she was to receive "[t]en on the bare doup" for plying her trade in the Union camp where Adam found employment as a sutler's assistant. In that position, with a stick laid across the back of her knees so that she couldn't move and her dress thrown up over the back of her head, her sex may well have been visible, but for the prurient leers of the audience her bare buttocks would suffice. Adam, however, found it impossible to look. At first, he "found himself staring at the woman's shoes," which, like that part of her he could not bear to see, "looked too big."

> But the pain of staring at the shoes was too great. If they had not been turned inward, pigeon-toed, it would not have been so bad. No, he couldn't bear to look at the shoes.
> He carefully looked at the faces of other men. They were all staring at the woman, some avid and intense, some with schooled detachment, some with idiotic grin and wet lips. They were all different, the faces, but the eyes of all were fixed there where he, Adam Rosenzweig, did not dare to look. (205–6)

As Perseus could only look at Medusa through the image reflected in Athene's shield, so Adam wisely substituted its reflection in the spectators' eyes for a view of the thing itself. That the thing itself was very close to being what Medusa's head may ultimately stand for certainly helps to sustain the illusion.

Yet, in the context of the novel, even this scene is a substitute for something else, precisely that something else for which the thing itself stands: castration. This pilloried victim recalls another, the hanged black man Adam saw when he arrived in New York at the height of the draft riots. "It hung there like an empty sack, with the top tied together and the loose part of the top fluffing out and falling to one side, over the tight cord. That was what it first reminded him of. His mind clung to that image as long as possible" (44). What Adam first saw of Mollie, some time before her public punishment, was a similarly shapeless parcel, tied at the neck with a cord: "The form was swathed in an army blanket, much patched, fastened at the neck with a cord. From under the shapeless huddle of blanket the feet moved in the mud. The feet wore army shoes, in obvious disrepair. The head was wrapped in a turban . . ." (166). Those shoes would later be the part of Mollie on which he would try to focus his attention in the effort not to look at that which he would have found more troubling, a substitution that proves unsuccessful because of what was wrong with her feet: "If they had not been turned inward, pigeon-toed, it would not have been so bad."[1] Similarly, the mutilated feet of the hanged man claimed so much of Adam's attention that they apparently distracted him from the even more horrible mutilation that is never named but must have been the ultimate aim of his executioners. The way the text describes those feet suggests that the narrator, at least, is not unaware of the castration the victim must have undergone: "Then he saw that one last, slow, tumescent drop was falling from one foot. He looked at the foot. The toes had been cut off" (45). Just as Mollie's feet could stand for her sex, so does this tumescently dripping foot stand for what else must have been cut off, which Adam neglects to notice, or chooses not to see.

When Adam recounts what he had seen of the hanged man to Aaron Blaustein, the way he begins suggests what he may have found most significant: "It was a lamp post. He was hanging on a lamp post. They had cut off his toes and——" (58). Now this persistent attention to feet has another basis other than just that of his aversion to looking at actual castration. For Adam, to stare at this amputation was tantamount to beholding castration for a very personal reason, as his own left foot stands (not very well, given its infirmity) for his penis. At the close of the novel, in the glade in the Wilderness where so many things are finally revealed to him (that he was responsible for Blaustein's death, that his father "betrayed" him by "what he gave me"—the foot lame from birth), he will come close to realizing even this, when he looks at his bare feet and calls them "stupid, ugly, unlovable children" (300). "Children," in the book Warren will later imagine his father reading ("Freud on dreams ...", in the poem "Reading Late at Night ..."), "in dreams often stand for the genitals; and, indeed, both men and women are in the habit of referring to their genitals affectionately as their 'little ones.' ... Playing with a little child, beating it, etc., often represent masturbation ..." (392). The tumescent quality of what drips from the mutilated foot, and the fact that the body of another riot victim will soon "lay across the very toes of Adam Rosenzweig" (50), already underscore the threat the hanged man's fate must have posed to Adam's unconscious. Pursuing the later connection to children would be superfluous were it not that the narrative itself moves in the same direction, in the immediate aftermath of the scene in which Adam gazes at the hanged man. "He went across the street and sat on the curb, staring at the body. Perhaps it would happen yet.... Three children, very dirty, frowzy-headed, and unkempt, two little girls about seven and nine dragging a naked-butted boy of some two years, came and stood to stare up at the body. He rose again, and went toward them, waving his arms, he did not know why" (46). If *Wilderness* recalls Freud's book on dreams when it shows us Adam calling his feet children (a connection further underscored when he focuses his attention on the foot of little Hans, Maran Meyerhof's infant: "One of the baby's feet gave a little rhythmic kick, over and over" [113]), after having already set up the analogy between the hanged man's mutilated feet and his unnarrated castration, then this sudden appearance of three children tempts us to recall another observation from the same source: "In any case the number three has been confirmed from many sides as a symbol of the male genitals" (393). The analogy is strengthened by the fact that the central figure here is a halfnaked boy, his parts exposed (particularly that part of the body Mollie had also to expose), being dragged against his will by two females to the scene of castration, with the result that, not only are these intruders upon Adam's meditations (his staring at the body and his waiting "for something to happen" in his heart) genital both by virtue of being children and being three, but at the same time they represent the fear, and the danger, of castration itself.

What is it Adam is waiting for as he stares at the body on the lamppost, deep in the meditation which the children interrupt? As so often happens in Warren, the moment a protagonist feels on the brink of an insight may also be the moment readers aware of a larger context can make their own discoveries. Thus it was when Jeremiah Beaumont kept returning to the childhood memory of the beech tree, and dreamed about the trees whose name he knew but could not remember, making it possible for us to discover the ultimate significance of their name. Given, then, the parallels between Mollie and the hanged man, what is there to see in their juncture that Adam's patient expectancy should encourage us to seek but that he could never know (since, for one thing, he could not yet be aware of their parallels)? The children may be a clue. Adam's first vision of Mollie, as we have seen, was of a shapeless huddle tied at the neck with a cord, which is strikingly reminiscent of the empty sack tied at the neck with a tight cord that was his first impression of the hanged man. Mollie is elsewhere described as a *parcel* ("nothing but a pore old broke-down parcel of Irish clap" [207]), a term not innocent of other connotations in the novel, for the narrative's one description of an infant, Maran Meyerhof's baby, is as "a soft ill-wrapped parcel" (117). And the fact that it is ill-wrapped sends us back to another bundled baby, one that was poorly, and strangely, wrapped, the child in disintegrating newspaper that appeared to Perse (and now we begin to suspect the significance of his first name) Munn in a dream.

Maran's child is worthy of interest for another reason: it displays something like a father's wink: "[W]ith abandoned truthfulness [its head] flopped over against her breast. Adam could see that the lid of the one eye visible to him was drooping.... The baby's name, he remembered with sudden precision, was Hans—Hans, like the father" (177). Adam will spend several days, on a pause on his way south as assistant to the sutler Jedeen Hawksworth, talking with the infant's dying father, who had fought in the same European revolution as Leopold Rosenzweig. In him he will see an idealized version of his own father, one who had not rejected his secular idealism to return to the Law. "He felt as though his life were curving backward on itself.... He felt as though, again, he sat beside a dying father, a father who had handled a musket at Rastatt but who, in dying ... would not repudiate the old truth" (120). It is Meyerhof's eyes that most catch Adam's attention, for the body was so wasted by illness that they were the only thing still alive: "the body was nothing more than a heap of bones, lying almost as starkly obvious as they would lie on the earth, if a spade ... broke open the coffin.... Life showed only in the eyes" (119). They would sporadically glitter with "astonishing brilliance, as though some great excitement, some commanding thought, were taking hold," yet that semblance of meaning behind their glitter was, he realized, not caused by "anything that had passed between them" (Hans and Adam) but was "only some fluctuation of the fever or the transitory flicker of some old event in that fading brain" (120). Like the twitch on the mummy-hided face of the old man that Jack Burden thought was the prelude to a wink, this phenomenon of seeming thought, this glitter in the eye, is purely physiological, empty of meaning and intent. Like the mummies Sweetwater was reminded of by the fetus in Sue Murdock's womb, whose eyelids were squinting in their preserved state "because there was nothing under them any more," these old eyes have the look of intent ("like the faces of the fetuses, the same look, intent, contorted, the same invincible, painful abstraction"), but inside they are as empty as Duncan Trice's coffin in Cass Mastern's fantasy ("I had the impulse to hurl the coffin to the ground and see its emptiness burst open"), a fantasy Adam comes close to sharing when he looks at Hans's dying body and thinks of how it would not look any different "if a spade, some years from now, broke open the coffin."

The hanged man, once Adam got past the image of an "empty sack" (an image "to which his mind clung . . . as long as possible"), gave a similar semblance of thoughtfulness for purely physiological reasons: "the head, hanging pensive, quizzical, abashed" (44). This pensiveness and quizzicality recall the wise puzzlement of Sweetwater's mummylike fetuses ("faces . . . intent and, for all their wisdom, contorted in profound puzzlement"). And it may also remind us of the way in which Hans's eyes showed a glitter of astonishing brilliance that seemed to reveal "some commanding thought" but was in fact the result of some kind of synaptic twitch. The hanged man is thus the site of the intersection of a great deal of imagery: of fetal fathers and phallic feet, and of thoughtful yet puzzled expressions that give the deceiving semblance of intent. Likewise puzzled, though more sure that we are, we have reason to wonder if the text of these intersections, like the thing it represents, only seems to mean something when in fact that was never its intent. In other words, in retracing these parallels (and thereby bringing into play much that happens elsewhere not only here but in the rest of the Warren corpus), do we run the risk of altering the text? Perhaps so, but this risk of rewriting a received and paternal text is anticipated by the novel itself, for *Wilderness* is the story of a son who tries to be true to his reading of his father's poem. And this may offer some comfort and assurance that there is an intent behind what we think we see that, like an all-seeing father, already knew this rewriting would happen.

For Adam Rosenzweig's quest for the worthiness his father's poem first named will culminate in his discovery of a rewritten paternal text, specifically, in his encounter with the debased incarnation of the paternal text to which his father had betrayed his own poem to return, the Law of Moses. "You have lived without the Law," his father's older brother (who had raised Adam during his father's thirteen-year imprisonment, and was thus a second, rival father) had told Leopold Rosenzweig; "I have prayed that you may die within the Law" (8). Now Adam will find that rewritten paternal text in the person of a Moses—Mose Talbutt, his fellow assistant to Jedeen Hawksworth—upon whose skin a letter has been inscribed, an initial that stands for the very word most able to contradict the word that best sums up the text his father had written, the thrice-expressed "worthy" of his poem: "On the man's right thigh, puckering and crinkling crudely up from the dark slickness of skin, was the brand. It was a big W.... 'You know what that is?' Jed Hawksworth demanded, turning to Adam. 'Reckin that's one letter your prize scholar can read. W—W for worthless! That's what the Yankees put on 'em. Put on a soldier that ain't worth a damn.'" (217). Mose's true identity[2] was discovered by Hawksworth, who had reason to suspect it already (from the commander of a black regiment's having recognized him), when he tore off the underclothes Mose would never remove and revealed the guilty letter. His real name was not Talbutt but Crawfurd, and he had deserted from the Union army. But this revelation of hidden identity, of the Crawfurd beneath the Talbutt—like those other moments in Warren when the protagonist discovers one thing and the reader something else—may remind us not only of the constancy of his first name but of its identity with that of the author of the received paternal text that Leopold Rosenzweig in his last days adopted as the palinode to the poem he had written, the Law of *Moses*. If one Moses can stand for another (if there is a reason for Mose's first name and this is it), then the text that contradicted the father's poem (the Mosaic Law, transformed by its black incarnation into a palimpsest, a rewritable text) is now canceled out by something like the very text it annulled. The degree to which it is something like (as "worthless" is like "worth"), like the degree to which Mose's name is like that of the author of the Law, is what gives impetus to this interpretation, to the sense that behind this similarity of situation and name there is some semblance of intent. But neither the nature nor even the existence of that intent is clear; much more apparent than either is the fact that both this reading and its sense of its own liability to error seem to have been anticipated by the text itself, for what could be more tenuous than the official interpretation that the text offers us, Hawksworth's reading of this solitary W? Could it not just as well have stood for the opposite of what he says it did, for worth instead of worthlessness?[3] Hawkesworth, of course, knew what he was talking about if the letter is to be interpreted in its specific military context. But what does it mean in the context of the two paternal texts, Leopold's and Mose's, to which it seems to allude?

And what does it mean that the word for which it stands (or which it contradicts) should also appear in the name of this privileged interpreter? What, in other words, is the *worth* of this *hawk?* The publication a decade and a half after *Wilderness* of the poem Harold Bloom has termed "a deliberate and overwhelming self-interpretation of [Warren's] obsessive hawk-imagery" (review of *Now and Then*, 74)[4] has made that question a little less difficult to answer. "Red-Tail Hawk and Pyre of Youth" is the story of the murder and subsequent preservation of the corpse of a hawk who bears an astonishing resemblance to the recurring and complex figure of fetus, mummy, and paternal text. Like the newspaper-wrapped infant in Perse's dream, the hawk is "cuddled / Like babe to heart.... Like a secret, I wrapped it in newspaper." As a "chunk of poor wingless red meat," the body shares qualities with the stillborn fetuses of *World Enough and Time* (where Rachel's dead child was "Nuthin but a pore little piece of meat" [204]) and *The Cave* (where what Jack Harrick fathered on Mary Tillyard was "a piece of something like a dime's worth of cat meat from the butcher shop" [380]). As a preserved corpse (the object of the poet's boyish taxidermy), the stuffed hawk has something in common with the mummies that the fetus Sweetwater imagined reminded him of; the fact that it was their eyes, with their semblance of intelligent intent, that made him think of their resemblance is not without resonance here, for the yellow eyes of the preserved hawk are what most haunt the poet: "the yellow eyes, / Unsleeping, stared as I slept" in the room where he had placed the hawk, like a text among texts, "on the tallest of bookshelves," in the company of "Blake and *Lycidas*, Augustine, Hardy and *Hamlet*." And later, after he had left home, books, and hawk behind, "with / Eyes closed I knew / That yellow eyes somewhere, unblinking, in vengeance stared."

It is in those eyes that the hawk is most alive, his vengeful intent made apparent. Yet, paradoxically, those eyes are the poet's own creation: "glass eyes / Gleaming yellow" he had substituted for the unpreservable original "Gold eyes, unforgiving, for they, like God, see all." Not gold but yellow and not flesh but glass, they are perhaps the most visible sign of the taxidermist's artifice, of the absence of the real. In this regard they resemble the eyes in the mummies Sweetwater remembered, which squinted and thereby seemed intent "because there was nothing under them any more," for there was nothing beneath the glass eyes either, only the skull "now well scraped / And with arsenic dried." All that poor red meat gone too, replaced by "the clay-burlap body built there within." As *Wilderness* makes apparent, where Hans Meyerhof's eyes glitter with an astonishing brilliance that is merely the visible sign of a fading brain, this quality of seeming intent belongs to the eyes not only of Sweetwater's mummies but of Warren's fathers, too. In *Wilderness* a certain winking can be expected from a father's eyes (withheld by Duncan, offered in the fading of Aaron Blaustein's cigar), and in "Red-Tail Hawk" the hawk eventually becomes one-eyed (which is essentially what winking does), too: the poet returns years later and finds it, no longer on the bookshelf but still among books—though with a difference, for it now lies not only with Milton and *Hamlet* but with a text that he has since then written: "a book / Of poems friends and I had printed in college."[5] If the bookish company the stuffed hawk had always kept since it was first enshrined on that bookcase suggests that it was a text among texts, might the fact that it is now gathering dust in the company of poems like the one in which it appears mean that over the passage of time it has become something like the poet's poem, his text? as it already is clearly an object of his own making, a reconstructed version of a dead original, a model perhaps for the kind of rewritten (paternal) text that may be at the origin of what this poet writes: "the chunk of poor wingless red meat, / The model from which all was molded"?

It is true that in the hawk's present timeworn state, in its one-eyedness, the poet does recognize something of himself:

> That night in the lumber room, late,
> I found him—the hawk, feathers shabby, one
> Wing bandy-banged, one foot gone sadly
> Askew, one eye long gone—and I reckoned
> I knew how it felt with one gone.

Like the secret, skeletal articulation in "The Circus in the Attic" that only Time can reveal, the fact that Warren is blind in one eye has had to wait a long time to become part of what is publicly known about him,[6] part of that text of which he says, in *Being Here,* "it may be said that our lives are our own supreme fiction" (108). What is the significance of the fact that the poet shares this one-eyedness with the stuffed hawk that is his own creation, or recreation? It is more than a family resemblance. Warren would never have become a writer, according to the family romance his sister Mary tells,[7] had it not been for the accident that led to his half-blindness, had not his brother Thomas thrown the rock in the air that sailed over the hedge to where Robert Penn was lying on his back, eyes open. It kept him from going to the Naval Academy, where he had already won an appointment and ultimately sent him to Vanderbilt University instead, where he came under the influence of such teachers as John Crowe Ransom and Donald Davidson and such friends as Allen Tate.[8] One would like to think the writer in Warren would have won out over the admiral in him anyway, but certainly the accident intervened like a stroke of fate. Of more interest than the biographical fact alone is the articulation it finds in Warren's published work, of which his belated revelation in "Red-Tail Hawk" is a highly privileged example; for it is not just that this is the first time the secreted truth has broken through into direct expression in his text, but that it takes place in a poem where all the elements of the recurring pattern are present: the father as preserved corpse with paradoxically expressive eyes, as text (and rewritten text), and as newspaper-wrapped infant (and fetal) bundle.

The resemblance between the stuffed hawk and the poet is indeed a family one, though—as we now know—artificial, for this half-blindness was not inherited from father to son. But the fact that the accident happened to the son alone and yet Warren's fiction is about fathers giving or refusing to give one-eyed looks to their sons, and fathers whose eyes give the semblance of intent when they don't necessarily mean to,[9] suggests a hidden motive for that fiction, one in which the son projects his own one-eyedness onto the father, thereby giving him the enforced wink that was really his own, and so invents the text he will pretend to decipher.

A similar reverse inheritance is accomplished in "The Leaf," where the poet climbs up to the nesting place of the hawk and finds that "I am the father / Of my father's father's father. I, / Of my father, have set the teeth on edge. But / By what grape?"[10] The fruit of such effort in *Wilderness* is the reappearance of the initial letter of the word, so insistently present in Adam's father's text, on the skin of a Moses, so that by such stigmatization the text of his father's father might be rewritten, reinscribed with the letter of worth or unworth that in his father's text it had, until now, effectively obliterated. That Adam was aiming, though without realizing it, at the grandfather is already apparent from the fact that he inflicts an eventually mortal blow on Aaron Blaustein—grinding the winking flame to extinction with his boot, refusing to be his adopted son, and later realizing that that refusal was responsible for his death—in the shadow of a mythic Perseus who (likewise unintentionally) killed his own grandfather. That Adam's ultimate grandfatherly target is the Moses whose text overthrew his father's is evident from Blaustein's first name, for what better scripturally sanctioned substitute could there be for Moses than Aaron, his brother and indispensable stand-in on that other wilderness journey?

Chapter 9

Continent in Flood *Flood,* 1964

Book I

Chapter 1   Screenwriter Bradwell Tolliver, originally of Fiddlersburg, Tennessee, is driving his white Jaguar to the Nashville airport to pick up Hollywood producer Yasha Jones. He approaches the Seven Dwarfs Motel; its garish decor occupies the spot where something whose nature we'll not learn about until later happened twenty years before, in 1941. He stops for gas and has an unsettling conversation with a young black employee dressed in a grotesque costume appropriate to the theme of the place.

Chapter 2   Waiting at the airport, Brad remembers old Izzie Goldfarb, a Jewish tailor in the Fiddlersburg of his youth who had taken an interest in him, but died when Brad was away at college. Now that a dam is going to flood Fiddlersburg, he thinks he will look for Goldfarb's grave and take charge of moving it. Yasha Jones appears, preternaturally bald, with a "ghostly continent" of a pink mark running up the left side of his skull. Brad is convinced that he is Jewish.

Chapter 3   Brad has been back in Fiddlersburg for three weeks. We read more of his recollections about his first wife, Lettice Poindexter, and his second, Suzie Martine. He had lived with Lettice in Fiddlersburg and remembers driving her past the present site of the Seven Dwarfs Motel to the train for Reno when that marriage ended.

Chapter 4   Yasha wants to make a film about Fiddlersburg and the impending flood. On the strength of *I'm Telling You Now,* a short-story collection Brad wrote about his hometown when still in college, Yasha has hired him to write the script. They arrive at the town—the river below, the state penitentiary on a hill above.

Chapter 5   Brad's sister, Maggie Fiddler, plays hostess to Brad and Yasha in the house that Brad grew up in. Lawyer Blanding Cottshill tells of Miss Pettifew's midnight exhumation of a fetus in a Mason jar in the yard of the house where she used to live.

Chapter 6 In bed the next morning, Brad recalls Telford Lott, the editor who read and liked the title story in *I'm Telling . . .* (about Israel Goldfarb) and published the book, and who was the matchmaker for Brad and Lettice Poindexter. He recalls, too, his father's casket in the living room and his sister asking how can Brad hate him now.

Chapter 7 Brad takes Yasha to church, where Brother Potts preaches on the text of Amos 9:15. Brad points out the blind but beautiful Leontine Purtle. Yasha later peruses Brad's file on other townsfolk, among them Harvard-educated black preacher Leon Pinckney, who refused Potts's request for a joint religious service uniting all Fiddlersburg residents to say farewell to the town. Maggie brings lemonade and cookies up to Yasha's bedroom and remarks that his (Japanese) robe makes him look like an Egyptian pharaoh.

Chapter 8 Brad reveals to Yasha that Maggie's husband, Calvin, is in the pen on the hill above the town. He doesn't say why.

Chapter 9 Brad tells Yasha about Frog-Eye, who lives in the swamp and had been the companion of his youth, and two anecdotes about his father, Lank Tolliver, who came out of the swampy backwoods to get rich in Fiddlersburg. (1) When he foreclosed on the house of Dr. Amos Fiddler—Calvin's father—he took possession of his extensive collection of books; when young Brad saw him idly tearing up the pages to make spills for the fireplace, he braved his father's blows to rescue the books. (2) Lank would on occasion retreat to the swamp; Frog-Eye once took Brad there to show him his father out cold, with tear-tracks streaking his dirty face.

Brad leaves a social message for Digby, the army engineer in charge of the flooding, in the room he rents at the house of Leontine Purtle and her father. He tries out a subplot for the movie on Yasha, in which Digby, fascinated by her blindness, falls in love with Leontine; Brad gives Digby's character a purple birthmark on his face that he realizes, too late, is based on Yasha's scar.

Book II

Chapter 10 Flashback to Brad's affair with Lettice Poindexter, who had formerly been Telford Lott's mistress. Dissatisfied with his writing, in a burst of idealism (and in search of identity) he volunteers to fight in the Spanish Civil War.

Chapter 11 Flashback continues: Stricken with typhus, Brad must quit fighting, recovers in France, returns, feeling "that all his experience came to nothing." Telford gives him a two-thousand-dollar advance for a novel on Spain. Six months later, unable to write, Brad tells Lott of his failure and of his decision to return to Fiddlersburg. Lettice accepts his proposal of marriage and a life in Fiddlersburg, but (though she had been faithful during Brad's entire Spanish adventure) has a one-night stand with Dr. Ramon Echegaray, a one-eyed Loyalist veteran on the lecture circuit.

Chapter 12 Brad takes Yasha on a tour of the pen, where Pretty-Boy Rountree, scheduled for electrocution in eight weeks, still has not prayed, despite Leon Pinckney's regular visits. The whole town is anxious to know whether he'll crack.

Chapter 13 Yasha and Brad talk about lonesomeness—the cons', Maggie's; Yasha recalls (to himself) his experiences in the French Resistance.

Chapter 14 Brad's mother had died giving birth to his sister. Her will left money for the children to receive a proper education outside of Fiddlersburg. When Brad announced to his father that he was going to the same Nashville prep school Calvin Fiddler attended, Lank Tolliver refused; but Brad pointed out the clause in the will, and furthermore told him that he had seen him weeping in the swamp and knew he couldn't bear to have his son in the house knowing that.

Chapter 15 Digby's social call (at Brad's invitation in chapter 9) resurrects Maggie's memory of how her husband, Calvin Fiddler, shot another young engineer, Alfred Tuttle.

Book III

Chapter 16 January 1939: Brad goes to Fiddlersburg to prepare the house for Lettice. He stares at the spot where his father's coffin had rested. He has a reunion with his sister, now in a Nashville girls' school. Lank Tolliver had committed suicide in the swamp when his late wife's Nashville cousin, in charge of the children's educational trust, threatened him with financial ruin if he refused to let Maggie go away to school. Upon Brad's return to New York, Lettice confesses her fling with Ramon Echegaray the night before. Brad forgives her and goes ahead with the marriage.

Chapter 17 The summer of 1939 in Fiddlersburg: Brad and Lettice are deliriously happy; Maggie joins them at the end of the school term and falls in love with young doctor Calvin Fiddler.

Chapter 18 Leontine Purtle invites Brad in, plays him a recording of his early story about Izzie Goldfarb. He doesn't want to hear it; he wants to know what it's like to be blind.

Chapter 19 Brother Potts comes to the house to recite more of the hymn he's been writing for the final Fiddlersburg farewell service; he has found poetic inspiration in Pretty-Boy's spitting on him when he came, with Pinckney's permission, to try to induce him to pray.

Chapter 20 Brad goes wandering through Fiddlersburg in the moonlight and runs into Yasha at the Confederate monument. He tells him Maggie suggested they make Brother Potts the center of the film. Yasha is enthusiastic; Brad had worked on it all night but got nowhere.

Chapter 21 Yasha's recollections (to himself) of his marriage to Lucy Spence and her death in a car accident. She was from a small town in Iowa, about which he used to ask her to recall as much as she could; his interest in Fiddlersburg derives from that.

Chapter 22 Brad visits Calvin in the pen; the latter is jealous of Yasha's interest in his wife.

Chapter 23 At Blanding Cottshill's law office, Brad learns from Pinckney that Pretty-Boy finally broke down and prayed. But this wouldn't have happened had he not spit on Potts's face. Brad asks Blanding for the record of the Calvin Fiddler trial.

Book IV

Chapter 24 In April 1940, Brad and Lettice decide to go to Mexico in the fall, and perhaps conceive a child there. In September, Telford Lott sends Brad an advance copy of *For Whom the Bell Tolls,* the book Brad might have written on Spain. On the evening of October 5, just after Brad had finished reading Hemingway's novel, he and Lettice, Maggie and their guest, Alfred Tuttle, were dancing. Calvin was in Nashville, doing his internship. Frog-Eye, whose portrait Lettice had been working on all summer, had passed out in a corner. In an atmosphere of increasing eroticism, Brad made Tuttle dance with Lettice, and then with Maggie, before disappearing upstairs with his wife. He had inadvertently put a scratch on a record of "The Continental," which kept repeating the words of its title over and over—until Tuttle could restrain himself no longer.

Chapter 25 Maggie and Tuttle had wound up under the hydrangeas, making love. When Calvin found out, he shot and killed Tuttle. He confessed, though there was a trial anyway, and was sentenced to a term in the pen (he would have been out by now, but a bungled escape attempt had compounded his sentence). Lettice conceived a child that night but had a miscarriage the following spring. When she reads in *Time* magazine that Ramon Echegaray has been executed by Franco, and Brad is not in a consoling mood, they realize the marriage is over. Brad drives her to Nashville for the train to Reno; she persuades him to stop on the way and make love one last time—that is what he was remembering took place on the present site of the Seven Dwarfs Motel.

Chapter 26 Brad throws away the screenplay based on Brother Potts and writes one that features a man like Calvin married to a woman like Maggie and who escapes from prison. Yasha rejects it as lacking verisimilitude as well as the feeling for Fiddlersburg that he is counting on the author of *I'm Telling You Now* to produce.

Chapter 27 Brad runs into Leontine Purtle, offers her a ride, and winds up in bed with her at the Seven Dwarfs Motel. Afterward, he learns from Mortimer Sparlin, the black attendant, that she comes there often, and not alone either.

Chapter 28 Brad pays a visit to Frog-Eye in the swamp and finds out that he had only been pretending to be asleep that night twenty years before, that he had been aware of all that transpired between Maggie and Tuttle and Brad and Lettice.

Chapter 29 Back in town, Brad crosses paths with Blanding Cottshill, who is on his way to say farewell to Pretty-Boy, scheduled for execution at midnight. Returning to the house, Brad finds a letter from Maggie: She and Yasha have run off together. The sirens are blasting at the pen; the screen door opens.

Chapter 30 Yasha and Maggie have returned. Brad is glad about their happiness, but he accuses Yasha of having rejected his screenplay (detailed in chapter 26) to spare Maggie's feelings. He himself had earlier abandoned the manuscript of a novel based on Tuttle's murder for the same reason. Yasha replies that they will go ahead with Brad's version because it is now apparent that it is where his deepest feelings are invested. Calvin appears, having escaped from the pen. When Brad is wounded trying to knock the pistol from his hand, Calvin suddenly becomes a doctor again, performing an emergency tracheotomy with a ballpoint pen.

Book V

Chapter 31 Brad recovers and visits the reincarcerated Calvin, who proudly shows him his new medical facilities at the pen (paid for secretly by Yasha). He explains that he had not been able to practice medicine in the pen before because his memory of the information in his medical books would dissolve whenever he was confronted with a patient. But the moment the gun that wounded Brad went off, he could suddenly see his father's anatomy book as clear as day, and it had been that way ever since.

Chapter 32 Maggie and Yasha are happily married, living in Greece. Yasha has abandoned the film, but another producer, Mort Seebaum, has picked it up and offered Brad a handsome salary to write it.

Chapter 33 With the farewell service in the background, Brad reads a letter from Lettice to Maggie that his sister has sent on to him and learns that she has devoted her life since the breakup of their marriage to working for the poor in a Catholic mission in Chicago. She also recounts a dream she had already told Brad long ago: three men try to kill her; she tries to elude them by hanging herself. Brad tears up Mort Seebaum's telegram, with its lucrative offer. And he realizes that now he will not have to find Goldfarb's grave after all.

When old man Bascomb went out on his back porch at 2:00 A.M. to shine his flashlight on whatever it was his dog was barking at, he was more than a little surprised to see "a female form, white in the face, clutching something to the bosom" (49). He was even more surprised to learn that it was old Miss Pettifew, who had returned to the backyard of the house she had lived in fifteen years before to dig up the sealed jar that contained "the thing she could not bear to leave lying in the ground, under the weight of water, when Fiddlersburg goes under," the stillborn fetus that was the secret issue of the one and only love affair of her life. "That, ladies and gentlemen of the jury," said Blanding Cottshill to Yasha Jones, Brad Tolliver, and Brad's sister, Maggie Fiddler, "is Fiddlersburg" (50).

"'Old Izzie Goldfarb,'" Brad will later say to Yasha Jones, "'he is Fiddlersburg. I have been ten thousand miles away and I have shut my eyes and I have said the word *Fiddlersburg,* and what I saw was Old Goldfarb'" (164). These two apparently diverse statements about what Fiddlersburg is are ultimately not in disagreement; for Goldfarb is to Tolliver as the fetus was to Miss Pettifew: the body he intends to dig up before the flood arrives. "Would that be another death, a drowning, an eternal drowning, a perpetual suffocation, a crushing weight on the chest that would never go away? Bradwell Tolliver, with a sudden swelling of the heart, thought that he himself, by God, if nobody else did, would take care of Izzie Goldfarb" (18–19). Goldfarb, "crouched in his tailor shop . . . pained eyes bowed over the needle that moved slower every year," had been not only Brad's friend—the only man in Fiddlersburg who would "speak to you as though you were a man. Later he played chess with you and did not let you win" (16)—but also a source of fascination because of his command of texts to which no one else had access: "Several of Old Izzie's books were in a language which occasioned some debate in Fiddlersburg—was it Yiddish or real Jew or German or what? But the others were in French," as Brad knew because he had studied a little French in high school. Brad spent a lot of time with him; in fact, as Barnett Guttenberg observed, he "makes Izzie Goldfarb his surrogate father" (123). From time to time in the course of the novel, Tolliver will wander the town cemetery making less-than-systematic searches for Izzie's grave—until in the final pages he will discover that he didn't need to find it after all.

But Yasha Jones, who has come to Fiddlersburg to gather material and get the proper feel for the movie he is thinking of producing about the disappearance by government-engineered flood of this Tennessee town, has yet a third definition of what Fiddlersburg is. "Fiddlersburg," he says to himself as he sits at the base of the Confederate monument and notices how the buildings on River Street shift and heave in the moonlight, "was a Mystery Spot" (273), a place like one he knew in California, where a buried meteorite emits a magnetic field that causes "a profound disorder of the senses.... Perspectives shift, equilibrium is impaired, the gut goes cold."

To a reader of *Flood* familiar with some of the recurring images traced in earlier chapters of this book, Yasha's simile comes uncannily close to describing what Fiddlersburg is—comes closest, that is, to describing what it is like to encounter once again a haunting fetus (haunting both Miss Pettifew and this reading of Warren), along with a fatherly figure who bears some parallel relation to the fetus—in this instance the need for exhumation. And Yasha's image of Fiddlersburg as a Mystery Spot of meteoric origin points as well to the possibility of a reality beyond the apparent narrative, beyond the world of this single novel, as if the source of its attractive force came from somewhere else in Warren's universe. Images are buried here that exert a disordering influence on these fictional characters, making them reenact rituals whose meaning they may not entirely understand, gestures that may make more sense in a larger context than that of their own story. *Flood* may provide yet another metaphor for this insistent repetition in the central event upon which its plot turns: a stuck record that keeps saying the same word over and over again.

This repetition eventuates in adultery and murder. Back in 1940, twenty years before Brad Tolliver returned to his hometown with Yasha Jones to make the movie, Brad and his first wife, Lettice Poindexter, were dancing to records in the old Fiddler house (thus named because Brad's father had acquired it by foreclosing on Dr. Amos Fiddler's mortgage) with his sister, Maggie, whose husband, Dr. Calvin Fiddler, Amos's son, was in Nashville doing his internship, and their guest, the young engineer Alfred O. Tuttle, whom they always called "Tut." Brad put on "The Continental" "and he never changed it, just flipped the needle back up near the beginning ... there was nothing but that same record over and over, saying, 'the Continental—the Continental,' just that one crazy word ..." (316-17)—as Maggie was to recall it later. And to make matters worse, "Brad must have scraped it—the record, that is—the last time he shifted the needle back to the start. The record, all at once, was stuck. Stuck in one groove and going on and on, with just that one word: 'the Continental—the Continental—'" (319). Brad had made Tut dance with Lettice, then with Maggie, while he danced with Lettice, "his hand on the bareness of her behind, under that tight purple cloth." The combination of this bold example and the insistence of "that one crazy word" was too much for young Tut. Brad dragged Lettice upstairs to bed, unwillingly, "her left arm straight ahead of her as though it were a rope Brad was pulling her by" (318), and Mrs. Calvin Fiddler and Arthur Tuttle were left to dance alone. Maggie suddenly heard him make "a sound like a painful, breathed-out groan. It was as though something had given way.... Then, in a sort of grinding whisper, he was saying: 'That God-damned record—if the record hadn't got stuck—if it hadn't got stuck...'" (319). The drift seems to be that Tut came in his pants, which incontinence did not prevent his subsequently taking Maggie outside to make love "right on the grass under the hydrangeas." When Calvin found out, he shot and killed him and was tried and sentenced to the penitentiary on the hill in the heart of Fiddlersburg.

These incidents in 1940 are not unlike Yasha's buried meteorite; for, though deep in the past of these characters, it exerts its influence on subsequent events. In 1960 Maggie is still married to Calvin but has not visited him in prison in all that time, although she has been devotedly faithful to him and has sacrificed herself to the care of his aged and senile mother. When, in the course of his research visit with Yasha Jones, her brother invites another younger engineer, Digby (who is working on the proposed flooding of Fiddlersburg), for drinks one evening, Maggie is painfully aware of the irony of the coincidence. "'Why did Brad bring him!' she cried. 'I hate him for that.... It was a long time ago.... That other young engineer off the river. His name was Al Tuttle—Alfred O. Tuttle—they called him Tut—and my husband shot him'" (190).

It is not Digby, however, but Yasha Jones who comes closest to replaying the role of Maggie's seducer, Tut (not that Digby will not have a role of his own to play in the working-out of the implications of Brad's scratching needle). For the reasonably happy ending of the story is that Yasha wins Maggie away from Cal, although not without very nearly sharing Tut's fate at the hand of a gun-wielding, angry husband.

Some hint that this is going to happen occurs early on when Maggie makes a mistake concerning Yasha Jones's bathrobe. She enters his bedroom bearing a tray of refreshments and remarks how Egyptian he looks in what is, in fact, a Japanese kimono. "'It's a very pretty robe,'" she says. "'[I]t makes you look like pictures in the Old Testament, Egyptian, you know—like Pharaoh, or something.' 'Just dug up,'[1] he said" (95), suggesting she thinks he looks like a recently exhumed mummy. Later that evening she tells everybody else the same thing:

> "You know," she said, "I most indecently stumbled into Mr. Jones' room this afternoon... and there he was propped up in an Egyptian robe, like a Pharaoh in the pictures in the Old Testament part of the Bible, and there—"
> "Japanese," Yasha Jones interrupted, "the robe, I mean."
> She ignored him.... (100–101)

And still later she will persist in her error:

> "I thought you were an Egyptian," Maggie said. "In your robe of state I thought you were an Egyptian Pharaoh."
> "No," he laughed, "not even the mummy of one."
> She laughed too, but a very peculiar thing, even before she laughed, had happened to Yasha Jones . . . he suddenly thought of himself . . . lying on the big tester bed, the bed where, he remembered, that strongly made, thick-skulled man there had once grappled, in darkness, with a tall, slim, yearning girl who happened to have had a CP card. He thought of himself . . . lying there in late afternoon light . . . wrapped in that russet and black robe . . . with, somehow, the head of Maggie Tolliver quietly on his arm. (104)

The thick-skulled man was Brad and the tall, slim Communist, Brad's former wife, Lettice. What Yasha is doing here, without in any way realizing it (for Maggie has not yet told him the story of what happened twenty years ago), is to fantasize himself into Maggie's arms, in the same way Tut had done that evening when Brad led his wife up to bed and left him alone to do the same with Maggie. It is a bit more understandable that Maggie should keep insisting that Yasha looked Egyptian, for it makes him like Tut[2]—as in King Tutankhamen, the mummy of a Pharaoh, whose discovery had been big news several years before (1922). But the resemblance that their nicknaming of Tuttle made possible had to wait twenty years to find its realization in the person of Yasha Jones in a falsely Egyptian robe.

However, the fullest realization of that resemblance lies outside *Flood*. For Yasha, in his "russet and black Japanese robe of coarse silk" (88), looking Egyptian, remarkably resembles Bogan Murdock in Warren's second novel, who likewise wore "a Japanese robe of russet silk" and, what is more, displayed "an Egyptian delicacy of bone," looking "like a carved figure on a tomb, or . . . a dead body laid out ceremonially" (182–83).[3] The likeness is striking, and at the very least it is a reminder that Yasha was right in saying that what happens in Fiddlersburg is like the magnetic effect of a hidden object from another world—in this instance from another novel. One could also point to the underlying connections in *At Heaven's Gate* linking Murdock to the other mummies there, those Sweetwater envisioned when he thought of their resemblance to certain exhumed fetuses. The most promising avenue of inquiry, however, is to pursue how it may be that Yasha Jones is to Brad Tolliver as Bogan Murdock was to Jerry Calhoun—that is, as fatherly employer to sonlike employee.

One does not have far to look. Yasha, of course, is the man who hired Brad to write his movie. Brad has to write a text—the script, the treatment—that will please Yasha; and that is by no means an easy task, as Brad learned when he tried out a scenario that called for a " '[s]on in prison, rather like Calvin Fiddler,' " to be married to a woman " 'rather, I suppose, like Maggie,' " who stays home to care for the son's father (rather like Calvin's mother). A " 'dam will flood them out. . . . Then the prison break. The husband, crazed by rumors—' " (342)—in other words, what really will happen later when Calvin escapes, arrives at the Fiddler house brandishing a pistol, and finds Maggie and Yasha in love with each other. Brad wrote his script in four days and five sleepless nights and left it under Yasha's door. When Yasha came down to talk it over with him the next day, he was once again "wearing the black Japanese kimono" (341), a costume whose appropriateness is only now fully emerging. He tells Brad that despite the fact that he has never read anything more "expert," and that things do have a way of happening like this, the plot just does not capture the feeling of Fiddlersburg, in particular the feeling Yasha remembers from *I'm Telling You Now*, the book of short stories in which Brad had lovingly detailed life in the town of his youth, and of which the title story concerned old Izzie Goldfarb. What Yasha Jones wants is a repeat performance.

The editor Telford Lott had played a similar role at an earlier stage in Brad's writing career, though his seemingly uncritical acceptance of what Brad had written but did not like was troubling. Tolliver had come under Lott's aegis while in college, when Lott arranged the publication of a collection of his stories to follow up the success of "I'm Telling You Now," his story about Izzie Goldfarb. It was Izzie's death, and Brad's guilt over not having gone to tell him goodbye before leaving for college (hence the title), which had awakened his literary gift. Telford, on his part, saw in Bradwell Tolliver a son, "a way, however modest, to touch the future" (61). However, Brad was at least dimly aware that his memories of a Fiddlersburg boyhood were not going to be enough to sustain him as a writer. Feeling the need for some lived experience, and caught up in the ideology of the Loyalists, of which his involvement with Lettice Poindexter—Lott's former mistress—had provided a heavy dose, Brad went to fight in the Spanish Civil War. "His fear of having no story was one of the motives that impelled him. . . . He did not yet know that the true shame is in yearning for the false, not the true, story" (68). When Brad returned, Telford gave him a handsome advance to write a novel about his experience. Six months but only eighty-three pages later, Brad was in terrible shape and unable to write his assignment with any conviction. He was suddenly seized by the impulse to return to Spain, thinking, "with a flash of elation, of killing a faceless enemy. Then in that split second, the faceless enemy wore the face of Telford Lott" (145). He went to Fiddlersburg instead and married Lettice, hoping to start a new life and resume a writing career untrammeled by Telford's sincerely meant[4] but unwanted assistance.

Brad's rage at Telford Lott may well have had its origin in his editor's demanding a text he could not produce. Given Lott's paternal role in Brad's life, this was not only an oedipal rage but also an interesting, and new, variation on the relationship among father, son, and text that has so consistently undergirded the plots of Warren's novels. Here once again the plot turns upon a paternal text. Not, as before, one written by the father for the son to read, but one the father demands the son write. Yet, once produced, it will become the father's text because the father has paid for it. Telford had given Brad a two-thousand-dollar advance on the novel about Spain; Yasha Jones will pay him handsomely for the script of the Fiddlersburg film. And the very first text Brad Tolliver wrote literally embodied just such a paternal demand:

> On good evenings in spring, when the light began to hold late, Abraham Goldberg—Old Abie, with his stooped shoulders, pale brow, paper-thin nose and dark pained eyes—would come out of the tailor shop on River Street, and prop himself in a split-bottom chair to read. . . . What does an old Jew sitting in front of his tailor shop, alone in a lost town . . . think as he stares in the red sunset?
> I do not know. Now I shall never know.
> All I know is that, when the time came for me to go away from that town . . . I did not tell you goodbye. But I am telling you now. (230)

"I'm Telling You Now," with its self-referential title, is precisely what it says it is, the text that must take the place of the goodbye not spoken in time. It is the least the writer can do. He owes it to the man who had been such a father to him.

This may go a long way toward explaining why it is that when Brad meets Yasha for the first time at the airport, knowing him only from his photographs, he is convinced he is a Jew (a mistake Yasha clears up later [103–4]) and is reminded of Israel Goldfarb. Waiting for the plane, Brad knew he "was enough the true-born son of Fiddlersburg to carry the image of a Jew in his head as the archetypal image of all exoticism, especially of that exoticism of secret wisdom and slightly sinister learning. . . . So the image that came into his head now, after that of Yasha Jones . . . was the image of little old Mr. Israel Goldfarb . . ." (15). For Goldfarb, with his books in languages that no one in town could even identify, perfectly embodied that archetype of secret, and sinister, wisdom.

Brad's relationship to his biological father was overshadowed by a desperate struggle over texts. Having foreclosed on Dr. Amos Fiddler, Lancaster Tolliver had come into possession of the house and its furnishings, including Amos's extensive collection of books. Young Brad had acquired the habit of going into the house's library and reading everything he could lay his hands on, but one day he discovered that his father had a different use for the books—he was tearing out pages and rolling them into spills for the fire. Thirteen-year-old Brad walked over to take a book out of his father's lap. Lancaster snatched it back, tossed it into the fire, and struck his son a glancing blow on the head, all in the same gesture. The son slid to one knee to save the book from the fire. The father took another from the shelf and repeated the process, and everything happened as before. On the fourth attempt, the boy, dazed, could no longer get up. The father "leaned over and thrust his own hand into the fire and jerked out the book. He stared at the book very curiously. It was as though such an object were preposterously strange to him. Then he flung the book to the floor, in front of the crouching boy, and with no word, was gone" (117). Lank Tolliver then fled to the swamp, as it was his habit to do, not to return for days. The son had won, in a way; he was to win again, more dramatically, when he discovered something about his father's flights into the wilderness. It was from Frog-Eye, a veritable swamp creature whose one good eye bulged like a frog's, that Brad learned the truth about his brutal, but not omnipotent, father. Frog-Eye led him "to the spot where Lancaster Tolliver lay in the mud of the deep swamp, unconscious, with the marks of tears yet on his cheeks" (176).

Like Ham in the aftermath of the story of another Flood, Brad has had the privilege, and the burden, of gazing on his naked, drunken father (it was in emotional, if not literal, nakedness that Lank Tolliver lay in the mud). Although he "could not bear the knowledge that his father, in his brutality, could lie in the mud and weep," he turned what would have been Noah's curse into, if not a blessing, at least a tactical advantage. For when the time came for Brad to try to enforce that clause in his mother's will that stipulated a sum to be used to educate her children "at some institution of standing, not situated in Fiddlersburg," he was ready. He cooly made it known one morning at breakfast that he was going to the Maury Academy in Nashville in the fall. It was with some measure of joy—he was "exhilarated with the image"—that he saw "the purple rush of blood to the father's face," for he knew that this time his son had the perfect answer to the expected refusal, the revelation of what he had learned in the swamp.

> "I have seen you crying," the boy said.
> The man stared at him. The purple of the face was, all at once, streaked with white. But the hand was still raised.
> "Yes," the boy said. "I've seen you lying in the mud, in the swamp where you go to cry. You had been crying."
> The man's hand was quivering in the air. (177)

The father's face would turn purple once more, and for the last time, when the banker cousin on Brad's mother's side who managed the children's trust fund in Memphis told Lank it was time to fulfill the mother's bequest for

Maggie's schooling. He hinted at Tolliver's imminent financial ruin, and Brad's father once more fled to the swamp, this time for good. His body was found two days later, rather as his son had found it the time before, "sprawled face down in the damp black earth" (198).

It would seem that the unconscious memory of the purpling of his father's brow that had so "exhilarated" Brad on one occasion and presaged his father's death on another had something to do with the extraordinary embarrassment Brad felt when he suddenly realized that the purple scar with which he endowed a fictional character in an imagined scene for the movie was in fact based on the very real scar Yasha Jones bore on the side of his bald head. When Brad had first laid eyes on Yasha at the Nashville airport, he did not at first realize who he was, even though he was the last to get off the plane. "But no: this couldn't be Yasha Jones—not this figure in the tousled nondescript gray suit, nondescript gray hat . . ." (19). But the "instant the hat came off, it was, of course, Yasha Jones. The skull was not merely bald. . . . On the left side . . . was a strange irregular shape, outlined in the faintest pink tracery on the tan skull, lying there on the bulge of the skull to suggest a pale, bleached-out, pink, ghostly continent on a somewhat elongated parchment-colored globe. Within that continent, almost imperceptible lines ran crisscrossing, faintly crazing and hatching the surface . . ." (20). Now the birthmark Brad invented was not pink, like Yasha's scar, but purple (like the flush he liked to see on his father's brow). Yet Brad was painfully aware of where the idea came from and was afraid that Yasha would take offense. Brad was imagining Digby, who in reality lived in a rented room in the Purtle household, falling in love with the blind but beautiful Leontine Purtle.

> "Here is the gimmick. The guy is a perfectly decent-looking guy. But for one thing. He has a—"
> He stopped.
> He found that his glance had fallen upon Yasha Jones. Yasha Jones was not wearing his hat. His left side was toward Brad Tolliver, who, in that instant, with a sickening swoop of his guts, saw the scar on the skull and thought: *Christ, that's where I got it! Christ, he'll know I got it there.*
> "Yes," Yasha Jones was asking, courteously, "a what?"
> "A birthmark—" Brad said.
> And thought: *Did I come in fast enough?*
> Saying: "—a hell of a thing, purple, on one side of his face. It comes up under the eye, too high for a beard to help . . . a hell of a thing—" (125)

Perhaps he was going to say *pink,* and caught himself in time. But that he said *purple* made it resemble the discoloration of another father's face (and we remember what was fatherly about Yasha Jones—and Telford Lott, and Izzie Goldfarb).

But although the scar on Yasha's skull (along with the color of Brad's enraged father's brow) lay behind the birthmark on Digby's fictive face, it is quite likely that something else lies behind that pink, ghostly continent of a scar crazed by almost imperceptible lines—that is, behind the words Brad uses to describe it. That something else is what, borrowing Yasha Jones's terminology, we could call the buried meteorite of the story: Brad's inadvertent scratching of the surface of the record to which he and Lettice, Maggie and Tut were dancing so that all it did was repeat "just that one crazy word,"[5] the *Continental;* continental as in "pink, ghostly *continent*"; continental, too, as in *content*—so that, thanks to what Brad accidentally inscribed on the record with the stylus of the phonograph, the name of the song ("The Continental") becomes as self-referential as the title of Brad's first story, naming its own content (the only content it had left after Brad was done with it).

That the novel is concerned with such things is evident from another scene with a record, a record from which, in this case, the title has been removed, in contrast to "The Continental," of which only the title remained. Leontine Purtle has enticed Brad to come to her room so she can show him a surprise. She tells him to close his eyes and puts on the phonograph a recording of his famous short story "I'm Telling You Now," taking care to start the needle after the announcement of the title, so that it will start precisely at the first line of the story and thus not spoil the surprise. This is no mean feat for someone who is blind. Brad does not like hearing his own story read back to him but is nevertheless amazed at what Leontine can do with the needle. " 'I'm damned if I see how you got that thing started right off. No title, and all' " (230).

If we pursue the coincidence of these needles, they point us in the direction of not only another needle but possibly the original one, the needle plied by Fiddlersburg's fatherly tailor: "little old Mr. Israel Goldfarb, crouched in his tailor shop on River Street . . . pained eyes bowed over the needle that moved slower every year as the arthritis did its work" (15–16). Its gradual retardation and eventual stop may or may not have anticipated the stasis Brad's phonograph stylus achieved in its eternal return to the same, but Goldfarb did teach Brad something he was eventually able to put to good stylistic use, as Leontine was clever enough to point out:

> "And that part where you go back to the grave. I could just cry. The first time or two I played it I did cry."
>
> "I'll tell you something to dry your tears," he said. "I never went back. I just made that up. I had to end the story some damned way. . . . [W]hen you are writing a story or doing a

movie script, you hit some logic, and it is that logic, not the
heart business, that drives you to a certain end. It is like chess,
and—"
"Old Mr. Goldfarb," she said softly, "he left you his chess
set—you, that part of the story is—"
"To hell with Goldfarb," he said. "What I'm trying to say
is—"
But she was looking at him from the serene, blue, forgiving
distance.
He shut up. (213)

In calling attention to the gift of the chess set Leontine may still be reacting, in her untutored way, to "the heart business," although her esthetic is not that far removed from Telford Lott's penchant for being "moved to tears by fiction presenting images of generosity or of human suffering patiently borne." But it is from the mouth of Brad himself that we learn that the logic of narrative is like the logic of chess, and that he learned the logic of chess from the old tailor to whom he is also indebted, in another way, for his first successful fiction. If Goldfarb is a father who demands a text from his son, he also is a father who gives his son some instruction in how to write it.

Brad learned logic from the tailor and transferred its relevance from chess to writing stories. But he also may have learned how (or how not) to ply a needle, the tailor's implement that, in the form of a record stylus (a term that sounds like a writing instrument), he made yield up the record's empty, self-naming content. Of course, it also put into train the disastrous events that drive the plot of the novel: Maggie's infidelity, Tut's death, and Calvin's incarceration—perhaps even a stillborn fetus, Brad's counterpart to the one that had haunted Miss Pettifew. For when he led Lettice up the stairs, leaving Maggie and Tut with the repeating record, they conceived, for the first time, a child. That action was not directly caused by the scratching of the record, but it was of a piece with it, in that both were the result of Brad's drunken frenzy. " 'I told you,' " she complained to him later, " 'as soon as you dragged me upstairs. I struggled with you. I told you I wasn't fixed' " (328). The miscarriage, however, was evidently brought about by the stress of Calvin's trial, as it occurred three days after the sentence (332)—and thus could ultimately be attributed to Brad's abuse of the needle.

It was in imagining a love life for Digby—the young engineer who, in Maggie's eyes, came uncomfortably close to resembling the other young engineer who had been so moved by Brad's accidental editing of the recorded song—that Brad realized he was projecting the image of Yasha's pink, continental scar where it did not belong. But he was really doing for Digby what he would like to have done, and eventually did do, for himself.

He imagined Digby as being fascinated by Leontine Purtle's blindness, and asking her what it was like to be blind; this is precisely what he himself asks her the day she plays him the record on his own story. And he will in fact sleep with her, at the Seven Dwarfs Motel, in a scene in which he once more encounters the paternal mark of Yasha's pink scar. On a bed with a pink chenille bedspread, "made pinker by the pink-shaded bed lamp"[6] (359), "he saw the scar. It was, clearly, the scar from an appendix operation; expertly done, old, healed. There was only the faintest line and slightest pucker against the motionless perfection that glimmered opalescently in that dimness" (362). As the "faintest line" of a scar seen in a pinkish light, this expert result of a surgical procedure recalls the "faintest pink tracery" of "almost imperceptible lines" on Yasha's skull. But why in the world would the distinguishing mark of the movie producer show up here, on the belly of a woman whom our hero is about to enter?

The answer lies in the other surprising thing Brad notices about Leontine. She is not as inexperienced as he first thought. This begins to dawn on him when, to his considerable surprise, he encounters her diaphragm: "In that cold burst of awareness in which everything had exploded into meaning, he felt his erection sag. "'For Christ's sake.' . . ."" It was confirmed when Mortimer Sparlin, the black attendant at the Seven Dwarfs, later asked "'Tell me, Mac, how do you like blind tail? . . . Sure, everybody knows Miss Purtle. . . . Lots of boys, it would seem, like blind tail'" (363, 364).

Now the discovery of the appendectomy scar goes hand in hand with the revelation of the truth about Leontine Purtle. She is not, as it were, without blemish. And it is significant that the discovery of the scar comes as his hand is reaching for something else: "he . . . touched a forefinger to the upper swell of the right breast, and traced the curve down the narrowing, gracile sweep of the waist to the swell of the right hip. His hand was shaking. He felt that his breath was not coming right. Then he saw the scar" (361–62). What the scar tells him and what he is soon to learn from other sources is that someone else has been there before him. What the striking continuities between this scar and one we have seen before tell us is that the predecessor is the father.

The scar, "expertly done," is the mark of the father. The mark, for example, of the kind of work Brad Tolliver, under the guidance of the fathers for whom he had produced the texts they demanded, had himself proved capable of achieving. For it was precisely because Yasha Jones had referred to Brad's story (the one that had someone like Calvin Fiddler escaping from the pen, the one Yasha rejected) as *expert* that Brad was so upset that he went with Leontine to the Seven Dwarfs Motel:

> "I wrote what is called a treatment—that is the story you later make the scenario from—and I showed it to my dear colleague

and employer, and he says it stinks. He says, in fact, that it is expert."

"But that—" she began.... "But expert," she began again, "that's a nice thing to say."

"Not the way Yasha Jones says it." (353)

Brad should not, perhaps, have been too surprised to find a paternal inscription on the body of the woman he is about to bed, since if he had realized what he was doing when he signed the motel register he would have seen that he came close to adopting the name of one of his fathers, Telford Lott: "Bradwell Tolliver scribbled something that looked like *Redfill Tellfer* ..." (357).

The particular expertise, of which the scar on Leontine Purtle is an example commanding Brad's respect, belongs to a domain of paternal textuality that is the oldest Brad knew, as well as being of greatest importance for the resolution of the plot of the novel. The texts for which Brad struggled with his father over the fire had belonged to Calvin Fiddler's father, Amos, and Amos was a doctor (while a verse from the text of the biblical Amos serves as inscription to the novel). The climactic scene in which Calvin, as Brad had predicted in the text rejected by Yasha Jones, breaks out of prison, confronts Yasha and Maggie, wields a pistol, and unintentionally wounds Brad in the neck when he tries to grab the gun, is given a satisfactory resolution because of the intervention of a paternal, surgical text. Calvin was a graduate of The Johns Hopkins Medical School but had lost his ability to practice medicine in prison because he could not remember his medical texts. So, unfortunately, he could not perform the kind of operation Leontine Purtle had once needed, and which Calvin's father evidently did. As Calvin recounts the event:

> "There was a man up here with a ruptured appendix and they couldn't get a doctor in time, and I just let him die because I didn't have the nerve—or something. Night after night, I'd lie up here in my cot and shut my eyes and try to see the pages of my old medical books, the way I used to before an examination. Well, at night, here in the pen, I'd see them clear as could be.... But when daylight came it would all disappear.... But as soon as that gun went off, it was different. I stood there and looked down and saw the wound in the throat, and at the same instant I saw a page in the book—the big old chunky, falling-apart, red *Anatomy,* by Piersol, the book my father had used, the book I always used because he had used it. Yes, I saw the page right there ... and it said: 'Digital compression may be used in the case of a stab wound....'" (410)

And so he was able to perform an emergency tracheotomy on Brad with a ballpoint pen from Yasha Jones's coat pocket (398). If there were any doubt about whether it is legitimate in the context of Warren's *Flood* to equate the surgeon's scalpel with the writer's pen, it is surely negated by this detail.[7]

The contrivance is remarkable: Calvin combines his reading of his father's text with the instrument with which Yasha Jones—paternal in his own way to Brad—writes; his reading, furthermore, of a paternal text whose author's name says it can *pierce all,* in a novel in which the working tool of another father figure is a piercing needle, and in which the father's mark which the son finds on the woman he wants to bed appears, not only in the form of a scar met on the way, but even in what he finds when he gets there. Brad reveals this second sign when he thinks back to Suzy Martine and her "orchidaceously blossoming, brown-petaled, self-offering, immolation-inviting, crimson-*winking,* crimson-hearted slash" (420; emphasis added). It's the wink that catches one's eye, if one has seen it before, in *The Cave,* when "you-know-what winked like glory" (20). And in case one still does not identify it, Warren will tell us, as plainly as can be, in the poem "Homage to Theodore Dreiser": "the cunt / Winks." But how can it be that the wink the father ambiguously flashes in *All the King's Men,* and elsewhere, now emerges from the essence of woman? Because it is the result of the father's piercing penetration—because it is his mark.

It is perhaps significant in this regard that Brad Tolliver should have found himself in the bizarre situation of wanting to communicate with blind Leontine Purtle through an exchange of winks, a clearly impossible feat: "He had the crazy impulse to wink at her. To wink at her because it was a joke.... And she would wink back, because it was sure a joke" (231).

Now Mortimer Sparlin, the black gas station and motel attendant who clearly knew so much about Leontine Purtle that Brad did not, does know how to wink. As Brad was about to drive away from his first visit to the site of the Seven Dwarfs Motel in chapter 1, " 'Yassuh, boss,' the man in the trick pants murmured, and looked up at the enormous black face on the second sign, with the bloated minstrel-show lips; and winked" (11). Sparlin is not what he seems—not the obsequious black servant the sign represents but a graduate student in literature. And he has a pretty good idea what it is like to lie with someone like Leontine Purtle in a bed in the Seven Dwarfs Motel. For example, there had been the woman with out-of-state plates who propositioned him when he brought ice and Seven-Up to her motel room at 1:00 A.M., and whose looks were improved by the characteristically pink light that would later shine on Leontine Purtle's scar: "the face promised to be acceptable, especially with the only illumination that from the pink-silk-shaded bed lamps cunningly arranged by the management of Happy Dell" (11). When Brad was on his way to the motel office to pay for the room he had enjoyed with Leontine, he came close to sparring with

Sparlin when the latter asked him how he liked blind tail and, when Brad started an irate response, "with a motion like a flick of a cat's paw, had knocked him down" (363).

Brad suffered at the hands of another man with a one-eyed look in the person of Dr. Ramon Echegaray, who was literally one-eyed—one eye covered by a black patch, the other "black as the hole in the muzzle of a gun" (148)—and who was responsible for the collapse of Brad and Lettice's marriage. We recall that Echegaray was a veteran of the Spanish Civil War with whom Lettice had a one-night stand just before she and Brad were to be married. She confessed to Brad, who forgave her. But later, when Brad finds her grieving over news of Echegaray's death in an outdated issue of *Time* and does not share her sadness, they know it is the end of their marriage (all this in the aftermath of Calvin's conviction for murder).

Now Echegaray, with his "black hole" of an eye, is, I believe, a version of the one-eyed father—the father who has a prior claim on the son's bride, as winking Mortimer Sparlin had on Leontine Purtle. For that black hole is also, precisely, all that is left of the father who is God, "the black hole in the sky God left when He went away," of which Brad speaks when he tries to explain Fiddlersburgian theology to Yasha Jones (166).[8] And on the very night when Lettice back in New York was having her adventure with the man whose single eye was a black hole, Brad was venturing downstairs in his boyhood home in Fiddlersburg in the dark with his flashlight to gaze upon the black hole in the library his father left when he went away, "the spot where the coffin had rested on its trestles" (196). He wept, but could not understand why.

If Mortimer *Spar*lin's surname seems to echo his boxing talent (he "danced back in his boxer's crouch, grinning. . . . 'Skip it, Mac—I'm high-rated in Golden Gloves' " [363]), his first name aligns him with the last text-demanding father Brad Tolliver will confront in the novel, Mort Seebaum, the Hollywood mogul who wants to hire Tolliver for the Fiddlersburg script after Yasha Jones's resignation. On the next-to-last page, Brad finally breaks free from the constraints of all these paternal texts (those demanded by Yasha Jones, Telford Lott, and even Israel Goldfarb) by tearing up the telegram in which Mort Seebaum confirms his offer: "With a sudden motion he thrust his left hand into the inner pocket and seized the telegram. . . . He grasped the telegram in both hands and tore it across. He carefully laid the yellow halves one on top of the other, and tore again. He let the pieces flutter away from him, to the grass . . ." (439). This decisive gesture is soon followed by the realization that he is absolved, too, of another paternal obligation: "he knew that now, at this moment, he did not need to try to find the grave of Israel Goldfarb."

In other words, Brad will not have to perform the work of yet another Mortimer, the one who gave notice of his intent to take charge of the physical burial of Israel Goldfarb (the one that took place when Brad was away in college, a quarter-century before) through the same kind of message Brad tears up here, a telegram:

> Mr. Goldfarb, he heard later, had got a bang-up funeral. On the wall above the cot where he slept in the back of his shop they found an address pinned to the wall, some Goldfarb in Cincinnati, and the Methodist preacher . . . had telegraphed. The answer had been prompt:
> PLEASE HOLD BODY TILL ARRIVAL ALL EXPENSES GUARANTEED
> MORTIMER GOLDFARB
> (17)

Tearing up Mort Seebaum's telegram and desisting from the search for Goldfarb's grave are intimately related: Brad is both refusing to be Mort's (Seebaum's) son and refusing to become a filial Mortimer (Goldfarb). As either Izzie Goldfarb, who knew the language well, or Yasha Jones, who successfully assumed a Frenchman's identity in the Resistance, could have told him, "Le père est *mort*."[9]

Chapter 10
Christmas Gift
Meet Me in the Green Glen, 1971

Book I

Chapter 1 Angelo Passetto, a twenty-four-year-old Sicilian immigrant, is walking down a muddy road in Tennessee when an eight-point buck leaps out of the undergrowth, mortally wounded by an arrow from the bow of Cy Grinder. Cassie Killigrew Spottwood, standing with a shotgun on the porch of the house where she cares for her immobilized husband, Sunderland, who suffered a stroke years before, tells Grinder he cannot have the deer if it was shot on her land. She asks Passetto and he confirms that it was not killed, as Cy had claimed, on the road. She enlists Angelo's help in dressing the deer and says he can stay on as long as he likes.

Chapter 2 Murray Guilfort, a lawyer who has given up frequenting whores in Chicago and now longs to be on the state supreme court, had grown up with Sunderland Spottwood and always been jealous of his strength and virility. But now that Sunder is a helpless, speechless invalid, Murray feels some "cold, justifying joy" when he makes his regular visits to bring money to Sunder's wife and to gaze on the living corpse of his once omnipotent friend.

Chapter 3 Angelo becomes infatuated with Charlene, a black girl he saw drawing water not far from the Spottwood farmhouse. She rejects his advances.

Chapter 4 Angelo is haunted by the memory of the man whom he had fingered in court as the one who held the gun in a robbery to which Angelo had been an unwitting accomplice, threatening vengeance beyond the grave. The inevitable happens between Angelo and Cassie when he spies her lying face down on the bed still warm from his presence; they begin a morning ritual of wordless intercourse. Flashback to Cassie's love for Cy Grinder, of whom her mother disapproved, making Cy flee west. He later returned in despair and married obese Gladys Peegrum, who had once been the confidante of Cassie's love for him. Cassie's mother made her daughter care for her dying aunt Josephine Killigrew, who was Sunderland Spottwood's first wife; Cassie soon became his second. In 1941 Sunder was rejected by the army because of high blood pressure; in 1946 he suffered his debilitating stroke. In between, Cassie learned that Arlita Benton was his mistress (Charlene would be the fruit of that union); she kept him from evicting Arlita from his farm when her husband left to go to war. Cassie had been hospitalized for mental illness when she laughed uncontrollably at her mother's funeral, but was released to care for her invalid husband when he had his stroke.

Book II

Chapter 5   Four months pass, during which Angelo and Cassie continue their silent sex every morning and Angelo buries himself in farmwork, repairing everything he can lay his hands on. At night he lies in bed, alone, and reads through the mass of detective magazines he found upstairs behind the mirrored door of the armoire, and that had once belonged to Sunderland, whose rasping breath he can hear but whom he has not yet seen.

Chapter 6   Murray Guilfort tells Cassie that Angelo is out on parole from the Fiddlersburg penitentiary, that he had squealed on his confederates in an armed robbery, and that they have been executed for the crime. Cassie finally asks Angelo his name, and their relationship deepens.

Chapter 7   Angelo speaks Cassie's name for the first time. He dresses her in red and black, with lipstick and perfume; they dance to the radio after supper every evening and sleep together at night. She finally lets him into the room where Sunderland lies paralyzed, and says she hates her husband. Yet Angelo is still smitten with Charlene and finally succeeds in winning her confidence, and more. His Sicilian skin, he points out, is actually darker than hers.

Chapter 8   Angelo staggers home bleeding from a fight. He had picked up Charlene on the road, driven her into town, tried to buy two tickets to the black entrance of the movie theater, and was beaten up by locals. Guilfort tells Cassie that Angelo has to leave or he will be put back in prison for breaking parole. Cassie follows Angelo and Charlene to the dairy house where they make love; Arlita finds her there clawing the wall in despair and tells Cassie how she once came close to murdering Sunder with a butcher knife. Later, in bed with Angelo, Cassie tells him he is free to do what he wants (implying Charlene) and says she could hide him upstairs and tell Guilfort he is gone. Hearing a noise from Sunder's room, she goes to see to him; on her return, she discovers that Angelo has locked her out.

Chapter 9 Several months have passed. Sunderland Spottwood has been murdered with Angelo's switchblade, but immediately after the jury declares him guilty Cassie leaps up and confesses. Guilfort, who oversees the prosecution but has an associate try the case, had found the red dress and black lace underwear Angelo used to make Cassie wear half consumed in the kitchen stove at the murder scene; he secretly took them home, and their existence never comes out at the trial.

Book III

Chapter 10 Angelo's lawyer, Leroy Lancaster, is unable to get a retrial, the judge discounting Cassie's confession because of her evident mental instability. Guilfort has her committed to an asylum. Lancaster writes an article for a national magazine in hope of provoking the governor into granting a pardon.

Chapter 11 The governor refuses a pardon. Having been released from the asylum into the care of the elderly Miss Edwina Parker, whom Guilfort has paid to keep an eye on her, Cassie manages to slip out on the day before Angelo's execution and to persuade Cy Grinder to drive her to the capital to plead with the governor in person. But they cannot find him. Passetto is executed, and Cassie is found semiconscious outside the wall of the penitentiary.

Epilogue

Chapter 12 Spottwood Valley is flooded by a dam; Cy Grinder becomes a game warden in the surrounding park. Murray Guilfort finally makes it to the state supreme court but dies from an overdose of sleeping pills after having gazed upon the paper bag with its half-burnt clothing and shoes he had taken from Cassie's stove. Cassie is institutionalized but no longer claims to have killed her husband.

"But I did follow him, all the years," the narrator of "Blackberry Winter" told us in the end—even though the passing stranger, with his city ways and his black pointy-toed shoes so inappropriate for muddy rural roads and his "little parcel wrapped in newspaper," had threatened Seth with a knife if he did. Angelo Passetto, whose passage through *Meet Me in the Green Glen* provokes nearly everything that happens in that novel, is less menacing than the tramp Seth met in "Blackberry Winter." But he is a foreigner in the same rainy landscape, wearing the same kind of shoes ("His eyes were fixed on the pointed tips of his patent-leather shoes as they were set, one after the other, neatly in the mud" [6]), and, more intriguingly, he bears the same kind of burden: "holding in his hand a parcel wrapped in disintegrating newspaper" (8). We never learn what the stranger in "Blackberry Winter" was carrying wrapped up in his newspaper parcel, though we might wonder if that was one of the things Seth was to find out by following him all those years. We do not exactly know, either, what it was that motivated the boy to follow him. But nevertheless, something about Seth's lifelong pursuit is very familiar. For we, too, have been following, if not the traveler, at least the package.

We first saw it in Warren's first published novel, when Percy Munn dreamed of a package "wrapped in old newspaper" that began "to flake away from the bundle, as though disintegrating from its own sodden weight." What it contained in that novel was by no means certain; Munn thought that, when the last shreds of paper fell away, he could see the face of Bunk Trevelyan. But that face, we found, could just as well be a dream's disguise for another face—that of the black man who, through Munn's unwitting intervention, was hanged for the crime Trevelyan had committed; while the bundle's other attributes—that it was a fetus carried in Percy's wife's arms, that it was wrapped in newspaper—made other claims on its identity. We knew all along that the body in Percy's dream was of "a foetus like those which he had seen suspended in liquid in great glass jars"; but it was only through its recurring appearances in Warren's subsequent novels that we could begin to realize the full nature of the contents of his dream's newspaper-wrapped package: that fetal eyes in their semblance of intent are like the eyes of a father who seems to be communicating something but who in fact may not be, either because he refuses to say whether he really winked or not or because, as he lies in the grip of death, his eyes glitter with the appearance of some commanding thought that may (like Hans Meyerhof's) be merely "some fluctuation of the fever or the transitory flicker of some old event in that fading brain."

Meet Me in the Green Glen gives us another glimpse at the disintegrating newspaper bundle in Percy's dream—seen here as "the soaked and disintegrating newspaper parcel" (15), as "a paper package [in n]ewspaper, soaked and giving way" (37)—and thus another chance to guess its contents. This novel is almost the continuation of the episode told in chapter 7 of *Wilderness*, where a traveling stranger enters the life of a woman nursing an older, dying husband who reminds him of his father and whose eyes show the semblance of some commanding thought. Adam Rosenzweig did not remain long with Mrs. Hans Meyerhof but continued his journey south; Angelo Passetto, however, does stay on with Cassie Spottwood, becomes her handyman and lover and, when she murders her invalid husband, is executed for the crime, despite her last-minute confession. But one can see another story being acted out here, one that has taken much longer to tell.

Warren's "I Am Dreaming of a White Christmas: The Natural History of a Vision"—which I quoted in the introduction and in which the poet dreams of a Christmas morning, of his father's eyes that are not there yet see ("Not there, they stare at what / Is not there"), of the package he is not allowed to open, and in which he seeks to discover the logic of this original dream—was first published just two years after *Meet Me in the Green Glen*.[1] These two ways of describing Warren's own quest—the narrator's lifelong pursuit of the stranger in "Blackberry Winter" and the search for the logic of the original dream in the poem—can also be taken as models for the task his text imposes on its readers, for the voyage of discovery to which they are invited. What is intriguing about the opening scene of this novel is that here these two images of the quest converge in the figure of the wandering tramp who suddenly thinks of Christmas. For what in fact draws Angelo Passetto into Cassie Spottwood's life is a mistaken symbol of Christmas, the sudden emergence of what Angelo, not knowing what else to call it, calls the giver of such gifts as the poet in "I Am Dreaming . . ." wants to open but cannot: "And there, in the air, over the road, seeming, for all its flash of speed, to float timelessly and without substance as without effort, was the creature. For that instant, as Angelo Passetto froze in his tracks, it was unidentifiable. Then he thought: *Sandy Claws!*" (7). Because it seems to fly through the air, the deer, which Cy Grinder will shoot with an arrow before its hooves touch the ground, reminds Angelo, whose English is poor, of a Cleveland Christmas where he had seen "a whole string of such creatures floating in the air and behind them the sleigh with the fat little red-nosed, red-dressed son-of-a-bitch grinning out." But his mistake is in another sense accurate, for Angelo, who will enter Cassie Spottwood's life through the coincidence of passing her house at just this moment and at the spot where Cy Grinder shoots the deer, will become for her what he mistakenly called the buck, a giver of gifts. He will later have occasion to evoke another gift-giving holiday when he embarks on the project of making Cassie beautiful. "The dress was red, and shiny like silk. The belt was black patent leather. The stockings were black and shiny. The slippers were black patent leather and pointed, and the heels were very high. . . . 'Happy birth-a-day,' he said" (168–69). It really was Cassie's birthday, her forty-third, and to celebrate it Angelo had secretly bought the clothes and cosmetics that would both give her back her youth and satisfy his erotic fantasy.

And the gift keeps on giving. On the day Sunderland Spottwood died, when Murray Guilfort found the patent-leather heels and the red dress and the black lace undergarments only partially consumed in the firebox of the kitchen stove (where Cassie had put them after she stabbed her husband), he hid them in a brown paper sack and locked them in the trunk of his car. He neither told the sheriff nor revealed them at the trial, for fear they would suggest what was really going on between Angelo and Cassie, thereby making it a little less apparent to the jury who it was who had killed Cassie's husband. But the brown sack and its contents made him uneasy. Sitting in the courtroom at the trial, he could see them locked up in his safe at home, "glowing in that enclosed darkness. And at that moment, the crazy fear struck him that another eye than his might even now pierce all the miles of distance, and pierce the steel, to see those objects glowing like live coals in the enclosed darkness of the safe" (251).

Later, with Angelo safely dead and even Cassie driven crazy enough to forget she had ever confessed, Guilfort will be so haunted by the mental picture of the charred remnants of those gifts, despite their double enclosure in the brown paper sack and the safe, that he will take an overdose of sleeping pills and, just before the end, experience "one more flicker of consciousness. He seemed to see a hand reaching into the darkness of the safe, where, like fox-fire, the red dress, the slipper, the letter,[2] lay gleaming coldly in the darkness" (371).

As we now know, this is not the first time Warren wrote a novel in which someone is shadowed by a brown paper parcel. Like Guilfort, Jack Burden was pursued by the brown paper package containing his notes and unfinished manuscript on Cass Mastern, which his landlady thoughtfully forwarded even though he was trying to throw it away (paralleled by the brown manila envelope that contained the truth about his father, the Judge); and Amantha Starr was followed by the brown envelope with the manumission papers Hamish Bond had drawn up for her, which she once left behind without ever opening, and which he had to give her a second time (freedom papers that were Bond's substitute for the ones her father might have given her but never did). If the contents of the brown sack Guilfort hid could have incriminated Cassie, his withholding of their evidence made him guilty too, all the more so because he was an officer of the court, the local district attorney; and though he did not try the case himself, he did oversee its prosecution.

Guilfort had long been a friend of the family, a boyhood companion of Sunderland Spottwood, but his recollection of that friendship was not free from a certain discomfort. Murray had been making visits to Sunderland's bedside ever since the latter's massive stroke more than a decade before, and each time he came into the room where the invalid lay in total paralysis he would stare into his friend's eyes and experience a thrill of justifying joy in the knowledge that Sunder was as good as dead.

> Murray was looking into the man's eyes.
> The eyes, a clear boyish blue, stared up at him. He could see nothing in them. Something might be there, if only he could read it.
> Then the shadow came over the eyes.
> The left side of the face began to twitch, the shadow in the

eyes darkened, like storm over water. Then the heavy, pale lips parted and the sound came. It was a grinding, rasping exhalation. It came three times. It was merciless and unappeasable.

It stopped. Then Murray knew that today it was going to happen. He felt, deep in himself, that stir, then that burst of cold, justifying joy. He had felt the moment that justified all.

It was Sunderland Spottwood who lay there. (44)

Yet as long as Sunder was alive Murray was not entirely at ease, nor safe from what it was he feared about the man with nothing in his clear blue eyes. "*God damn him,*" Guilfort would think on a later visit, "*why can't he die!*" If Spottwood were dead, "then there would be nobody who could remember the Murray Guilfort who had once been the boy who had been afraid to mount the gray stallion" or dive off the high bluff or whatever boyish feat Sunder would dare Murray to do, "nobody to remember that earlier self whom Murray Guilfort now sought to forget, expunge, bury, or absorb into the man who was now called Murray Guilfort" (134-35).

It is Sunderland Spottwood's eyes that, even though it is impossible to say whether they could really see anything when he was still alive, Guilfort fears when he thinks about what he left at home in the bag in the safe and is possessed by the dread "that another eye than his might even now pierce all the miles of distance, and pierce the steel, to see those objects glowing like live coals." And it is Sunderland's dead hand that Murray will see in his own last moments, "reaching into the darkness of the safe, where, like fox-fire," the contents of the brown paper sack coldly gleamed.

But was the transformation Angelo's gifts to Cassie underwent, becoming in Guilfort's hands his burden of guilt and, in his safe, fox fire coldly glowing with a self-generated light, preceded by another transformation? Were the bundles with the clothes and shoes inside that Angelo had secretly brought into the house on the evening of Cassie's birthday themselves a transformed version of the other bundle she had seen him carrying when she watched him coming down the road that first day "like a torch coming through the rain, like a lightwood torch and the flame so pale you could hardly see it in daylight, but I saw it, and the rain couldn't put it out" (297)? Isn't the rain-splattered newspaper package, "soaked and giving way," the most recent version of one we see recurring in Warren, and of whose contents we might gather some clue from the fact of the fox-fire it may in the end have become? We shall have seen that fox-fire before, too, if we have read the poem with that title in the sequence which, like Guilfort's final vision of the coldly gleaming parcel in the safe, has a dead hand in it. For what burns with a self-begetting light in "Fox-Fire: 1956," in the "Mortmain" sequence in *You, Emperors, and Others,* is a paternal text, the poet's father's Greek grammar book posthumously discovered.

> Years later, I find the old grammar, yellowed. Night
> Is falling. Ash flakes from the log. The log
> Glows, winks, wanes.
> ... The world lives by the trick of the eye, the trick
> Of the heart. I hold the book in my hand, but God
> ... will not let me weep. But I
> Do not want to weep. I want to understand.
> ... There must be a way to state the problem.
> The statement of a problem, no doubt, determines solution.
> ... I put the book on the shelf, beside my own grammar,
> Unopened these thirty years, and leave the dark room,
> And know that all night ... in the dark,
> Amid History's vice and vacuity, that poor book burns
> Like fox-fire in the black swamp of the world's error.

Warren's recycling and recombination of the elements of paternal text, winking, and a father's dying fire may be, as this poem suggests, an attempt to state and restate the problem in the hope that the correct statement will emerge in the end and provide a solution. "Fox-Fire: 1956" itself provides at least two such statements, the winking and waning log with which it begins and the fox fire with which it ends. In the later poem "Heart of the Backlog," in *Now and Then,* the two phenomena become one when the burning back log glows "red in the living pulse of its own / Decay" as if it were decaying foxfire. And the first poem of the "Mortmain" sequence, whose title almost tells all—"After Night Flight Son Reaches Bedside of Already Unconscious Father, Whose Right Hand Lifts in a Spasmodic Gesture, as Though Trying to Make Contact: 1955"—states the problem, or part of it, in yet another way (though as a variant of Willie Stark's problematic wink and the semblance of intent in mummies' empty eyes), when the spasmodically raised hand that seems to want to make contact with the son but may be as empty of intent as the sporadic glitter of Hans Meyerhof's "large blue eyes" is compared, in its descent, to a closing eye:

> Like an eyelid the hand sank, strove
> Downward, and in that darkening roar,
> All things ...
> Were snatched from me, and I could not move,
> Naked in that black blast of his love.

But what if Warren's repeated attempts to restate the problem were themselves "nothing more than the old cycle repeated, the tale always empty of meaning" (122), as the paternal text *Meet Me in the Green Glen* proposes for our consideration? That text is the collection of old detective magazines that had belonged to Sunderland Spottwood and that Angelo discovers in the armoire in the uninhabited upstairs of Cassie's house, behind the tall mirror in which, when he first ventures into that bedroom, he is startled to see "the shadowy image of a man with the flame glimmering pale on his face. His blood froze, for in that instant he did not realize that there was a mirror, that the ... face ... was his own" (107–8). Angelo brings the magazines down to his room and stacks them on one side of his bed. He reads each one from cover to cover, "even the advertisements," and flings it over to the other side. The paper was disintegrating with time, "ready to flake under a touch" (122).

It remains to be shown that the original owner of the flaking newsprint with which Angelo surrounds his bed is a paternal figure, particularly for him. We have already seen that when Murray Guilfort stared into Sunderland's eyes he saw that there was "nothing in them" but that "[s]omething might be there, if only he could read it." He also noticed a twitch ("The left side of the face began to twitch, the shadow in the eyes darkened..."). Sunderland, whose "empty blue" (157) eyes have the quality that fathers' eyes in Warren always have of offering something to be read in them despite their emptiness, might be more of a haunting paternal presence for a younger man than for Guilfort. Spottwood is fifty-six, Guilfort fifty-four, Cassie forty-three, and Angelo twenty-four. She is old enough to be his mother, which is precisely what underlies the peculiar nature of their sexual relationship. Though what Angelo does with his birthday gift to Cassie is make her look younger, when he first began to live in her house he had wished she were older: she had "dark hair that, in a crazy way, you wished were gray" (47). When, later, he was to feel the cooling touch of her hand on his forehead (a gesture Jack Burden's mother also used to good effect on him), "there was the fleeting recollection of a night when, as a little boy after he had been sick for a long time, he had waked up in the dark and the fever was gone and he felt weak and sweet and floating, and a hand, his mother's, had been on his forehead" (147–48). When he prepared to make love to her, and told her to get off the floor and onto the bed, "like an old woman, her face now averted from him, she obeyed" (119). For her part, Cassie's affection for Angelo was at least in part maternal: "As she stared at the mouth and saw that tiny motion of the lips moving with the breath of sleep, she knew that it was the face of Angelo Passetto when he was a little boy, a little boy asleep, and somebody else had been watching him" (153).

Following these echoes, Cassie's husband would then be Angelo's father, but what form, exactly, does that paternal figure assume in his imagination? Like Murray Guilfort, he could stare down at Sunderland's eyes and see how empty they were: "He looked down into the empty blue of the eyes. But the eyes, he suddenly knew, they were looking up at him, they were alive, they were sucking him in. It was like losing your balance, falling into a deep hole" (157). Despite their blueness, these eyes are empty, and they have the irresistible gravitational force of a black hole—like the single eye of Brad Tolliver's rival, Ramon Echegaray, in *Flood,* and the black hole in the sky caused by God's disappearance, paralleled in that novel by the place where Brad's flashlight discovered the absence of his father's coffin— the empty spaces that threaten to swallow up the son who gazes into them. Because of their blueness, they resemble the blue eyes of Hans Meyerhof in *Wilderness,* the figure for the father into whose eyes Adam Rosenzweig stared, trying to grasp some flickering intelligence. And the "empty blue" of these eyes anticipates with some precision the vision in "I Am Dreaming . . ." of a father's eyes that are both empty and blue: "The eyes / Are not there. But, / Not there, they stare at what / is not there. / . . . His eyes / Had been blue."

When Guilfort stared into Sunder's eyes, thinking that something might be there if only he could read it, the side of the man's face began to twitch, a twitch that presaged the only voluntary gesture of which his body was capable (he could not, for example, wink), "a grinding, rasping exhalation . . . merciless and unappeasable." When Angelo heard that sound, it conjured up a specific image in his memory: "It was like the sound he remembered from his uncle's farm in Ohio, when you butchered a sheep. You hoisted the sheep up by the hind legs and slit the throat and suddenly the last bleat with the blood in it was like the sound from that room" (104). It was this grisly recollection that enabled Angelo to do what Cassie wanted him to do to the "Sandy Claws" that dropped dead at his feet on the road outside her house.

> "It's not like a lady is supposed to talk," she said, "but if you do a thing it don't matter much, I guess, how you say it. They say, bleed, nut, and gut." Her gaze swept the buck, from the sack of testicles, hanging forward now, down the cream-colored muscle-bulge of the belly, to the black muzzle. A little blood now drooled from the muzzle.
> "I'll get a knife," she said. . . . (16)

Passetto then proceeded to slit the throat of the deer and emasculate and eviscerate it with an agility that surprised Cassie.

> "If you know how to do things so well," the woman said, "how come you asked me what to do?"
> "Before I never do it to a—" He stopped. "To a Sandy Claws," he finished. (17)

And he told her how he had learned to butcher sheep in Ohio. There is not much difference between dressing a deer and dressing a sheep, but his hesitancy, his error of identification, and his later mental association of

Sunderland's groan with the last gasp of a slaughtered sheep provide the basis for an illuminating reading of this opening scene of the novel. Angelo's mistake in naming is actually a double one, for he not only mistook a Tennessee deer for a reindeer but the reindeer for the name of the man in the red suit who drives them. Warren's "I Am Dreaming . . ." offers some insight into the identity of the figure who, through this double error, becomes Angelo's name for the animal whose real name he cannot remember (like Jeremiah Beaumont, who could not remember the name of the trees in his dream), for in that recounted dream Father Christmas is the father, guarding the gifts the poet cannot yet open: *"No presents, son, till the little ones come."*

Meet Me in the Green Glen is full of containers, boxes, rooms to open: the one where Sunderland lies and groans, into which Angelo is not at first allowed to go; the upstairs of the house, where he does venture and finds "the gray, clotted viscera spilled out over the floor" of a mattress the rats had got into, as well as his own unrecognizable reflection in the armoire mirror in the room with the big tester bed where, had Cassie and Sunder really been his mother and father, he would have been conceived; the space behind that mirror where he discovered Sunder's collection of yellowing magazines; the eviscerated deer, and later, rabbits; the packages from town Angelo gave Cassie to open that were his way of dressing her, his gift of new clothing to replace that "brown bag of a sweater" (144) that made it impossible to tell anything about the shape of the woman inside (47); the "brown paper bag" (228) that became the wrapping for the gift that was itself a new wrapping for Cassie, a repackaging intended to reveal what her body had been concealing all those years, "the little girl inside her" (176); and the safe in which Murray Guilfort hid the incriminating brown paper bag, where in the end its contents began to glow like fox fire. If Warren's poem makes the father the presiding presence over the Christmas gift he wants so much to open, Passetto's linguistic error suggests that what he finds himself bleeding, nutting, and gutting on the road he had been innocently traveling along is the father he will later be accused of slaying, the Laius that his oedipal penetration of the maternal Cassie and his identification of Sunderland's cry with that of an eviscerated animal also suggests that this Sandy Claws has, or will, become. And when Sunder is killed, it is with Angelo's knife, though—in symmetrical counterpoint to the dressing of the deer, which Angelo performs with the knife Cassie gave him—it will be Cassie who wields it (312–13).

The detective magazines with which Angelo surrounds himself in bed and which he reads voraciously from cover to cover are, like the poem about worth that Adam Rosenzweig had committed to memory, an inheritance from the father, though with some differences: Adam's actual father had written the poem; Angelo's assumed father had merely possessed the magazines (though we have seen this form of paternal text before: in the case, for example, of Dr. Amos Fiddler's copy of Piersol's *Anatomy*). But the magazines are essentially for Angelo what the poem was for Adam, a text that becomes, as he reads it, his own life: Adam's journey became a search for worth, culminating in the letter about worth and worthlessness inscribed on a Moses; and Angelo finds that his own past—"the dream his own past now seemed to be"—and the story the detective stories kept retelling—"the tale always empty of meaning but charged always with the heavy atmosphere of gunsmoke and sweetly sweating flesh"—begin to "merge into one dream, not to be differentiated, and in that dream he was strong, he was real" (122). It is not surprising that he should find the text whose dream merged with the dream of his past behind a mirror that gave back his own reflection. But it is a mark of the peculiar insistence in Warren's fiction on the power of the paternal text that the text Angelo finds should not only have belonged to the man who becomes his father as he enters the house to which his ability to eviscerate the deer has led him, but should also be waiting to be discovered in the bedroom where, according to the fiction his entry into the house causes him to live out, he would find his own origin, on that big tester (an adjective suggesting the testicular activity that took place upon it) bed.

But if the Sandy Claws that dropped dead at Angelo's feet anticipates his adopted father, it also serves to evoke his biological father, the "dying hulk" (Sunderland Spottwood was likewise a moribund "hulk" [94]) back in Sicily, whose right foot "had always been twitching, just a little, inside the torn felt slipper . . . twitching with a rhythmic regularity . . . just that twitch that you waited for, and then it came, always in that feeble and merciless regularity that made you want to get up and yell and run out into the street, into the fields, up the mountains, anywhere" (124). For the deer's legs move, too, in a purely mechanical nervous reaction that, like the father's dying gesture in "Mortmain," is "spasmodic": "When he released the hind legs to get a better grip, one of the legs jerked spasmodically" (8–9). The mercilessly regular twitching that Angelo fled from in Sicily pursues him in a different, more inescapable, form in the snow on Cassie's farm: "his tracks . . . emerging from the invisibility of distance, marched up the slope at him. They came, sharper and darker, to the very spot where he stood, walking mercilessly at him, and all at once, as though his shoes had come alive with a life of their own, or the earth were alive under the shoes and seized the shoes and moved them forward, he was moving into the shadow of the trees" (186). If Angelo has the feeling that his shoes had begun to have a life of their own it may be because they are not his shoes. His pointy-toed black patent-leather city shoes had been so impractical for farm work that Cassie had given him a pair of Sunder's old brogans to wear. In the morning he would get up, "shivering in his nakedness [and] set his feet into the brogans, which had once belonged to another man . . ." (68); he was so accustomed to wearing them that he would even keep them on in bed under the quilt in the evening (51). Angelo's exchange of the patent-leathers for the brogans presages his substitution of one father for another; but the merciless regularity he fled from in Sicily cannot be so easily abandoned, and tracks him through the Tennessee snow in another father's shoes.

Seth, in "Blackberry Winter," was fascinated by the possibility of envisioning his own footprints as having been by somebody else: "you . . . make the perfect mark of your foot in the smooth, creamy, red mud and then muse upon it as though you had suddenly come upon that single mark on the glistening auroral beach of the world." Angelo Passetto is looking for "the perfect mark" too, though in this instance it really is the "perfectly formed" mark of someone else's foot. It becomes a beautiful image of pure emptiness, another version of the container with no content that we found in *Flood*:

> He moved forward, staring intently at the ground he was about to tread.
> Then he found one. . . . What he found was a single foot track, small, perfectly formed. . . . Water had seeped into the track, and now the water was frozen, and the shape was there, clear and perfect in the moonlight. . . . Carefully, he pinched off the stalk at the root and began to lift it. The foot track of bright ice came with it, keeping its shape. He held it high, letting the moonlight shine on it, then through it. . . . Then, all at once, with a fierce exhalation, he thrust his now parted lips against the icy shape. It shattered soundlessly beneath that kiss. (187–88)

The track belongs to Charlene, a black girl with whom, despite Cassie, Angelo is in love—and who, it turns out, is Sunder's daughter by Arlita Benton. But Passetto's affection for feet extends to Cassie, too; he took off her brogans to get her to dance, then "leaned and seized a foot in each hand . . . lifted them to meet his bowed face, and kissed them. Looking up at her, he said: 'Leetle feet—you got so leetle feet!' " (165). Yet what seems here to attract him in Cassie is a quality he embodies himself, both in name and in fact. *Passetto* means "small step," and Angelo lives up to the implication of this patronymic, as Murray Guilfort notices when he inspects the bedroom of Cassie's new hired hand: "He picked up one of the patent-leather shoes that sat neatly side by side on the floor and examined it. It was wadded with old newspaper to hold its shape. . . . 'He hasn't got a big foot,' he said, 'Is he a little man?' 'No,' she said, 'he's a right good-size. Bigger than most' " (38). Angelo's feet are evidently small in proportion to the rest of his body. So that Passetto's discovery of the "perfectly formed" foot-track is indeed a variation on Seth's feigned discovery in "Blackberry Winter" of the "perfect mark" that he pretended had been made by somebody else.

Given that we would like to know what is in the newspaper-wrapped bundle that first appeared in *Night Rider*, then in the hand of the tramp in "Blackberry Winter," and most recently in the possession of Angelo Passetto as he wanders onstage in *Meet Me in the Green Glen*, and given that all such unopened packages in Warren seem to have something important to do both with each other and with the Christmas gift he cannot yet open in "I Am Dreaming . . ."—which he has recently said contains "his whole life, of course"[3]—we should note that Angelo's newspaper-stuffed city shoes find an inverted counterpart in a newspaper package of which we do know the contents in another *Circus in the Attic* story. Mrs. Jeff York, in "The Patented Gate and the Mean Hamburger," had a pair of black high-heeled shoes that she only wore in town and that she carried "wrapped up in a piece of newspaper until their wagon had reached the first house on the outskirts of town" (125). Obviously, Angelo was not carrying his black patent-leather shoes in the newspaper bundle when he walked along the road that went past Cassie's house because he was wearing them at the time. But we have seen how that first package transmutes into the ones he brings home on Cassie's birthday, one of which contains, along with the red dress, black patent-leather shoes. It is virtual content that counts in the end; but what is most intriguing about tracking this package in Warren is the gradual realization that the direction in which it is taking us, like the direction in which the tracks that seemed to Angelo to have a life of their own led him, is toward a package, a wrapping, a container that has no content but itself—like the pure, transparent foot-track Angelo was led by his footprints to discover and embrace into nothingness, like the contents of the packages he brings home to Cassie that are themselves now wrappings for her, like the shoes in his closet that contain what elsewhere contains them: newspaper. Or like the stuck and repeating record in the novel just before this, which, by an abuse of the stylus, comes to express the entirety of its content as containment itself.

Or like the texts which, in this novel, a son inherits from his putative father—the pages, flaking away at a touch, that Angelo brought down from behind the mirror, whose content was a repetitive "tale always empty of meaning." Another flaking away reveals the emptiness in the eyes of Sunder's own father, the progenitor of the line, in the remarkable scene witnessed by Murray Guilfort in which inanimate objects seem to move, change, and disintegrate: "The shreds of the carpet raveled under his eyes, writhed like worms in anguish, burning in their lightless combustion. The leather of the Bible disintegrated and fell, like pollen, on the white marble of the tabletop. The paint scaled off the eyes of old Sunderland Spottwood, the arrogance fell away from those painted eyes in miniscule pale flakes that lay on the dark brick of the hearth, like dandruff. Everything was nothing" (35). The carpet, the Bible's leather, and the painted surface of the portrait's eyes disintegrate simultaneously, revealing once more that the shredding newspaper bundle and the father's eyes that move independently of his body are versions of the same thing—all tantalizing objects of the son's desire to decipher, to know "What present there was in that package for me, / Under the Christmas tree," to learn whether Willie Stark meant the wink or just had something in his eye. For perhaps we can guess why the carpet is burning, having seen "the red winking of the blackened strands of the fabric as they were consumed and parted" in that scene in *Wilderness* when a would-be father's torch fell from his grasp. Recall that the winking flame was about to go out; Adam Rosenzweig definitively extinguishes the paternal line it symbolized both by grinding out the dying flame with his boot and by refusing to comply with Aaron's plea to become his adopted heir.

The lightless combustion of the Spottwood carpet likewise symbolizes the extinction of paternity: it is yet another instance of the house falling into decay before the very eyes of the original Sunderland Spottwood, "who had grabbed the line, built the house, beat the niggers, and gone to Congress, and whose flat, painted arrogance of eye refused, in this dimness, to acknowledge what, over the years, had happened in his house" (35). But as lightless combustion it also evokes the young man whose presence there will bring about the final destruction of the Spottwood line (for Cassie would not have murdered her husband had Angelo not come into her life). When Cassie first saw Angelo coming down the road in the rain she thought he looked "like a lightwood torch and the flame so pale you couldn't hardly see it" (297), and this image of almost invisible burning makes such an impression on her that she later expresses it at the most inopportune time, with the result that those who hear her are convinced of her insanity and disbelieve her claim that she, not Passetto, killed Sunderland Spottwood. The image evokes its opposite as well, the combustionless light of the fox fire to which Angelo's gifts to Cassie are reduced; for, like fox fire, the carpet strands that unravel and burn like writhing worms represent death in the semblance of life, decay in the guise of fire—not unlike the painted eyes in which something is seen to move, but in a movement devoid of intent, because the arrogance that might have constituted the intent, by its disappearance, is precisely what gives the semblance of movement.

The third object in this list of things whose decay makes them seem to move, the Bible's leather binding, is not without its allusions to the action of the novel. We have seen text as container (the disintegrating newspaper wrapping the package Angelo carried) and as contained (the newspaper he stuffed in his shoes to make them hold their shape), and the latter was, like the Bible, enclosed in leather. This Bible is a paternal text in the same sense as Sunder's detective magazines, one whose ownership passes from father to son; but one also in the sense in which Adam's father's poem was in *Wilderness,* for it is a book in which fathers write something for their sons to read. It is a family Bible, a "big black leather Bible ... in which the names of all the Spottwoods were written, in ink long since gone brown, the black leather binding gone brown too" (34–35). The simultaneity of this color change makes the content of this text (that is, not Scripture but the inscription of the paternal line) visible on its surface, in the simultaneous decay of its container, effecting another version of the interchangeability of container and contained (or of the identity of same) that Angelo's putting the newspaper in his shoes enacted. The shoe leather began to change from black to brown, too, at the beginning of the novel, when Angelo set his feet on the muddy road leading to Cassie's house. And later, like the leather cover of the Spottwood family Bible, his patent-leathers start to decay: "He looked down at the shoes and saw that they had no sheen in the candle light. They were getting dry and cracked. Despair flooded his bosom" (106).

In "Blackberry Winter," Seth marveled at the effect one's own footprint makes in the mud, and at how it could come to look like a trace that someone else had made. He knew this was possible because he had read it in a book: "You have never seen a beach," he reflected, "but you have read the book and how the footprint was there." It is as if the reading of books had already corrupted the boy to the extent that he could see texts where they did not exist, or perhaps they had enlightened him to the extent that he knew that the reader's perception creates them. Angelo has a similar experience, walking in the mud of the road to Cassie's house: "Angelo Passetto watched the water flow into and fill the tracks. He did not know what this fact meant—the water flowing into the fresh tracks—but he felt somehow that it confirmed the new bleak strength in his own being. Soon he would go up that road, and the water would flow into the tracks made by the pointed toes of the patent-leather shoes, and he would not look back to see the water fill their emptiness" (14).

Gradior, ergo sum: making tracks is one way of making one's mark on the world. This much Angelo knows, but he does not yet know what it means for them to acquire a content, although he does know it must mean something. Later, however, we—if not Angelo—will learn some of what it means when he comes across the transparent but tangible track of ice formed by the very process begun here, for there, too, "Water had seeped into the track." When this emptiness made visible becomes the object of his emotion, shattering under the force of his kiss, that emotion turns out to have been self-love. Smitten with what he calls "such leetle feet," he will seem not to realize that he practically names himself in that exclamation. But we can realize it, just as we can also see that these two scenes reenact the two moments of the single scene in "Blackberry Winter" when Seth first made the perfect mark of his foot in the mud (admiring its perfection and knowing that he had made it himself) and then pretended that someone else had made it and he was merely its discoverer—its reader.

The *Passetto* that is fleshed out in the "leetle feet" of these water-filled tracks is, however, not only Angelo's name but his father's too. It is the nature of surnames that they are shared equally by father and son until they are passed on from one to the other. But the nature of this particular surname is its special resonance in the context of Warren's novels, and furthermore the fact that it stands for the very thing of which it is an example: inheritance, indeed the very organ of inheritance. In *Wilderness* we saw how Adam Rosenzweig denounced his feet as "stupid, ugly, unlovable children" and, bearing in mind the naked, toeless feet of the hanged man, together with the three children who came to stare at the castrated victim, we recalled that Freud found that both children and the number three could stand for the genitals—specifically, as "little ones" (392, 393). Freud also found that the male organ, in particular, can be represented in dreams by a foot (394). The feet of which Adam was ashamed and in which Angelo took such delight (though only Charlene's) evidently represent their own genitals, their closest tie to their fathers, the organ that could make them fathers too. For, in addition to their Freudian resonance, feet are, for both characters, the essential paternal inheritance: Adam had "stared down at the twisted whiteness of his poor foot . . . *My father,* he thought, *this is what he gave me.* He felt that he was on the verge of a great truth" (303). While the clue in Angelo's case is what his inherited surname actually names, "little step."

By using dream logic to make sense of these pieces of the original dream, we may finally be in a position to discover what really was in that Christmas present that Warren could open in "I Am Dreaming of a White Christmas." The answer may have been there all along, in the words of the parental command that delays its disclosure, a paternal text that may now at last yield to interpretation: "*No presents, son, till the little ones come.*" For *little ones* may be just what that package contains: the organ of inheritance, the genitals with which the father endows the son so that he too may be capable of giving such a Christmas gift—the "leetle feet" Angelo so loved, the "unlovable children" Adam so hated, and what Freud found "in dreams often stand for the genitals" (as "both men and women are in the habit of referring to their genitals affectionately as their 'little ones' ").

Not only does the delaying command contain within it a hint of the contents—hidden in plain sight like the purloined letter in Poe's story—but so does the other impediment to their discovery, the fact that there were "*three* packages. Identical in size and shape"—so identical that the poet cannot tell which is his: "My breath comes short. For I am wondering / Which package is mine. / / Oh, which?" The threeness stands in his way, preventing him from picking up the one meant for him; but is also a clue to the contents of the package—given the Freudian context evidently evoked by the sudden appearance of three children (two girls and a trouserless boy) at the foot of the castrated victim in *Wilderness:* "In any case the number three has been confirmed from many sides as a symbol of the male genitals."

The fact that Warren, at the end of the poem, is no longer trying to open the present but instead is "trying to discover the logic of" this "original dream" surely means that the contents of the package can be deduced from the dream itself, from the logic of its dreamwork in conjunction with a certain context of specific symbolism ("little ones" and the number three) in the book Warren left for his father to read in "Reading Late at Night . . ." later in the same poetic sequence (*Or Else*), "Freud on dreams." And thus we see what it means for the boy to step across the hearth to reach for the present, the act that provokes the forbidding voice:

I have stepped across the hearth and my hand stretches out.
But the voice:
No presents, son, till the little ones come.

As we saw in "Prime Leaf" when Thomas Hardin "stepped to the center of the hearth" and found that his father "looked very small before him" (252), the hearth is the woman's space and there comes a time when the son must take possession of it and defy his father. The flame in that fireplace is phallic, as we saw in *World Enough and Time,* and in "Prime Leaf" Thomas Hardin becomes phallic himself when he stands "on the hearth, rigidly erect" (272). It is the son's task to bring new life to that fire, as Aaron Blaustein wanted Adam Rosenzweig to do, and Thomas Hardin in fact does: "It was Thomas who first reappeared, to kneel on the hearth and begin rebuilding the fire. When the door closed behind his father he did not even glance up from his task. 'I've told Edith,' he said into the black hollow of the chimney" (271). (Here, the parallel between the Edith whom he told and the black hollow of the chimney into which he says these words underscores the fact that Edith and the fireplace are one, this "black hollow" anticipating the "black hole" that both a fireplace and a woman will be in *A Place to Come To.*)

In the poem, "There is no fire on the cold hearth now. . . ." But then the package remains opened, for the son has not yet claimed his inheritance, which is the gift of inheritance itself, the ability to be a father. This inheritance of inheritance parallels the container as pure container in the stuck record in *Flood* that repeatedly named its content as "just that one crazy word," *Continental*—which is to say, characteristic of a *continent,* "a containing agent or space" (*O.E.D.*), a word that was in fact the mark of the father in Yasha Jones's "ghostly continent" of a scar. After *Night Rider,* when Perse Munn's wife gave birth to a boy he would never see except in dreams and whose name he would never know, no Warren protagonist manages to open that Christmas gift to assume paternity until, in his next, and last, novel, the protagonist fathers a son who in the end of the story will be recognized as having a Perseus-like grace. A circle finally closes, a long tale at last ends, and we may finally know the identity of the fetus in Perse's dream.

Chapter 11
Old Buck's Golden Shower: Or, the New Perseus *A Place to Come To,* 1977

Book I

Chapter 1 Jediah Tewksbury recalls the death of his father, who stood up on a mule wagon to urinate and, being drunk, fell off. The wheels passed over his neck. Jed, who appears to have been born circa 1917, was eight at the time.

Chapter 2 His mother sells the farm and they move to nearby Dugton, Alabama, where she finds work in a canning factory. Boys at school tease Jed about his father's having died, as they jokingly tell it, while masturbating, but later, in graduate school, he turns the tale to good social advantage. In Nashville in 1951 an unexpected phone call from Rozelle Hardcastle prompts Jed's recollection of the time she had made him take her to the senior prom even though he was immune at the time to her considerable charms. He later learns that she had done it to spite her boyfriend.

Chapter 3 This chapter and the next recapitulate Jed's past between high school and Rozelle's phone call. He attends a miserable Alabama Bible college, good only for the Greek he learned there (Latin had been his salvation in high school). After graduation he talks his way into graduate school at the University of Chicago, befriended by the imposing Dr. Heinrich Stahlmann, who introduces him to the *imperium intellectus*—the cosmopolitan life of the mind, detached from history. But Stahlmann becomes increasingly dissatisfied with this academic ideal because of its irrelevance in the face of the Nazi horror then overrunning Europe and takes his own life. From a news clipping his mother sends, Jed learns that Rozelle has married a much older, and wealthier, man in Florida, Michael X. Butler.

Chapter 4 Jed joins the army, serving with Italian partisans behind German lines. In 1946 he resumes his studies in comparative medieval literature at Chicago. A letter from his mother informs him that Rozelle's husband has drowned in a boat accident; Rozelle was steering. Displacing Perry Gerald in her affections, Jed marries Agnes Andresen of Ripley City, South Dakota, whose death from cancer a few years later will make it possible, as if it were a Faustian pact, for him to write a brilliant article on "Dante and the Metaphysics of Death." He accepts a post at a college in Nashville.

Book II

Chapter 5   There is a return to Rozelle—now Mrs. Lawford Carrington—on the telephone: having heard of Jed's arrival in the Nashville paper, she invites him to Sunday supper with friends. Among them are Bill Cudworth, a lawyer who has come home from New York, and his wife, Sally; young, intelligent Maria McInnis; and the fiftyish Mrs. Jones-Talbot, Lawford's aunt. Carrington is wealthy (though from Rozelle's Florida inheritance) and an artist; Jed realizes that a sculpted head of a woman in orgasm is Rozelle.

Chapter 6   Jed drifts into dating Maria and gives Mrs. Jones-Talbot a weekly tutorial in Dante.

Chapter 7   Cudworth is trying to get Jed to buy a neighboring farm, and Jed senses that his new friends are expecting him to marry Maria McInnis. He appreciates their friendship but is in no way inclined to put down roots in Nashville. Lawford Carrington unveils a new sculpture: the bronze head of an older man with his mouth open as if to scream. Asked to tell an Alabama story, Jed recites the death of his father. Later the next day he finds Rozelle waiting for him in the dark, at his house.

Chapter 8   Maria tells Jed in a letter about the skeleton in her closet—her mother is insane—and that, now she has heard him tell the story about his father, she has found the strength to live her own life; she is leaving town for a while to find herself. Jed and Rozelle begin a torrid affair; he continues to be part of the Carringtons' social circle so as not to arouse suspicion.

Chapter 9   Jed asks Rozelle to leave her husband. She insists she loves Jed but refuses.

Chapter 10   The Friday Dante sessions with Mrs. Jones-Talbot continue—and the afternoon trysts with Rozelle. When Lawford goes to New York to exhibit his sculpture, she invites Jed to spend the night.

Chapter 11   Rozelle flies to New York to join her husband; on her return, she tells Jed that the reviews were bad and that Lawford has taken to drink and to abusing her sexually. She adds that the sculpted head of the screaming man was molded on the death agony of her husband who drowned in Florida.

Chapter 12 Jed witnesses Mrs. Jones-Talbot's stallion Dark Power performing stud service; inspired by the sight, she and Jed wind up in bed together. She hints at something fishy about the death of Rozelle's first husband.

Chapter 13 Jed, in Florida to give a lecture, does a little investigating concerning Rozelle's late husband. Upon his return, Rozelle tells him that Lawford, with whom she had been having an affair, was on the boat when the sail knocked Butler off; Lawford may or may not have tried to catch him, but he clearly had not thrown the life preserver in time (claiming that Butler had suffered a heart attack and it would have done no good). Lawford had set off in the dinghy, ditched it, and swum to shore, pretending that his own sailboat had capsized and keeping his presence on Butler's a secret. He then married Rozelle. Jed, no longer in love with her, quits his Nashville job and leaves for New York.

Book III

Chapter 14 After a penurious summer in Paris, Jed is offered a position at the University of Chicago. Sometime later he reads in the newspaper that Lawford has died of a heroin overdose, and that "a swami had been indicted for trafficking in dope"—a reference to a turbaned Hindu poet who had been present at numerous Carrington parties when Jed lived in Nashville. Rozelle was free of suspicion.

Chapter 15 Jed marries Dauphine Finkel, who had been his mistress years before, in graduate school, and is now a photographer of some repute. They have a son, Ephraim; but in a few years she leaves him, citing feelings of emptiness. His academic career prospers; in 1976 he is invited to Rome for an honorary degree. He looks up his old partisan comrades.

Chapter 16 Jed has a reunion with Rozelle, who just happens to be in Rome. She has married the "swami," who is actually a southern black who taught himself Hindi in India and is now fantastically wealthy from arbitrage. She had allowed Lawford to fall in love with another woman in Nashville, whom the swami supplied with drugs; it was a double suicide. In a letter from Perk Simms, his mother's husband, Jed learns of her death.

Chapter 17 Jed spends a summer in Paris, goes on a Canadian canoe trip with his grown-up son, Ephraim, then takes the trip to Dugton to visit his stepfather and his mother's grave. In the end, he writes to Dauphine asking if they couldn't get together again.

A Place to Come To, like *Meet Me in the Green Glen,* begins with the spectacular death of a buck—Buck Tewksbury, that is, the father of protagonist Jediah.[1] On his way home one night he stood up in his wagon, as was his custom, to relieve himself on the hindquarters of the nearer mule; but, being drunk, he fell off, and both left wheels passed over his neck. "Throughout, he was still holding on to his dong" (3), which was reputed to have been the biggest in the county. This dying gesture gave rise to some uncertainty at his funeral as to what exactly his last act had been:

> "All his r'aren and skirt-tearen round Claxford County and he ends like tryen to jack off in the middle of the night on the gravel on Dugton Pike."
> "Naw," Mr. Tutwayler sepulchrally uttered, "naw, he must of been standen up to piss...." (7)

A few months later, nine-year-old Jed is humiliated by a schoolyard raconteur who has opted for the fancier version: " '... and his daddy, he stood up in the wagon and—' and here he dropped a hand down to crotch level, but held out from his body, '—and jacked off—' he made a motion with his hand, '—and fell in the road and killed his-self!' " (20). It was at this moment, Jed says, that "I had discovered my hatred of my father" (24).

Yet later Jed would realize that "I should have been grateful to the wicked father" for dying that way, since "He was, through that very schoolyard scene, in its very pain, to provide me later with the first—I almost said, only—social success I was ever to know" (21). For Jed was to make a considerable social splash among his fellow graduate students at the University of Chicago by acting out, "in much the same spirit as his old torturer of the schoolyard, the hilarious episode of his father's death, complete with hand on hypothetical dong and the lethal plunge" (22). It was to make him popular with the Yankees, particularly with Dauphine Finkel, who comes over to sit beside him immediately after the performance, evidently curious "as to what the Son of Old Buck—as I had fondly termed my father in my little interlude—would be like in the clutch" (23). She becomes his mistress, and though they do part company for a while, she eventually becomes his wife and the mother of his only son. That marriage will suffer divorce, but in the last pages of the novel Jed, as old age approaches, seeks a final reunion with the woman the story of his father's death had first won him.

What reconciliation and closure the novel offers in its conclusion thus involves a return to the fruit of that original fiction about the father—a story that, when first invented in the schoolyard, brought the discovery of "rage at the father who had brought it all upon me" (21) but would later inspire filial gratitude for what was, in effect, Jed's only paternal legacy. "I should have been grateful," he realized, paralleling Jeremiah Beaumont's gratitude and rage at reading the handbill he thought Fort had written ("grateful ... with ... the gratitude of a good son to a father").

Jed's reworking of his father's story is based on a physiological ambiguity that finds resonance in ancient myth; it is not for nothing that Jed, fascinated early on by the study of Latin and Greek, goes on to pursue the kind of classical education that will enable him to appreciate such an allusion. The myth in question is one evoked by an insistent background detail that is repeatedly connected to the memory of his father's demise—the golden shower of "the torrent of gold-bodied August sunlight, perfectly transparent but somehow as substantial as lava, pouring inexhaustibly down from the sky" (8), seen as he heard his father's contemporaries debating the nature of his last gesture on the day of the funeral. That gold, lava-like torrent will be remembered years later when, fighting with Italian partisans behind enemy lines in World War II, Jed will recall "the men, the weeping child, the golden lava of sunlight pouring down" (9), and, still later: "I could close my eyes and see the scene of the child weeping ... with summer sunlight pouring down like golden lava" (84).

There are two remarkable things about this golden torrent. One is that it echoes what his father was in truth—if not in fiction—doing: urinating. The son had on at least one other occasion seen him do so, even though then, too, the gesture had also evoked his sexual potency. Riding back from town on the mule-drawn wagon with his father, Jed had seen him stand up, "fumbling at the front of his overalls to extract his member ... clutching his great member ... crying out in manic glee: 'Got the biggest dong in Claxford County—and what the hell good does it do me!' ... And now, in the midst of the wild mirth, he was relieving himself on the hindquarters of the near mule, playing the stream on that target, a gleaming arc in starlight ..." (15). And on yet another occasion, Jed had witnessed a genuinely golden stream fall on the same spot—this time from a different, though still paternal, source: "Then he had spat, the long golden stream of amber—tobacco juice, that is—lancing precisely out to spatter on the off-rump of the near mule" (227). The other remarkable thing about the golden torrent is that by calling attention once more to the image of a golden shower, and giving it a celestial origin (the sun in fact is the father in *Flood*), it evokes in a more particular way the locus classicus of all such golden showers: Zeus's insemination of Danaë, his successful penetration of the concealment in which her father, Acrisius, had placed her.

In a remarkably down-home way, Warren rewrites that myth while keeping intact the original double nature of Zeus's golden yet seminal stream. And he does so by having Jediah Tewksbury rewrite what—given all that has happened in Warren's previous novels between fathers and sons—we have a right to call the paternal text: the father's unwitting gift to the son, an event that becomes a text (if it was not, as in *Wilderness*, one already) by dint of the son's reworking it into a rewarding narrative.

It is not the first time the myth has surfaced. In *Wilderness*, Adam Rosenzweig came to, after lying unconscious from hunger and exhaustion, to discover a "great bronze of Perseus meditatively holding the head of Medusa" in Aaron Blaustein's house. When Jed Tewksbury recovers consciousness from malnutrition and whiskey in the house of Professor Heinrich Stahlmann, what happened then will come close to happening again: Blaustein's living room had had a "great gilt mirror above the screened fireplace," while Stahlmann's is similarly furnished with "a fireplace, very large" featuring "an extraordinary hearth" (62) surmounted by "an enormous mirror" (60). But more to the point is the circumstance that while Blaustein's living room had its statue of Perseus contemplating the head of Medusa, in Stahlmann's there is "a life-size copy, in white marble, of the Venus de Milo, and . . . a matching copy of the Discobolus" (61). One statue matches, in the context of Stahlmann's house, another; but within the larger context Warren's novels consistently construct for themselves, the second of these matches yet another statue; for, in the myth to which Blaustein's statue alludes, Perseus, in the sequel to his decapitation of Medusa, is a dangerous thrower of the discus. After his heroic labors, Perseus returned to Argos in search of his mother's father, Acrisius. But his grandfather fled at his approach, fearing the prophecy that he would die by his grandson's hand; the same prophecy had made him keep his daughter, Danaë, shut up in a tower (or underground, in another version of the myth) so that she would not conceive a son. The oracle was nevertheless fulfilled when Perseus, taking part in the funeral games of another son for another father, threw a discus that missed its target and fatally injured Acrisius.

It is possible that the wagon wheels that were the instrument of Jed's father's death—he hit "the pike in such a position and condition that both the left front and the left rear wheels of the wagon rolled, with perfect precision, over his unconscious neck" (3)—are a latter-day version of that discus. Be that as it may, in the context of *Wilderness* I argued, quoting Ernest Jones, that Perseus's unwitting slaying of his grandfather could be viewed in an oedipal light: "When the grandson in the myth avenges himself and his parents by slaying the tyrannical grandfather . . . he slays the man who endeavoured to possess and retain the mother's affections, i.e. his own rival . . . the primordial father, for whom to him the grandfather is but an *imago*." What happens to Jed and Heinrich Stahlmann lends support to this view. For one thing, Stahlmann had a curious name for his house: the "Castle of Otranto." Jed recalls that it was "a reference that, at the time, escaped me" (59), though he "did sense that everything around me [in Stahlmann's house] was generous with mysterious meaning" (62). Jed never does say what sense he made out of the allusion to Horace Walpole's novel about a father who profits from his son's untimely death to steal his bride.

We are, however, given enough clues to draw our own conclusions. If Stahlmann said his castle was Otranto, then he was giving a quite different message to Jed than what his otherwise fatherly solicitude conveyed.

Their first encounter was not, in fact, without its hint of violence. Jed, hoping that if he could demonstrate his prowess in classical languages the eminent professor would allow him into his classes at the University of Chicago, lay in wait for Stahlmann on the street outside his house, tracking him as he kept up his vigorous pace and running the risk of being taken for an assailant. The professor was armed with an impressive alpenstock, and Jed noticed "the way he clutched the walking stick well down below the head" (58), as once his father had been "*clutching* his great member, with a force that must have been painful, waving it at the stars" (15).[2] " 'What do you want, sir?' he demanded in a firm voice, his stick now grasped at the head . . ." (58). Jed responded with the opening lines of the *Aeneid* in Latin and—perhaps with greater relevance—a chorus from *Oedipus at Colonus* in Greek. Despite Jed's Alabama accent, the professor was appropriately impressed and took him under his wing, not only arranging his acceptance at the University of Chicago but also giving him a job and living quarters in his "Castle of Otranto." Jed became for Stahlmann, who was childless, not only a disciple but a son.

But two events cast a shadow on this idyll of paternal and filial devotion. One is Stahlmann's suicide—like Judge Irwin, he shoots himself neatly in the heart.[3] The other is the strange delight with which Jed kills another German professor. Immediately after Stahlmann's death Jed had volunteered for the army; three weeks into his service with Italian partisans, it was his duty to interrogate a captured SS lieutenant who, as it happened, "had been a classical scholar—an *Assistent* at Göttingen" (80). He was troubled then (and would still be long afterward, as Jed would confess to Mrs. Jones-Talbot [235]) by the fact that there was more than military necessity on his mind when he shot the German in the back of the head. Just before he pulled the trigger, he had, "in a tone of ironic question," set his victim up for a classical allusion: " ' . . . *dulce et decorum est?*' I was hating the bastard" (82). The hate seems to have originated from something other than an abhorrence of Nazis; evidently it had more to do with the manner in which his prisoner had recited to Jed the rules of the Geneva Convention, with all the authority of a German classics professor condescending to speak to a less-than-adequate student—"in the tone he must have used in dealing with dullards at Göttingen" (81). Jed saw it as jealousy: "I had hated him simply because I envied him" (83). But the coincidence of attributes between his victim and the fatherly (or grandfatherly, given the allusion to Perseus's lethal discus) German professor under whose roof Tewksbury had been living for the last two and a half years, and from whom he had suddenly been orphaned, suggests another interpretation, although it is not one of which Jed ever seems consciously aware.

But then there is a great deal going on in the novel of which Jed is unaware. Take, for example, the scene in Nashville where Jed makes passionate love to Rozelle Hardcastle Carrington on a bed of beech leaves. He is a wearing a raincoat, a "black slicker" (270), "and the black slicker, unlatched but still on its owner, outstretched like the wings of a monstrous black bat, wounded and fallen, heaved and flapped, stirring the carpet of bleached-gold beech leaves in its pain, while the rain fell" (271). Jed does not appear to be aware that he had earlier laid quite a bit of emphasis on the fact that Stahlmann owned a black cloak that Jed had first taken to be a raincoat. It was when he caught his first glimpse of the professor, outside a classroom (and before the incident in the street): "what, over his arm as he approached earlier, I had taken to be a dark topcoat or raincoat, had turned out to be a black cape that now, draped loosely over his shoulders, regally swayed and swung as he withdrew into infinite distance" (57). The fact that Jed wore a similar outfit when he made love to Rozelle would not be significant were it not for the fact that he had specifically spoken of Stahlmann's black cape as the emblem of his professorial authority and—what is more—of how ridiculous it would look on the back of a disciple who tried, without meriting it, to assume that mantle of authority. For, thinking of the cape on Stahlmann, he thought of poor Mr. Pillsbun, his classics professor at Blackwell College—Pillsbun, who had studied one summer with Stahlmann and who had pretended to have enough pull with his former professor to get Jed admitted to the University of Chicago (when Jed arrived on campus, he learned that no letter from Pillsbun had been received). Pillsbun, Jed was sure, must have secretly purchased a black cape like the one the master wore. "The cape, I suddenly knew, was what he had wanted most for his dream. . . . And knew that at night, behind locked door and drawn shades, he would put it on. Standing there in his grubby little rented room, he would regard himself in the mirror" (57).

There is no indication that Jed grasps the irony inherent in his lovemaking costume. But that does not mean the irony isn't there. And one more detail from that scene deserves close attention, for it too provides evidence of connections in the novel of which the protagonist is unaware, as well as evidence of the continuity between Warren's novels and his poetry: the carpet of golden beech leaves that provide the setting for the heaving of that monstrous black bat. A few pages later, as it happens, a monstrous black "bat" of another sort will be engaged in precisely the same activity: the "big, black dong, rigid and looking like a baseball bat" (277) that belongs to Mrs. Jones-Talbot's stallion preparing to render stud service to a waiting mare. There, too, "the bright sunlight poured down" (276) as it had, lava-like, when the son heard how his father died clutching his dong. The stallion's black bat of a dong (a word whose only other appearances mark it as belonging to the father) and his prowess with the mare inspired Jed and Mrs. Jones-Talbot to go and do likewise, thus placing Jed in the role he had assumed six pages earlier of a lovemaking black bat, or rather the wielder of one.

Now the poem "No Bird Does Call," appearing in the sequence *Being Here: Poetry 1977–1980* (and thus contemporaneous with the publication in 1977 of *A Place to Come To*), unites the two major themes of Perseus and beech in such a way as to provide a long-awaited key to the puzzle of their presence in Warren's fiction. The poet wanders into a hollow surrounded by beeches. It is a place reminiscent of the setting in *The Cave* near Beecham's Bluff, where the entrance to the cave lay under the roots of "the biggest beech of all" (6), for in the poem the "roots of great gray boles crook'd ... down / To grapple again, like claws, in the breathless perimeter / Of moss, as in cave-shadow darker and deeper than velvet." There he lies down on the beech leaves' "carpet of gold, for then / The hollow is Danaë's lap lavished with gold by the god...." Lying there "With closed eyes I fell so slowly ... as though / / Into depth that was peace, but not death...." If the mother is Danaë, the poet must be Perseus, returning to the womb that is peace but not death; and, most remarkably, the father, source of the golden shower that lavished Danaë's lap, is not only Zeus but the beech.

That he is a beech is consonant with the name of the father in the novel: "Old *Buck*—as I had fondly termed my father in my little interlude" (23; emphasis added). Though the name obviously comes from the *buck* that originally meant "goat" and has come to signify the male of many species, including deer, in Warren it is inextricably tied to the *buck* that means "beech," a form of the Old English *bóc*, still present in such words as "*buck*mast" (beechnuts) and "*buck*wheat" (because of the resemblance of buckwheat seeds to beechnuts). In light of the way Warren's sons consistently ground their identities in their father's texts, it is significant that *beech* and *book* were originally the same word, the aforementioned *bóc*, because "inscriptions were first made on beechen tablets, or cut in the bark of beech-trees" (*O.E.D.*). There originally was, in other words, a textuality to beeches. So it is perhaps no accident that the boy in "Blackberry Winter" who made a footprint in the mud and then pretended to be reading someone else's mark was also capable of imagining it imprinted on a *beach:* "as though you had suddenly come upon that single mark on the glistening auroral beach of the world. You have never seen a beach, but you have read the book and how the footprint was there." We have seen how, in "Aspen Leaf in Windless World," Warren himself muses upon beach-inscriptions, wondering if they form a text: "Look how sea-foam, thin and white, makes its Arabic scrawl / On the unruffled sand of the beach's faint-titled plane. / Is there a message there for you to decipher?" Is there not a message for us to decipher in Warren's Buck/beech/beach/Beecham/Beauchamp connection?

Nor is it any accident that the verb in the poem that tells what the god did to Danaë to bring this Perseus into existence—*lavish*—should be phonically and etymologically related to the likewise golden *lava* that poured down from the sky the day Jed heard how his father died: "the torrent of gold-bodied August sunlight, perfectly transparent but somehow as substantial as lava ... the golden lava of sunlight pouring down ... summer sunlight pouring down like golden lava." This insistent connection between sunlight and lava may find its origin, given the contemporaneous context of the poem's retelling of the Danaë myth, in the fact that Zeus was originally a solar deity (*Larousse*, 98, 106); he was, in any case, god of the sky (as Poseidon was god of the sea and Pluto, the underworld). And in the golden shower itself, "which penetrates to the subterranean Danaë it is easy to recognise the rays of the sun which germinate the seed buried in the ground" (*Larousse*, 106). The curious fact underlying the connection between *lava* and *lavish* is that the latter, like the former, is actually liquid, deriving from "*lavasse, lavache,* deluge of rain. Cf. OF *lavis* torrent" (recall "the *torrent* of gold-bodied ... sunlight"), while *lava,* from *lavare,* to wash, was originally " 'a streame or gutter suddenly caused by raine' (Florio 1611), applied in the Neapolitan dialect to a lava-stream from Vesuvius; hence adopted in literary Italian" (*O.E.D.*), whence it acquired the fiery content it has today. We should not forget that, when Dr. Stahlmann laid out a program of study for Jediah Tewksbury, "It was his idea that I begin intensive work *in Italian* . . ." (63; emphasis added).

Nor should we ignore that soon after Stahlmann's death Jed found himself in the company of men from a *volcanic* Italian region. "A number of the desperadoes," Jed says of his partisan comrades in the war, "were from the city and zone of Siena, especially from the region of the great volcanic cone of Monte Amiata . . ." (80). And their very identity is grounded in that lava-based soil, as he learns when one of them tells him that his *politica* is his *terra.* Jed asks if by *terra* he means Italy.

> " 'No, la mia terra.' He closed his hand over the fist and gravel, his dirt, his *terra,* is whatever it was, and shook the clenched hand at me to show possession—or the being possessed, identity or whatever you want to call it. 'La mia,' he added. He was from that desert-like country near Siena, and that is one hell of a patch of country to have to call *la mia terra.*" (233)

When he returns to Italy some three decades later to pick up an honorary degree in Rome, Jed travels to Siena to look up his wartime comrades. The climax of this pilgrimage is his visit to Gianluigi, who has become a religious hermit—and has also come to incorporate a remarkable number of the qualities attributed to fathers in Warren's fiction. He is one-eyed; his face is "empurpled" (recall Brad Tolliver's fascination with the purple rage in his father's face and its echoes in the purple birthmark that, inspired by Yasha Jones's scar, he gives Digby) by scars from Nazi torture; and he lives in a cave below beeches (the cave entrance in *The Cave* lay beneath the roots of "the biggest beech"): "He lived in a cave in the great band of conifers below where the beeches start on the mountain" (356), a volcanic mountain, the Monte Amiata whose "great volcanic cone" defines the Sienese landscape. The Italian journey is thus a symbolic return to the father in a lava-incrusted landscape.

If lava's paternity is stressed by this pilgrimage, its sexuality is suggested by what lava can do for Mrs. Jones-Talbot, the mother-figure with whom Jed once found himself in bed. It is, in fact, the lava of a certain *Roman* history: " 'The only trouble is that when you suddenly get old and have to go to bed early, there's less and less reason for going to bed at all. . . . I've taken up reading Gibbon—oh, what lovely, crystalline lava flowing over all the centuries up to your first old-lady snore when you drop the book' " (385). Just as Danaë in the poem was lavished with gold, this other figure for the Warrenian mother finds lava the next best thing to sex.

The revelation the poem provides of the beech's paternal quality casts some light on what Jebb Holloway found in *The Cave:* the stalagmite that felt like a beech ("It was like a beech. . . . If you leaned up against this thing in the dark, durn it, you'd think it was a beech"). Recalling that the mouth of the cave was located under the roots of the biggest beech, an opening "flanked by the great humping"—a word that now reveals its sexual resonance—"gray roots of the biggest beech," remembering how powerfully the cave in *The Cave* functioned as maternal space, and aware that Danaë's lap was lavished with (and ravished by) beech leaves, we can now imagine what that beech is doing in that cave: it is the father's phallus in the mother's womb, a version of the primal scene in Warren's text (of which another is the father's golden shower).[4]

And it may illumine as well a minor but quite possibly telling detail concerning what happens between Jed and Mrs. Jones-Talbot. Jed had accumulated some debts during his graduate studies at the University of Chicago that he had not yet paid off when he accepted the teaching position in Nashville. Mrs. Jones-Talbot, Lawford Carrington's aunt, wanted to pursue her study of Dante, a specialty of Jed's, and was willing to pay for weekly tutorials. The minor detail in this instance is her friend Mrs. *Beacham,* who took part in the lessons too. Her name, in the context of the argument I have made concerning the locally correct pronunciation of the historical Beauchamp on which the protagonist of *World Enough and Time* was modeled, as well as the Beecham's Bluff that marked the location of the cave in *The Cave*—but most especially with regard to the paternity of the beech— is a provocative riddle. An examination of exactly what it is Mrs. Beacham does—or rather doesn't do—suggests the answer. Although she is an eager student ("The middle-aged ladies," Jed reports, speaking of both, "worked so hard at the self-imposed task . . ." [215]), nothing she says is recorded, and more appears to flow from her absence than from her presence. The third time she appears she is no sooner mentioned than she "announced that she had to run . . . and was gone" (231). In the next sentence Jed notices that "The little fire that had been set to knock off the unseasonable chill had died, and the fireplace was a black geometrical hole. . . ." Quite possibly she left to allow her friend some time alone with Jed; she was even more thoughtful on the following Friday, for on that occasion, "before we settled down to work, Mrs. Jones-Talbot explained that my other pupil, Mrs. Beacham, would not be coming today" (272)— and this was the day that, inspired by the action of the stallion's big black bat of a dong, they wound up together in bed.

In terms of the plot, that outcome may in fact have been Mrs. Beacham's kindly intent. But on a deeper level, this chain of events suggest a somewhat different reading. Her earlier departure, as I noted, coincided with the disappearance of the flame in the hearth. Now in the struggle at the hearth between Jeremiah Beaumont and his grandfather in *World Enough and Time,* and at the moment in *Wilderness* when Aaron Blaustein tried to make Adam his son, we saw the significance of the extinction of a flame that was in fact paternal. Does that imagery carry over here? Jed's observation, at the same moment he saw the fire had died, that the fireplace was "a *black* geometrical *hole*" suggests that it does, for just a few pages before he had described the experience of making love to Rozelle Carrington as one of falling into a black hole: "I understood that the orgasm was like the 'black hole' of the physicists—a devouring negativity" (220).

There is evidence elsewhere in Warren for the femininity of a fireplace. In "The Unvexed Isles" Alice Dalrymple's throat and her cigarette paralleled the "black chimney throat" and its flame, while in "Prime Leaf" Edith Hardin was just as closely identified with her hearth. The hearth was, for Jed Tewksbury's mother, her ultimate weapon against his father's drunken rage: It was "onto the stone hearth" of their house that Old Buck one night "took a header" (as, by the way, he would later take "his header" on the Dugton road and fall victim to the wheels of his wagon) "and successfully laid himself out like a stunned beef," while Jed's mother "would sit and regard the finished product with a face as noncommittal as a boulder washed bone-white in a creek bed and then dried in the August sun when the drouth came" (4), an extended simile that draws out the passive power of the maternal hearthstone. Dorothy Cutlick handled her drunken father in much the same way in *The Cave*. He too fell into unconsciousness on the stone of the fireplace as he rushed toward her, threatening violence: "his head nearly knocked a chunk of limestone out of the chimney.... He lay on the hearth, and she let him lie" (38).

At the time of his afternoon interlude with Mrs. Jones-Talbot, Jed was thirty-four and she was "fiftyish" (147). She was therefore old enough to be his mother—and quite possibly the age of his own, who had married young: "in the early days of marriage . . . she [was] little more than a girl" (17). What happened between Jed and Mrs. Jones-Talbot could only take place in the absence of Mrs. Beacham, whose name, despite the sex of its bearer, strongly suggests the power of the beech to stand for the father, who had to be evoked, yet absent, for the oedipal goal to be reached.

When Jed arrives in Nashville he discovers that he has not really left the Castle of Otranto, for the converted barn where Lawford and Rozelle Carrington do their entertaining is strangely reminiscent of the house Professor Stahlmann called by that allusive name. "There, at the south end, appeared a jungle of plants . . . and at that moment, I had felt a disturbing sense of déjà vu, or reliving—until I remembered what now seemed such a poor little token of a jungle in the conservatory off the erstwhile dining room of Dr. Stahlmann's house" (132). There is more to this resemblance than even Jed realizes. The entrance to Stahlmann's conservatory, which at the time had seemed to him "a wildly improbably surrealistic jungle dream," was, we recall, "flanked by two mahogany pedestals, on one a life-size copy, in white marble, of the Venus de Milo, and on the other a matching copy of the Discobolus." Now statues abound in the Carrington household, for Rozelle's husband is a sculptor. Jed turns his attention to a new group Lawford has just finished:

> There were six, each mounted on a black boxlike structure, all in a silvery metal of dull patina, all of the same subject: a pair of female arms. A plate of the same metal was attached to the nearest black stand. It read: BALLET: A SUITE. . . . The arms, and hands, too, I should add, spectrally suggested—not crudely, quite subtly, in fact—the ballet of love. (157–58)

Later, the other five pairs of arms will have "all leaped, by contagion, into more precise significance" when some joker adds a finishing touch: "in the middle of the circle defined by the forefinger and thumb of the silvery right hand of 'Number 5,' a splendid banana reared" (182–83). That contagion of complementary significance may not, perhaps, stop there, for these pairs of female arms supply precisely what the Venus de Milo in Stahlmann's Castle of Otranto lacked: arms.

Later, another sculpted product of Carrington's art will leap into a more precise significance of its own:

> It was a man's head, in bronze, the head of an aging man . . . the big round skull almost bald, the head thrown back, eyes wide with outrage, the mouth straining open in a soundless scream. . . .
> "Oh!" Rozelle uttered, in a breathy exhalation, and in the long moment while she stared at the object . . . and while Lawford stared at her, there wasn't a sound. (183)

As Rozelle knew immediately, and Jed learned only later, the head frozen in the moment just before death was modeled on that of Michael X. Butler, Rozelle's rich and older husband who had drowned under suspicious circumstances. It is not clear whose fault Butler's death was, if anyone's, but clearly by creating this sculpture Lawford was trying to provoke some sort of shock of recognition from Rozelle, even a feeling of guilt. What he also accomplishes, without intending it, is to make Rozelle into a kind of Medusa who kills her lovers and turns them into stone.

Jed experiences something like that petrifying power at one stage of his own love affair with Rozelle, comparing himself to a man transformed into statuary by Vesuvius's lava, an image "suggested by the plaster casts at Pompeii of men who died even in some obsessive private concern . . . [a man] who, as he entered upon the long dark slide toward bliss, didn't even miss a beat as the ashes fell" (207). But in the end he does escape the Medusan glance of Rozelle, née Hardcastle (a maiden name that evokes both petrification and the Castle of Otranto), and returns to the woman—Dauphine Finkel—he had first won with his fiction about his father's death.

Who, then, gets Rozelle? The strangest sort of character: an American southern black who passes for Indian—the turbaned "swami" who had been a constant feature at Carrington parties and recited his own poetry in Hindi. But the oddest thing about him—from the perspective of a reading of Warren's novels that keeps encountering winks and other one-eyed looks—is that he *winks* at the protagonist: "I swear to God," Jed tells us, "that as my eyes momentarily engaged those of the swami, he almost winked—or maybe did wink—and gave some sort of complex smile that seemed to be full of ironical dimensions involving, among other things, camaraderie, amiable contempt and brotherly knowingness—as though he were just trying to indicate that if I didn't mess with his racket, he wouldn't mess with mine" (253–54). Carrington later dies from an overdose of drugs supplied by this "swami" to Amy Dabbitt, who had become Lawford's mistress; when Rozelle and Jed cross paths in Rome in 1976, she reveals that she is very happily married to the former swami, who is now fabulously wealthy. That Jed should lose Rozelle to the man who winked at him parallels what happened to Brad Tolliver in *Flood* when he lost his bride to one-eyed Ramon Echegaray—or rather to his memory, for the Spaniard was already dead. We saw there that, because both Echegaray's one eye and the space left when the father (and God) left were called a "black hole," Echegaray was a version of the one-eyed father—the father who, like Mortimer Sparlin at the Seven Dwarfs Motel, has a prior claim on the son's bride. The fact that Sparlin was black—as is the "swami," despite his disguise—makes it quite likely that the same symbolic logic is working itself out here. And thus the prophecy embodied by the name of Stahlmann's house, a place Jed found recreated in the house where Rozelle lived—the Castle of Otranto where a father steals the bride of his son—is finally fulfilled.

This is not the first "Indian" to give a Warren protagonist a one-eyed look.[5] In his 1969 poem *Audubon: A Vision,* "The Indian, / Hunched by the hearth, lifts his head, looks up, but / From one eye only"—having lost the other when an arrow rebounded off his bowstring—and silently warns Warren's protagonist of the murderous intent of the woman in whose cabin they have sought shelter: "he becomes aware / That the live eye of the Indian is secretly on him, and soundlessly / The lips move, and when her back is turned, the Indian / Draws a finger, in delicious retardation, across his own throat." The Indian was not lying. Audubon sees the woman honing her knife and knows that he must leap up and defend himself before it is too late, but "He cannot think what guilt unmans him, or / Why he should find the punishment so precious," as though he wanted to die at her hands. Three men enter just in time to save him. Later, when he gazes on the woman hanged, he has his Perseid moment: "the face / Is, he suddenly sees, beautiful as stone, and / / So becomes aware that he is in the manly state." She is Medusa, her beautiful stoniness a displacement for the stoniness she inflicts on those who gaze upon her—which is precisely what happens to Audubon, who gets an erection from the sight of her face.

Jediah Tewksbury, too, finds his Medusa in the end. And when he does she tells him she is his mother. Many years after the events in Nashville, having returned at last to the place "where I always started my thoughts" (385), the castlelike house where Stahlmann had lived near the campus of the University of Chicago, he saw ahead of him on the sidewalk the "classic shape" of an immigrant grandmother. And then he was suddenly aware of two youths, one struggling with her shopping bag, the other with her purse. He hurried to her rescue but was no match for the young men, and was in fact knifed by the one who was trying to grab the purse. The last thing he recalled seeing before losing consciousness was a vision of the youth "as he leaped, rather as he seemed to drift with ineffable, slow, floating godlike grace—godlike, truly, it seemed—to the hood of the nearest halted automobile, to stand beautifully balanced there with the purse—like Medusa's head hanging from the hand of Cellini's Perseus in Florence.... I remember thinking how beautiful, how redemptive, all seemed. It was as though I loved him. I thought how beautifully he had moved, like Ephraim, like a hawk in sunset flight" (387). At least one circle is closed here, for the woman's purse in this Perseus's grasp becomes the mystical icon of horror that stands for—as it does in *Wilderness*—what Freud suggested women's purses can also sometimes represent (*The Interpretation of Dreams*, 393, 419). But this allusion to the myth of Danaë's son is also overlaid by another legend, a biblical one. At least that is suggested by the names the immigrant grandmother insists on calling Jed in the hospital, before she dies: "*figlio mio*" and "*Giuseppino*, which is Little Joseph" (388). And although Ephraim is Jed Tewksbury's son by Dauphine Finkel, and who increasingly occupies his thoughts in these closing pages of the novel, the father of the Ephraim for whom Jed's son is (directly or indirectly) named is precisely who the old immigrant grandmother says *he* is, Joseph, son of Jacob, famous for his knowledge of the science of interpreting dreams.

Now the biblical story of Ephraim involves, of all things, another error made by a dying parent. Joseph thought Jacob would be wrong to give his formal blessing to Joseph's son Ephraim who, being the youngest, was not entitled to receive it. As Jacob's sight was dim, Joseph thus placed Manasseh at his right hand and Ephraim at his left, so that he would bless the appropriate son. But Jacob was not about to be manipulated by his son as he himself had once manipulated his own blind father by disguising himself as his brother Esau, although by avoiding such manipulation he was repeating his act of dispossessing the rightful heir. Jacob crossed his hands.

> And when Joseph saw that his father laid his right hand upon the head of Ephraim, it displeased him: and he held up his father's hand, to remove it from Ephraim's head unto Manasseh's head. And Joseph said unto his father, Not so, my father: for this is the firstborn; put thy right hand upon his head. And his father refused, and said, I know it, my son, I know it; he also shall become a people, and he also shall be great: but truly his younger brother shall be greater than he, and his seed shall become a multitude of nations. (Gen. 48:17–19)

So Ephraim not only took precedence over Manasseh against Joseph's wish, but he—and Manasseh—took precedence over Joseph himself, for Jacob turns his grandfatherly blessing into a fatherly one:

> And now thy two sons, Ephraim and Manasseh, which were born unto thee in the land of Egypt before I came unto thee in Egypt, are mine; as Reuben and Simeon, they shall be mine. And thy issue, which thou begettest after them, shall be thine, and shall be called after the name of their brethren in their inheritance. (Gen. 48:5–6)

Thus Joseph's sons became Jacob's sons, and attained a rank of seniority more exalted than Joseph's. "In consequence of their adoption by Jacob, Joseph's two sons acquire the status of Jacob's sons, on a par with that of Reuben and Simeon (Jacob's oldest)" (Speiser, 357). "In the first blessing of Jacob, Joseph was replaced by his two sons, Ephraim and Manasseh, thereby doubling Joseph's portion" (Wintermute, 986), for Joseph's descendants would now receive both what Joseph was entitled to and what his two sons would inherit as sons of Jacob. On the one hand, Joseph is dispossessed by his own sons in terms of seniority among the sons of Jacob, but on the other, he gains, as he will have more to pass on to his later descendants.

In addition, Joseph is granted a small compensatory inheritance in the final verse of chapter 48: "Moreover I have given to thee one portion above thy brethren, which I took out of the hand of the Amorite with my sword and with my bow." Speiser observes that for this troublesome passage "no plausible solution is in sight." The chief difficulty is the word *shechem,* here translated as "portion," but which really means "shoulder." It could mean the shoulder of a mountain, either as a common noun or a place name, and thus allude to a conquest on Jacob's part for which there is no other record. Yet even this last bit of an inheritance, which appears to be Jacob's attempt to compensate Joseph for what he lost in the deal, seems to have worked its way into Warren's text. For the thieving youth who became, for Jed, a vision of his own son left his mark in the form of a wound in Jed's *shoulder* (386); that scar, inscribed by the son on the body of the father, is what Jed will inherit from this encounter with the future.

This allusion has consequences for Tewksbury's vision of the youthful thief as Perseus, Ephraim, and sunset hawk—which is to say, in the context of the hawk imagery in Warren's poetry, as *father*. (We saw this in *Night Rider* and *Wilderness,* as well as how the "Red-Tail Hawk" was simultaneously father and infant progeny.) The purse-snatcher is even more obviously a vision of the father because of his graceful leap "to the hood of the nearest halted automobile, to stand beautifully balanced there with the purse," like Perseus with the head of Medusa. For this clearly echoes the opening paragraph of the novel, in which Jed's father stands, somewhat less gracefully balanced, on a historically earlier vehicle ("standing up in the front of his wagon") and enacted the godlike gesture of making a golden shower. Like father, like [grand]son.

But where does this leave Jed? Like Joseph, it appears, he is the disinherited testator, getting only a wounded shoulder for his pains. Not only younger than his son (as Joseph became "younger" than his sons, who were made as "old" as his eldest brothers, Reuben and Simeon), he is the son of his son, who is now the father—as the protagonist in Warren's poem "The Leaf" is "the father / Of my father's father's father."

There is also an analogue to this in the novel, the "teaser," the horse who may well be under the impression that he is about to do to the mare what only the black stallion has the right to perform. " 'But the gentleman in the case, he is only a stand-in,' " Mrs. Jones-Talbot explains. " 'It's not for him, poor fellow' " (275). Jed does get to do it, of course, though he does not know it, at that moment, as he will soon spend the rest of the afternoon in the bed with Mrs. Jones-Talbot. But in a sense he does not, for she too, as we have seen, is a stand-in. And she is not the only one, for the almost clinical description of the copulation of Dark Power and the mare serves more than the purpose of graphic realism; the more graphic it is, the more allegorical it becomes, the more the two horses become symbols for the players in a kind of primal scene. We have seen how Dark Power's "big black dong . . . looking like a baseball bat" recalls the "dong" that Jed's father had displayed in death and the big black bat Jed himself seemed to become when, wearing a raincoat like his adopted father's, he made love to Rozelle on a carpet of gold beech leaves. To that picture we could add another feature of Old Buck's last moments, the fact that he was spilling his golden stream, as was his habit, "on the hindquarters of the near mule, playing the stream on that target." Mutatis mutandis, the black stallion approached his task from the same perspective, as Warren's graphic account makes clear.[6]

But what the mare is doing at the time is perhaps the most striking instance of a graphically depicted reality that is at the same time a haunting, and recurring, image with larger implications.

> The mare's bound tail had lifted.
> "She's a-blinken," Uncle Tad said.
> Then I saw what he meant. The tail of the mare being lifted, the aperture about which all the ritual centered, was indeed blinking, with a flash of inner flesh-red visible at every blink. *Blinking*—there was no other word for it. (275)

The closing of the eye, be it wink or blink, has been at issue for a long time in this reading of Warren's fiction. It began, with Willie Stark, as a father's ambiguous sign; more recently, in *Flood* (and, somewhat less prominently, in *The Cave*), it has been seen as the father's mark, the sign that he has already been there. In *A Place to Come To* it becomes the mother's ambiguous sign in precisely the same way that it was the father's in *All the King's Men*—that is, the wink is a message its sender refuses to authenticate, as Jed will learn from his stepfather, Perk Simms:

> "She could stop anything she was doing . . . and just for a second give you a look that made you feel you and her had a wonderful secret. Sometimes I might be helping her make up a bed on Saturday and she'd give me a wink, *and then pretend she hadn't never.*" (393; emphasis added)[7]

Like Jed's mother, Rozelle had a way with her eyes: "eyelids drooping ever so little in a way to remind me of the biblical words 'she taketh thee with her eyelids' " (128–29). So, in a different way, did Jed's first wife, Agnes Andresen, who used her eyeglasses to get him to propose: "She still had the horn-rims on and drove the sharp corner through fabric and flesh ... while she twisted the spikelike corner of the horn-rims into the bleeding wound, I was taking a deep breath, and saying, 'Listen ... what about marrying me and just forgetting the hell out of this little Perry?' " (90–91). The Perry in question was the boyfriend Agnes left for Jed, the Perry Gerald who could well, as he told Jed after Agnes's death, have loved her better. There must be more than a coincidence behind these echoing names, Perry and Perk, Jed's first and last rivals, both of whom share the first three letters of Perseus (as did the original dreamer, Percy—or, as his friends called him, *Perse*—Munn). As Jed's son, in his fleeting vision of the thief of the mother's purse (the mother who claimed she was *Jed*'s mother), becomes the Perseus the manner of Jed's father's death had promised Jed would have been, so does Perk displace him from that mythic role: he is the only man to see the mother's wink, just as Perseus was the only man to see Medusa's gaze—by reflection, in Athena's shield—and live.

As the lover of Jed's mother, Perk was privileged to gaze upon the nakedness that Jed first discovered, to his horror, when he came home from college unannounced. Finding there a whiskey bottle and two glasses, one lipstick-stained, he at first thought he must be in the wrong house. Then he heard a sound, turned, and saw her. "She stood there with her long black hair down loose ... holding the robe tight over herself with both hands. I looked down at her feet. I wasn't ready yet to look at her face" (52). In *Wilderness* Adam Rosenzweig, encountering his Medusa—the naked Mollie about to be flogged—had taken exactly the same evasive action: "Adam found himself staring at the woman's shoes. He thought that if he kept his eyes firmly fixed on the shoes he would be all right." Jed eventually did look at her face, and then looked down and realized his mother's nakedness: "I looked from her face down to the hands that were clutching that silky-pink robe together, and I knew, quite suddenly and quite coldly, that there wasn't a stitch under it. I knew this as clearly as though, even while I was gazing into her face, she had drawn the garment apart to expose what was beneath, and then, instantly, but somehow deliberately, had again closed the cloth over what I had seen" (52).

Freud insisted that what was visible, and petrifying, in Medusa was maternal: "in the myth it is the genital of the mother that is represented" ("The Infantile Genital Organization," 174n4). "The terror of Medusa ... occurs when a boy ... catches sight of the female genitals, probably those of an adult, surrounded by hair, and essentially those of his mother" ("Medusa's Head," 212). Warren leaves little doubt about the Medusan quality of

Jed's mother, for that long, unconstrained hair is very much in evidence: "She stood there with her long black hair down loose...." In a (literally) striking earlier scene, "her black hair" was likewise "flying loose" when she had hit him on the nose, and broken it, with his own shoe (46). It had happened when he was a teenager and had come home drunk, fresh from having consorted with a black prostitute in the poor section of town; the attack was apparently a punishment for that expression of his sexuality. Jed bore the mark of what was essentially a castrating gesture—Freud points out in *The Interpretation of Dreams* that "Comparisons between nose and penis are common" (422)—for the rest of his life. His mother never forgot it either, recalling her handiwork in nearly every letter she would write him in the years to come:

> "I aint had no call to break no more noses yet, ha ha. I do not mean to make no joke how I broke yore nose. I am sorry I done it. But it seemed like something I had it in me to do at the time. Have you tole the new wife how it is broke and who?" (98)

"Anybody broke yore nose lately?" (159)

This destructive contact with his own shoe is yet another variation of Seth's "discovery" of the footprint that was in fact his own, in "Blackberry Winter," and Angelo Passetto's loving embrace of the "leetle feet" and the ice-formed footprint that turned out to be the image of his own, in *Meet Me in the Green Glen*.

This journey through Warren's fiction began with a dream to be deciphered and will draw to a close with three more, one in *A Place to Come To* and the other two evoked by it. Just as he is about to fall into a love affair with Rozelle Hardcastle in her husband's Nashville mansion, Jed Tewksbury will feel imprisoned in a dream: "For a fleeting instant I stood in the middle of the floor, my feet on the rose-and-gray geometry of the deep-piled rug, and heard my heart beating. It was, for that instant, like being powerlessly trapped in an indecipherable dream" (157). He may not be able to decipher the rose-and-gray geometry of that fireplace rug ("On the other side of the chimney was another fireplace, much smaller, with easy chairs gathered round on a great rug of rose and gray in geometrical design" [132]), but we can see that it anticipates the "black *geometrical* hole" of Mrs. Jones-Talbot's fireplace (231), which itself echoed the "black hole" that orgasm with Rozelle Hardcastle turned out to be (220)—"a devouring negativity" that entraps him, as does the indecipherable dream. The geometry of the rug seems to be part of what draws him, just as logic of another sort—the logic of dream—draws us further into the meshes of these interlocking images.

But what about the rose and the gray? *Rose* immediately suggests *Rozelle* Hardcastle, who has become *Rose* Carrington. It recalls, too, something about the robe Jed's mother wore that parted to reveal her nakedness: "She stood there with her long black hair down loose, wearing a new-looking pink silk robe with pink *roses* sewed to it.... I could almost feel how that slick silky pink stuff would slip and slide on the bare skin" (52; emphasis added). The loose hair that contributed to the Medusa effect of this naked mother will be evoked in the sentence that immediately precedes the one that places Jed on that rose and gray rug: "It is as though you half-expect to turn around and find a woman there, innocently naked, *hair loose*, face illuminated by tenderness and desire, one hand with a warning finger laid to the lips. For a fleeting instant ..." (157; emphasis added). It, too, may be part of the dream.

So may be the moment Mrs. Jones-Talbot drew off her kerchief "—snatched it off, really—and tossed her *hair loose* in a quick, irritable motion. She flung the kerchief toward a chair, and when it fell wide, I made a movement to pick it up. 'Oh, leave it alone!' she burst out. When I proceeded to pick it up and lay it on the chair, she did not even the notice the act, much less acknowledge it" (278; emphasis added). It is curious that Jed is so anxious to pick up the kerchief, given that Perse Munn was so concerned to retrieve his handkerchiefs from Thebes and that we have been so eager to pick up all the ones dropped since then. We saw in Perse's story that the newsprint falling off the bundle in his dream was part of a network of handbills and handkerchiefs; does this mean that here the dream has returned once more, to reveal what used to be a fetus but has now become Medusan hair?

That hair caused the death of the men who gazed upon it, but it did so by making them hard as stone—which is to say, according to Freud, that it gave them a sexual rise: "The sight of Medusa's head makes the spectator stiff with terror, turns him to stone. Observe that we have here once again the same origin from the castration complex and the same transformation of affect! For becoming stiff means an erection. Thus in the original situation it offers consolation to the spectator: he is still in possession of a penis, and the stiffening reassures him of the fact" ("Medusa's Head," 212). Jed did not die, but he did get an erection in the sequence of events that began when Mrs. Jones-Talbot "snatched"—a verb suggesting the *snatch* Medusan hair signifies—off her kerchief to reveal the same kind of loose hair that his mother had displayed the night he glimpsed her nakedness.

And it is at this juncture that the gray of that geometrical design comes into play. Jed's mother had worn a pink silk robe with roses on it; Mrs. Jones-Talbot's silk robe was *gray*—and so, of course, was her hair: "a long dark gray raw silk robe—or what looked like that—with dark red piping and sash.... Her gray-streaked hair had been brushed now, no longer in the disorder left when she had snatched off the kerchief and flung it, so inaccurately, at the chair" (281). As Jed stood on that hearth-rug in Rose Carrington's house and felt trapped in an indecipherable dream, he was standing between the rose and the gray, the rose of his disrobing mother's robe and the gray of the coeval Mrs. Jones-Talbot's.

This is not the first time the reader will have seen the kerchief Jed was so persistent about picking up after Mrs. Jones-Talbot "snatched" it off her head to reveal her Medusan hair. In the scene, several chapters back, of the unveiling of Lawford Carrington's sculpted depiction of his wife's former husband's death by drowning, both the snatching and Jed's retrieval of the covering cloth had already occurred. It was not, of course, a kerchief, but "a white cloth, almost as big as a sheet, that shrouded" the bronze head until Carrington "*snatched* the cloth free, and flung it carelessly behind him in my direction. I caught it" (183; emphasis added). Now not only is that scene recalled by Mrs. Jones-Talbot's gesture, but the subject of the sculpted head will come up in their postcopulative conversation, with her suggestion to Jed that there was something not quite right about the official story that Butler's death had been an accident. In the very next chapter Tewksbury goes to Florida, the scene of the crime, and discovers the truth: that Butler had accidentally fallen off the boat when a boom swung around but that Carrington had intentionally not thrown him the life preserver in time.

Butler's death resembles Old Buck's in that they were both (1) accidental (2) falls (3) from a moving vehicle. The roundness of the life preserver that sealed Butler's fate because it wasn't thrown in time even resembles the wagon wheels that ran over Jed's father's neck, while both suggest the discus with which Perseus *accidentally* killed his grandfather. Just as the snatched-off kerchief repeats the moment in Perse's dream when the newspaper falls away to reveal what it concealed, so does the snatched-off white cloth that covers the statue. What it reveals in this instance is "the head of an aging man, perhaps an old one, the big round skull almost bald" (183). That baldness insists here, for just a few pages earlier it had appeared combined with carelessly tossed white sheets in the person of Bill Cudworth, as he recounted his experience of parachuting into Normandy on D-Day. "He was grinning at me ... with his strong-looking near-bald skull cocked to one side, one eye squinting quizzically" (175) and telling Jed about the only two times he had ever "felt real": the first when he told his boss and prospective father-in-law that he was walking out of his comfortable Wall Street job to move to Tennessee, and the second when "the night sky was full of floating bed sheets like God-a-Mighty had inadvertently kicked over the laundry basket of the whole goddamned Heavenly Hotel, and I was counting for the pull on the rip cord" (174). Cudworth's quizzical, one-eyed squint joins the list of other Warrenian winks (along with the "eyelids *squinting* because there was nothing under them any more" that belonged to the Indian mummies in *At Heaven's Gate*). He winks at Jed, it appears (as did Tiny Duffy), because he has defied the father and gotten away with it—defied, that is, the prospective Wall Street father-in-law, who was doubtless as stunned as Aaron Blaustein had been when he heard Adam Rosenzweig decline the invitation to become his adopted son. In the process Cudworth achieves not only a sense of reality but eventually fatherhood, too. Just before he told Jed those two stories, he had announced to all of Carrington's guests the happy news that his wife had been "knocked up" (171). So it is a father—a newly announced one—whose bald head we see beneath the white cloth of his parachute. If the falling white sheets from God's kicked-over laundry basket anticipate the "white cloth ... flung ... carelessly" from the sculpted bald head later in the same chapter, both bald heads and both white cloths recall the "handkerchief / On great bald skull spread ..." of another father, *the* father in Warren, *his own* father reading "Freud on dreams, abandoned / By one of the children," in "Reading Late at Night, Thermometer Falling."[8]

Ultimately, despite our best efforts to keep autobiography out, it will, like the repressed, return. Although surely whatever appears in a poem, for example, can be analyzed in the same context as a work of fiction, especially in the case of such a writer as Warren, whose work in all genres is so remarkably of a piece, having the same underlying symbolic network. Still, we are analyzing the work, not the man.

So, in the light of that "bare hundred-watt bulb that glares / Like truth" above the handkerchief and the great bald skull, we need to trace one more set of connections. In *A Place to Come To* Warren twice names his protagonist a Joseph: by making him the father of Ephraim and by arranging for the Perseus-mugged woman to call him "*Guiseppino*, which is Little Joseph." Now the Freud of the book the poet leaves behind for his father to read, the filial text given in exchange for the paternal one later named in the same poem—the "poems. Not good" which his father had written in his youth—also identified himself with Joseph, his biblical forerunner in the art of interpreting dreams. "It will be noticed that the name Josef plays a great part in my dreams. . . . My own ego finds it very easy to hide itself behind people of that name, since Joseph is the name of a man famous in the Bible as an interpreter of dreams" (522n). Freud might also have mentioned that he shared something else with Joseph, a father named Jacob.[9]

The remarkable thing is that the book Warren pictures himself as leaving for his father to read in "Reading Late at Night" provides not only a key to understanding his novels, obsessed as they are with dreams, but also a strangely prophetic anticipation of the opening scene of Warren's last novel—what Old Buck was doing with his hand when he fell off the wagon—and of the way it combines with the recurring image of the one-eyed father. It happens in a dream Freud has about his own father:

> Once more I was in front of the station, but this time in the company of an elderly gentleman. I thought of a plan for remaining unrecognized; and then saw that this plan had already been put into effect. It was as though thinking and experiencing were one and the same thing. He appeared to be blind, at all events with one eye, and I handed him a male glass urinal (which we had to buy or had bought in town). So I was a sick-nurse and had to give him the urinal because he was blind. If the ticket-collector were to see us like that, he would be certain to let us get away without noticing us. Here the man's attitude and his micturating penis appeared in plastic form. (This was the point at which I awoke, feeling a need to micturate.)[10] (244)

The dream is patricidal to the extent that Freud's unconscious is expressing the disguised wish that his father "come to nothing." For that is the phrase he recalls his father once saying to him when as a boy he suffered incontinence in front of his parents.

> One evening before going to sleep I disregarded the rules which modesty lays down and obeyed the calls of nature in my parents' bedroom while they were present. In the course of his reprimand, my father let fall the words: "The boy will come to nothing." This must have been a frightful blow to my ambition, for references to this scene are still constantly recurring in my dreams and are always linked with an enumeration of my achievements and successes, as though I wanted to say: "You see, I *have* come to something." This scene, then, provided the material for the final episode of the dream, in which—in revenge, of course—the roles were interchanged. The older man (clearly my father, since his blindness in one eye referred to his unilateral glaucoma) was now micturating in front of me, just as I had in front of him in my childhood.... Moreover, I was making fun of him; I had to hand him the urinal because he was blind.... (250)

Like Freud, Jed Tewksbury made fun of his father's art of urination, reenacting in graduate school "the hilarious episode of his father's death" (22) in order to win friends and seduce women. And, like Freud, Warren's sons either have or encounter one-eyed fathers, for as we learn from Freud's interpretation of his own dream, his father was blind in one eye from glaucoma.

Furthermore, there is in Freud's dream as well as in the two accounts of Jed's father's death—the one on the first page of the novel versus the one Jed will concoct when he makes fun of it—the same ambiguity about whether the urination was not in fact something else. Marianne Krüll points out, "From the Fliess correspondence, we know that Freud replaced all references to his own sexuality with '*drekkologikal*' (fecal or urinary) statements, so that conscious censorship is probably the more likely explanation" of why Freud's father said "the boy will come to nothing" in the scene Freud tells us occurred in his parents' bedroom: "the discovery that his son, in whom he had placed such great hopes, was guilty of 'self-abuse' must have filled him with doubts about all his ambitious plans for Sigmund's future" (112). Krüll argues that

> the various urination scenes in Freud's dreams, which he himself associated with ambition, must either have been screen memories for masturbation or else conscious attempts to censor the dream content.... Now, if these urination scenes were in fact masturbation scenes, then Jacob's reaction becomes much more understandable. He was afraid that "the boy will come to nothing." The association of masturbation with ambition is in any case much more convincing than that of urination with ambition. (112)

And thus the father who urinates in the dream may likewise be engaged in a much less innocent activity—which would account for why the dreamer hopes he and his father will pass unnoticed:

> It is remarkable that, in his associations, Freud should have ignored an important element of the dream, the double attempt at concealment: "I thought of a plan for remaining unrecognized" and "the ticket-collector ... would be certain to let us get away without noticing us." Might Freud as a child have surprised his father in the act of masturbation? Or had he perhaps merely come upon him during urination but had so startled him as to gain the impression that he had caught him in some forbidden act? (113–14)

Now if this dream strangely anticipates the way in which Warren's last novel gives such special—indeed mythic—prominence to the doubly charged image of the father's golden stream, as well as to the son's mocking use of that response to nature's call (whichever call it was), another dream in the "Freud on dreams" Warren gave his father anticipates just as uncannily the primal myth that we have found to underlie all of Warren's fiction, the very ambiguity of Burden's forever imponderable question: was it a wink or not? And it appears as a text printed on something very like Perse's handbills (which, like the one in Freud's dream, were stuck up as posters:

"Over at Thebes they got 'em all over the settlement, on walls and telephone poles . . .") and also the printed notice that Jeremiah Beaumont interpreted as a message from the father:

> During the night before my father's funeral I had a dream of a printed notice, placard or poster—rather like the notices forbidding one to smoke in railway waiting-rooms—on which appeared either
>
>   "You are requested to close the eyes"
> or, "You are requested to close an eye."
>
> I usually write this in the form:
>
>   the
>   "You are requested to close eye(s)."
>   an
>
> Each of these two versions had a meaning of its own and led in a different direction when the dream was interpreted. I had chosen the simplest possible ritual for the funeral, for I knew my father's own views on such ceremonies. But some other members of the family were not sympathetic to such puritanical simplicity and thought we should be disgraced in the eyes of those who attended the funeral. Hence one of the versions: "You are requested to close an eye," i.e. to "wink at" or "overlook." (352–53)

Freud had earlier recounted this dream with some significant differences in a letter to Wilhelm Fleiss dated 2 November 1896, in the immediate aftermath of Jacob Freud's death on October 23:

> I must tell you about a very pretty dream I had on the night after the funeral. I found myself in a shop where there was a notice up saying:
>
>   You are requested
>   to close the eyes.
>
> I recognized the place as the barber's to which I go every day. (*Origins*, 171)

  What can account for the fact that in 1900, when *The Interpretation of Dreams* appeared, the locale of the dream had changed from a barbershop to a railway station and that a new ambiguity had been introduced into the request to close the eyes, making it impossible to decide if one is supposed to close one or both?[11] The editors of the Fleiss letters comment, with somewhat circular reasoning, that "Freud described this dream in slightly different terms, obviously with the aid of notes" (171n), apparently concluding that the 1900 version is more accurate because it is more detailed. But it is precisely the added detail—the alternative of one eye—that poses the problem. Wouldn't the letter, closer in time to the context of the dream, have been the more accurate account?[12] One can certainly, however, imagine an excellent reason for Freud's having changed the barbershop to a train station in the context of *The Interpretation of Dreams,* which is after all not just a scientific treatise but a literary work, and that is to tie it more closely to the other major dream about his father—which took place in a train station. Actually, in *The Interpretation of Dreams* Freud does not in fact say where he read the notice about closing the eye(s): by simply omitting all mention of a barbershop, and by saying that the notice is "like" the kind of notice one can see in a railway waiting-room, he is able to *suggest* the same locale in which the other dream takes place without actually lying. And for the same reason we can see why he might have wanted to add the part about closing just one eye, for the other father-dream made specific reference to his father's one-eyedness, although the result of that added detail is to create even more ambiguity in an already ambiguous text within the text of the dream. In the letter, Freud says that the command to close the eyes "has a double meaning. It means 'one should do one's duty towards the dead' in two senses—an apology, as though I had not done my duty and my conduct needed overlooking, and the actual duty itself" (*Origins,* 171). In the *Interpretation of Dreams* version, Freud no longer speaks of the second of these alternative meanings, the duty of closing the eyes of the dead, but locates the ambiguity in the conflicting commands. "Here it is particularly easy to see the meaning of the vagueness expressed by the 'either—or.' The dream-work failed to establish a unified wording for the dream-thoughts which could at the same time be ambiguous, and the two main lines of thought consequently began to diverge even in the manifest content of the dream" (353).

Warren, as we have seen, introduces "Freud on dreams" into the text of "Reading Late at Night"; but the close connections between that poem, with its handkerchief-covered father's bald skull and the white cloth-covered ones in *A Place to Come To,* not to mention all the ways those connections stretch out to include images recurring in all his novels, compel us to ask how much of that book is in fact introduced there, both in the poem and in the wider context of his fiction. Was it just the method of dream analysis, the concept of the dream-work of the unconscious, whose relevance for an analysis of Warren's novels, and particularly of the way dreams flow in and out of his work, is undeniably genuine? Or is some of the specific imagery of Freud's book on dreams introduced into Warren's text as well? The parallels between Freud's dreams about his father and the one long dream about the father that Warren's novels (and some of his poems) appear to embody are strong enough to make us think it might be so.

Perhaps it is as impossible to know the answer to these questions with any certainty as it is to determine whether what Willie gave Jack was a wink or not (or whether the command in Freud's second version of his dream was to wink or not, or even if the version with the wink is more accurate than the one without). Yet it is doubtless more prudent to assume that Warren knew well the text of which he spoke, the one he left behind for his father to read, than not. One thing he would surely have known is that the dream Freud experienced at the time of his father's death is the most important one in *The Interpretation of Dreams*. For in the preface to the second edition Freud says that the motivation for the entire book was his father's death:

> An equal durability and power to withstand any far-reaching alterations during the process of revision has been shown by the *material* of the book, consisting as it does of dreams of my own ... by which I illustrated the rules of dream-interpretation. For this book has a further subjective significance for me personally—a significance which I only grasped after I had completed it. It was, I found, a portion of my own self-analysis, my reaction to my father's death—that is to say, to the most important event, the most poignant loss, of a man's life. Having discovered that this was so, I felt unable to obliterate the traces of the experience. (xxvi)

This book on dreams thus begins with the declaration that the dreams it analyzes are to a large degree the author's own, that it is therefore an exercise in self-analysis, and that this self-analysis began with his father's death. So that the dream he had on the occasion of that death is itself the origin of the book. It is, as Jean-Louis Baudry has pointed out, the "inaugural dream" that began his self-analysis and that "caused him then to write the book on dreams" (145–46; my translation).

Thus Warren's last protagonist, the Jediah Tewksbury who eventually becomes a Joseph, may in the end turn out to be the fullest revelation of a Warrenian son. For Warren is that son, that Joseph, the same Joseph with whom Freud identified. And Freud on dreams is not just a text that can be usefully applied to Warren's but is already inscribed within it. Everything we think we can discover is already there.

Conclusion
"at the end of . . . life's long sorites"

The last of the paternal texts we shall try to read is perhaps the first one to appear in Warren's work, the "taciturn tall stone, / Which is your fathers' monument and mark," in a poem he wrote before his twentieth year. "To a Face in a Crowd" occupies a peculiar place in the canon Warren has created for his poetry. It is always the last poem in his self-selected anthologies, the *Thirty-six Poems* of 1935 and the four editions of *Selected Poems* published since 1943. The sequences from which selections are made in the *Selected Poems* appear in reverse chronological order, although the poems within each sequence do not, since such sequences as *Promises, Incarnations,* and *Being Here* have always been organized on something other than a chronological basis. "To a Face in a Crowd" not only always has the last word, and is Warren's oldest consistently republished poem, but it also has the distinction of being named in the title of each of the *Selected Poems,* as it alone accounts for the *1923* in *Selected Poems 1923–1943, . . . 1923–1966, . . . 1923–1975, . . . 1923–1985.*

"To a Face in a Crowd" marked the beginning, in Warren's estimation, of his literary career. For the reader of these backward glances at his significant production, thanks to the choice he made over forty years ago, it is the taciturn text, the blank stone at the end of the journey that says little or nothing, in the same implacable monotone.

> Brother, my brother, whither do you pass?
> . . . .
> In dream, perhaps, I have seen your face before.
>
> A certain night has borne both you and me;
> We are the children of an ancient band
> Broken between the mountains and the sea.
> A cromlech marks for you that utmost strand
>
> And you must find the dolorous place they stood.
> Of old I know that shore, that dim terrain,

And know how black and turbulent the blood
Will beat through iron chambers of the brain

When at your back the taciturn tall stone,
Which is your fathers' monument and mark,
Repeats the waves' implacable monotone,
Ascends the night and propagates the dark.
....

Warren's partly autobiographical 1980 essay *Jefferson Davis Gets His Citizenship Back,* by stressing the importance of another blank monument as a screen for the projection of his youthful literary desire, presents a tantalizing parallel to this taciturn stone. In 1917, when he was "nearly twelve," Warren kept returning to Fairview, Kentucky, just up the road from Guthrie, "to stare at the ... gray-white shaft" (23), the "great monolith" (12) of the unfinished concrete monument to the president of the Confederacy. It seemed to be trying to speak: "Was the blank shaft that was rising there trying to say something about that war of long ago ... ? Was the tall shaft, now stubbed at the top, what history was?" (24). And it seemed as well that the boy was trying to force some significance out of that blank stone by the effort of staring at it: "In any case, as I fumble at recollection and try to immerse myself in the dark flow of that moment, it seems that in facing the blank-topped monument I was trying to focus some meaning, however hard to define, on the relation of past and present ..." (25). Six decades later, recently refurbished, the Jefferson Davis monument seemed "somehow, suddenly, meaningless" (110).

The parallel between the Davis monolith that seemed to have something to tell that it never disclosed and the fathers' taciturn tall stone is uncannily enhanced by the fact that Davis—as Warren takes the trouble to mention no less than three times in this brief book—was, like so many father figures in his fiction, blind in one eye: his face "twitched with neuralgia"—one thinks of the old hitchhiker in *All the King's Men* whose twitch presaged a wink that never came—and his "left eye was bleared in blindness" (31). "He was now past fifty, erect but even more gaunt-cheeked, blind in one eye ..." (51). "Davis's blind eye—blind for years now—prompted him ... to reach back into his memory for Milton: 'Oh dark, dark, dark, amid the blaze of noon; / Irrevocably dark, total eclipse without the hope of day'" (77).

The same conjunction had already occurred in Warren's "Folly on Royal Street Before the Raw Face of God" (in *Or Else*). That is, these very lines were the response he made to a certain one-eyedness then, though in this instance it was not semiblindness but a wink, and not his own wink but the Father's: "God's / Raw face stared down. / / And winked. / / We / Mouthed out our Milton for magnificence." The "Milton" there mouthed was, evidently, these parodying first lines of Warren's poem: "Drunk, drunk drunk, amid the blaze of noon, / Irrevocably drunk, total eclipse. . . ." We saw in *Flood* how this eclipse of God is thematically linked both to the disappearance of the father and to the father's missing eye. There God has vanished into the death of the sun; all that is left is the "black hole in the sky God left when He went away" (166). "It looked like the death of the sun. . . . It was like last week's *Time* magazine. The sun was already, in fact, dead" (28)—for it was precisely from an outdated copy of *Time* magazine that Brad Tolliver learned of the death of Ramon Echegaray (334), the rival who had seduced Brad's wife by staring at her with his black hole of a missing eye (148). So that, through the *Time* connection, it is clear that Echegaray and God occupy the same space. And that the empty space God left behind is same place where Brad looks in vain for his father's corpse: "hunched, shivering, in that room, in his overcoat, the beam of the flashlight on that spot, the same spot over there where the coffin had been . . ." (196). The same coffin, ultimately, that Cass Mastern "had the impulse to hurl . . . to the ground and see its emptiness burst open" (172).

In its very first appearance, in the June 1925 issue of *The Fugitive*, "To a Face in the Crowd" (as its title was then) was immediately preceded by another of Warren's poems, which has never been republished. Because he evidently wrote both at the same time in his life, and because they share some of the same imagery, "Mr. Dodd's Son" may help us to interpret its one-time companion. In the now-forgotten poem the protagonist comes off sounding very much like a young Penn Warren from rural Kentucky who regrets having been born so far from such more poetically inspiring regions as windswept beaches—like young Seth of "Blackberry Winter," for whom the red mud of that same landlocked region would have to make do for "the glistening auroral beach of the world."

> He was born far inland in a little town
> That sent no men in ships down to the sea,
> And beyond her dusty streets had only known
> Green mains of the wheatfield tossing silently.

Only by putting his ear to a shell imported from such a shore can he hear that authentic sound that has the power to remind him of what he has heard before, in a dream, where it was, even then, something that reminded him of something else:

> If in her steeples never there tolled a bell
> For lovely keels that left her but to be lost,

> At least in chambers of the deep whorled shell
> Reverberation lingered like the ghost
>
> Of reminiscent music in a dream.

Yet, as he must have surely been aware, since it is one of the most universal of childhood realizations, what one hears in a seashell is the magnified echo of one's own blood. Indeed, he evidently was aware, for in "To a Face in the Crowd" this is precisely what one will hear if one goes to the beach to stand between the paternal monolith and the sea, as the "chambers of the deep whorled shell" in the first of these two poems will become what they originally echoed, the "iron chambers of the brain" in the other ("And know how black and turbulent the blood / Will beat through iron chambers of the brain . . ."). Mr. Dodd's son will finally get to that beach, but when he does he will be afflicted with speechlessness:

> Before he died unto the sea he came;
> He could not speak—as one who suddenly
> Hears in the night beyond the coasts of time
> Faintly the surges of eternity.

"In the Turpitude of Time: N.D.," from the "Mortmain" series in *You, Emperors, and Others,* shows us the poet, as in "To a Face in a Crowd," on the beach by a stone that tries to speak and, like "Mr. Dodd's Son," is unable to give utterance. "Can we—oh, could we only—know / What annelid and osprey believe, / And the stone, night-long, groans to divulge? / If only we could, then . . . might . . . between the stone and the wind's voice / A silence wait to become our song. . . ." The stone is evidently the taciturn one by the ocean in "To a Face in a Crowd" that was the "fathers' monument and mark"—all the more so because of the fact that the "Mortmain" series tells the story of his father's death. The first poem recounts the death itself, with the last gesture of a hand that "Like an eyelid . . . sank"; the second imagines the father as a young man "Circa 1885"; in the third the son finds the paternal text he left behind, a Greek grammar; while the fifth imagines him again in his youth, "Circa 1880." "In the Turpitude of Time: N.D.," the fourth in the series, seems at first glance to have no immediate reference to the father—until, that is, we realize that he is there in the stone that groans, night-long, to speak.[1]

The groaning that is the attempt to speak may be all the speech one gets to hear, for already implicit in the conjunction of those two poems in *The Fugitive*—which are printed on the front and back of the same sheet, as it happens (pp. 35–36)—and especially in the echo of the *chambers* that reverberate from one poem to the next, is the suspicion that what the father's stone has to say has no intention in it, that it is nothing but the automatic echo of the waves' implacable monotone, just as the ghostly dream music Mr. Dodd's son hears in the chambers of the shell is nothing more than the echo of the blood beating in his brain. What the father's monument and mark has to say may thus be no more than the reflection of something else, as the eyes of the fathers in the novels display a glimmer of intent that may have a trivially physical cause—just the warmth of the blood, in fact: "only some fluctuation of the fever . . . in that fading brain" (Hans Meyerhof, in *Wilderness,* in this instance).

That paternal monolith is nevertheless the object of the poet's pilgrimage, particularly in the sense that he keeps returning to the poem in which it appears at the end of every edition of the *Selected Poems.* However, what "To a Face in a Crowd" actually recounts, or projects, is not the poet's journey to that beach and that stone (for he has already been there) but someone else's—the brother he passes, whose face he has seen in dream before, the reader he here encourages to make the same voyage: "you must find the dolorous place," he tells us, and if you do "we must meet / As weary nomads in this desert at last. . . ." If, that is, we take the risk of wandering the deserted beach and listening for the father's lithic text to speak, even though we may never know for certain if its taciturnity means it has, in the end, nothing to say, we will at least have met the author on his own terrain.

Another *Fugitive* poem, never since reprinted, recounts a similar pilgrimage, whose goal is defined by a similarly ambivalent void.[2] In "Crusade," published in the June-July 1923 issue (pp. 90–91), the young poet has to all appearances donned the clanking armor of romantic medievalism in an impetuous attempt to storm the battlements of poetry by telling a "poetic" tale—the poetry supposedly inherent in the subject. Yet even in this product of his immaturity Warren, with what in retrospect seems remarkable consistency, discovers what the protagonist of *Flood* will still be thinking about forty years later, the hole God left when he went away: "We have not forgot the clanking of grey armors / . . . The close hush of the rabble as we made our vow / To win the Tomb of God—that was our mission / . . . . We have now won through . . . to the Tomb of God; / Here is a hole where once lay sacred bones." And the ambiguous emptiness of that hole (ambiguous because it might not mean that God is dead but that he is risen) is remarkably like the taciturnity of the father's monument and mark that Warren was discovering at about the same time.

Placing the poem with the father's stone at the end of every *Selected Poems* is one way Warren has of saying what is left in the end, a taciturn paternal text that may just be an empty screen for his own imagination;

another way is to pose the question and answer it, as he does at the end of "Aspen Leaf in Windless World," in *Being Here*:

> What image—behind blind eyes when the nurse steps back—
> Will loom at the end of your own life's long sorites?
> Would a sun then rise red on an eastern horizon of waters?
> Would you see a face? What face? Would it smile? Can you say?
>
> Or would it be some great, sky-thrusting gray menhir?
> Or what, in your long-lost childhood, one morning you saw—
> Tinfoil wrappers of chocolate, popcorn, nut shells, and poorly
> Cleared up, the last elephant turd on the lot where the circus had been?

The sorites spoken of here is evidently a "series of propositions, in which the predicate of each is the subject of the next, the conclusion being formed of the first subject and the last predicate" (*O.E.D.*); in Greek it originally meant "heaped up": "a *sorites* or *heap of syllogisms,* the conclusion of one forming the premiss of the next" (Liddell and Scott). The last image one sees acquires a sense of finality from nothing but chance; it just happens to be the last thing one sees, and the chain could have been indefinitely continued. Yet, in this instance at least, each of the four elements in the chain, as haphazardly as they may seem to have been chosen, could be taken to represent the father. We have seen how the death of the sun parallels his disappearance; the face could certainly be his; while the menhir is clearly a version of his taciturn tall stone. The paternal resonance of the last of the four is a little harder to see, but that makes it all the more interesting.

If we were to explore what connotations elephants have here—not just in this poem but in the poetic sequence in which it appears, *Being Here*—we would have to consider "Snowshoeing Back to Camp in Gloaming," where "Hillward and sky-thrust, behind me, / Leafless and distanced to eastward, a huge / Beech clung to its last long twinge / Of pink on the elephant-gray...." The elements of the "sun" that would "rise red on an eastern horizon," the first of those four possible last visions, appear here in "eastward" and in the "pink" of this sun. Elements of the "sky-thrusting gray menhir" repeat the "sky-thrust" "gray" beech, while the elephantine quality of that gray anticipates the "last elephant...." Even that "last" had already appeared in the "*last* long twinge...." That what is elephant-gray is a beech is also meaningful in *Being Here*, for elsewhere in this sequence, in "No Bird Does Call," we learned that the beech was the father, whose gold engendered the poet upon Danaë's lavished lap. Thus the "sky-thrusting gray menhir" is even more clearly the equivalent of the "sky-thrust ... / Beech."

We can now understand how something that comes from an elephant could qualify as a meaningful last glimpse at the end of life's long sorites, but why this particular thing? In "Reading at Night, Thermometer Falling," another account of his father's death, the son discovers something strangely like it. His father

> ... aged eighty-six, fell to the floor,
> Unconscious. Two days later,
> Dead. Thus they discovered your precious secret:
> A prostate big as a horse-apple. Cancer, of course.
>
> No wonder you, who had not spent a day in bed,
> Or uttered a single complaint, in the fifty years of my life,
>
> Cried out at last.

"Horse-apple" has two senses, the fruit of the osage tree and equine excrement. Here it is more likely the former; but the latter should not be entirely ruled out, given the importance elsewhere assigned its elephantine equivalent. And given, too, what happens in *Band of Angels*. There, as in the poem, a father dies after giving birth to a horse-apple (with the difference that there the son acts as midwife). When the boy Hamish Bond told his mother that he didn't believe her constant boasting about having been born into a wealthy slaveholding family, he provoked a sudden outburst from his father. " 'The laugh was awful. His face wasn't laughing, but his mouth was open and that awful sound was coming out.... Maybe now that I got him free of the horse-apple of a lie he had lived with all that time, maybe there wasn't anything to live for now' " (183). This, too, is evidently the vegetal definition. But, significantly, the other meaning had already appeared in Hamish Bond's New Orleans courtyard when Amantha Starr saw a horse "letting two or three great golden apples of manure drop with solid ripeness to the brick" (99). Within the novel the instances of horse-apple answer each other, one occurring before the other in the narration but succeeding it as an event in Bond's life; indeed, the wealth Bond accrues and displays in the luxuries of his New Orleans mansion (especially his slaves) is the real opulence to which his mother had only pretended, in that "horse-apple of a lie."

The horses from which these apples come have a paternal resonance in Warren. In "The Mission" (from *Now and Then*) they stand silently by the ocean like the taciturn ancestral stone, "like gray stone" (like the elephant-*gray* beech), "like stone primitively hewn":

> ... I wake from a dream of horses. They do not know
> I am dreaming of them. By this time they must be long dead.
>
> Behind barbed wire, in fog off the sea, they stand.
>   ... like gray stone, stand ...

> . . . if I stare at the dark ceiling
> And try to remember, I do not have to go back to sleep,
> And not sleeping, will not again dream
>
> Of clumps of horses, fog-colored in sea fog. . . .
> . . . standing like stone primitively hewn. . . .

This is a dream about the father, not only dead but possibly murdered, which may explain why the poet does not want to go back to sleep to dream that dream again. The poem begins its own dream analysis as the poet realizes that the motionless stone horses are standing in a specific place, on the shore of the Bay of Biscay in southwest France, and that he must have remembered that "*La boucherie chevaline,* in the village, / Has a gold horse-head above the door." The dreamer knows that he has dreamed of horses because he saw the sign (that it was the "day residue" that brought horses to the dream), and that the reason he is so certain that "They are dead" is because of what the sign really means: equine butchery. The reader of Warren's poems who is willing to read them like dreams will realize that the poet dreams of dead stone horses for another reason as well: because when the father died, what he left his son is what a horse leaves, a "precious secret" as worthy of the son's (and our) attempt at decipherment as the last heap of elephant dung discovered among "Tinfoil wrappers of chocolate, popcorn, nut shells . . . on the lot where the circus has been."

That last detail from "Aspen Leaf"'s last vision recalls the other dream, the "original dream which / I am now trying to discover the logic of," in "I Am Dreaming of a White Christmas." There, too, the poet found himself staring at what was left after the giver of gifts had come and gone:

> On
> The ashes, gray, a piece of torn orange peel.
> Foil wrappings of chocolates, silver and crimson and gold,
> Yet gleaming from grayness.

Among the detritus on the Christmas hearth and that in the circus lot one can find least one common remnant: tinfoil wrappers of chocolate. Could it be that the original dream and the last item in life's sorites are not only linked but the same thing, another attempt to name "What present there was in that package for me, / Under the Christmas tree?" In other words, could the logic of that original dream be in part soritic logic, where the first and last terms of an indefinitely long series turn out to be the same ("the conclusion being formed of the first subject and the last predicate"): could the content of the package that his dream would not let him open be what can ultimately be discovered behind the troubling object of life's last glimpse? Could the ultimate text bequeathed from father to son, nourished for years inside him, growing in secret, finally reveal itself, in a parody of childbirth, as a kind of ancient fetus?

The "precious secret" the father reveals in death assumes, in "One I Knew" (from *Rumor Verified*), the form of something living, like a fetus, and straining to be born.

> It was as though he leaned
> At a large mysterious bud
> To watch, hour by hour,
> How at last it would divulge
> A beauty so long withheld—
> As I once had sat
>   . . . watching
> The bud of a century plant
> That was straining against the weight
> Of years, slow, slow, in silence,
> To offer its inwardness.

The son finds that he himself had already performed an unwitting parody, before the event ("As I once had sat . . ." puts his century plant vigil in a more distant past than his father's death), of his father's secret study of the growth of his cancer, as he waited for it to emerge and blossom forth into its parody of life that is in fact death (when it blooms, too, the century plant dies). The son discovers, in other words, that he had already been reading something like the text—the century plant, the horse-apple, the inner fetus—that had been the object of his father's most secret scrutiny.

That what the father leaves the son in this instance is indeed a text is made clear by what the father was doing at the very moment the blossoming of that mysterious bud caused him to lose consciousness:

>   he
> Collapsed and, unconscious, slid
> To the floor, pen yet in hand.
> They revived him only for
> The agony of the end.
>   . . . Later,
> I found the letter, the first
> Paragraph unfinished. I saw
> The ink-slash from that point
> Where the unconscious hand had dragged
> The pen as he fell. I saw
> The salutation. It was:
> "Dear Son."

> The shimmering
> White petal—the gold stamen—
> Were at last, in triumph,
> Divulged. On the dusty carpet.

Although the letter is unfinished, something is divulged: the triumph of the flower, its "inwardness" brought to light, opened at last to the gaze of the poet, who elsewhere was for so long denied the knowledge of what "was in that package for me...." And something else is divulged, at last: The taciturn father's text that keeps appearing in so many other forms in Warren's oeuvre is now quite literally a text, the briefest imaginable, addressed to the only reader who can answer its incompleteness: "Dear Son."

Notes

Introduction

1. The beeches acquire more and more reason for being where they are as the story subtending his fiction unfolds. They will not appear here until chapter 5 (where they are the name in a dream the dreamer knows he knows but cannot remember), but from that point on they begin to form a subplot to that story, whose main plot has to do with the recurring images of the dream in *Night Rider*. In the end, the name of the original dreamer reveals—or acquires—its true meaning, one that in the final chapter is shown to bear a filial relation to the name in the other dream, which made its first appearance as a forgotten name. Like Warren's protagonists, then, we too will be engaged in a search for that paternal text, the father's name—and the son's.

2. This anticipates Paul de Man's more recent declaration that "the only irreducible 'intention' of a text is that of its constitution" (65).

3. According to which the creative process is a basically rational mining of the unconscious and not "merely an expression of the unconscious" (287). I agree that it is not the latter, for to say that the creative process is governed by the rules by which the unconscious works is not to say that it is merely the unconscious speaking.

4. My understanding of Warren is indebted to such precursors as James Justus, Marshall Walker, Barnett Guttenberg, and Leonard Casper—Justus in particular, because of the comprehensiveness of his reading of Warren and the accuracy of his insights into his declared, as well as unconscious, intent.

5. It will be important to remember that in "I Am Dreaming of a White Christmas" Warren did not say he wanted to recover the dream itself, but its *logic*. And though this search is echoed in both the figures of the Christmas present he is forbidden to open and the unwrapped object in *Night Rider*'s dream, I wish to caution the reader not to hope to find a *presence* in that present, some hidden truth, some tangible—say—biographical detail in Warren's life that will explain all. It might be more reasonable to expect the revelation of an *absence*. Shoshana Felman has recently written of such an absence of meaning when she contrasts Jacques Lacan's approach to Edgar Allan Poe's "The Purloined Letter" to the more traditional one of Marie Bonaparte, who represents the school of psychoanalytic literary criticism that seeks ultimate answers in the biography of the author. The

latter sees the analyst's job as being to uncover the content of the stolen letter in Poe's story, "which she believes—as do the police—to be hidden somewhere in the real, in some secret biographical depth. For Lacan, on the other hand, the analyst's task is not to read the letter's hidden referential content, but to situate the superficial indication of its textual movement, to analyze the paradoxically invisible symbolic evidence of its displacement, its structural insistence, in a signifying chain. . . . The history of reading has accustomed us to the assumption . . . that reading is finding meaning, that interpretation can dwell only on the meaningful. Lacan's analysis of the signifier opens up a radically new assumption, an assumption that is an insightful logical and methodological consequence of Freud's discovery: that what *can* be read (and perhaps what *should* be read) is not just meaning but the lack of meaning . . ." (44–45). In the case of Poe's "Purloined Letter" this means that Lacan is more interested in the triangular structural relationships that duplicate themselves in the text among those characters involved in the letter's circulation than he is in its actual content, which Poe (quite rightly, surely, for Lacan) never reveals. Poe's story spectacularly illustrates this way of reading any literary text—and so can Robert Penn Warren's. All the more so because Warren will, in the end, make absence itself thematic.

Chapter 1

1. Yet the buzzards in "Pondy Woods"—who, like the sun-gazing hawks and eagle, drift "high in the pure sunshine / Till the sun in gold decline"—do possess at least the nobility of "hieratic" eyes ("Then golden and hieratic through / The night their eyes burn two by two").

2. The words with which *Night Rider*'s sentence about the buzzard begins—"At a great height"—are the last words of the poem in which Warren contemplates the flight of wild geese, "Heart of Autumn": "I stand . . . my arms outstretched in the tingling / Process of transformation, and soon tough legs, / / With folded feet, trail in the sounding vacuum of passage, / And my heart is impacted with a fierce impulse / To unwordable utterance— / Toward sunset, at a great height." Just as Munn would have liked to repeat the Senator's eloquence but could not (at least not at first), so here the poet yearns to duplicate the flight of the geese. And as Munn made the nothingness he perceived the substance of his speech, here the poet speaks of a vacuum that sounds—and of an unwordable utterance. On birds in Warren, see Harold Bloom, "Sunset Hawk: Warren's Poetry and Tradition," and Sister Bernetta Quinn, "Gull Against a Crimson Sky: Birds in the Later Poems of Robert Penn Warren." Bloom argues that the stuffed hawk in "Red-Tail Hawk and Pyre of Youth" is "text" (72); while for Calvin Bedient the red-tail hawk is the father (190). I agree with both (as I argue in *The Braided Dream*): it is the father, transformed by the poet's taxidermy into text. This conjunction of father and text is at the heart of my reading of Warren.

3. Leonard Casper's implied answer to this question—"Ball . . . keeps his own hands disguised under antiseptic bandages" (102), that is, the Professor manages in this symbolic way to keep his hands clean—is plausible, but cannot account for all that echoes his bandages elsewhere in the novel.

4. The "patches of white cloud no bigger than a man's hand" echo a well-known biblical verse from the story of Elijah, 1 Kings 18:44: "Behold, there ariseth a little cloud out of the sea, like a man's hand." At a time of drought, the prophet had predicted rain from a sky as cloudless as the one in whose empty blue incandescence the Senator lifted his hand. What happened at the command of that hand—the first spatter of applause that broke out sporadically like the first drops of a rainstorm ("like the first heavy, individual, tumescent drops exploding upon the dry roof before the storm breaks in full volume")—seems, too, a retelling of the long-delayed rain announced by the hand of cloud. Warren does, in fact, retell it in the poem"Elijah on Mount Carmel": "sky darkened, / Rain fell, drouth broke, for God had hearkened. . . ."

5. Mr. Morphee's name was evidently Morphée in its original French, which is Morpheus in that tongue to which Warren will continue to have recourse in subsequent novels for the slyly hidden meanings of proper names.

6. Although he might have noticed as he rode out that night, had he been paying attention, that his assiduous search for the truth was leading him into something like a trap: "The almost bare boughs of the trees made a *web-like* pattern of shadow on the road" (58).

7. The distancing ability that writing has—of which newspapers are but one example—is a recurring theme in Warren. Any medium will do, even mud, as the boy Seth proves in "Blackberry Winter" when he seeks to make on it the "perfect mark" of his foot. Once the mark is made, it ceases to be *his* mark. The distancing has been accomplished, and you can "then muse upon it as though you had suddenly come upon that single mark on the glistening auroral beach of the world" (*The Circus in the Attic,* 64).

8. Discovering the father's texts, both those he owned and those he wrote, is a scene Warren will later retell more than once. In "Fox-Fire: 1956" it was his father's old Greek grammar: "Years later, I find the old grammar, yellowed. . . . [I]n the dark, / Amid History's vice and vacuity, that poor book burns / Like fox-fire in the black swamp of the world's error." In the quite recent *Portrait of a Father,* he recalls the discovery of *The Poets of America,* a vanity anthology in which his father had published several poems. "The discovery was, in itself, a profound and complex surprise" (41).

9. This symbolism is all the more resonant because of yet another literary allusion, and a suppressed name. Isabella Ball, the loyal daughter who contributed to the framing of Percy Munn for her father's crime by pretending to do him the favor of telling him to get out of town, was originally supposed to have been called Desdemona (remember that the Professor gave all his daughters Shakespearean names). But when Mrs. Ball asked her husband, "didn't the book say that the man she ran off and married was colored?" Ball decided "to spare even the tenderest sensibility. So we named the baby Isabella" (257). And so the woman who gives Munn the advice to leave town, thereby completing the illusion that he was guilty of a crime he did not commit, was meant to have been named for one who was likewise framed for a crime she did not commit, and against whom the most incriminating piece of evidence was a missing handkerchief. A handkerchief from Thebes is missing in Munn's story too, although he doesn't know it. And there is some measure of poetic justice here, for Munn, though not guilty of that murder,

is responsible for the deaths of four other men: the black on Mr. May's place who was hanged for Treveylan's crime, Trevelyan, Benton Todd, and Bill Christian, who died from the stroke brought on by Munn's adultery with his daughter. The very fact that Isabella was *not* named Desdemona makes this all the more intriguing, as well as making it all the more apparent that something in *Night Rider* is doing what the unconscious does in dreams: disguising the truth the better to express it.

Chapter 2

1. Richard Law points out the irony of Warren's casting "Slim Sarrett, who is a pathological liar, poseur, and murderer, as a New Critic." Sarrett's talk about pure and impure poetry sounds remarkably like what Warren was writing in "Pure and Impure Poetry" in 1943, the same year *At Heaven's Gate* was published. "Not only do these ideas obviously resemble Warren's," Law continues, "but Sarrett's narrative style becomes at times a parody of the author's mannerisms: his attempts to catch the fullness of the moment in the impurity of its components exaggerate Warren's familiar techniques (see, for instance, Sarrett's life story as told to Sue Murdock)" (93–95).

2. Leonard Casper, too, notes some other common ground between *At Heaven's Gate* and the contemporaneous *Eleven Poems* (107).

3. There is, in fact, a key to the gate in the title's allusion to its original source, for in *Cymbeline* Cloten obscenely jokes with his musicians about how he hopes their efforts will open up erotic opportunities for him with Imogen: "If you can penetrate her with your fingering, so; we'll try with tongue too" [2.3.14–15], suggesting what kind of heaven lies beyond those gates.

Chapter 3

1. By calling this gesture a wink here and elsewhere in this chapter, I do not mean to conclude that it was one. It might, after all, as Stark suggested, have been a blink. There is no more convenient term, "ambiguous eyelid closure" being more accurate but somewhat cumbersome. Imagine that "wink" appears here within quotation marks.

2. Taken by itself, Willie's ambiguous eye movement can prove irritating to a reader, who may conclude from its inconclusiveness that Warren made a mistake in leaving it so unresolved. Thus Erwin R. Steinberg cites the wink as evidence that "[n]either Jack nor the reader is ever to be sure of what motivates Willie Stark or of what he thinks" (18) and finds it "a cause for dissatisfaction, even for frustration. Perhaps it is this frustration that makes one feel that the devices used by Warren to prevent the reader from understanding Willie Stark . . . are artificial" (27–28).

3. John Edward Hardy writes that "Jack Burden . . . is in his relationship to Willie both Odysseus [that is, father] and Telemachus [son] by turns. (One can hardly miss the significance of the transformation of Stark from 'Cousin Willie,' the 'plowboy' and 'teacher's pet,' who was glad to meet '*Mr.* Burden' to 'the Boss' who,

when some years later they reminisce about the occasion of their first encounter, specifically addresses Jack as 'boy.')" (165).

4. John Edward Hardy, though he claims that "it is both Willie and Jack ... who are Humpty" (161), has noticed the resemblance to Duffy, who "teeters precariously for an instant on the edge of the stand before crashing to the ground—enacting here, obviously, a slapstick comic version of the Humpty role" (162). He notes as well that the way Willie "picked up the pieces and put him back together" is "a variation on the nursery-rhyme imagery."

5. Like Uriah (2 Sam. 11:15), Bellerophon was the unwitting bearer of his own death warrant. His story is told in the sixth book of the *Iliad*.

6. Not only his name but that of the place where he fell contains fragments of the name to which the novel's title alludes: DUffY, UPTon.

7. Jack pleads guilty to the deaths of both Adam and Stark, "of having delivered his two friends into each other's hands and death" (436). Tiny Duffy, of course, and Sadie Burke, are more immediately blamable; but it should also be pointed out that in the end the responsibility for the death of both of Jack's fathers, Stark and Judge Irwin, really belongs to a *fetus*—the one inside Sybil Frey. It is how the plot works: it was to counter the advantage MacMurfee had acquired from his knowledge of her pregnancy and Tom's possible paternity that Willie made Jack confront the Judge with the information about Mortimer Littlepaugh, which led to Irwin's suicide. Willie had counted on that information to force the Judge to make MacMurfee give up his plans. But with the Judge dead, the only card Willie had left to play was to give the hospital contract to Gummy Larson, which Tiny Duffy had been trying to get him to do all along, because Tiny stood to profit handsomely from the kickback. That would be a blow against MacMurfee, in his whose camp Larson had been. So he does, but then when Tom is gravely injured in a football game, Willie reneges on the deal because now he wants to name the hospital for Tom and cannot bear to have any "evil" involved in its construction. Stark's abominable treatment—abominable even to Jack's jaded eyes—of Tiny Duffy is most prominent in the scenes connected with this incident: when he first awards the contract to Larson but manages to splash a drink in Tiny's face all the same (362) because he is taking out his anger on him for having to do what he doesn't want to do; and later, when he tells Duffy that Larson cannot have the contract after all (387). It is immediately afterward that Duffy calls Adam Stanton to tell him all about Anne and Stark. And even though it was Sadie who told Duffy to do it, his disappointment over losing what he had striven for for so long surely fueled his eagerness to comply. Had the fetus not existed, Stark would never have been forced to give Larson the contract on which he later reneged, and Duffy would not have had to endure the ultimate disgrace of telling Larson the deal was up.

8. Mastern's impulse, in fact the entire novel (and quite possibly the two that precede it), is anticipated by yet another mysterious package, one that in "*All the King's Men*: The Matrix of Experience" Warren says he found in the hand of a "mythological figure" who stands at the origin of his novel. In September 1934, Warren left Tennessee to begin his new teaching assignment at Louisiana State University. "Along the way I picked up a hitchhiker—a country man, the kind you call a red-neck or a wool-hat, aging, aimless, nondescript, beat up by life and hard times and bad luck, clearly tooth-broke and probably gut-shot, standing beside the

road in an attitude that spoke of infinite patience and considerable fortitude, holding a parcel in his hand, wrapped in old newspaper.... He was, though at the moment I did not sense it, a mythological figure" (76). He was such a figure because he represented the countless poor who loved Huey Long and were grateful for all he had done. But in the context of all the other newspaper packages and their equivalents in Warren's first three novels, the myth he embodied may have had another dimension of which Warren might not have been consciously aware. In any event, this hitchhiker "became, it would seem, the old hitchhiker whom Jack Burden picks up returning from Long Beach, California, the old man with the twitch in the face that gives Jack the idea for the Great Twitch. But my old hitchhiker had had no twitch in his face" (81).

9. I refer to the logic of the *recurring* dream: Munn's original dream of a package whose contents he thinks he can identify as its torn newspaper wrapping shreds away, together with the way handkerchiefs and newsprint become interchangeable both there and in *At Heaven's Gate*, contribute to the enormous resonance of the gesture Jack's mother makes when she discloses his father's true identity (Judge Irwin): "Her hands twisted and tore the handkerchief she held before her at the level of her waist.... She flung down the shredded handkerchief and ran off..." (429). She had appeared to him at the beginning of this scene "like somebody who has fallen into deep water" (428); in the recurring dream Munn's wife approaches him slowly, as though her feet were weighted with lead, echoing the deep-water scene of the ballad he had just heard of Pretty Polly, who had sunk beneath the sea and held out her infant before her—at waist level, surely, as Munn's wife "held out" (317) the disintegrating bundle and Burden's mother the shredded handkerchief. To both the dreamer and Jack Burden what is ultimately revealed is the father.

Chapter 4

1. I have taken that risk in *The Braided Dream: Robert Penn Warren's Late Poetry*.

2. *Being Here: Poetry 1977–1980*, one of Warren's most closely integrated poetic sequences, bears a similar, though more informative, notice concerning the rearrangement its contents have undergone: "The order of the poems is not the order of composition.... The order and selection are determined thematically, but with echoes, repetitions, and variations in feeling and tonality" (107). Although we do not know in exactly what order the stories were written, we do know that "Testament of Flood" and "The Love of Elsie Barton: A Chronicle," which first appeared in print in 1935 and 1946, respectively, were originally meant to appear together in chapters 2 through 4 of the untitled, uncompleted, and unpublished novel Warren wrote in 1933–34.

3. He is also in chapter 9 of the unpublished novel "God's Own Time."

4. I hope it will be understood that by equating femininity with passivity I am dealing with a certain set of stereotypes accepted by the citizens of a fictional town, Bardsville.

5. Substitutability reigns here, as it does in dreamwork: Bolton's wife is a stand-in for Sara Darter, who is likewise one for Bolton's mother, as the fact that they both utter wild and uninterpretable cries suggests.

6. James Scott notes Viola's awkward gait, as well as some of the instances of foot and shoe symbolism, in *The Circus in the Attic*.

7. Warren suggests a similar linkage in " 'Blackberry Winter': A Recollection" when he notes the irony of the resemblance between Old Jebb's name and that of the "dashing Confederate cavalryman" J. E. B. Stuart (642).

8. Shakespeare was older than Webster, a point the book Steve was reading stresses: "After Shakespeare there developed a drama which, in comparison with the broad sympathy and humanity of the great bard, rightly deserves the name of decadent. But John Webster is sometimes capable of real poetic feeling, if not scope . . ." (168). Steve's feeling of triumph after he repeats the line from the play consists in large measure of feeling older—"much older; older than Frank Barber" (169)—as if he had experienced an anxiety of belatedness.

9. What Steve is projecting here, upon a flat surface, is in fact Frank Barber's sexual prowess, for later in the paragraph someone will make a joke about Barber's probable intimacy with Helen by metaphorizing it as "spring plowing." The line that follows the one cited here hints at the same sexual imagery: "Behind the man the earth split open like a ripe melon."

10. In the untitled novel Steve is in fact Thomas Adams's son.

11. It is not perhaps by chance that the engagement in which Bolton's father received his wound was the Battle of *Franklin* (18), the one part of Robert Franklin Warren's name that was entirely his own and not inherited by his son, nor fortuitous that it was Warren's *left* eye that was lost in a childhood accident (see chapter 9 on this point, where a deformed leg will likewise play a significant role).

Chapter 5

1. Jeremiah had, in the short-lived land speculation venture with Josh Parham, traveled to western Kentucky to do some surveying; this is evidently "the West" to which he refers in the dream.

2. I am fudging a bit here, but I think justifiedly. The dream speaks of "the names of the trees" in the plural, whereas I am reducing these names to one: the beech. I believe the plurality in the dream is part of the disguise, a disguise partly lifted at the other end of the dream when the narrator speaks of another "name" (singular) whose impossibility to recall is compared to that of the trees'.

3. Actually, Warren's own command of French is not perfect either. When he has the Gran Boz tell Beaumont " '*Autrefois—autrefois—*you tell me *autrefois—*how you keel—*maintenant j'ai sommeil,*' " he evidently means *une autre fois*, "some other time"; *autrefois* would mean "formerly," "once, in the past"—unless Warren intended the Gran Boz to speak his native tongue incorrectly.

4. Robert Berner cites this passage and notes its womb symbolism (69–70).

5. Note that the beech bough is a symbol of his authority. A similarly imposing father figure, the Gran Boz, is also connected to a beech, in an almost mythic way. According to the legend of his origins, he had been a trader between the

whites and the Indians, who played both sides against each other, particularly on the occasion when "He arranges at least one truce with a white outpost, and then, when it has been lulled by his gifts and has bought corn from him, he sits under a tree, at night—a beech tree, according to the story—and watches the flames and hears the screams of the massacre" (433).

6. If it appears that certain elements of Oedipus's story surface at times in Beaumont's, it is not only because Jeremiah murders the man who had been like a father to him or marries that man's mistress, or because he sees his mother's face when he gazes into his wife's in his dream, but also because the narrator makes explicit reference (as he had in the case of Thebes in *Night Rider*) to that ancient myth when he speaks of the Sphinx and its riddle. It is Rachel who plays this role, thereby reminding us that Jeremiah did not murder Fort for love of his wife so much as for reasons that have more to do with solving a mystery and fulfilling his destiny; nor was Rachel the ultimate object of his desire. Because of the crookedness of her smile, Miss Jordan was, in Beaumont's words, a "Sphinx that would not slay the traveler who could not guess her riddle and leave his bones whiten on the Greek road, but would let him pass on in peace except for the memory of her face" (45). The specific content of that riddle and its answer may have something to do with why walking sticks are so prominent in the novel (even Munn Short's lame leg becomes one when he stretches it out before him "like a stick" [384]). And it might have some bearing on a curious detail concerning Jeremiah's feet. In Beauchamp's *Confession,* the posse that came to take him back to Frankfort had a drawing of a footprint at the murder scene, and to his horror his foot fit into it; but in Warren's version, the drawing makes Beaumont's foot larger than it really was. It is as though his oedipal crime had given him oedipal—that is, swollen—feet.

7. The name of Runnymede, that place of ultimate origin, has a possible origin of its own in the novel, in a "Runnion" and a "Mead"—two men with whom Jeremiah once went hunting as a boy ("It was Jim Runnion who took Jeremiah when he was thirteen on his first big hunt . . ."). As they camped under the stars, "Jeremiah would lie awake . . . and 'wickedly' wish he had no family to go back to and that he could stay forever in the forest" (15). This is precisely what Morton Marcher could not get him to wish at Runnymede, which finds its first mention after the Runnion-led hunting trip. Colonel Mead was the largest landowner in the vicinity where Jeremiah grew up; Runnion, "the chief disgrace of the settlements" (14), was (possibly like the Kentucky descendant who is writing this book) a most irresponsible character, though he had been one of the original pioneers. Then there is the other Runnymede, of course. Like the kingdom of the Gran Boz, it was originally an island, like the maternal space Jack Burden's mother created for him in *All the King's Men* when he lay with his head in her lap, her cool hand covering his eyes: "she had the trick of making a little island right in the middle of time" (112).

8. The evidence, not falsified, of another assassin's guilt will appear in a handkerchief in *Brother to Dragons:* "The Sheriff pulled a parcel out of his pocket, / Wrapped in a rag, his handkerchief I guess. / . . . And Lil, he unwrapped it slow. It was a bone. / It was a jawbone, black where fire had burned" (1953: 156; 1979: 97). And what was wrapped in that handkerchief was, astoundingly (considering

the manner in which historical fact once more intersects the cluster of haunting images *Night Rider* began), fetal: Lilburn's victim "sort of curled up there, / Drew up his knees to make himself all little, / To lie all on that hunk of tulip-wood / And not hang over, and be little there, / A-lying sidewise, and his eyes squinched shut" (1953: 129–30; 1979: 87).

9. Fort, in his fatherly way, had tried to give another text to Jeremiah earlier in the novel (back when they were on good terms)—a volume of Byron. "But Jeremiah would take it only as a loan" (37). Beaumont encounters it again in Rachel's library, at a time when he is not having much success in courting her. The "inspiration" comes to him to take the book from her shelf and read aloud to her from it. "It was the blue book with the name Byron stamped in gold on it, the book Colonel Fort had given him long back. 'As I held it in my hand,' he wrote, 'I felt a great excitement and thought . . . how the book which he had put in my hands and hers might be sent as the instrument to fulfill the lives of us all. . . . I opened the book to find, as I knew I would find, the leaf torn out at the first and the pages loosened. "Look," I said, "look what somebody has done. They have ruined the book"'" (105–6). He has guessed, correctly, that the page held a dedication from Fort to Rachel, and that after the tragic outcome of their affair she had torn the page from the book. His beau's stratagem is to make her tell him what he already knows about her past, so that he can gain entry into her closed heart. It works, after a fashion; she "'flung it into the fire, and the flames leaped up to take it'" (107)—though it is not until the next scene, that of her mother's death, that Rachel tells him her secret.

In the end, Beaumont will find himself writing in that space where the father had first written, on the blank pages at the beginning and end of books. On the Gran Boz's island, he will keep working feverishly on his autobiographical manuscript, even though he is running out of paper. "[H]e tore out blank pages from books and gathered the scattered papers on the floor in the corner. The last of his manuscript is on these, on the end pages and title pages . . ." (441).

There is yet another example of Fort's gift of a text to Jeremiah, and it is his paternal ability to handle fire that makes it possible. It took place when he was instructing Beaumont in the law: "'Colonel Fort opened my eyes,' Jeremiah writes, 'to the law as mankind's servant. . . . So the book that had been dull now glowed before my eyes as though it had been a drab, dead coal he leaned to blow upon with his breath and bring to flame'" (42).

10. Warren could have found Fort's surname in the Beauchamp story. In fact, it is more than likely that he did, for a certain French [sic] Fort did what Cassius Fort is said to have done (but didn't): he said the baby was black. And he would have been in a position to know, for he was the man who buried Ann Cook's stillborn fetus (Kallsen, 352).

11. The mention, for what it is worth, comes from a doubtful source, as the jailer, McIntosh (actually, Sharp's brother, who printed McIntosh's statement and had his own axes to grind), put words in Beauchamp's mouth that directly contradicted what the prisoner maintained until his dying breath in the manuscript of his confession: namely, that he had worn the handkerchief on his hand when he killed Sharp and had dropped it there, and that Patrick Darby (the original of Sugg Lancaster) had been a co-conspirator in the murder.

Chapter 6

1. In Warren's *Portrait of a Father*, his own father would speak just such a gabble of a foreign tongue while shaving in front of his son. "A few times over those years he simply seemed to be gabbling something. At one time, as he told me, what he was saying came from the opening of the Gospel of John. To the boy ... the words coming forth were just a gabble. Then, cleaning the razor, the wielder remarked: 'That's Greek. Now you know how it sounds' " (38).

2. The name of the poem that disappeared one night and left a pale rectangle as its mark could have contained Amantha *Starr* as well within its cenotaphic embrace, for not only was *vedetta* at first a place to view the stars, but *vedette*, since before Sears's time, has meant, in the language Amantha was studying with Prieur-Denis, "star" in the other, nonastral sense (from the practice of inscribing the name of the headliner in larger type, so that it stood out from the rest, like the honored name on a monument).

3. Raphael told Tobias to burn the viscera, thus creating a smoke that would scare off the evil demon who had killed her previous husbands. Tobias's reincarnation in several other twentieth-century texts is the subject of my *Fowles/Irving/Barthes: Canonical Variations on an Apocryphal Theme*.

4. Seth Parton, too, is involved in a possible echo from the Book of Tobit. " 'Hannah,' " he tells Amantha, " 'is the name of my wife. In the godly language the name means grace' " (226). It is also the name of Tobit's wife. Tobias's last name, whose connection to sight has already shown its relevance to "The Dead Vidette," may also, ironically, allude to his namesake's (or his namesake's father's, depending on which version of the story we read) inability to see.

Chapter 7

1. Thus, most recently, Madison Jones speaks of "the cave image, which furnishes the center around which the novel turns and to which all the characters, for better or worse, are finally drawn" (52).

2. What we learn on page 139 is that Jack Harrick had been baptized by MacCarland Sumpter "in Elk Creek, in the big still pool below where the creek came boiling white over the gray limestone of Beecham's Bluff Falls." It is not until page 376 that we learn that the cave and the falls are in the same vicinity. There, Jack Harrick recalls how at the age of seven or eight "he had climbed up the Sumpter Ridge, and had gone swimming in the pool below the falls, and then he had climbed on up to the glade where the big beeches were, and the little hole in the ground under the roots of the biggest beech." That hole is the entrance to the cave, although until Jack's son, Jasper, discovered it decades later no one realized that the hole led to such a cave. There the young Jack Harrick had lain on the ground "and wondered if the sun would dry his hair enough so his mother wouldn't give him a whaling for getting in the creek"—which indicates how close the creek, and the falls, were to the cave. Earlier, however, Isaac Sumpter had mentioned the cave and the falls in the same breath, thinking of the commercial possibilities of these scenic—and historic, in the sense in which Jasper's tragic entrapment would consecrate the cave as Floyd Collins's had hallowed another—elements: " 'It will

be big. It will stay big. There is a cave here about like Mammoth or something. This is a scenic location. There is the falls' " (200).

3. Jasper is a sacrificial ram of another sort for his own father, who realizes that "I did not want my son to come out of the ground, because somebody always has to go in the ground. If he was there I would not have to go" (385); and likewise for Nick Pappy, who "felt a flood of sweet gratefulness" for the thought that "He is suffering for me. Jasper Harrick, he is in the ground suffering for me" (270).

4. Isaac's willingness to sacrifice Jasper's life for his own journalistic glory, and in particular his tricking the authorities into drilling from above instead of attempting a quicker rescue through the mouth of the cave, both suggest a more recent, and specific, source for the plot of *The Cave* than the story of Floyd Collins. Billy Wilder's 1951 film *Ace in the Hole* starred Kirk Douglas as Chuck Tatum, a newspaperman fallen on hard times who stumbles across the story of a man trapped in a cave near Albuquerque, New Mexico. Tatum makes a deal with the sheriff to obtain exclusive rights to the story in exchange for ensuring the latter's reelection by making him look good in the papers; he even gets the sheriff to insist that they drill from above, which will take seven days, instead of shoring up the walls to rescue the man through the way he came in. The result is that Leo Minosa dies before the drilling is completed; he otherwise would have been rescued in sixteen hours. Minosa's blonde wife, Lorraine, like Giselle Fontaine in the novel, is a former nightclub dancer; like Fontaine's husband, Papadoupalous, she profits handsomely from selling food and drink to the gathered crowds.

5. The word crops up in conversation as well. Monty Harrick, for example, talking to Jo-Lea about Jasper and his father says: "[H]e had just come out of Pappy's room. I told you how it is. When he goes in to sit with Pappy" (23).

6. Only later, when we consider Warren's last novel (*A Place to Come To*), will it be possible to determine the ultimate significance (or what appears to be such) of the fact that it was in the shadow of a beech—and while pretending to urinate by its trunk—that Isaac retrieved the scrap of paper Jasper had left behind.

7. The slick-faced boy thought Jebb Holloway was referring to Jasper when he was talking about Pappy; when Timothy Bingham asked Nick to make the arrangements for an abortion, Nick thought that Bingham had got Dorothy Cutlick pregnant, not realizing that he was referring to his daughter, Jo-Lea. And it was only when Jo-Lea herself seemed to have gotten confused about who was the father of her child—when she stood up and announced that she was the unwed mother she thought Jasper was referring to (even this error was induced by Isaac's fiction)—only, that is, through another misplaced referent, did Papadoupalous realize his mistake (324–25).

Chapter 8

1. If Mollie's feet were "turned inward," then her toes would have been somewhat less visible than the rest of her feet. The fact that the hanged man's fingers seemed "curled inward" to Adam until he realized that "There were no fingers" (45) suggests a further connection between the particular nature of Mollie's pedal deformity—her pigeon-toedness—and the way the man's extremities looked to Adam. The "pain of staring at the shoes" in Mollie's case could, even on the

level of the story itself, very well have been caused by an unconscious recollection of the sight of the man with the missing toes.

2. Mose's other scars suggest yet another identification: Rau-Ru and what his scars stood for in *Band of Angels*. The scene where Mose reveals the whip marks on his back to Adam and the one where the old beggar in Halesburg shows his to Amantha are strangely alike. Amantha "saw . . . how the shirt was tattered, and . . . saw on the half-exposed shoulders and upper back the neat herringbone pattern of old welts and scars on the gray-black flesh" that she identified with what she had earlier imagined to be "scars . . . interlacing"; Adam saw, when Mose twisted "his shoulder down, stripping the calico shirt back . . . the old welts plaited and crisscrossing grayly on the dark skin" (85–86).

3. Not to mention a kind of author's signature, an initial he shared with *his* father, as well as with the title of the novel.

4. Other poems also hint at the equation of father with hawk. Calvin Bedient has recently argued that in "Evening Hawk" the hawk is "the phallus, here winged" as well as "both father and son, in a crackling synthesis. . . . It is poetry as the son, seeking to be consubstantial with truth and glory, the father" (167). Similar conclusions, as we will see, can be drawn from "Red-Tail Hawk."

5. Warren contributed five poems to such a book, *Driftwood Flames* (Nashville: Poetry Guild, 1923; Grimshaw, 248).

6. "Until recently," Floyd Watkins writes, "it has not been widely known that Warren is blind in one eye, yet the accident was perhaps the most momentous event in his younger years" (54). Possibly the most revealing account of this incident and its significance can be found in Daniel Joseph Singal's chapter on Warren in *The War Within:* "Imagery having to do with eyesight, blindness, darkness and light, night and day would recur frequently in his writings" (344).

7. Mrs. Mary Warren Barber, in an address to The Nomads, a literary society in Maysville, Kentucky, 13 February 1985 (recorded by Mrs. Jane Alexander Smart, my mother-in-law).

8. In a 1977 interview, Warren lends support to his sister's version of how he became a writer: "Then I had an accident. I couldn't go [to Annapolis]—an accident to my eyes—and then I went to the university instead, and I started out in life there as a chemical engineer. That didn't last but three weeks or so, because I found the English courses so much more interesting" (*RPW Talking*, 243).

9. Hans Meyerhof, whose eyes were not only such signifiers without a referent, but who had the habit of lying on his back with his eyes open, in the same pose that had proven so unlucky for the young Warren: "I don't worry about him so much when he's asleep," his wife told Adam. "It's when he just lies with his eyes open, looking out the way they do" (123).

10. Harold Bloom has recently demonstrated this in a brilliant analysis of the topos in Warren, in "Sunset Hawk: Warren's Poetry and Tradition."

Chapter 9

1. Making a joke on the word that figures in a pun Brad will make on Digby's name, he points out to Maggie that the name suits his profession, and that "when he gets through digging, they will call him Dugby" (174).

2. The following excerpt from the transcript of Calvin's trial shows the degree to which the nickname had taken precedence. "Q: Who was on the porch when you came down? A: There was Tut, and—Q: Who? A: Al Tuttle—they called him Tut. Q: Is this Tut—or all Tuttle—the person legally known as Alfred O. Tuttle? A: I reckon. Q: What are you reckoning for? Haven't you seen his legal signature?" (308).

3. Barnett Guttenberg finds another basis for their similarity: "Like Bogan Murdock . . . Yasha is an artifact . . ." (129).

4. The trouble, perhaps, with Telford Lott's literary esthetic was that it was too enamored of sincerity: "he was sometimes moved to tears by fiction presenting images of generosity or of human suffering patiently borne" (60). That is why he so admired Brad's story "I'm Telling You Now," but it is also why he was such a potentially bad influence on his career. Lott's idea of what literature is was noticeably lacking in irony, in the "awareness of that doubleness of life" without which, accord to Blanding Cottshill, "no real conversation, conversation of inner resonance, is possible" (294)—nor, from what is known of Warren's esthetic, any similarly resonant literature. It is instructive to compare what fictional reviewers said of Brad's short story collection with what real ones said of Warren's *The Circus in the Attic:* "The author had, it was said [of Tolliver's book], great compassion. He had reported, without flinching, extenuation, or romanticism, the degradation of life in his native region. He exhibited an instinctive awareness of social problems" (61). Warren's reviewers said nearly the same thing—unaware of the irony, for example, of the two Seths and of the possibility that there may have been something else going on in that book other than just an unflinching depiction of the decline of southern society.

5. Note that "Within that continent [i.e., Yasha's scar], almost imperceptible lines ran crisscrossing, faintly *crazing* and hatching the surface" (20). *Crazing* here has the sense of having cracks in the surface ("making it look like some piece of precious china that has been shattered, then painfully and scrupulously reassembled and glued"), but even this word for the process through which the almost imperceptible lines seem to have appeared on the continent of Yasha's scar recalls (for Brad, for the reader anticipates) the adjective *crazy,* which at least three times is applied to the word *Continental* in the account of the stuck record: "just that one crazy word . . . that record with the one crazy word over and over" (317); "The stuck record was yammering it over and over, that crazy word" (319).

6. Actually, the pink chenille bedspread was off by then. But the pink bed lamp was still on, casting its roseate glow over the proceedings.

7. In his recent essay on Thomas Eakins's *The Gross Clinic,* Michael Fried focuses on the same topos, finding "the association of scalpel with pen literally inescapable" (178n). We should not lose sight of the fact, either, that Yasha's scar appeared "on a somewhat elongated *parchment*-colored" surface—as if it were a kind of writing. That Warren is comfortable with the analogy of scalpel to pen is also evident in a letter to me (see Introduction, p. 2) in which he compared the critic's work (mine, in this instance) to a surgeon's.

8. Unconsciously at least, Brad seems to be remembering the article in *Time* magazine about the death of Echegaray and to be connecting Echegaray's black hole of an eye with the black hole God left in the sky when, driving Yasha from Nashville to Fiddlersburg early in the novel, he puts on his Beverly Hills sunglasses and

observes that "Over Tennessee, the light, on the stroke, changed. . . . It looked like the death of the sun. The sun was dying. No—the wave of light that brought this news had left the point of origin light years ago. The news was, therefore, outdated. It was like last week's *Time* magazine. The sun was already, in fact, dead" (28). Like the sun that itself is like the blackness in the sky God left when He departed, Ramon Echegaray was already, in fact, dead: "The magazine—a copy of *Time*—was almost a year old" (334).

9. Although if the sun—as the black hole imagery linking its disappearance to fathers, and to fathers' eyes, suggests—is the father, then in the very last sentence of *Flood* Brad is still just beginning to learn how to recognize what messages his own eyes, as opposed to those fathers', can convey: "And for a moment he mistook the brightness of moisture in his eyes for the flicker of sun, far off, on the chrome and safety glass of cars passing on the new highway, yonder across the lake" (440).

Chapter 10

1. In the *Atlantic Monthly,* December 1973. It appeared in the collection *Or Else* the following year.
2. This is the letter that Angelo wrote to Cassie from prison just before his execution and that she never received, in which he thanked her for trying to save his life by confessing the truth. Guilfort, who had intercepted it, stuffed it in the safe with the rest of Angelo's gifts to Cassie.
3. Quoted in Watkins, 164.

Chapter 11

1. The buck whose death begins *Meet Me in the Green Glen* had paternal qualities, too, as I argued in chapter 10.
2. The verb has phallic applications elsewhere in the novel: when Rozelle Hardcastle called Jed up on the telephone and identified herself, "as that name came over the wire, out of time and distance, I was *clutching* my cock" (19); and when he cited his version of how his father had died with his hand similarly engaged, Dauphine Finkel wanted to know what "the Son of Old Buck. . . . would be like in the *clutch.*" It is insistently connected to his father's dying gesture: telling the story to Stahlmann (the true—urinary—version), Jed recounts that " 'They found him in the middle of the road, next morning, *clutching* his prick' " (66); at the end of the novel Jed wants to go back to Dugton to "see the spot where Buck Tewksbury had taken his lethal header with the noble dong in *clutch*" (399). In sum, when Stahlmann first spoke to Jed, he was making a gesture associated in Jed's memory with his father's last act on earth. And the walking stick is clearly phallic—as it was when Jeremiah Beaumont wrested it from his grandfather's grasp in *World Enough and Time.*
3. The suicide had nothing to do with Jed but, rather, with Stahlmann's despair over the death, some time before, of his Jewish wife and the feeling that he had betrayed his homeland by not defying the Nazis.

4. When Jeremiah Beaumont in *World Enough and Time* finally encountered the beeches that had figured in his dream, it was only after passing through what now appears to have been the mother's vagina, up into her womb: "Into a constricted valley, then up the stream where the valley narrowed like a gorge, with dank stone walling each side. Then suddenly, there was a little open space, with grass and a few trees like great blobs of denser blackness. From the shape, Jeremiah decided that they must be beeches" (417). Those walls of dank stone recall the caves he had explored as a boy, "dank and unvisited by sun" (315), that we have already identified as the mother's internal space. Now that we know that the father is not only the beech but the sun (the golden shower that impregnated Danaë), we can understand why Jeremiah preferred that this space be "unvisited by sun." The missing father is clearly identified with the sun when Beaumont, holed up in the cave, imagines "how my father might at that moment be standing in a field full of sun . . ." (315), wondering where his son could be. Yet, as we know from *Flood*, the father, like God, is also a black hole in the sky—a dead, black sun. That blackness is visible here, in the "great blobs of denser blackness" that Jeremiah decides must be beeches.

5. Recall that the mummies whose eyelids, according to Jason Sweetwater in *At Heaven's Gate*, like those of fetuses, were peculiarly expressive because there was nothing in them any more—an emptiness we have come to recognize in Warren as an essential characteristic of the father—were (American) Indian too. And the turban that was essential to the swami's disguise has appeared before as a sign of the father in *Band of Angels*, when Amantha saw Jimmee's bandaged head and thought he was Old Shaddy, who had once held her in his lap like a father: "the head preternaturally big with swathing of white cloth, *like a turban*, all familiar, terribly familiar . . . it must be Old Shaddy. . . ."

6. As he approached the mare, the stallion repeated what had been the dying gesture of another *buck* (one, as I argued in the last chapter, with connections to the father), the one whose death opens *Meet Me in the Green Glen* (as Old Buck's opens this novel): Dark Power's "front hooves [were] *pawing* the air as though to *climb* the empty bright blueness" (277), while "The buck was in the air . . . the forelegs making an awkward *pawing* motion as if they were trying to *climb* up a wooden ladder into the air" (8; emphasis added).

7. According to the Midrash, when Joseph produced his sons before his father, Jacob (Gen. 48:9), he also produced his wife in order to prove they were really his. His spouse, Asenath, was an Egyptian, daughter of the priest Potiphera. So, unlike Dauphine Finkel, she was not Jewish, which was enough of a scandal for legends to have arisen claiming that she was. "In one recension she is pictured as a Hebrew (daughter of Shechem and Dinah) who was adopted by Potiphera; elsewhere it is claimed that although she was Egyptian, she was converted to Yahwism by Joseph" ("Asenath," in *The Interpreter's Dictionary of the Bible*). Like Rozelle, however, whose eyelids could hieratically close (255), she had Egyptian eyes; and like Jed's mother (who, thanks to his oedipal outlook, was in some measure his bride), she had a certain one-eyed look, for according to the same source she "was blind in one eye" (935).

8. In *Portrait of a Father*, Warren writes at some length of his father's baldness. It had begun early, at age twenty-nine; when he spoke of its premature onset, "there was the angry and despairing expression on his face which I had

never seen before, nor have ever seen since" (10). When Warren thinks back to what his father looked like to him when he was a boy, the baldness is especially prominent, and even makes him look like the kind of statue Carrington made of Butler: "Even as I now think of him in his forties he was somewhat memorable, with the dignified calm of his face, the thrust of his Roman nose, and, especially in the glint of artificial light, the bald head seeming to be carved from some stone, even marble. Not that in my boyhood I had ever seen a bust, or any statuary, except in pictures" (11).

9. Marianne Krüll points out some further similarities. The biblical story of Jacob and his sons is "a 'family romance' with striking resemblance to [Jacob Freud's] own story. Like Jacob Freud, the Jacob of the Bible had children from several marriages. Of his twelve sons he loved Joseph best because—like Sigmund Freud—he was the fruit of his father's old age.... I feel certain that ... he saw himself as the biblical Jacob, and cast his son in the role of Joseph. Sigmund, for his part, must have realized that his father wanted him to be a second Joseph: upright, clever, the support of his father in old age, and—I would add—a son who did not enquire into his father's past..." (161).

10. Warren also needs to urinate in "Literal Dream" (part of *Altitudes and Extensions*, in *New and Selected Poems: 1923–1985*), after having dreamed of the blood about to drop from the ceiling in *Tess*: "I woke at the call of nature. It was near day. / Patient I sat, staring through the / Wet pane at parse drops that struck / The last red dogwood leaves." The connections between the need to pass water and the dropping liquids, both in and out of the dream, are obvious and betray a profound understanding of Freud's theory of how dreams are made.

11. Or why had the date of the dream changed from the night after to the night before the funeral? Krüll comments that by "changing the original version and claiming that he had dreamed this dream before, and not after, the funeral, Freud was able to dissociate his lateness from the impulse to flee the scene and his consequent guilt feelings" (42). In the letter to Fliess, Freud mentions this lateness: "On the day of the funeral I was kept waiting, and therefore arrived at the house of mourning rather late. The family ... took my lateness in rather bad part" (*Origins*, 171). But he makes no mention of it in the subsequent version. Krüll continues: "He could accordingly relate the 'winking at' requested in the dream to the trappings of the funeral ... his lack of filial piety was conveniently forgotten."

12. Peter Rudnytsky comments that the editors' "explanation is at best disingenuous, since it seems clear that the alteration in *The Interpretation of Dreams* is a deliberate attempt to minimize his self-disclosure on Freud's part" (366n31).

Conclusion

1. The last word of the first line quoted above (not the first line of the poem) became *know* in the *Selected Poems* of 1966 and 1975; quite recently Warren apparently revised it back to *believe*, when he reprinted "Mortmain" in the 1988 edition of *Portrait of a Father*. It makes a considerable difference: *believe* implies that the knowledge exists and all we have to do is accept it; with *know*, that knowledge is much farther from our grasp, perhaps unattainable.

2. The void sought in the youthful "Crusade" is related to the nothingness at the heart of Warren's poetry that Richard Jackson, in two remarkable articles, discusses from a Heideggerean and Derridean perspective. He cites the stones in the stream in "Dream of a Dream," which sing, but "What they sing is nothing, nothing, / But the joy Time plies . . ." and such Warrenian paradoxes as "the glittering metaphor / For which I could find no referent" ("Time as Hypnosis") and Time as "a concept bleached of all content" ("Heat Wave Breaks"). Some, but not all, of Derrida's deconstruction of Western notions of the origins of writing is relevant to Warren. In "Plato's Pharmacy" he articulates the oedipal force of authorship: "Writing is parricidal" (166). "The specificity of writing would thus be intimately bound to the absence of the father . . . the desire of writing is indicated, designated, and denounced as a desire for orphanhood and patrical subversion" (77). According to Socrates in the *Phaedrus,* the written text is an orphan, bereft of a father to defend it and to guarantee its meaning—as Jack Burden is deprived of Willie's guarantee as to the meaningfulness of the wink. To write is indeed to engender, for both Socrates and Warren; but there is a significant difference between the two with regard to the issue at the heart of Derrida's deconstruction of Plato.

In the *Phaedrus* and elsewhere, living speech is the father of this orphan, and father is to son as speech is to writing (and as Socrates is to Plato). But in Warren the father does not, like King Thamus, reject writing; nor does he, like Socrates, only speak and not write. For he is a writer too. Robert Franklin Warren, who becomes part of Warren's literary universe in "Mortmain" and *Portrait of a Father* and elsewhere, wrote poems in his youth and would have written more had family obligations not prevented him (as Warren tells the story in *Portrait of a Father*). Prophetically, one of the two poems his son discovered announced the inversion of generational authority that Warren would embrace in such a declaration as "I am the father / Of my father's father's father," in "The Leaf," and predicted, too, that sons would one day be doing the dictation: "We are marching to that lovely land, / Where . . . children command" ("Our Pilgrimage"). In fact, the father is so much a writer in Warren that in his late long narrative poem, *Chief Joseph of the Nez Perce,* the Derridean situation is precisely reversed: there it is the son who rejects the father's infatuation with writing in favor of pure orality. The elder Joseph was too much taken with "The New Book of Heaven," the white man's Bible, for the son's taste, and committed as well the foolish mistake of writing his signature on a treaty with the enemy (I discuss this at greater length in *The Braided Dream*). What the son elsewhere in Warren writes is certainly, to use a Derridean term, a *supplement* to what is lacking in the father; but it is a supplement to the father's text, not to his speech. Yet, for Warren, the father is indeed a vanished *presence,* his tomb the black hole the *sun* left behind, as in Derrida's reading of Plato "the disappearance of the god-father-capital-sun is . . . the precondition of discourse" (168).

Works Cited

Works by Warren

Fiction

All the King's Men. New York: Harcourt, Brace, 1946; Reprint. New York: Bantam, 1974.
At Heaven's Gate. New York: Harcourt, Brace, 1943.
Band of Angels. New York: Random House, 1955.
The Cave. New York: Random House, 1959.
"The Circus in the Attic" (short story). *Cosmopolitan,* September 1947, 67–70, 73–74, 76, 78, 80, 83–84, 86, 88.
The Circus in the Attic and Other Stories. New York: Harcourt, Brace, 1947.
Flood: A Romance of Our Time. New York: Random House, 1964.
"God's Own Time" (unpublished novel). 1932–33. Typescript. University of Kentucky Library.
Meet Me in the Green Glen. New York: Random House, 1971.
Night Rider. New York: Random House, 1939; Reprint. New York: Vintage Books, 1979.
A Place to Come To. New York: Random House, 1977.
Untitled (unpublished novel). 1933–34. Typescript. University of Kentucky Library.
Wilderness: A Tale of the Civil War. New York: Random House, 1961.
World Enough and Time: A Romantic Novel. New York: Random House, 1950; Reprint. New York: Vintage Books, 1979.

Poetry

Being Here: Poetry 1977–1980. New York: Random House, 1980.
Brother to Dragons. New York: Random House, 1953.
Brother to Dragons, A Tale in Verse and Voices: A New Version. New York: Random House, 1979.
Chief Joseph of the Nez Perce. New York: Random House, 1983.
"Crusade." *Fugitive* 4 (June 1925): 36.
Eleven Poems on the Same Theme. Norfolk, Conn.: New Directions, 1942.
"Images on the Tomb. III. Evening: The Motors." *Fugitive* 4 (Sept. 1925): 91.
"Mr. Dodd's Son." *Fugitive* 4 (June 1925): 35.

New and Selected Poems: 1923–1985. New York: Random House, 1985.
Now and Then: Poems 1976–1978. New York: Random House, 1978.
Or Else: Poem/Poems 1968–1974. New York: Random House, 1974.
Promises: Poems, 1954–1956. New York: Random House, 1957.
Rumor Verified: Poems 1979–1980. New York: Random House, 1981.
Selected Poems: New and Old, 1923–1966. New York: Random House, 1974.
Thirty-six Poems. New York: The Alcestis Press, 1935.
"To a Face in the Crowd." *Fugitive* 4 (June 1925): 36.
You, Emperors, and Others: Poems, 1957–1960. New York: Random House, 1960.

Other

"*All the King's Men:* The Matrix of Experience." *Yale Review* 53 (Winter 1964): 161–67. Reprinted in *Robert Penn Warren: A Collection of Critical Essays,* 75–81. Ed. John Lewis Longley, Jr. New York: New York University Press, 1965.
"Author's Note" to the poem "Terror." *Modern Poetry, American and British,* 542–43. Ed. Kimon Friar and Jon Brinnin. New York: Appleton-Century-Crofts, 1951.
" 'Blackberry Winter': A Recollection." *Understanding Fiction,* 638–43. Ed. Cleanth Brooks and Robert Penn Warren. 2d ed. New York: Appleton-Century-Crofts, 1959.
"Introduction to the Modern Library Edition of *All the King's Men,*" i–vi. New York: Random House, 1953. Reprinted in Chambers, 93–97.
Jefferson Davis Gets His Citizenship Back. Lexington: The University Press of Kentucky, 1980.
Letter to the author. 10 June 1985.
Letter to the author. 7 December 1988.
New and Selected Essays. New York: Random House, 1989.
"A Poem of Pure Imagination: An Experiment in Reading." *New and Selected Essays,* 335–423. New York: Random House, 1989.
Portrait of a Father. Lexington: The University Press of Kentucky, 1988.
"Pure and Impure Poetry." *New and Selected Essays,* 3–28. New York: Random House, 1989.
Robert Penn Warren Talking: Interviews 1950–1978. Ed. Floyd C. Watkins and John T. Hiers. New York: Random House, 1980.

Works about Warren

Baumbach, Jonathan. "The Metaphysics of Demogoguery: *All the King's Men* by Robert Penn Warren." *The Landscape of Nightmare,* 16–34. New York: New York University Press, 1965. Reprinted in Chambers, 126–42.
Bedient, Calvin. *In the Heart's Last Kingdom: Robert Penn Warren's Major Poetry.* Cambridge, Mass.: Harvard University Press, 1984.

Berner, Robert. "The Required Past: *World Enough and Time.*" *Modern Fiction Studies* 6 (1960): 55–64. Reprinted in Gray, 67–75.

Bloom, Harold. Introduction. *Robert Penn Warren (Modern Critical Views)*, 1–11. New York: Chelsea House Publishers, 1986.

———. Rev. of *Now and Then: Poems 1976–1978*, by Robert Penn Warren. *The New Republic*, 30 September 1978, 34–35. Reprinted in *Critical Essays on Robert Penn Warren*, 74–76. Ed. William Bedford Clark. Boston: G. K. Hall, 1981.

———. "Sunset Hawk: Warren's Poetry and Tradition." In Edgar, 59–79.

Bohner, Charles. *Robert Penn Warren, Revised Edition*. Boston: Twayne Publishers, 1981.

Casper, Leonard. *Robert Penn Warren: The Dark and Bloody Ground*. Seattle: University of Washington Press, 1960.

Chambers, Robert H., ed. *Twentieth Century Interpretations of All the King's Men*. Englewood Cliffs, N.J.: Prentice-Hall, 1977.

Edgar, Walter B., ed. *A Southern Renascence Man: Views of Robert Penn Warren*. Baton Rouge: Louisiana State University Press, 1984.

Gray, Richard, ed. *Robert Penn Warren: A Collection of Critical Essays*. Englewood Cliffs, N.J.: Prentice-Hall, 1980.

Grimshaw, James A., Jr. *Robert Penn Warren: A Descriptive Bibliography 1922–1979*. Charlottesville: University Press of Virginia, 1981.

Guttenberg, Barnett. *Web of Being: The Novels of Robert Penn Warren*. Nashville: Vanderbilt University Press, 1975.

Hardy, John Edward. "Robert Penn Warren: The Dialectic of Self." *Man in the Modern Novel*. Seattle: University of Washington Press, 1964. Reprinted in *Robert Penn Warren's All the King's Men: A Critical Handbook*, 157–67. Ed. Maurice Beebe and Leslie A. Field. Belmont, Calif.: Wadsworth Publishing, 1966.

Harmon, William. "Three Italians Visit Monticello." *Robert Penn Warren's Brother to Dragons: A Discussion*, 263–79. Ed. James A. Grimshaw, Jr. Baton Rouge: Louisiana State University Press, 1983.

Jackson, Richard. "The Deconstructed Moment in Modern Poetry." *Contemporary Literature* 23 (1982): 306–42.

———. "The Generous Time: Robert Penn Warren and the Phenomenology of the Moment." *Boundary 2* 9 (1981): 1–30.

Jones, Madison. "Robert Penn Warren as Novelist." In Edgar, 39–57.

Justus, James H. *The Achievement of Robert Penn Warren*. Baton Rouge: Louisiana State University Press, 1981.

Law, Richard G. "*At Heaven's Gate:* 'The Fires of Irony.'" *American Literature* 52 (1981): 87–104.

Meckier, Jerome. "Burden's Complaint: The Disintegrated Personality as Theme and Style in Robert Penn Warren's *All the King's Men*." *Studies in the Novel* 2.1: 7–21. Reprinted in Chambers, 57–72.

Quinn, Bernetta. "Gull Against a Crimson Sky: Birds in the Later Poems of Robert Penn Warren." *Southern Literary Journal* 16.1 (1983): 11–23.

Runyon, Randolph Paul. *The Braided Dream: Robert Penn Warren's Late Poetry*. Lexington: The University Press of Kentucky, 1990.

Scott, James C. "The Theme of Betrayal in Robert Penn Warren's Stories." *Thoth* 5 (1964): 74–84.
Shepherd, Allen. "Carrying Manty Home: Robert Penn Warren's *Band of Angels*." *Four Quarters* 21.4 (1972): 101–9. Reprinted in Gray, 78–84.
———. "Prototype, Byblow and Reconception: Notes on the Relation of Warren's *The Circus in the Attic* to His Novels and Poetry." *Mississippi Quarterly* 33 (1979–80): 3–17.
Singal, Daniel Joseph. "Robert Penn Warren: The Southerner as Modernist." In *The War Within: From Victorian to Modernist Thought in the South, 1919–1945*, 339–71. Chapel Hill: University of North Carolina Press, 1982.
Snipes, Katherine. *Robert Penn Warren*. New York: Frederick Ungar, 1983.
Steinberg, Erwin R. "The Enigma of Willie Stark." *All the King's Men: A Symposium*, 17–28. Pittsburgh: Carnegie Institute of Technology, 1957.
Strandberg, Victor H. *A Colder Fire: The Poetry of Robert Penn Warren*. Lexington: The University Press of Kentucky, 1965.
Walker, Marshall. *Robert Penn Warren: A Vision Earned*. Edinburgh: Paul Harris, 1979.
Watkins, Floyd C. *Then and Now: The Personal Past in the Poetry of Robert Penn Warren*. Lexington: The University Press of Kentucky, 1982.

Other works

"Alexis Carrel." *Encyclopedia Britannica*. Chicago: University of Chicago Press, 1948.
Baudry, Jean-Louis. *Proust, Freud et l'autre*. Paris: Editions de Minuit, 1984.
De Man, Paul. *Allegories of Reading: Figural Language in Rousseau, Nietzsche, Rilke, and Proust*. New Haven: Yale University Press, 1979.
Derrida, Jacques. *Dissemination*. Trans. Barbara Johnson. Chicago: University of Chicago Press, 1981.
Felman, Shoshana. *Jacques Lacan and the Adventure of Insight*. Cambridge, Mass.: Harvard University Press, 1987.
Freud, Sigmund. "The Acquisition of Power over Fire," trans. Joan Riviere. In *Character and Culture*, ed. Philip Rieff, 294–300. New York: Collier Books, 1963.
———. "The Infantile Genital Organization of the Libido," trans. Joan Riviere. In *Sexuality and the Psychology of Love*, ed. Philip Rieff, 171–75. New York: Collier Books, 1963.
———. *The Interpretation of Dreams*. Trans. James Strachey. New York: Avon Books, 1965.
———. "Medusa's Head," trans. James Strachey. In *Sexuality and the Psychology of Love*, ed. Philip Rieff, 212–13.
———. *The Origins of Psycho-analysis: Letters to Wilhelm Fliess, Drafts and Notes: 1887–1902*. Ed. Marie Bonaparte, Anna Freud, Ernst Kris. New York: Basic Books, 1954.
Fried, Michael. *Realism, Writing, Disfiguration: On Thomas Eakins and Stephen Crane*. Chicago: University of Chicago Press, 1987.
Ibsen, Henrik. *The Lady from the Sea*. Trans. Frances Archer. In *The Works of Henrik Ibsen*. Vol. 4. New York: Willey Book Company, 1912.

———. *The Lady from the Sea*. Trans. not given. Everyman Library. New York: E. P. Dutton, 1910.
Jones, Ernest. *Hamlet and Oedipus*. New York: W. W. Norton, 1976.
Kallsen, Loren J. *The Kentucky Tragedy: A Problem in Romantic Attitudes*. New York: Bobbs-Merrill, 1962.
Krüll, Marianne. *Freud and His Father*. Trans. Arnold J. Pomerans. New York: Norton, 1986.
Liddell, H. G., and Robert Scott. *An Intermediate Greek-English Lexicon*. Oxford: Oxford University Press, 1889.
Midrash Rabbah: Genesis II. Trans. H. Freedman. London: The Soncino Press, 1939.
New Larousse Encyclopedia of Mythology. New York: Hamlyn, 1968.
Oxford English Dictionary (Compact Edition). Oxford: Oxford University Press, 1971.
Le Petit Robert: Dictionnaire. Paris: Société du Nouveau Littré, 1972.
Ross, J. F. "Asenath." *The Interpreter's Dictionary of the Bible*. 4 vols. Nashville: Abingdon Press, 1962. Vol. 1.
Rudnytsky, Peter L. *Freud and Oedipus*. New York: Columbia University Press, 1987.
Runyon, Randolph Paul. *Fowles/Irving/Barthes: Canonical Variations on an Apocryphal Theme*. Columbus: Ohio State University Press, 1981.
Shakespeare, William. *Cymbeline*. *The Riverside Shakespeare*. Ed. G. Blakemore Evans. Boston: Houghton Mifflin, 1974.
Speiser, E. A. *The Anchor Bible Genesis*. Garden City, N.Y.: Doubleday, 1964.
Walpole, Horace. *The Castle of Otranto: A Gothic Story*. Ed. W. S. Lewis. London: Oxford University Press, 1964.
Webster, John. *The Duchess of Malfi*. Ed. John Russel Brown. Cambridge, Mass.: Harvard University Press, 1964.
Webster's New World Dictionary of the American Language, Second College Edition. Ed. David B. Guralnik. New York: Simon and Schuster, 1982.
Wintermute, O. S. "Joseph Son of Jacob." *The Interpreter's Dictionary of the Bible*. Nashville: Abingdon Press, 1967. Vol. 2.

Index

Ace in the Hole (film), 271n. 4
Acrisius, 171–73, 226, 227, 243
"After Night Flight Son Reaches Bedside of Already Unconscious Father . . . ," 210, 253
All the King's Men, 5, 36, 60–81, 113, 122, 123, 131, 133, 138, 142, 150, 151, 161, 169, 178, 200, 208, 210, 217, 228, 239, 244, 246, 251, 252, 268n. 7, 277n. 2; Introduction to the Modern Library Edition, 74
"All the King's Men: The Matrix of Experience," 265n. 8
Altitudes and Extensions, 86–87
"Aspen Leaf in Windless World,"64, 230–31, 255–57
At Heaven's Gate, 37–59, 63, 64, 65, 66, 79, 122, 140, 141, 178, 191, 210, 244, 266n. 9, 275n. 5
Audubon: A Vision, 236
Author's Note to Friar and Brinnin, 50

Band of Angels, 127–45, 151, 159, 162, 208, 256, 272n. 2, 275n. 5
Barber, Mary Warren (sister), 181, 272nn. 7, 8
Baudry, Jean-Louis, 249
Baumbach, Jonathan, 81
Bedient, Calvin, 262n. 2, 272n. 4
Beech (tree), 3, 114–15, 116, 119, 121, 147, 149, 159, 177, 229, 230, 232–33, 234, 239, 255, 256, 261n.

1, 267n. 5, 270n. 2 (chap. 7), 271n. 6, 275n. 4
Being Here: Poetry 1977–1980, 181, 255, 266n. 2
Bellerophon, 68, 71, 98, 113, 265n. 5
Berner, Robert, 267n. 4
"Blackberry Winter," 82–83, 89–90, 91, 96, 97, 98, 99, 100, 103, 134, 162, 205–6, 207, 215, 216, 218–19, 230, 241, 252, 263n. 7
"'Blackberry Winter': A Recollection," 267n.7
Bloom, Harold, 179, 262n. 2, 272n. 10
Bohner, Charles, 153–54
Bonaparte, Marie, 261n. 5
Brother to Dragons, 268n. 8

Carrel, Alexis, 50–52
Casper, Leonard, 110, 261n. 4, 262n. 3, 264n. 2 (chap. 2)
Castle of Otranto, The (Walpole), 227–28, 236
Cave, The, 5, 146–62, 165–67, 180, 200, 230, 232, 233, 234, 239
Chief Joseph of the Nez Perce, 14, 277n. 2
"Christian Education, A," 84, 99
"Christmas Gift," 83, 91
"Circus in the Attic, The," 82, 86–97, 103–4, 134, 181
Circus in the Attic, The, 5–6, 82–106, 121, 263n. 7, 273n. 4

"Confession of Brother Grimes, The," 84–85, 94
"Crime," 50, 52–53, 162, 166
"Crusade," 254, 277n. 2
Cymbeline (Shakespeare), 46–48, 264n. 3 (chap. 2)

Danaë, 171–72, 226, 230, 231, 232, 255
de Man, Paul, 261n. 2
Derrida, Jacques, 277n. 2
"Dream of a Dream," 277n. 2
Driftwood Flames, 272n. 5
Duchess of Malfi, The (Webster), 98–99, 267n. 8

"Eagle Descending," 14
Eleven Poems on the Same Theme, 49–53, 162
"Elijah on Mount Carmel," 263n. 4
Ephraim, 237–38, 244
"Evening Hawk," 14, 272n. 4

Father's eyes, 1, 36, 53, 63–64, 66–67, 70–71, 72, 77, 79–80, 144, 150, 169, 170, 173, 177, 178, 180, 181–82, 201, 206, 207, 209–12, 216–17, 232, 235–36, 239, 243–44, 245, 247–49, 251–52, 253, 254, 274n. 9, 277n. 2
Father's text, 2, 6, 13, 14–15, 23, 35, 36, 63, 64, 67, 70–71, 72–73, 77, 79–80, 102, 123, 133, 137–38, 142, 151, 159, 163, 166–68, 170, 178–82, 193–94, 197, 198–200, 201, 209, 210–11, 213–14, 216, 217–18, 219, 226, 230, 249, 250, 254, 258–59, 262n. 2, 263n. 8, 269n. 9, 272n. 2
Felman, Shoshana, 261n. 5
Fetal imagery, 11, 18, 19, 21, 24, 25–27, 29, 30, 31, 34–35, 49–50, 52, 53, 63, 66, 70–71, 72, 79, 107, 112, 122, 125, 126, 140, 142, 155–56, 158, 161, 162, 166, 178, 180, 181, 183, 188, 189, 191, 197, 206, 221, 242, 258, 265n. 7, 268n. 8, 275n. 5
Flood, 6, 183–202, 212, 214, 215, 216, 220, 226, 232, 235–36, 239, 252, 254, 275n. 4
"Folly on Royal Street Before the Raw Face of God," 251–52
"Fox-Fire: 1956," 209–10, 253, 263n. 8
Freud, Sigmund, 276n. 9; "The Acquisition of Power over Fire," 117; "The Infantile Genital Organization," 240; *The Interpretation of Dreams*, 1, 2–5, 19–20, 24, 25, 26, 45, 46, 94, 170, 176, 219, 220, 237, 241, 244–49, 276nn. 10, 12; letter to Wilhelm Fleiss, 247–48, 276n. 11; "Medusa's Head," 174, 240, 242
Fried, Michael, 273n. 7

"God's Own Time" (unpublished novel), 140, 266n. 3
Guttenberg, Barnett, 261n. 4, 273n. 3

Hardy, John Edward, 264n. 3, 265n. 4
Harmon, William, 14
"Heart of Autumn," 14, 262n. 2
"Heart of the Backlog," 210
"Heat Wave Breaks," 277n. 2
"Her Own People," 85, 95–96
"History During Nocturnal Snowfall," 86–87, 89
"Homage to Theodore Dreiser," 200

"I Am Dreaming of a White Christmas: The Natural History of a Vision," 1–2, 36, 81, 206–7, 212, 213, 216, 217, 219–20, 257, 259, 261n. 5
Iliad, 265n. 5
"Images on the Tomb," 5, 19, 20
"In the Turpitude of Time: N.D.," 253

Index

Jackson, Richard, 277n. 2
Jacob, 237, 244, 275n. 7, 276n. 9
Jefferson Davis Gets His Citizenship Back, 2, 251
Jones, Ernest, 169–72, 227
Jones, Madison, 149, 270n. 1 (chap. 7)
Joseph, 237–38, 244, 249, 275n. 7, 276n. 9
Justus, James, 57, 130, 148, 150, 261n. 4

"Kentucky Mountain Farm," 14
Krüll, Marianne, 246, 276nn. 9, 11

Lacan, Jacques, 261n. 5
Lady from the Sea, The (Ibsen), 38, 47–48, 53, 54–55, 59
Landor, Walter Savage, 6, 23
Law, Richard, 264n. 1 (chap. 2)
"Leaf, The," 73, 182, 238, 277n. 2
"Life and Work of Professor Roy Millen, The," 85, 98, 105
"Literal Dream," 276n. 10
"Love of Elsie Barton: A Chronicle, The," 84, 90–91, 93, 94, 95, 100–101, 266n. 2

Meckier, Jerome, 73
Medusa, 171, 174–75, 227, 235, 236, 237, 238, 240–41, 242
Meet Me in the Green Glen, 162, 203–21, 224, 241, 274n. 1 (chap. 11), 275n. 6
Midrash, 275n. 7
"Mission, The," 256–57
"Mortmain," 209–10, 214, 253, 276n. 1, 277n. 2
Moses, 166, 178–79, 182
"Mr. Dodd's Son," 252–54

New and Selected Poems: 1923–1985, 86–87, 250
Night Rider, 2, 5, 6, 9–36, 40, 42, 43–47, 49, 51, 52, 63, 73, 102, 111, 112, 121–22, 123, 126, 162, 177, 180, 206, 216, 220–21, 240, 242, 243, 246–47, 261n. 5, 266n. 9, 268n. 8
"No Bird Does Call," 230, 255
Noah, 194

Oedipus, 2, 14, 15–16, 22, 32–34, 73, 117, 118, 193, 213, 227, 228, 234, 268n. 6, 277n. 2
"One I Knew," 258
Othello (Shakespeare), 263n. 9
"Our Pilgrimage" (Robert Franklin Warren), 277n. 2

"Patented Gate and the Mean Hamburger, The," 83–84, 93, 216
Perseus, 171, 173–75, 177, 182, 221, 227, 230, 231, 236–37, 238, 240, 243, 244
Place to Come To, A, 171, 220, 222–49, 271n. 6
Plato, 277n. 2
Poe, Edgar Allan, 78, 81, 219, 261n. 5
"Poem of Pure Imagination, A," 2–4
"Pondy Woods," 262n. 1
Portrait of a Father, 263n. 8, 270n. 1 (chap. 6), 275n. 8, 276n. 1, 277n. 2
"Prime Leaf," 85–86, 99, 100, 101–3, 220, 233
"Pure and Impure Poetry," 39, 65, 131–32, 264n. 1 (chap. 2)
"Pursuit," 50, 52

Quinn, Sister Bernetta, 262n. 2

"Reading Late at Night, Thermometer Falling," 1, 176, 220, 244, 248, 256
"Red-Tail Hawk and Pyre of Youth," 14, 179–82, 238, 262n. 2, 272n. 4
Rudnytsky, Peter, 276n. 12

Scott, James, 267
Shepherd, Allen, 95, 130
Singal, Daniel Joseph, 272n. 6
"Snowshoeing Back to Camp in Gloaming," 255
Steinberg, Edwin, 264n. 2 (chap. 3)

"Terror," 50–52
"Testament of Flood," 84, 91, 97–99, 100, 266n. 2, 267nn. 8, 9, 10
"Time as Hypnosis," 277n. 2
"To a Face in the Crowd," 14, 250–59
Tobias, 143–45, 270nn. 3, 4

Untitled novel, 91, 266n. 2, 267n. 10
"Unvexed Isles, The," 85, 100, 101, 104–6, 233

Warren, Robert Franklin (father), 244, 263n. 8, 267n. 11, 270n. 1 (chap. 6), 275–76n. 8, 277n. 2
Watkins, Floyd, 1
"When the Light Gets Green," 83, 95–97
Wilderness, 64, 163–82, 206, 210, 212, 213–14, 217, 218, 219, 220, 226–27, 233, 237, 240, 244, 254
"Winter Wheat: Oklahoma," 86, 87
World Enough and Time, 3, 5, 64, 107–26, 139, 149, 150, 151, 159, 162, 171, 173, 174, 177, 180, 213, 220, 225, 232–33, 247, 274n. 2 (chap. 11), 275n. 4

"Youthful Picnic Long Ago: Sad Ballad on Box," 86–87

www.ingramcontent.com/pod-product-compliance
Lightning Source LLC
Chambersburg PA
CBHW030108010526
44116CB00005B/149